To: Professor Slade

from: William

05/08/2011

REFRAMING CORPORATE SOCIAL RESPONSIBILITY: LESSONS FROM THE GLOBAL FINANCIAL CRISIS

CRITICAL STUDIES ON CORPORATE RESPONSIBILITY, GOVERNANCE AND SUSTAINABILITY

Series Editor: William Sun

CRITICAL STUDIES ON CORPORATE RESPONSIBILITY, GOVERNANCE AND SUSTAINABILITY   VOLUME 1

REFRAMING CORPORATE SOCIAL RESPONSIBILITY: LESSONS FROM THE GLOBAL FINANCIAL CRISIS

EDITED BY

WILLIAM SUN
Leeds Metropolitan University, UK

JIM STEWART
Leeds Metropolitan University, UK

DAVID POLLARD
Leeds Metropolitan University, UK

Emerald

United Kingdom – North America – Japan
India – Malaysia – China

Emerald Group Publishing Limited
Howard House, Wagon Lane, Bingley BD16 1WA, UK

First edition 2010

Copyright © 2010 Emerald Group Publishing Limited

Reprints and permission service
Contact: booksandseries@emeraldinsight.com

British Library Cataloguing in Publication Data
A catalogue record for this book is available from the British Library

ISBN: 978-0-85724-455-0
ISSN: 2043-9059 (Series)

Emerald Group Publishing Limited, Howard House, Environmental Management System has been certified by ISOQAR to ISO 14001:2004 standards

Awarded in recognition of Emerald's production department's adherence to quality systems and processes when preparing scholarly journals for print

INVESTOR IN PEOPLE

CONTENTS

**PART III: IMPLEMENTATION OF CSR:
REGULATORY MODELS AND MANAGERIAL
FRAMEWORKS**

LIST OF TABLES

LIST OF FIGURES

LIST OF BOXES

LIST OF CONTRIBUTORS

Lawrence Bellamy	Leeds Metropolitan University, Leeds, UK
Justyna Berniak-Woźny	Polish Open University, Warsaw, Poland
Colin Fisher	Nottingham Trent University, Nottingham, UK
Hershey H. Friedman	Brooklyn College, City University of New York, New York, NY, USA
Linda Weiser Friedman	Baruch College, City University of New York, New York, NY, USA
Brian Jones	Leeds Metropolitan University, Leeds, UK
Tineke Lambooy	Nyenrode, The Netherlands; Business University, Breukelen, The Netherlands and Utrecht University, Utrecht, The Netherlands
Paul Manning	Leeds Metropolitan University, Leeds, UK
Alex Nunn	Leeds Metropolitan University, Leeds, UK
David Pollard	Leeds Metropolitan University, Leeds, UK
Robert J. Rhee	University of Maryland, Baltimore, MD, USA
Simon Robinson	Leeds Metropolitan University, Leeds, UK
Jim Stewart	Leeds Metropolitan University, Leeds, UK
William Sun	Leeds Metropolitan University, Leeds, UK
Ralph Tench	Leeds Metropolitan University, Leeds, UK
Wayne Visser	CSR International, London, UK; Cambridge University, Cambridge, UK; Birmingham Graduate School, Birmingham, UK and La Trobe University, Melbourne, Australia

EDITORIAL ADVISORY AND REVIEW BOARD

ACKNOWLEDGMENTS

This edited volume is the result of a collective effort of the Corporate Governance and Sustainability Research Group (CGSRG) at Faculty of Business and Law, Leeds Metropolitan University, and scholars from other universities in the United Kingdom, the United States, the Netherlands, and Poland. We wish to thank all the contributors for their intellectual contributions, collaborations, and support of this work.

For their academic support or engagement, we wish to thank Dr. Suzanne Young, Associate Professor, La Trobe University, Australia; Dr. Richard W. Leblanc, Associate Professor, York University, Canada; Dr. Roger Barker, Head of Corporate Governance, Institute of Directors, UK; James McRitchie, Publisher of CorpGov.net (Corporate Governance), USA; Laura Berry, Executive Director, Interfaith Center on Corporate Responsibility, USA; Professor Eamonn Judge, Poland Open University, Poland; Professor Hongtao Yang, College of Economics and Management, Harbin Engineering University, China; and Dr. Dayong Niu, Associate Professor, College of Economics and Management, Harbin Engineering University, China. A special thanks is to the volume editorial assistant Maggie Meng.

This work was supported by the Faculty of Business and Law, Leeds Metropolitan University. We particularly thank Professor Ian Sanderson, the Faculty Director of Research, and Lawrence Bellamy, Leader of the Strategy and Business Analysis Subject Group, for their kind support throughout the research process.

At Emerald Group Publishing, special thanks are to the Commissioning Editors Chris Hart and Emma Whitfield, Assistant Commissioning Editor Sarah Baxter, and the Corporate Communications Manager Arnaud Pellé. The strong support to the volume publication from the Emerald Board and the four anonymous reviewers of the volume proposal are greatly acknowledged.

The volume chapters were double-blind reviewed by the following reviewers, and their contributions to the volume are specially acknowledged:

Dr. Ralph Bathurst, Lecturer, Department of Management & International Business, College of Business, Massey University, New Zealand

Lawrence Bellamy, Principal Lecturer, Leader of Strategy and Business Analysis Subject Group, Faculty of Business and Law, Leeds Metropolitan University, UK

Dr. John Bottone, Senior Lecturer, Faculty of Business and Law, Leeds Metropolitan University, UK

Dr. Barry A. Colbert, Reader, Director of CMA Centre for Business & Sustainability, School of Business & Economics, Wilfrid Laurier University, Canada

Dr. Brian Jones, Senior Lecturer, Faculty of Business and Law, Leeds Metropolitan University, UK

Dr. Elizabeth C. Kurucz, Assistant Professor, College of Management and Economics, University of Guelph, Canada

Dr. David Pollard, Reader, Faculty of Business and Law, Leeds Metropolitan University, UK

Dr. David Russell, Head of Department of Accounting & Finance, Leicester Business School, De Montfort University, UK

Dr. Greg Shailer, Reader, School of Accounting and Business Information Systems, College of Business and Economics, the Australian National University, Australia

Professor Jim Stewart, Director of HRD and Leadership Research Unit (HRDL), Faculty of Business and Law, Leeds Metropolitan University, UK

Dr. William Sun, Leader of Corporate Governances and Sustainability Research Group (CGSRG), Faculty of Business and Law, Leeds Metropolitan University, UK

Dr. Crystal Zhang, Senior Lecturer, Faculty of Business and Law, Leeds Metropolitan University, UK

PART I
INTRODUCTION

REFRAMING CORPORATE SOCIAL RESPONSIBILITY

William Sun, Jim Stewart and David Pollard

Corporate social responsibility (CSR) has been a serious concern over the past three decades in media reports, public forums, academic debates and governmental policies, mainly because of the increasing careless corporate behaviours, poor and failed corporate governance practices together with continually rising social expectations and stakeholder pressures. However, issues like corporate fraud, greed, selfishness, short-termism, corporate failure and collapse, abuse of management power and the excess of executive remuneration would not have been so exacerbated and exposed, had it not been for the global financial and economic meltdown of 2008. Did CSR play a significant role in the financial crisis? Though many people have started to link CSR issues to the financial crisis, very little research has been done so far to explore the key question. Time does not allow us slow reactions to the CSR failure in preventing the current financial crisis and slow reflections on the limited existing knowledge of CSR that did not prepare well for the crisis, if we have to urgently cope with the moral and environmental challenges we are facing today. This volume brings together leading scholarly thinking to understand why CSR failed to prevent the global financial crisis, how corporate social irresponsibility contributed to the financial crisis, and how we may reframe CSR or improve CSR frameworks to help prevent or mitigate any future financial and economic crisis.

Reframing Corporate Social Responsibility: Lessons from the Global Financial Crisis
Critical Studies on Corporate Responsibility, Governance and Sustainability,
Volume 1, 3–19
ISSN: 2043-9059/doi:10.1108/S2043-9059(2010)0000001006

Although encouraging a critical rethinking of CSR issues in relation to the financial crisis, this volume is not to simply describe the correlation between CSR and the financial crisis, but to explore underlying issues of CSR such as perspectives, approaches and implementation mechanisms. Although it emphasises critical reflections on the role of CSR in the financial crisis, it does not stop there, but further explores how CSR could function well to reduce risks and threats from business and increase public trust and confidence in businesses. A new perspective of CSR, namely, an embedded CSR, is suggested in this volume.

DEFINITION OF CSR

The fierce debate on CSR is often linked to different understandings of CSR from different perspectives. Although there is no strong consensus on CSR, Carroll's pyramid of CSR encompassing economic, legal, ethical and philanthropic responsibilities (Carroll, 1979) is a good starting point for discussion.

Conventionally, private business exists with its basic purpose and function to make profits for business owners. When making profits under a legal framework of protections and constraints, business not only benefits the owners, but also other people and the whole society. This is because the survival and growth of any business is dependent on the support of stakeholders such as customers, suppliers, employees, government and communities, involved in enabling and generating business. In turn, those who support business must have a reason so they gain some benefits (though the benefits gained may be unsymmetrical). Such mutual benefits between business and its supportive environments are the fundamental justification for a legitimate business. In other words, business must show its responsibility to other stakeholders and the society to gain support from them. Ideally, some basic elements of CSR are inherently within business and they are DNAs of a good business. In this sense, neoclassical economists might be right for arguing that the social responsibility of business is to make profits while staying within the rules of the game (e.g. Friedman, 1970).

However, neoclassical economists' claim, while only involving the economic and legal responsibilities in the Carroll's pyramid of CSR, is built on the 'ideal' and abstract business society with an implicit assumption that businesses do good and do no harm to society. The reality is that not all businesses are 'good' and business can be 'bad', even though their actions might be 'legal'. For example, businesses might manipulate their supporters and markets, exploit employees, corrupt governmental officials, lobby legislators and governments and pollute environments and damage the ecological system to gain more profits and other benefits for business owners and their managers at the cost of others, society and natural environments. This is a real issue of CSR and a great concern to the public since the Industrial Revolution in the 19th century (Carroll, 2008).

What is more concerning today is that unlike early business firms, the size of many corporations nowadays has so increased that their economic power is much more than many national states. The potential for and actual abuse of the huge economic and political power of large corporations can be dangerous to society. Hence, CSR since the mid-20th century has become a more serious public debate due to the massive impact of large businesses on society. Corporate operational disasters (e.g. Union Carbide's gas leak in Bhopal in 1984, and BP's oil spill in the Gulf of Mexico in 2010), corporate fraud (e.g. Enron in 2001 and WorldCom in 2002), corporate collapse and failure (e.g. the failure of the US investment banks like Lehman Brothers, Merrill Lynch and Bear Stearns in 2008), the abuse of managerial power (e.g. careless risk taking, extreme short-termism and excessive remuneration) and market manipulations (e.g. speculative and artificial market bubbling and bursting) are some of the key fundamental problems of CSR.

Basically CSR is concerned with corporate attitudes and behaviour towards its responsibility beyond its immediate profit gain and other benefits pursued for its owners, beyond its limited legal obligations and liabilities, and beyond the passive benefits brought from business operations to society. The economic and legal obligations are a very narrow and incomplete version of CSR. CSR is more about caring for any possible negative impact of business on society, avoiding harm to other people and the public at large, meeting increasing and changing social and stakeholder expectations, contributing resources to communities and helping improve the quality of life in society. That means business should not just do what is legally, economically and morally right, and avoid what is legally, economically and morally wrong, but also hold social and moral obligations to help build a better society. Social and moral values infused into business philosophy and business values embedded in society are the key of CSR.

Although CSR can be defined normatively, the understanding of CSR is always dynamic, evolving and contextual, rather than homeostatic, mechanistic and context-free. CSR at a time and in a society has its specific meanings subject to societal conditions, traditions, values, cultures and political forces. Thus, while CSR may have some converged principles across the world such as universal human rights, the practical perception of CSR is always embedded in societal context of place and time. For example, the current global financial crisis has fuelled more public concerns with specific CSR issues like Wall Street greed, executive overpay, moral hazard of financial derivatives, and excessive risk taking, while other CSR issues have temporarily been cast aside. Surely, societies with different value systems and cultures, or different crises, have differing understandings of CSR.

THE FAILURE OF CSR

Did CSR exist before the 2008 financial crisis? It was shown that CSR did exist more or less in business practice if defined by the Carroll's pyramid. Many businesses had fulfilled their economic, legal and philanthropic obligations. Some had made efforts towards moral obligations, such as the rapid growing socially responsible investment (SRI), green business, fair trade, supply chain screening, social accounting and auditing and stakeholder dialogue and involvement in business decisions. A number of CSR-related world and local organisations, business principles, standards, indexes and codes of practice had been established to guide business operations. Most large corporations had initiated publishing their CSR-related annual reports on websites available to the public.

However, the truth was simply that CSR failed to prevent the global financial crisis. Furthermore, many people, including the contributors of this book, believe that corporate social irresponsibility contributed, at least in part, to the financial crisis. Wayne Visser (this volume) vividly illustrates how executive greed, banking greed, financial market greed, corporate greed and capitalist greed had together acted like a cancer in the body which ended up destroying the heath of its host society. He comments that

> CSR has undoubtedly had many positive impacts, for communities and the environment. Yet, its success or failure should be judged in the context of the total impacts of business on society and the planet. Viewed this way, as the evidence already cited shows, on virtually every measure of social, ecological and ethical performance we have available, the negative impacts of business have been an unmitigated disaster, which CSR has completely failed to avert or even substantially moderate. (Visser, this volume)

The failure of CSR could be measured in terms of public trust and faith in business. The European Economic Advisory Group (EEAG) at Ludwig-Maximilians-Universität, Germany, shows that the percentage of randomly selected people that reported having full trust in banks, brokers, mutual funds or the stock market was 40% in the late 1970s, about 30% just before the financial crisis, and only 5% after the financial crisis (EEAG, 2010).

> When trust is missing, financing disappears and economic activity suddenly stops. This is what happened in October 2008 and the subsequent months. (EEAG, 2010)

Ralph Tench (this volume) also shows that the British public has lost trust in both politics and business because of their poor ethical behaviour. A recent survey indicates that only 38% of British people trusted business to do what was right and 17% trusted the information provided from corporate CEOs.

This has led many to believe that 'CSR is dead' (see Visser, this volume). Malcolm McIntosh observes that

> In one sense this ['CSR is dead'] is true because many of those banks awarded good corporate citizenship prizes over the last ten years and more have proved to be lacking in any principles other than greed and fraud. On the other hand, much of what the corporate citizenship movement has been arguing has come true: that greater accountability and transparency is needed, particularly when trust evaporates. (McIntosh, 2009, p. 9)

CURRENT THEORETICAL MODELS ON CSR

The current practice of CSR has been framed and informed by three CSR models: the shareholder value model, the stakeholder model and the business ethics model.[1]

The shareholder value model, a perspective represented by the Nobel laureate Milton Friedman (1970), argues that the only social responsibility of business is to increase its profits while following legal rules. Neoclassical economists like F. A. Hayek assert that the function of business is doing business that contributes to economy and society, and its function should not be confused with other social functions performed by governments and not-for-profit organisations. Otherwise, it is not the most efficient way of allocating resources in a free market. Economists like agency theorists believe that the owners of the corporation are its shareholders, and managers as agents have fiduciary duty to serve the interest of shareholders (i.e. principals) rather than any others. Although maximising shareholder profit is justified as the only or the most important corporate responsibility, corporate social obligations are often regarded as strategic instrument for more profit gain and corporate competitive advantage.

The stakeholder model has become popular since the 1990s, as a direct challenge and alternative to the shareholder value model. It argues that the number of stakeholder pressure groups has increased rapidly since the 1960s and the influence of stakeholder forces on business should not be underestimated. Pragmatic and ethical as it ought to be, business success must consider wider interests of stakeholders than the interests of shareholders alone. The stakeholder model emphasises special social responsibility of a corporation to the stakeholders of the corporation only, rather than any others unrelated to the corporation (without a stake in the corporation). Thus, CSR is interpreted as 'company stakeholder responsibility' (Freeman & Velamuri, 2006).

The business ethics model is concerned with broader social obligation and the moral duty business has to society. This model justifies CSR on three slightly different but interrelated ethical grounds: (1) intrinsic or eternal ethical values, often inspired by Kantian deontological ethics and expressed as some normative and universal principles like human rights, social justice and fairness; (2) emerging and changing social expectations and social responsiveness to specific social issues and (3) corporate citizenship, i.e., corporation as a good citizen in a society to contribute to social wellbeing. The business ethics model views CSR more as ethical and philanthropic responsibilities rather than economic and legal responsibilities. CSR begins where legal obligation ends (Davis, 1973).

LIMITATIONS OF CSR THEORIES

Theories are explanations and understandings of practices. Although theories are usually generated, inspired or derived from practices, in turn, they may inform, influence or guide practices. The theoretical models of CSR are more or less reflections of business practice. For example, many companies in the United States have been following the shareholder value model, many companies in Japan and Europe follow the stakeholder model, and some companies have adopted the corporate social performance model and the corporate citizenship model (Mele, 2008). If CSR has failed in business practice, it does suggest corresponding failings, or at least severe limitations, of current CSR theories.

Indeed, the mainstream CSR theories have been frequently criticised in academic circles. For example, the main criticism against the shareholder value model is that this model presupposes a very narrow functionalist vision of business and regards business purely as self-interest and profit maximisation, with little attention to the interconnection and complex relationships between business and other stakeholders, and to the negative impacts of business on society. Such attitudes and behaviours of businesses and executive managers would eventually destroy business and the efficiency of markets (e.g. Davis, 1960; Arrow, 1973; Preston & Post, 1975; Kay, 1993). It was evidenced in the current financial crisis that an over-pursuit of self-interest brought about selfishness and greed, and an over-concern with profit maximisation led to excessive risk taking and short-termism.

The stakeholder model seems to be more ethical, as it requires business to consider much wider interests of stakeholders rather than shareholder value only. However, apart from many other issues, the shortcoming of this model is that it only recognises and emphasises or prioritises narrow interests of some particular stakeholder groups of the firm, who may have exerted or will exert large influence on the firm, or who just shout to the firm from the sidelines (Gioia, 1999), whereas the interests of other stakeholders, the whole society and natural environments are often marginalised or simply ignored by the firm. This leads to 'different distribution of benefits and burden, of pleasures and pain, of values, rights and interests' (Hummels, 1998, p. 1404). Hence, the stakeholder model is more a political model than a genuine and broad ethical model.

In this volume, Sun and Bellamy show that the financial crisis was actually triggered by the US government's national homeownership policy from 1994 through 2006 when the housing bubble burst. From the beginning, the mortgage finance industry was pressed to follow the governmental policy to serve the interests of low-income and minority families with compromised mortgage loan lending standards. Although priority was given to the interests and benefits of the US government and the low-income people, other stakeholder groups like investors, shareholders, employees, taxpayers and the general public finally assumed the huge risks and costs. Sun and Bellamy indicate that the stakeholder model prescribed by the national homeownership policy also provided the finance industry and managers with room and opportunities to manipulate the policy, abuse mortgage underwriting standards, justify the transfer of huge risks in mortgage loans to investors and pursue their own interests. In this sense, such a stakeholder model could destroy corporate social responsibility as business is not required to consider wider social interests beyond few specific stakeholder groups of the firm. Similarly, Etzioni argues that

> While all stakeholders and not only shareholders have fair claims to a voice in corporate governance, recognizing such claims may be damaging to the well-being of the economy,

and hence injurious to the common good. It might be further maintained that such consideration should outweigh the fairness claim. (Etzioni, 1998, p. 688)

The business ethics model tends to be an ideal model for capitalism that is often criticised as 'an inherently amoral system, concerned only with money making money' (Jackson & Carter, 1995, p. 883). But the key issue with this model is that it regards business and ethics as two distinct and separate conceptual frameworks as well as realities, known as the 'separation thesis' (Freeman, 1994; Wicks, 1996; Sandberg, 2008; see also Stewart, 2007), and thus lacks integration of ethical normative aspects and business activity (Mele, 2008). For example, in business ethics, the firm is believed to have two different roles, i.e., the private economic role and the public social role; two different responsibilities, i.e., economic responsibility and ethical responsibility; and two different norms, values and codes, i.e., business values and ethical values. To quote Sandberg (2008), 'There is a genuine difference between matters of business and matters of ethics, at least insofar as there is a genuine difference between descriptive and normative matters' (p. 227).

Although many scholars in business ethics have attempted to integrate business and ethics, their dichotomised modes of thinking tend to reinforce the separation thesis rather than overcome it (Wicks, 1996). In this regard, ethics is conceived as external to business, as normative values added or attached to business values, and business is considered as the first order and ethics second. In the Anglo-American business environment, business ethics is highlighted only in addition to the shareholder value model. With the globalisation movement in the 1990s, the paradigm of shareholder value plus (or minus) ethics has influenced business around the world, including Europe and Japan where the stakeholder model is traditionally oriented.[2] Thus, with the separation thesis, CSR in business practice has been used as window dressing, a PR tool, a strategic instrument, a voluntary measurement, a managerial discretion and a philanthropic gesture. Why did CSR fail in practice and in preventing the 2008 global financial crisis? We may find the theoretical root of this failure in here: business discourse and values are independent from ethical norms, and ethics has never been truly integrated into business.

In sum, the key limitations of the current CSR theoretical frameworks are that they essentially talk about business without ethics (in the case of the shareholder value model), ethics without business (in the case of the business ethics model), or business with narrow-minded responsibility (in the case of the stakeholder model).

FROM ALIENATED CSR TO EMBEDDED CSR

The drawbacks of current theoretical models reflect the fact that CSR is commonly perceived to be added on to business from the outside. This is understandable, given that business in capitalism tends to be inherently lacking in morality, as many critics insist. CSR seems to be alienated from what should be integrated and embedded in business, for business and society are actually inseparable. However, it is arguable that the alienation of CSR from business is not what must occur in the first place in the history of society, just like greed as a disease is not normally pre-born or pre-given. The disease of greed and corporate social irresponsibility is acquired. In this volume, Sun and Bellamy demonstrate that before the subprime mortgage crisis, poor standard of subprime mortgage lending, risk transfer and redistribution from the mortgage finance industry to investors and the US housing bubble, which together caused the subprime mortgage crisis, were actually co-constructed by the US homeownership and low-interest rate policies, the mortgage finance industry, financial market investors, housing market speculators, shareholders and other interested stakeholders. It was a social construct, as all those participants accepted and justified those 'realities', and actively participated in the process of social construction. CSR failed in the subprime mortgage process, not because there was no CSR, but because CSR was artificially split and the mortgage finance industry was encouraged to serve few particular stakeholder groups rather than a balanced interest of whole society.

As the narrow-minded interest of individual stakeholder groups were pursued at the cost of all others, there was no genuine CSR. As Sun and Bellamy note, we are living in an artificially constructed world informed by a separation thesis, and the ontological assumption of atomistic individual entity and the alienated egoic view of self (Driver, 2006) have been ideologically constructed to separate self from others and isolate business from society. This justifies excessive self-interest at the expense of others for competitive advantage or for a political agenda. This is the fundamental reason of CSR malfunctioning in practice, yet, mainstream CSR theories failed to address this key issue.

The future success of CSR depends on to what extent we can move away from the artificial separation thesis towards a genuine connection thesis; a thesis grounded on the interconnectedness of all members of society, mutual interests of self and others, inseparable business from society and the purpose of business to serve the common good. What is needed for business is to depart from an alienated and split CSR towards an integrated and

embedded CSR, and view CSR not as an add-on, but as an intrinsic value
and inherent building block of business. Business is embedded in society as
its functional parts to serve the common interests, rather than dominate and
hijack society for their own purposes and interests. This is a general
direction for CSR that some scholars have suggested in recent years
(e.g. Gioia, 2003; Stormer, 2003; Solomon, 2004; Driver, 2006; Kueucz,
Colbert, & Wheeler, 2008). We believe that in the wake of the global
financial crisis, the reality of CSR is facing some fundamental challenges,
such as public distrust and lack of faith in business, social unacceptability
and intolerance of some corporate irresponsible behaviours, increasing
business risks with complex financial systems and products, globalised
competition, uncertain business and economic reality and degraded and
deteriorated ecosystem and unsustainable natural resources. Those are
serious challenges to the conventional business model that aims to maximise
profits over a rather short-term time horizon and for the very narrow
interests of shareholders and/or few stakeholder groups at the expense of all
others and the society as a whole. Such a business model has proved to be
unsustainable in itself and disastrous to the whole economy and society.
Business has to respond quickly to the challenges, particularly in a time of
economic, ecological and social crises, in order to gain legitimacy and social
license to operate, and move forward accordingly to increase public
confidence and trust in business and meet social expectations. Reframing
CSR is not just necessary but urgent, if we are to learn important lessons
from the current financial crisis and attempt to prevent any further financial,
economic and ecological crises in future.

THEMES OF THE VOLUME

As a general framework for the future, an embedded CSR should be an
evolving and dynamic process rather than a static state. An embedded CSR
is not an abstract CSR, but always a living CSR in a society. Societal values,
cultures, and various conditions and forces will shape what CSR could
actually emerge. How to understand embedded CSR in a societal context at
a particular time and apply embedded CSR perspectives into business
practice is always a key task for research. The current global financial crisis,
for example, as a significant challenge to traditional CSR understandings is
a core context for exploring the meanings and implications of embedded
CSR. Reframing CSR also requires multidisciplinary efforts to explore CSR
issues in depth and to examine it from different angles.

Although CSR involves a variety of issues, this volume concentrates on three key themes: (1) the role of CSR played in the financial crisis and its underlying thesis, (2) institutionalising CSR in codified rules and the application of CSR into business and management and (3) the future direction of CSR as post-crisis agenda.

The first theme examined in the volume is that the global financial crisis was characterised by a lack of corporate responsibility in many aspects and that CSR issues are inseparable from institutional environments surrounding business. Thus, understanding why CSR failed to prevent the financial crisis needs to examine the wider context of business environments and the social reality we have collectively constructed. Simon Robinson notes that while the financial crisis was due to a complete lack of responsibility, there is no clarity on what responsibility means. He makes the concept of responsibility clearer by referring to three interconnected elements of responsibility: imputability, accountability and moral liability. With this definition, he finds that the key industry actually denied any responsibility, for there has been a lack of responsible agency and leaders (subjects), a general lack of awareness of plural accountability to stakeholders and wider community (relationships), and an absence of moral liability in relation to the wide effects of different projects (objects). He argues that business without responsibility is the key reason why the financial crisis occurred.

The contribution of Ralph Tench takes a contextual approach in understanding the financial crisis and CSR. Tench notes a significant shifting of social mood and cultural climate in recent years that society has lost trust and faith in both politics and business. The instability of social, political and cultural environments has affected how the role of business was/is played in society and will influence what business will do with CSR in the future. He argues that the financial crisis was not caused by CSR alone, but by a range of stakeholders including business executives who made such a reality. Although the financial crisis has created a new environment, business managers have to respond to it by taking a strategic and refreshing approach to continue working with stakeholders through openness and constructive dialogue. Taking the idea from Argandona (2009), Tench suggests that to make business trustable, managers' personal trust, namely, 'ethical benevolence based' trust, is key. This is an element missing in business.

Brian Jones takes a further contextual examination into the political ideology of neo-libalilism and market fundamentalism promoted by the UK and the US governments since the 1980s. He argues that the move from the post-war tri-partite based consensus politics to the new right, neo-liberal conviction politics led to loss of public scrutiny and accountability ushering in increasing levels of irresponsibility. He suggests that from the wreckage of the financial crises will emerge a stronger, differently shaped and more resilient form of capitalism, which will be shaped by political, economic, social and technological imperatives as well as the needs and demands of stakeholders. At times it will need more as well as less state intervention and regulation.

Similar to Jones' argument, Alex Nunn's analysis of performance management in labour market governance in the United Kingdom vividly illustrates that the social responsibility of the public sector in recent years has been deeply shaped by the Anglo-American neo-liberal ideology that promotes cost-based efficiency and market approaches, creating tensions among different objectives and priorities towards CSR. For example, in labour market governance, efficiency was gained at the expense of lower wages of workforces and poverty, labour market expansion favoured at the cost of marginalising social inclusion and labour upskilling. Nunn points out that there is a fundamental ethical issue with the neo-liberal model employed in government policy, and a consideration towards balanced and harmonised CSR objectives in both public and private sectors is a necessity.

Along with the key theme that the traditional business model and the managerial perception of CSR are embedded in political, social and cultural contexts, William Sun and Lawrence Bellamy further demonstrate how the financial crisis has been fueled by a separation thesis, that is, the business-related reality has been artificially constructed as a split world where all shareholding and stakeholding groups are perceived as naturally separated with their own identities, objectives, values and vested and desired interests. With the separation thesis, excessive self-interest, transfer of risks, externalisation of social costs, managerial dominance and hegemony and other immoral and irresponsible behaviours are justified. All of those are treated as reasonable and rational in the name of shareholder value or the very narrow interest of some stakeholder groups. For Sun and Bellamy, the failure of CSR is rooted in the separation thesis; unless the separation thesis is reconstructed and replaced by a connection thesis, fundamental issues in CSR are hardly resolvable.

Traditionally, CSR is often perceived as ethical values, as what people think in their minds, as invisible principles, as voluntary codes. This reflects the prevalent belief that CSR exists more in theory than practice, and its application into practice only deals with some abstract values added to business, rather than concrete measures and engaged models merged with business and management. Hence, little attention has been paid to how CSR is or should be institutionalised in codified rules and in corporate governance practice. The second theme of this volume is that an embedded CSR is inseparable from corporate governance and management practices regulated by soft and hard laws, and its effective implementation depends on how CSR is integrated into the frameworks of corporate governance and management.

Robert J. Rhee's contribution shows how US corporate laws give corporate boards authority to assume broad principles of CSR. Through the examination of the Bank of America – Merrill Lynch merger case in 2008, Rhee informs us that under American corporate law, corporate boards have both fiduciary duty and social obligation, particularly during a public crisis. Unlike what many people have believed in that the US pursues a shareholder value model, the corporate laws have actually directed companies towards the maximisation of social wealth and welfare, rather than the narrow interest of shareholder profit. The shareholder value model is outdated and was used in the 19th century and early 20th century. With recognition that the modern corporation is integrated into the fabric of society rather than a separate, discrete nexus of contracts removed from the surrounding context, the US legal framework has since attempted to reconcile and align profit with CSR.

Although the US regulatory model is somewhat unique, Tineke Lambooy shows that in Europe, the Dutch model has full CSR provisions in corporate governance codes, which is very different from the 'comply or explain' approach used in the United Kingdom. The Frijins Code published in 2008 and becoming effective in 2009 makes CSR explicit and concrete. CSR promotes long-term business plans, the internalisation of external costs, the accountability of corporate conduct, stakeholder engagement and the transparency of Environmental Social and Governance (ESG) factors. This is in line with the Dutch concept of the corporate role in society to satisfy the interests of multiple stakeholders and society as a whole.

An embedded CSR requires CSR to be likewise embedded in managerial commitment and decision making. Colin Fisher proposes a normative debating scheme for managers to discuss the ethical issues and respond to ethical and social challenges to their business model. For Fisher, an open and transparent debate and dialogue on CSR issues prepared by management is a preliminary test of whether a company has embedded CSR in its decision making. There are two questions in the debating scheme: the virtue question (whether it is the right thing to act) and the objectivist question (whether it is in the company's interest to do so). Using two case studies,

Fisher suggests that companies seldom have a single motivation, and a powerful combination of virtues and interests is required for a company to change its core business model.

In recent years, social capital has been recognised as one of the most important resources for business success and competitive advantages. For many, social capital (or social relations, social networks, social interactions and sociability) is almost equal to CSR. However, Paul Manning's contribution makes it clear that social capital is not always CSR positive. Social capital is ethically neutral and can be manipulated by business and managers to serve their self-interests at the cost of their social relations and others. Madoff's 'Ponzi' scheme, revealed in the financial crisis as the biggest ever fraud in American history, has demonstrated this. Hence, when we say that CSR is always embedded in social relationships, we cannot assume inversely that corporate social relations are necessarily favourable towards CSR.

The third theme of this volume is regarding how we may redirect CSR in the future as a post-crisis agenda. It also indicates how an embedded CSR might appear in the future. Wayne Visser indicates that the global financial crisis represents a multi-level failure of responsibility – from the individual and corporate level to the finance sector and entire capitalist system. Unless CSR itself is fundamentally transformed, it will be unable to prevent an equally devastating crisis of responsibility from recurring in future. He presents a new model of CSR 2.0 to replace the failed version of CSR 1.0. For Visser, CSR 2.0 comes down to one thing: clarification and reorientation of the purpose of business. Ultimately, the purpose of business is to serve society, through provision of safe, high-quality products and services that enhance our wellbeing, without eroding our ecological and community life-support systems. Profits are simply a means to this end. Visser informs us that CSR 2.0 is a search for the Chinese concept of a harmonious society, which implies a dynamic yet productive tension of opposites – a *Tai Chi* of CSR, balancing *yin* and *yang*.

Further to Visser's view that CSR 2.0 comes to stand for 'Corporate Sustainability and Responsibility', Hershey H. Friedman and Linda Weiser Friedman make it clear that the current economic model, focusing on extreme materialism and overconsumption, is unsustainable and destroying the true values that result in a healthy and happy society. One of the key lessons from the financial crisis is that we need a new economics; one that is moral and considers more than profit and growth. They argue that voluntary simplicity, a life style philosophy that is to become less materialistic in order to lead a life that has more meaning and purpose, can help lead us on a path towards sustainable development and corporate social responsibility, and away from the greed-is-good credo that nearly caused another Great Depression.

Since the beginning of the new century, CSR has increasingly become popular in developing countries. Yet, it is clear that while the global model of CSR failed in developed countries, a simple transfer of the model to developing countries to ignite and activate CSR could not work. An embedded CSR is contextual-based, since it merges with societal values, traditions and cultures, and emerges from country-specific conditions. Justyna Berniak-Woźny's chapter examines the development of CSR in Poland and demonstrates that successful adaptation and implementation of CSR concept requires continuous dialogue and cooperation among key local partners in the process. Berniak notes that the development of CSR is facing significant challenges in developing countries during the global financial crisis. However, she argues, a change of the quality in CSR promotion supported by key social partners would aid corporations to better cope with the financial crisis.

CONCLUSION

CSR issues could not be more seriously important than in a time of crisis. CSR obviously failed in preventing and mitigating the global financial crisis and the financial crisis has severely challenged our conventional understanding of CSR and exhibited the very limitations of mainstream perspectives on CSR. It is time to rethink the CSR concept and its dominant models, to understand CSR as embedded in social, political and economic contexts and redirect CSR towards a better perspective that integrates business into society rather than separates business from society. This collection brings together a group of contributors to explore the role of CSR for the financial crisis and the underlying issues, examine the institutionalisation of CSR and application of CSR into business and management, and discuss the future agenda for CSR. This volume proposes a way forward towards an embedded instead of an alienated CSR; a way of merging business into society and its context. We believe that this is a general direction for future research. This volume is only a start to explore the core theme. Owing to limited space, this volume cannot cover many topics and aspects of CSR but serves to ignite interest in this research direction, challenge conventional modes of thinking and inspire further discussion. The financial crisis has taught us important lessons from which we have learned to rethink CSR deeply and critically.

NOTES

1. Domenec Mele (2008) summarises four CSR theories, i.e., corporate social performance theory, shareholder value theory, stakeholder theory, and corporate citizenship theory. We think that both corporate social performance theory and corporate citizenship theory can be incorporated into the business ethics model, as both are grounded purely on business ethical principles.

2. It was evidenced that since the 1990s, under the pressures of globalisation and world-wide competition, both Germany and Japan had signalled their changes in corporate direction from a more stakeholder-oriented model towards a more shareholder-valued and market-based model (Jüergens, Naumann, & Rupp, 2000; Stoney & Winstanley, 2001; Schilling, 2001).

REFERENCES

Argandona, A. (2009). *Can corporate social responsibility help us understand the credit crisis?* Working Paper, IESE Business School, University of Navarra, Pamplona, Spain, March.

Arrow, K. J. (1973). Social responsibility and economic efficiency. *Public Policy, 16*, 303–317.

Carroll, A. (1979). Three-dimensional conceptual model of corporate performance? *Academy of Management Review, 4*(4), 497–505.

Carroll, A. (2008). A history of corporate social responsibility: Concepts and practices. In: A. Crane, A. McWilliams, D. Matten, J. Moon & D. S. Siegel (Eds), *The Oxford handbook of corporate social responsibility* (pp. 19–46). Oxford: Oxford University Press.

Davis, K. (1960). Can business afford to ignore social responsibilities? *California Management Review, 2*(3), 70–76.

Davis, K. (1973). The case for and against business assumption of social responsibilities. *Academy of Management Journal, 16*, 312–322.

Driver, M. (2006). Beyond the stalemate of economics versus ethics: Corporate social responsibility and the discourse of the organizational self. *Journal of Business Ethics, 66*, 337–356.

EEAG. (2010). *EEAG report on the European economy 2010.* CESifo Group Munich, Munich.

Etzioni, A. (1998). A communication note on stakeholder theory. *Business Ethics Quarterly, 8*(4), 679–691.

Freeman. (1994). The politics of stakeholder theory; some future direction. *Business Ethics Quarterly, 4*(4), 409–421.

Freeman, R. E., & Velamuri, R. (2006). A new approach to CSR: Company stakeholder responsibility. In: A. Kakabadse & M. Morsing (Eds), *Corporate social responsibility (CSR): Reconciling aspirations with application* (pp. 9–23). Basingstoke: Palgrave Macmillan.

Friedman, M. (1970). The social responsibility of business is to increase its profits. *New York Times Magazine*, 13 September, pp. 32–33, 122, 124 and 126.

Gioia, D. A. (1999). Response: practicability, paradigms, and problems in stakeholder theorizing. *Academy of Management Review, 24*(2), 228–232.

Gioia, D. A. (2003). Business organization as instrument of social responsibility. *Organization, 10*(3), 435–438.

Hummels, H. (1998). Organizing ethics: A stakeholder debate. *Journal of Business Ethics, 17*, 1403–1419.

Jackson, N., & Carter, P. (1995). Organisational chiaroscuro: Throwing light on the concept of corporate governance. *Human Relations, 48*(8), 875–889.

Jüergens, U., Naumann, K., & Rupp, J. (2000). Shareholder value in an adverse environment: The German case. *Economy and Society, 29*, 54–79.

Kay, J. (1993). *The foundation of corporate success.* Oxford: Oxford University Press.

Kueucz, E. C., Colbert, B. A., & Wheeler, D. (2008). The business case for corporate social responsibility. In: A. Crane, A. McWilliams, D. Matten, J. Moon & D. S. Siegel (Eds), *The Oxford handbook of corporate social responsibility* (pp. 83–112). Oxford: Oxford University Press.

McIntosh, M. (2009). Editorial. *Journal of Corporate Citizenship* (33), 7–10.

Mele, D. (2008). Corporate social responsibility theories. In: A. Crane, A. McWilliams, D. Matten, J. Moon & D. S. Siegel (Eds), *The Oxford handbook of corporate social responsibility* (pp. 47–82). Oxford: Oxford University Press.

Preston, L. E., & Post, J. E. (1975). *Private managements and public policy: The principle of public responsibility.* Englewood Cliffs, NJ: Prentice-Hall.

Sandberg, J. (2008). Understanding the separation thesis. *Business Ethics Quarterly, 18*(2), 213–232.

Schilling, F. (2001). Corporate governance in Germany: The move to shareholder value. *Corporate Governance: An International Review, 9*, 148–151.

Solomon, P. A. (2004). Aristotle, ethics and business organizations. *Organization Studies, 25*(6), 1021–1043.

Stewart, J. (2007). The ethics of human resource development. In: C. Rigg, J. Stewart & K. Trehan (Eds), *Critical human resource development: Beyond orthodoxy.* Harlow: Prentice Hall.

Stoney, C., & Winstanley, D. (2001). Stakeholding: Confusion or utopia? Mapping the conceptual terrain. *Journal of Management Studies, 38*(5), 603–626.

Stormer, G. J. (2003). Making the shift: Moving from "ethics pay" to an inter-systems model of business. *Journal of Business Ethics, 44*(4), 43–64.

Wicks, A. C. (1996). Overcoming the separation thesis: The need for a reconsideration of business and society research. *Business Society, 35*(1), 89–118.

PART II
UNDERSTANDING THE ROLE OF
CSR IN THE FINANCIAL CRISIS

THE NATURE OF RESPONSIBILITY AND THE CREDIT CRUNCH

Simon Robinson

In the time since the so-called credit crunch, much has been written about responsibility. However, the discussion has often left the nature of responsibility untouched. Hence, often, there have been different aspects of responsibility referred to in debates without conceptual clarity. This chapter aims to develop some conceptual clarity about the nature of responsibility and how that relates to the credit crunch. Of course, there is not space in one chapter to develop a detailed appreciation of the credit crunch itself. Much of that work is played out in the rest of this volume. Hence, in this chapter, I will be content to provide illustrations from the credit crunch to underline the issue of responsibility, with a little more detail around the particular areas of bonuses and governance. In this chapter, then, I focus immediately on the nature of responsibility and from that reflect on elements of the credit crunch.

THE NATURE OF RESPONSIBILITY

Much of the work in business studies and responsibility has focused on the concept of corporate social responsibility (CSR). For a time, this was very much about the relationship of business to the community. This has developed further into the so-called triple bottom-line approach stressing

Reframing Corporate Social Responsibility: Lessons from the Global Financial Crisis
Critical Studies on Corporate Responsibility, Governance and Sustainability,
Volume 1, 23–41
ISSN: 2043-9059/doi:10.1108/S2043-9059(2010)0000001007

the importance of giving an account of the firm's relation to the social and physical environment as well as the financial state of the firm. Alongside this has been a stress on both the complexity of the external environment and the need to include the internal environment in any view of responsibility, not least in terms of health, safety, and well-being of the staff (Robinson, 2010). The concept of responsibility, however, goes beyond even these concerns.

Schweiker (1995) suggests three interrelated modes of responsibility, the first two of which originate in Aristotle's thinking: imputability, account-ability, and liability.

Imputability

There are strong and weak views of imputability. The weak views (McKenney, 2005) simply refer to the causal connection between the person and any action. Person A has caused, or was responsible for, action B. Such a view does not help in determining just how much the person is actually involved in and therefore fully responsible for the action. A stronger view then suggests that to be fully responsible for something, this necessitates a rational decision-making process. Taylor (1989) argues that this decision-making constitutes a strong valuation that connects action to deep decision making. This owning of the thoughts and related decision is what constitutes the moral identity of the person or group. Closely connected to this is the concept of moral or retrospective responsibility that focuses on blame for actions. Imputability, however, is not about finding blame but rather empowering an organization and its members to take responsibility for their values and practice, in effect developing rational agency.

Each of the modes of responsibility interconnects, and each is relational. Stress on agency might give the impression of a largely individualistic perspective. Hence, it would be easy to see imputability as simply concerned with the self, and accountability as a quite separate concern with the other, requiring a separate justification. However, responsibility, even as agency, is fundamentally relational. Focus on agency, such that the best decisions are taken, demands not simply rationality, but awareness and appreciation of ideas, values, and actions/practice.

Ideas
This demands clarity about the concepts that are used and the capacity to justify them rationally. We can hardly be said to be responsible for our thoughts if we cannot provide some account of and justification for them.

Core to this is some understanding of purpose. Any account and justification of thoughts and actions also demands openness to critical intellectual challenge.

Values
This demands the capacity to appreciate and value thoughts and actions. It is not just that they are coherent; it is also that they have distinct meaning and value, such that one prefers one practice to others. Even at this stage, responsibility involves a comparison with other practices and their values. Hence, deciding upon ones own values does not take place in social isolation, and to fulfill this aspect of responsibility demands a justification of the values. This also engages feelings, not least because values connect to purpose and identity and thus any sense of self-worth. Of course, to be truly aware of, and be in a position to justify, values requires critical reflection and the capacity to set out where the values come from. In turn, this requires critical awareness of the cultural context of values held, including narrative, worldview, and myth around purpose and value.

Practice
At the heart of the third focus is social awareness, of the effects of ones actions, and thus the connection between oneself and the other, be that the social or physical environment. In business, for instance, does one fully understand the practice of an organization and the effect that this might have on the wider social and physical environment?

None of this prescribes a particular response. What it does demand is awareness of what one is doing, how that fits into the purpose of the organization, and how that affects the internal and external environment. In other words, there is a relational context to agency that goes beyond the individual self and that demands awareness and responsiveness. The relationality is also about being answerable to the self.

Critically then, the idea of responsibility includes responsibility for meaning. Taylor (1989) argues that self-interpretation is key to identity. He distinguishes linguistic meaning, knowing what I am saying, and experiential meaning. He argues that the first of these is key to agency, and that this involves three things. First, it is tied to a subject in relationship. Meaning does not occur in vacuo. Second, meaning can be distinguished from any situation. While we find meaning in situations, such as a football game, we choose to give that situation a meaning, often based in the group identity and values. Third, meaning is only developed in relation to other things.

Hence, value, as noted, is espoused in relation to other value meanings. For Taylor, such meaning is at the heart of making any ethical decision.

All this is developed in critical dialog and thus engages plurality inside and outside the group. Only in that context is meaning articulated, defended, and developed. Responsible leadership then involves enabling the group and group members to critique their own and the group's myths – the big stories that give value and identity to the group – not least through engaging other narratives that provide a challenge. Responsible leadership has to provide that critical discourse both at the level of the organization and for the members of the organization. This is exemplified in the development of vision and value statements in organizations. It is increasingly accepted in the development of any organizations' values and mission statement that leadership should consult the members. It would be easy to see this as a matter of "harvesting" values, with the aim of reaching broad agreement, so that members can identify with the values of the organization. However, simply to state values is not to understand them. To understand them requires a critical reflection on the values in relation to the community of practice and any idea of purpose. Without that, it is difficult to develop real commitment to values. In the case of Enron, employees typically learned their values as a mantra, often having them printed out on their desk in case their manager came. There was no sense of responsibility for testing the meaning of those values. This is an exercise that would have to occur over time. In the 1980s, Johnson and Johnson, famous for their proactive credo, reacted rapidly and effectively when faced by the poisoning crisis involving Tylenol (Rehak, 2002). It was assumed that the company credo was the key to the strong ethical response, including the recall of the product. In fact, the CEO noted that it was the regular sessions held in the corporation to review and challenge the basic values that primed the leadership for action.

This also suggests a different approach to trust and leadership. For Solomon (2005), integrity was the basis of trust because it showed consistency and commitment. In other words, one could see from the behavior and attitude of the leader that he or she was positive and worthy of trust. The stress on critical discourse suggests that trust rests on the opportunity to test out the thinking and practice of the leader. In this case, trust is built up over a long period during which the leader can demonstrate the coherence and congruence of ideas, and the development of them in the light of critical challenge.

Bauman (1989) argues that most people seek to avoid taking that responsibility. The experiments of Milgram (2005) reveal almost 70% of participants who accepted the direction of authority figures even where the action of the participant seemed to be causing risk to another person's life. The experiment involved participants who controlled what they believed to be an electric current attached to a person they could either see or hear. They could see that what they perceived was pain in the other (who was actually an actor simulating pain) was being caused by their actions. However, they did not consider themselves responsible for this pain. The "actor" was seen as partly responsible, because they got the questions wrong, in an experiment that the participant was told was about the relationship between pain and learning. More importantly, the experiment director was a figure of authority who assumed overall responsibility, both for the practice and for the ideas and values behind it. Few of the participants took responsibility for questioning critically either the values or the practice. In relation to leadership, Hinrich (2007) has noted how easily this can lead to "crimes of obedience," committed through following the orders of the leader without question. The assumption of the follower in such cases is that the leader is responsible for any values held and any decisions based in those values. In effect, the follower accepts no responsibility for testing ideas and values and does not hold the leader to account for his ideas or values.

Accountability

The second mode of responsibility is accountability to another. This is focused usually in contract relationships, formal or informal. The contract sets up a series of mutual expectations. At one level, these are about discernible targets that form the basis of any shared project, and without which the competence of the person cannot be assessed. At another level, there will be broader moral expectations of how one should behave in any contract. This would include the importance of openness and transparency in relationships and other such behaviors that provide the basis for trust. Any contract can be modified and developed by the parties, and thus, contract between shareholders and executives, for instance, need not be confined to a single purpose. The contract also sets up the sense answerability to another. I give an account to that person or group of my thoughts and actions, thus connecting imputability to accountability. This aspect of responsibility involves roles or relationships and stresses a proactive stance, working out the meaning of this in practice.

Many writers argue that accountability is best understood through stakeholder theory (SHT). A stakeholder was initially defined as individuals or groups that were critical to the survival of an organization, especially business, including employees, customers, lenders, and suppliers. This has been further developed to "any individual or group who can affect or is affected by the actions, decisions, policies, practices or goals of the organization" (Carroll & Buchholtz, 2000). This widens stakeholders to government, the community, and beyond. For multinational corporations, this becomes even more complex.

It is possible to identify different versions of SHT, as argued by Heath and Norman (2004). These include the following:

- Strategic SHT: a theory that attention to the needs of stakeholders will lead to better outcomes for the business;
- SHT of governance: a theory about how stakeholder groups should be involved in oversight of management, for example, placing stakeholders on the board; and
- Deontic SHT: a theory that analyzes the legitimate rights and needs of the different stakeholders and uses this data to develop company policies.

It is possible, however, to see all these theories as simply aspects of a larger stakeholder's view that sees any organization as accountable to its stakeholders. Hence, leadership of the organization has to ensure that accountability and the means of fulfilling this accountability are clear, inside and outside the organization. Most organizations are in a position of having to handle quite complex multiple and mutual accountability. A commissioning firm is, for example, both a stakeholder to the tendering firms and vice versa. Equally, each company would have some very different stakeholders, with different and sometimes conflicting values. The company is accountable not only to its shareholders but also to its customers. By extension, the government and wider industry might hold them to account for professional standards, and even some nongovernmental organizations (NGOs) and consumer associations might call them to account for the effect of their products. Sternberg (2000) argues that strict accountability cannot be extended to groups such as NGOs. The thrust of her argument is that if accountability is extended to all stakeholders, it loses any meaning of responsibility to a particular organization. This is lost once one moves beyond specific contracts. Her argument, however, fails to grasp the interconnectedness of relationships and purpose. In the Nestle breast milk substitute case, for instance (Robinson, 2002a, 2002b), the narrow purpose of Nestle was to market this product in developing countries. In the light of that narrow purpose, it could be argued that Nestle was not accountable to the NGOs UNICEF or WHO. However, in both NGOs, their focus was on a wider health-centered purpose that was in direct competition with Nestle's marketing practice. The first focused on children's health and the second on the primacy of breast feeding for baby care. The wider social purpose made Nestle directly accountable to the both of these NGOs, precisely because the marketing practice seemed to be subverting this public good. Even a narrower view of the purpose of Nestle, as providing increased share value, would still support a form of accountability to these groups, not least because they had then power to effect that value through economic boycotts if Nestle did take account of the wider social concerns. Other firms have complex relations with professions and professional bodies. Engineering firms, for instance, relate directly to professional bodies that define their identity in terms of responsibility to clients, the profession, the wider society, and its future well-being (Robinson, Dixon, Moodley, & Preece, 2007). Accountability then does not involve a simple "line." It is worked out in the plurality of relationships within and outside any organization.

Liability

Moral liability (as distinct from legal liability) goes beyond accountability, into the idea of concern for others, of sense of wider liability for projects, people, or place. Each person or group has to work these out in context, without necessarily an explicit contract. Working that out demands an awareness of the limitations of the person or organization, avoiding taking too much responsibility, and a capacity to work together with others and to negotiate and share responsibility. This is responsibility for people and projects in the past, present, and future. Once again, this can have a strictly legal sense or a wider moral one encompassing the broadest possible view of stakeholders, from those directly affected by any business or project to the social and natural environment in which these operate. There are several aspects to this "mode" of responsibility.

First, it is possible to be accountable to someone or thing and also be responsible for them. A good example is the doctor who is accountable to her patient and for her patient.

Second, like accountability, there may be multiple responsibilities. These carry with them a sense of responsibility to a complex environment of which we are a part. Brown (2005) argues that this responsibility is part of corporate integrity and involves relational awareness. This involves five dimensions: cultural, interpersonal, organizational, social, and ecological. The organization is part of any of these dimensions, and thus in some part responsible for them. The cultural may be about responsibility for meaning and practice. It may involve several different meaning systems for any group or person, reflecting Taylor's (1989) point that individuals and organizations are "plural." The interpersonal involves friend and peer groups. Organizational involves what is often seen as the well-being of the group. The social moves into citizenship, responsibility in some sense of the civil and social environment. The person or organization is inextricably bound up in the networks of society and will influence that for bad or good whatever they do. The ecological is the physical environment, which all have a stake in and supports all groups. The integrity of the organization involves, Brown argues, the awareness of and responsiveness to each of these areas, all of which are interlinked.

Leadership, suggests Brown, enables the group to be aware of these intersecting environments, enables the group to recognize what they mean and the value base of response, and enables the different stakeholders of these environments to share responsibility for response, both by negotiating particular responsibilities and by developing partnerships.

The leader then is involved in enabling the development of meaning around responsibility, in ensuring a proper level of awareness of the group's social and physical environment, and ensuring a response.

Caldwell, Hayes, Bernal, and Karri (2008) argue that a key aspect of meaning in this third mode of responsibility is the idea of stewardship. This focuses on the recognition that resources are not totally owned by the leader or the group, that he and it act as custodian to use these resources for a greater good. Caldwell suggests that stewardship is found in covenant thinking rather than the contract of accountability. Covenant thinking is about a broader commitment over time to the wider environment. It tends to begin with this concern and then see how it can be fulfilled and who is best to do that.

Compared to this, contract is specific, calculative and limits relationships, and can be put to one side if the terms of the agreement are broken. It would be very easy to polarize the two approaches to agreements and lead to a battle between covenant and contract. Both are needed in working through responsibility.

Stewardship is, of course, expressed strongly in theological and philosophical terms. Jonas (1984) a philosopher from a Jewish background aims to provide an ontological rather than theological justification for responsibility for the whole global environment. Nonetheless, as Vogel

(2006) notes, his ontological grounding of this is an analog of Jewish creation theology. He argues, firstly, that living nature is good in itself, attested to by matter's capacity to organize itself for life (the analog of God attesting to the goodness of his creation). Secondly, he argues that the creation of humankind is an event of the highest importance, establishing a reflective stewardship responsibility for nature (the analog of man created in God's image). Thirdly, he argues that the imperative to be responsible is answered by the capacity of humankind to feel responsible for the whole (the analog of God writing in man's heart the consciousness of the good). Responsibility in this is based on an identification with the environment and an acute awareness of man's role in relation to it. Hence, H. Richard Niebuhr writes, "What is implicit in the idea of responsibility is the image of man – the answerer, man engaged in dialogue, man acting in response to action upon him" (1963).

This sense of responsibility can even take the form of universal responsibility. There are echoes here of a more mystical approach to responsibility as set out in Dostoevsky's *The Brothers Karamazov*. Markel recognizes his connection with everything and says "everyone is really responsible to all men, for all men and for everything" (Dostoevsky, 1993, p. 41), a view echoed by Father Zossima. Zossima, however, moves responsibility across from liability for consequences to liability for the sins of humankind,

> as soon as you make yourself sincerely responsible for everything and for all men, you will see at once that it is really so, and that you are to blame everyone and for all things. (Dostoevsky, 1993, pp. 78)

Arendt tempers this. She defines humanity as the view "that in one form or another men must assume responsibility for all crimes committed by men and that all nations share the onus of evil committed by all others" (Arendt, 1991, p. 282). Here, Arendt does not necessarily mean strict moral liability for the sins of others, but more the sense that human kind must take collective responsibility for learning from those sins.

In all this, one is not literally responsible for everything. Rather, one begins with the attitude of responsibility. This cannot be totally fulfilled by the one person. Hence, for Bauman (1989, p. 81), "the moral self is always haunted by the suspicion that it is not moral enough."

What this does mean is that if universal responsibility is to be genuine, then it has to be shared. This demands a process of negotiation, enabling all parties to see how their resources can be used to fulfill civil responsibility. This relates directly to all levels of decision making. Hence, even at the level of data gathering, it is critical to work together with other groups. When that does not happen, then the data tends to be dominated by the interest of the groups and it becomes eroded. Entine, through the Brent Spar case (2002) shows how this can lead to bad decisions, in terms of ethics and effectiveness.

THE CREDIT CRUNCH AND THE FAILURE OF RESPONSIBLE LEADERSHIP

The causes of the credit crisis in 2008 were many and cannot be covered in detail here, however, at its heart was a failure of responsible leadership at different levels.

First, leadership was characterized by a lack of agency as described earlier. Part of agency is about understanding the context, and part of that is about being responsible for understanding the past, and the implications this has for present actions and consequences. This links agency to wider responsibility. It is clear that leadership in the finance industries took no responsibility for this. Since the 1970s, there were over 120 bank-centered crises globally. Most of these followed booms in house prices and stock markets. Carroll and Mui (2008) note the example of Green Tree Finance who, in the 1990s, offered mortgages on mobile homes. The financial mismatch should have been obvious given that the average life of a mobile home did not exceed 15 years, and average length of mortgages sold was 30 years. No one, however, questioned the ever-increasing flawed loans. When problems began to occur with loan repayments in 1999, Green Tree Finance succeeded in selling the company to Conseco for almost $6 billion. Conseco subsequently became bankrupt. The leaders of the finance industry in 2008 made no attempt to examine the history of a sector that had made the same mistakes that led to the credit crunch. The only difference was that the early mistakes were restricted to individual corporations or a small number. For Aquinas, this would have been seen as a failure of prudentia, practical wisdom that relates directly to responsibility. The first part of prudentia is awareness of the past and the lessons that need to be learned from the past (memoria). Memoria requires that responsibility be taken for learning.

Second, the lack of responsibility as critical agency extended to little basic understanding about the products themselves. This was evidenced in different ways. There was no attempt critically to assess the sale of derivatives, in terms of theory or practice. Tett (2009) notes how attempts even to question practice, as a journalist, were dismissed out of hand. Repeatedly, firms made the mistake of buying into practices that were not thoroughly understood, or involved judgments outside their expertise. AIG, for instance, offered credit-default insurance on mortgage-backed securities that it did not understand. Merrill decided it would use instruments developed by Goldman Sachs to invest its own capital in what was subsequently revealed as toxic loans. Once again, the examples from the past revealed the same lack of critical thinking. Conseco in 1999 had a successful track record of taking over companies, all of which were insurance based. The corporation however had no understanding or experience of the mortgage business. The result was a complete lack of understanding about the business model that it had taken on, with all its problems. Despite this, Conseco increased the mortgage business. This continued up to the point of collapse. The only criterion for taking this on board was that it made money.

Companies such as LTCM and AIG claimed that their portfolios and securities were risk-proof. Even disregarding the subprime base of the securities, the very idea of a financial instrument as being risk-proof should be met with the same skepticism as we might afford Dr Dulcamara and his love potion in Donizetti's *L'Elisire d'Amore*. The lack of any critical thinking was also evidenced all through the business chain, not least in the way the original mortgage businesses approached their customers. Companies actively encouraged customers to make decisions that were not based in realistic and responsible thinking. There was thus little genuine agency.

Third, there was even less sense of accountability. The finance industry has in many respects been founded on the basis of trust. This has been strongly reinforced in the profession of accountancy. Recent work from the ICAEW (Institute of Chartered Accountants in England and Wales) has stressed that the profession is itself built around the virtue of integrity. Integrity, of course, is not simply one virtue but many, including honesty, transparency, and justice (ICAEW, 2007). These come together to help form a coherent character and identity, for the individual and the organization. This helps to establish trust in the profession. Key to such trust is the development of reliable information. Can the client trust the professional to present information that is true, relevant, and honest? It reminds us that the presentation of any such information is never free from interpersonal dynamics and related values. Are there other pressures that lead to lack of appreciation of the implications of the data? The Challenger Case, where health and safety was ignored leading to the explosion of the space shuttle, showed how political pressures led client and eventually engineers to ignore crucial information (Robinson, 2002a, 2002b).

By extension, clear and truthful information becomes critical for the wider financial markets. Participants in the markets depend on accurate information to make choices. Accurate information is also necessary if any organization is to plan effectively and sustainably. In turn, such information is necessary if public policy is to be effective.

In effect, the ICAEW is arguing that the functioning of the whole financial system relies on the practice of integrity. In that context, the leader has to give attention to the development and articulation of integrity. By extension, any wider financial services will be accountable to the wider financial system, not least because the financial services cannot operate in a system that has collapsed. Of course, when faced by a system that was collapsing, the finance corporations argued that the survival of the system demanded that they could not be allowed to fail, introducing the theme of moral hazard. The danger here is that by bailing out the banks, the issue of their responsibility is once more not addressed.

Fourth, in addition to a lack of accountability to the finance system and the stakeholders involved, there was a lack of awareness of and responsibility for the wider community. The thinking of leaders was insulated. Merrill Lynch and WaMu, for instance, built large portfolios of mortgage-related securities that were based on the assumption that housing markets were localized, and thus that failure in one area would not affect other areas. The credit crunch, however, showed that markets were interconnected, linking Kansas to Shanghai, and thus that leaders need to take responsibility for being aware of the possible effects of any practice. In the midst of all that was a naïve view of risk. Any risk assessment was based on a narrow view of risk, not connected to the wider environment of the product or industry. This reinforced little sense of liability beyond the immediate, and no sense of shared liability, for the industry or the wider community. Behind this, there was another, equally naïve, assumption, that things would not go wrong. LTCM, for instance, thought that, even in the event of problems, it could always unwind its projects in orderly fashion. In fact, all buyers disappeared at once. The same thing happened to Merrill, WaMu, and others. The market, however, unfolded so quickly that nobody would buy their debt portfolios.

In short then, the credit crunch was characterized by an almost complete lack of responsible leadership, with little agency, critical thinking, or awareness of the wider environment, of either the industry or the wider community, no sense of accoutantability other than to shareholders, and no sense of shared responsibility for other than the share price. The lack of responsibility was precisely reinforced by excessive remuneration that focused on immediate gains and gave no value long term for sustainability in the firm, the industry, or the wider environment.

REASONS OF IRRESPONSIBLE THINKING AND PRACTICE

It might be asked why the finance industry demanded no evidence of responsible thinking or practice. I will suggest three reasons. One reason was because they assumed a moral framework that simply did not take such responsibility into account. At the time of writing, Goldman Sachs is being sued by the US Securities and Exchange Commission.[1] The charge is one of fraud, based on a hedge fund who asked Goldman Sachs to put together a collateralized debt obligation (CDO). The hedge fund subsequently bet, successfully, on the CDO failing. There is no denying that something like this happened, and at the moment, the kind of arguments being used to rebuff the accusation are that this is simply what happens in the bond market, as distinct from the stock market, and the people who lost money were all part of this risk business and knew the score. At one level, the argument is curiously close to the long ago expressed view of Albert Carr (1968) that business really is not about ethics. Everyday ethics are left at the office door. The point, so the argument goes, is that everyone in business knows what the "game" is about, competition and deception and much that requires us to suspend "normal" ethics. Once one begins what is analogous to a game, one simply uses the rules of the game, much as one uses the rules of poker, to gain personal advantage. Allied to the idea of an alternative ethics of game rules is the argument that the only people who have been harmed are those who have chosen to play the game, and thus, by implication, those who chose to risk what resources they had.

As an argument, this has little merit, without much evidence of critical thinking. First, it is not clear that the analogy to games rules actually holds. The idea that one can determine the content of a CDO and then bet on it, regardless of any questions about how this relates to the law, would seem to be anything but about a game of chance. Games of chance are characterized by a level of fairness. All have a similar chance to win and no one knows what the deal will give them. Of equal difficulty is the idea that those who bet on the various deals will harm only themselves if things go wrong.

This is clearly false. At the very least, those who are involved in the bond market are connected to the firms that they work for. The fall out of the credit crisis amply demonstrated that failure in the area directly and adversely affected colleagues and coworkers. Extending beyond that are the shareholders large and small who invest in the finance organizations. I am left wondering then how if we suspend "normal" ethics in favor of the rules of the risk business just what those rules might be, who polices them, and who might ensure that none of this affects people who have mortgages and the housing industry, the non-speculative side of banking, the finance and banking industry, the governments who have bailed out the industry, and so on. The credit crisis showed that they are connected to all these groups and more and share responsibility for global financial well-being. The ethical imperative for the leadership of this area then is to work together with the other stakeholders to fulfill that responsibility. Minimally, this requires greater regulation in the bond market, to mirror the stock market, and probably dividing the speculative side of banking from other banking operations. Regulation in this sense would be to remind the firms involved that responsibility cannot be "suspended."

A second reason why many of the finance institutions did not practice any of the modes of responsibility was to do with the system of remuneration. At its most basic, the culture of remuneration reflected and determined the key values of the organizations. General remuneration and the large bonuses were tied directly to immediate profits. This reinforced a focus that that was concerned less with the nature of the product and more with any profit. The dynamic was already there in examples such as Green Tree Finance. This firm continued to deal in flawed loans because remuneration was tied directly to an increase in the number of mortgages. Key to the later subprime lending crisis was also the connection of immediate remuneration to the generation of flawed loans. These of course were then turned into securities and sold on. Remuneration of leaders was thus tied directly to a single and flawed means of making money. This clearly signaled that the firm was responsible for nothing but making money now, not for any effect of that decision on the firm a year or more down the line. The means of remuneration thus can have the effect of discouraging any sense of responsibility beyond the project in the moment. Aquinas's prudentia involved two more elements: awareness of the present and its environment (conscientia) and awareness of the future (solertia). This involved taking responsibility for present awareness and for the future, and thus for possible consequences of ones actions. This was absent in the practice of the banks.

The same dynamic is now repeating itself after the government bail outs. One report (Storey & Dash, 2009) notes that nine banks in the United States that were bailed out, having lost over $81 billion, were by late 2009 paying over $39 billion in bonuses. The justification from the banks has been that this was matter of reasonable reward. Wider issues of responsibility were once more not involved. The argument from figures such as Brian Griffiths is once more around utility rather than responsibility.[2] This includes the arguments that there is a limited market of leaders, that effective leadership demands high remuneration, and that the best leaders will leave if regulation of bonuses comes in.

There are several counterarguments to these. First, the empirical evidence does not support these assertions. Research suggests that openings for CEOs are scarce (Kolb, 2005). There is little evidence of many better jobs that would attract leaders away. There is evidence of available leaders who would take the job for considerably less pay. Many alternative approaches have simply not been tested across industry, such as hiring leaders from within the firm or recruiting from different countries. Second, research also suggests that the effect of leaders on the fate of business is often not as much as claimed. The fate of businesses is more often down to contingencies that the leader cannot control (Khurana, 2002). Third, any arguments about the justice of any remuneration all agree that the key to this is a transparent view and system of justice (Shaw, 2006). This includes discussion about and justification of pay differentials within the organization. This has increasingly led to demands in business for the development of "compensation philosophies."[3] The critical point about such philosophies is that they become part of the company's identity. Remuneration then becomes not simply functional but part of how the company makes sense of itself. More than that, it becomes a part of how the company develops its responsibility. Critically testing and working through a compensation philosophy develops agency, genuinely understanding what is meant by justice. By doing that, it is also giving an account of its meaning and practice to the stakeholders. It is also demonstrating a wider responsibility that acts as an example to other firms. The arguments from leaders such as Griffiths are characterized by an absence of any reference to responsibility of the firm or of the leaders. Quite the contrary, the dynamics of the argument are about setting up scenarios where firms have no choice but to pay massive bonuses. This asserts that there is not even room for the exercise of responsibility.

A third reason why there was little conscious reflection on responsibility was to do with leadership and governance. In many respects, the issues to do with compensation of the leaders are to do with how leadership is dispersed at the head of the business and how the firm is governed by the board of directors. Leadership in the charismatic model has tended to see the CEO acting also as the chair and as a result dominating the board. Much of the leadership style in the finance institutions has reflected this approach. Increasingly, however, it is argued that, no matter how committed the CEO is, he or she should be made more directly accountable to the board. It is precisely such accountability, and the distance that this implies, that would ensure that the leadership of the CEO could be questioned and assessed. Some have even argued that the CEO should not serve as a voting member of the board. In effect, this gives a strong leadership role to the board as a whole, such that it has oversight and is able to monitor: how the firm is achieving its results; how the firm's practices relate to the narrative of the adequate investments in the future; whether the firm's strategies still reflect its core purpose and are being implemented effectively; and what the effect of the firm's practice is across the social and physical environment.

The board then becomes the transparent environment in which the leadership of the CEO is framed, tested, supported, and developed. It would have a strong responsibility for dispersed leadership, and for critical discourse that would make sure that there was no element of leadership that could hide from external gaze. It is within that context that the compensation policy can be thoroughly tested and its philosophy developed.

It is precisely such developments that were recommended by the UK Combined Code of Governance (2006). This argued that the board should be effectively and collectively responsible. A core recommendation was that the Chairman and CEO should have a clear division of responsibilities, with the chair facilitating the leadership of the board, ensuring that board practiced its responsibilities to monitor and support the work of the CEO as manager and leader, carrying out what is determined by the board. A second major recommendation seeks to develop the most effective board composition involving a balance of executives and nonexecutive directors. The chair would then be responsible for ensuring that the different perspectives of the nonexecutive directors, valued most for their independent thinking, were fully brought out. Nonexecutive directors then provide a critical challenge essential to responsible leadership.

In effect, all this enables dispersed leadership, a sense of shared responsibility, and clear negotiation of responsibility. The board would then begin to reflect wider discourse and debate among stakeholders and in the wider community. Ultimately, the chair would be responsible for ensuring the practice of dispersed leadership.

All of this looks to build ethical thinking into the culture of the board and CEOs such that they take responsibility in all senses of the word: defining and continually reevaluating the purpose, aims, and values of the organization (King Report, 2002); being accountable to stakeholders; and embodying the shared responsibility for the social and physical environment. This includes then responsibility for plural stakeholders and also multiple function responsibility, with executive directors both responsible to the CEO but also with all other board member to the shareholders for the direction and operation of the firm.

The case of the so-called credit-crunch exemplifies precisely where leadership in the finance industry chose to ignore responsible practice in every aspect of governance.

CONCLUSION

There are, of course, many other reasons why the credit crunch came about. In this chapter, I have suggested that one key reason was that the industry in effect denied any responsibility, for knowing what they were doing, or the effects of their actions; for giving an account of their thinking and actions; and for accepting that they shared responsibility for wider social environments. This places the meaning and practice of responsibility at the heart of corporate leadership. The chapter concludes that business has to take account of all these factors, demanding a culture of critical thinking, clearer articulation and dialog around plural accountability, and more focus on how wider responsibility can be achieved in partnership. Business means responsibility, inclusive rather than exclusive.

NOTES

1. http://news.bbc.co.uk/1/hi/business/8625931.stm
2. http://www.guardian.co.uk/business/2009/oct/21/executive-pay-bonuses-goldmansachs
3. http://findarticles.com/p/articles/mi_m3495/is_1_50/ai_n11841250/pg_2/?tag = content;col1

REFERENCES

Arendt, H. (1991). Organized guilt and universal responsibility. In: L. May & H. Hoffman (Eds), *Collective responsibility: Five decades of debate in theoretical and applied ethics* (pp. 273–283). Savage: Rowbottom and Littlefield.

Bauman, Z. (1989). *Modernity and the holocaust*. London: Polity.

Brown, M. (2005). *Corporate integrity*. Cambridge: Cambridge University Press.

Caldwell, C., Hayes, L., Bernal, P., & Karri, R. (2008). Ethical stewardship – Implications for leadership and trust. *Journal of Business Ethics, 78*(1–2), 153–164.

Carr, A. (1968). Is business bluffing ethical? *Harvard Business Review* (January/February), 143–149.

Carroll, A., & Buchholtz, A. (2000). *Business and society – Ethics and stakeholder management*. London: Thompson.

Carroll, P. B., & Mui, C. (2008). 6 lessons we should have learned already. *Harvard Business Review* (September 12), 8–91.

Combined Code of Governance. (2006). *The financial reporting council*. London.

Dostoevsky, F. (1993). *The grand inquisitor*. Indianapolis: Hackett.

Entine, J. (2002). Shell, Greenpeace and Brent spar: The politics of dialogue. In: C. Megone & S. Robinson (Eds), *Case histories in business ethics* (pp. 59–95). London: Routledge.

Heath, J., & Norman, W. (2004). Stakeholder theory, corporate governance and public management. *Journal of Business Ethics, 53*(3), 247–265.

Hinrich, K. (2007). Follower propensity to commit crimes of obedience. *Journal of Leadership and Organizational Studies, 4*(1), 69–76.

ICAEW. (2007). *Reporting with integrity*. London: ICAEW.

Jonas, H. (1984). *The imperative of responsibility*. Chicago: Chicago University Press.

Khurana, R. (2002). *Searching for a corporate savior*. Princeton, NJ: Princeton University Press.

King Report on Governance for South Africa (King II). (2002). Institute of directors in South Africa, Capetown.

Kolb, R. (2005). *The ethics of executive compensation*. Oxford: Blackwell.

McKenney, P. (2005). Responsibility. In: G. Meilander & W. Werpehowski (Eds), *Theological ethics* (pp. 237–253). Oxford: Oxford University Press.

Milgram, S. (2005). *Obedience to authority*. New York: Pinter and Martin.

Niebuhr, H. R. (1963). *The responsible self*. New York: Harper and Row.

Rehak, J. (2002). Tylenol mad a hero of Johnson and Johnson. *New York Times*, March 23, 32.

Robinson, S. (2002a). Challenger Flight 5I-1 A case history in whistleblowing. In: C. Megone & S. Robinson (Eds), *Case histories in business ethics* (pp. 108–122). London: Routledge.

Robinson, S. (2002b). Nestle and international marketing. In: C. Megone & S. Robinson (Eds), *Case histories in business ethics* (pp. 141–158). London: Routledge.

Robinson, S. (2010). Can the marketplace be ethical? In: P. Wetherly & D. Otter (Eds), *The business environment* (2nd ed., pp. 187–212). Oxford: Oxford University Press.

Robinson, S., Dixon, R., Moodley, K., & Preece, C. (2007). *Engineering, business and professional ethics*. London: Heinemann Butterworth.

Schweiker, W. (1995). *Responsibility and Christian ethics*. Cambridge: Cambridge University Press.

Shaw, W. J. (2006). Incentives and executive compensation. In: R. W. Kolb (Ed.), *The ethics of executive compensation* (pp. 87–100). Oxford: Blackwell.

Solomon, R. (2005). Emotional leadership, emotional integrity. In: J. Ciulla, T. Price & S. Murphy (Eds), *The quest for moral leaders* (pp. 28–44). Cheltenham: Edward Elgar.

Sternberg, E. (2000). *Just business*. Oxford: Oxford University Press.

Storey, L., & Dash, E. (2009). Bankers reaped lavish bonuses during bailouts. *New York Times*, July 30, 15.

Taylor, C. (1989). *Sources of the self*. Cambridge: Cambridge University Press.

Tett, G. (2009). *Fool's gold*. London: Little Brown.

Vogel, L. (2006). Natural law Judaism? The genesis of bioethics in Hans Jonas, Leo Strauss, and Leon Kass. In: W. Schweiker, M. Johnson & K. Jung (Eds), *Humanity before god* (pp. 209–237). Minneapolis: Augsbursg.

THE ROLE OF CORPORATE SOCIAL RESPONSIBILITY IN THE FINANCIAL CRISIS

Ralph Tench

We live in interesting times. In the past few years Western economies have been hit by several tidal waves originated by poor or irresponsible corporate behaviour (see Tench, Bowd, & Jones, 2007) which have resulted in a dramatic global economic downturn.

Many of our usual reference points have been changed. We can no longer rely on institutions and organisations that for generations we have believed in and trusted. Think of our manufacturing giants such as the automotive industry; pension providers and most importantly our financial institutions (banks worldwide). Our confidence in all of these has been shattered. In essence we can no longer trust those that previously we have put great faith in and trusted. And this is a terrible indictment of contemporary business. This equates on a personal level to the revelation that a friend is unreliable; a partner prepared to cheat on you or a business associate who will steal from you or behave fraudulently. These are all examples of what can happen to us as individuals and business people in society. But we have not faced such a large scale, worldwide societal shift in confidence which permeates all levels irrespective of age, vocation, gender or demographic for decades. For example we have elementary school children who talk about the 'credit crunch' and understand the concepts of financial supply and demand. These

Reframing Corporate Social Responsibility: Lessons from the Global Financial Crisis
Critical Studies on Corporate Responsibility, Governance and Sustainability,
Volume 1, 43–56
Copyright © 2010 by Emerald Group Publishing Limited
All rights of reproduction in any form reserved
ISSN: 2043-9059/doi:10.1108/S2043-9059(2010)0000001008

are youngsters who in the United Kingdom know the name of pantomime business-stage 'baddies' such as Fred 'the shred' Goodwin (former CEO of RBS bank) and find his media nick name funny but his actions deplorable. There is a dissonance for many in society from the young to the old because this is a man who is perceived by the popular media as having put people out of work and yet he, the 'boss', has continued to be financially rewarded.

We then have the more detailed failings of the money markets and market makers such as executives from Lehmann Brothers, Merrill Lynch, Goldman Sachs and Morgan Stanley. These business managers have demonstrated poor business judgement and in some cases highly question-able corporate ethics. The case of Goldman Sachs' executives highlights the issue with their appearance before the US Permanent Subcommittee on Investigations in April 2010 when the bank's mortgage bankers were compared by the US lawyers to bookies. In further cross examination Senator Carl Levin asked why the firm sold securities the company itself called 'shitty' in internal email correspondence. According to a Bloomberg report (2010) in the comments to the executive, Levin was referring to a June 2007 e-mail to Sparks from Thomas Montag, the former head of sales and trading in the Americas at Goldman Sachs. The message described a set of mortgage-linked investments that his bank had been trying to sell as part of 'one shitty deal'. David Viniar, Goldman Sachs' chief financial officer, told the panel that 'we share responsibility' for the financial crisis. Without irony he also said 'we care very much about ethics at Goldman Sachs'. It is this kind of extreme corporate management irriesponsibility which has been identified as fueling the economic collapse during the credit crunch.

So what do these lessons and experiences of recent years tell us about corporations and their responsibilities and what can business leaders do in such times to respond to the new environment? This chapter will set the scene for the irresponsible behaviour of some executives in Western corporations as well exploring how this moral failure has led to the global financial crisis.

TRUST AND BUSINESS IN SOCIETY TODAY

In order to understand this new economic environment we need first to look at the context and some of the facts. Firstly society has lost a lot of faith with two important institutions, politics and business. There is a lack of trust in both. The UK political scene has been hit by several scandals involving poor ethical behaviour such as false and fraudulent expenses claims by members of the UK parliament. This has created distrust in politicians according to many surveys and polls such as for the BBC which found 80% of voters did not trust politicians to tell the truth (BBC News 24, 18 March 2010). This distrust arguably created political ambiguity and the country and contributed to the first 'hung parliament' in the United Kingdom for many years with no overall majority for one party in the 2010 general election. This subsequently resulted in the first coalition government since 1945 between the Liberal Democrats and the Conservatives (UK General Election, 6 May 2010). In the United States, Barak Obama in an attempt to differentiate himself from the cosy business-Bush presidential era developed a presidential campaign message about 'restoring trust'. Arguably companies need to do the same as we enter the second decade of the second millennium. According to the 11th annual Edelman Trust Barometer (2010) we have seen trust figures plummet with two-thirds of the study's public trusting companies less than a year ago. Furthermore in the context of organisations' responsibility, just 38% trust business to do what is right, which is down 20% from just the previous year. Perhaps most disturbing of all for corporations only 17% trust the information coming from a company's CEO (chief executive officer). For companies that is a terrifying statistic. In previous eras rolling out the organisational head was a sure fire way of getting media coverage as well as influencing key stakeholders such as institutional investors and also in building and developing credibility. This was achieved because organisational stakeholders when listening to corporate messages heard it 'from the horse's mouth', the CEO. Now these individuals are tarnished with the labels of greed, excessive pay and the abuse of managerial power.

So what does this tell us? Well arguably we have a changing cultural climate. We have experienced economic collapses and mass investment of national wealth to privatise and secure businesses worldwide. Examples can be tracked in the United States with interventions to support large corporations in 2008; in the United Kingdom with the government's loans and privatisation of independent banks again in 2008 and 2009 as well as the European Institutions' interventions to secure Greece's economic stability in May 2010 along with the Euro currency itself. Consequently, societal stakeholders are no longer prepared to take the values and attitudes of business for granted. An example in the United Kingdom is the attitude towards banking and bonuses. For decades it has been accepted that City employees 'worked hard and played hard' and as a result they got handsomely rewarded for their efforts with high salaries and bonuses – and they deserved it. Not any more it would seem. The public's tolerance for this type of selfish behaviour has declined. Now that many tax payers feel they 'employ' many of the bankers or have 'bailed them out' they feel these rewards systems should be challenged and reviewed. Similarly there has been a media and consumer support to call the bluff of many bankers who have suggested that the markets and the market makers who have had such rewards will leave the United Kingdom to seek their appropriate rewards and returns in other countries or markets if they are capped. To date, interestingly, this has not happened. The markets in reality know that historically the United Kingdom is an inherently stable and secure place to do business – and to make money! We may be in short-term leaner economic times with high public debt but the executives have not so far found a greener field elsewhere.

So we have a shifting social mood. As Alex Aitken (2008), Director of Communications for Westminster City Council, said at the height of the economic crisis in the autumn of 2008: '(we) should be explaining to fellow managers the mood of the country is changing and they must develop a corporate narrative that recognises these difficulties'. The directives for change are also coming from international voices such as Banki-Moon, General Secretary of the United Nations who stated that we 'need business to give practical meaning and reach the values and principles that connect cultures and people everywhere' (UN Global Compact, 2008, p. 4).

STAKEHOLDER RESPONSIBILITIES

We do not know the long-term implication of the economic downturn but the turmoil is forcing organisations to reassess how they communicate with key stakeholders. Therefore discussions about the mood of the nation have come to the fore and in turn how business should reflect on these swings and analyse and respond to the changing cultural climate. This changing climate is something Leeper (2001) wrote about at the start of the millennium before the economic turmoil saying:

> A loss of trust in others and loss of sense of community means that there is a loss of shared meaning that in turn affects the cultural standards and political participation.

So has the zeitgeist-spirit of the age-changed? Certainly the language and experiences of the credit crunch have influenced the cultural environment. For example in 2009 Asda Wal-Mart (third largest supermarket in the United Kingdom and part of the US Wal-Mart group) launched a 'Pulse of the Nation' survey in the United Kingdom. This involved 10,000 panel members and focussed on 10 issues that impact on people's personal lives including personal finance, relationships, education and safety from crime, job security, the environment, time pressure, diet, exercise and the economy. In summary, a multi-dimensional view of day-to-day living. They were interested in how given the economic climate these conditions were impacting on key aspects of family life, clearly with an eye on consumer attitudes and responses to key issues. The company has used the insights to inform its communications (tone and content) with key stakeholders.

So how does this unstable social, political and cultural environment influence the role of the organisation in its societal context, i.e., in terms of its corporate social responsibility? Put this another way, is this a bad time to be good? Should and are companies abandoning their CSR? Is it a luxury for the good times?

The interesting way to answer these questions is to consider some stakeholder perceptions. Firstly from business leaders generally. For them CSR in 2008 was clearly an important issue. And this sentiment goes right across Europe and the world. For example attitudes of business leaders in a McKinsey Global Leaders' Survey (2009 Feb) indicated agreement that environmental, social and governance programmes do create shareholder value, though the ongoing economic turmoil has increased the importance of governance programmes and decreased that of environmental and social programmes. Nonetheless, a significant proportion of respondents do not fully consider these programmes' financial value when assessing the attractiveness of business projects or companies. Some think the value is too long-term or indirect to measure, and others just are not satisfied with the metrics available.

Also from a European perspective, Zerfass, Moreno, Tench, Verčič, and Verhoeven (2008), Zerfass, Moreno, Tench, Verčič, and Verhoeven (2009), Zerfass, Van Ruler, Rogojinaru, Verčič, and Hamrefors (2007) (ECM, 2008, 2009, 2010) have surveyed Communication Directors from up to 42 countries. The research found that 3of 4 professionals are involved in CSR activities with 73% believing it will be even more important in 3 years' time. Perhaps unsurprisingly 4 of 10 practitioners think it is a strategic issue that communication management should deal with and this reflects the fact that reputation management is a key driver for CSR activities in all types of organisations and regions across Europe. Linked to this is the fact that main focus of CSR communication is in enhancing the corporate profile, i.e., the values and strategies of the organisation.

However healthy scepticism remains. This brings us back to the question: can companies still be good in the bad times? Should they bother? Or is it about returning to Friedman's (1962, 1970) 1960s neo-liberal views that the business of business is business, i.e., generating wealth and shareholder value. But today is different from when Friedman was first writing. Perhaps this is the time when business culture and philosophy will be changed away from the corporate responsibility to enhance shareholder value alone, to also recognising and being steered by the need for corporate social responsibility. In other words what Dicken called the 'race to the bottom line' (Dicken, 2003, p. 384) will end. This is when organisations put pressure on suppliers to lower costs of production. This in turn puts increased pressure on competition between suppliers and clearly somewhere something has to give, whether this is making employees redundant, using inferior products or exploiting cheap labour (e.g. children or unacceptable working conditions and hours).

A CSR CONTEXT FOR BUSINESS

CSR is on the political agenda if you consider the following examples of government and trade organisations from a UK and European perspective which are influencing the debates:

- Trades Union Congress (TUC)
- Confederation of British Industry (CBI)
- Department of Trade and Industry (DTI; Dept for Business Enterprise and Regulatory Reform BERR)
- European Union (EU)
- Business in the Community (BITC)
- Federation of Small Business (FSB)
- United Nations (Global Compact)

Furthermore as had already been discussed CSR is on the public's agenda:

> Social Responsibility is neither a fad nor an optional extra. The interest in it is reflective of a deeper change in the relationship between companies and their stakeholders ... Healthy business require a healthy community, and should be contributing to its creation and maintenance. The public increasingly wants to know about companies that stand behind the brands and products presented to them. And use their power to reward 'good' companies and punish the 'bad' ones. (Lewis, 2003)

Corporate social responsibility's position on the public's agenda is reinforced through consumers with many studies focusing on the ethical performance and behaviour of companies as a trigger and influence on the purchasing decision and then potentially the financial performance of the firm. Currently papers are appearing in academic journals and books exploring the sustainability of the ethical consumer in straightened economic times, for example Carrigan and de Pelsmacker (2009).

And of course CSR is on the business agenda as it is the 'license to operate' and a responsible business is 'one that has built-in to its purpose and strategy a commitment to deliver sustainable value to society at large, as well as to shareholders, and has open and transparent business practices that are based on ethical values and respect for employees, communities and the environment'. Tomorrow's Global Company (June 2007). And so Friedman's shareholders are just one of many stakeholders.

So this takes us back to basics of why organisations do CSR (Carroll, 1991). Carroll's model is simplistic but maybe organisations will regress and slide back towards the legal requirements for CSR in difficult economic times. If they do then we will continue to see a performance gap as reported in The Economist (2008) at the start of these economic conditions. CEOs were asked what they should do against what they actually do to address environmental, social and governance issues. The results demonstrate that the CEOs recognise and acknowledge the need to take action but also acknowledge the failings and shortcomings in what they were already doing. They also reinforce why they need to do this – i.e. to build and develop reputation through the responsibility agenda. So will businesses drop their CSR? Only if they want to damage their business and furthermore their reputation. Many companies have spent decades building a dialogue with stakeholders on societal issues. Also it is in difficult times that many business writers argue innovation and creativity excel (Grayson et al., 2008). But some companies do find it easier than others. Also for many organisations what drives CSR activities in all types of organisations (public and private) is reputation. This raises an important question about CSR activities: are they about image, substance or both? There is a real danger that the abundance of CSR programmes produces a cynical backlash for the society at large. Therefore authenticity, sincerity and legitimacy are and in the future will continue to be crucial. What business must be wary of is that a new trend of cynicism does not develop and both the concepts of CSR and also the communications of it are damaged. Managers need to become critical of the promotional uses of CSR programmes. For example sponsorship is a communication tool and not an ethical activity in itself. The self-delusion of management that it is being socially responsible if it invests in activities that communicate (e.g. professional sports) are self-defeating and have a negative impact. This does not detract from the fact that for communications and organisations more broadly responsibility and CSR are key elements in this discussion. As Heath and Palenchar (2009) have stated the key issues management for an organisation is to help keep it 'attuned to its community' (p. 15). And this community is working and communicating in a new media world which is online, interactive and 24/7. Until very recently news was something you received via newspapers radio or recently TV. Consumers were not in control and had no choice on what to receive or when to receive it. But this has changed since the 1990s and quite rapidly since the millennium. The power and influence of the media is well researched but in the context of financial and economic performance it also shows interesting effects.

ROLE OF THE MEDIA IN INFLUENCING CSR AGENDAS

It is interesting to look at trends in the media landscape and how they are influencing and moderating the behaviour of corporations and their executives. There are numerous examples of ethical misdemeanours by executives which have been splashed and highlighted across popular as well as business media forcing either changes in individual and corporate behaviour or even changes in management personnel altogether. But how we receive and interact with news is changing and this is important in the CSR debate. It changes our relationship with media suppliers and potentially our relationship with and power over corporations. As Steve Busfield (2010), Head of media and technology from the Guardian, stated:

> Media and communications are constantly changing. Little more than a decade ago most people in the UK had four TV channels and read a daily newspaper. Today the UK's online audience is around 35 million (figures from comScore, December 2008) (about 70% of the UK population), and most people are as likely to get their news from the internet, blogs, talkboards or Twitter as from a newspaper.

The impacts of these changes are becoming quite transparent to all organisations. We have to change how we communicate with a range of key stakeholders including customers, clients, competitors and others within our supply or relationship chains. These relationships are and must continue to be reviewed, evolved and changed. Furthermore, the recession of the past couple of years has had a significant impact on the UK and European media landscape. This can be measured by the collapse of advertising revenue and spend (although there is some evidence of a switch to on-line advertising).

This has led some media outlets to change their publishing format with 10% of media from a European Digital Journalism study (Oriella Survey of journalists across Europe, 2009) switching completely from traditional to on-line.

From this research nearly 60% of European journalists predict that the number of printed media will shrink dramatically. Perhaps worryingly 40% of journalists claim the dependence on public relations content will increase (note this is despite several published warnings by academics and journalist authors (Davies, 2008) of the impact on journalism practice e.g. 'churnsalism', the 'hidden persuaders' and 'truth manipulation'.

And then there is the important field of new and social media. Social media allow users to share ideas, information and personal detail (Baumann, 2006; Beer & Burrows, 2007). We no longer have the powerful media gatekeepers acting as editors and controllers through expert knowledge. The impact therefore of simplifying and sharing web technologies has been to encourage sharing and collaboration. It has also taken power from the media/technology controllers to support UGC (user generated content). This has had implications for business and the monitoring of business ethics and ethical (mis)conduct. Social media provides the opportunity and access to media outlets to break 'stories' of poor ethical standards and to whistleblow. Social media users are commonly referred to as generation C (Dye, 2007) where C stands for content, creation, consumption and connectivity. This generation want to be communicating with the world and they want everyone to be able to trace and track them through social media. A perfect example of this is Twitter. Twitter is being used to feed an international thirst for instant news. For example, Twitter allows publications to publish the headline of their story and disseminate wider and faster and to larger audiences than their 'normal' distribution channels would permit. This is a big contemporary threat and issue for companies that do not listen to stakeholders internally and externally. These stakeholders are potentially monitoring and scrutinising the actions and activities of the company and its executives and will be quick to debate and report on these through the social networks. To demonstrate this change and the impact it is having in practical terms, the biggest publications across Europe have tens of thousands of Twitter followers (*Financial Times, The Guardian, El Pais* and *Le Monde*). As such there is a move away from the web being a content archive to also being used to generate new material. And of course today much of this news material can be focused on the actions of corporations and their executives. Clear examples are evident in news and business pages daily but big issues do emerge that underline this focus on behaviour. In May 2010, consumers, stakeholders and political figures exerted pressure on BP after the Deepwater Horizon oil rig disaster in the Gulf of Mexico. The clean up was estimated to cost up to $450 million and President Barak Obama made several public statements the responsibility for this fell foursquare with the company, not the State, the government or the residents.

As a result, journalists are increasingly turning to UGC to satisfy demand for online content. Another interesting finding from the Oriella survey is that the majority (68% of journalists) encourage comments on stories online. Also a quarter quote bloggers in their original stories. This clearly highlights the blogosphere's influence as a resource for editorial content (see e.g. www.talkingpointsmemo.com). This has been reinforced recently with the UK parliament's agreement to supply lobby passes for 'approved' bloggers so that they can report on an equal footing with mainstream media. Clearly this endorsement in the formal political arena reflects their increased power which will be and is translated over to news monitoring through blogs within the business community (communities). Again this is translated to those who monitor, track and comment on social, political and business issues and behaviour.

AN ALTERNATIVE APPROACH TO CSR IN BUSINESS

CSR as previously argued needs to be careful of loosing its purpose and strategic value to business. Although arguments are made for the imporantance and value of CSR for sustaining and devleoping reputation and goodwill it is impertative that it does not become viewed as a label associated with 'greenwash' and superficialitiy of responsibility messaging. For example think of the work invested in environmental and social responsibility campaigns by petroleum companies over the past two or three decades. Then consider the communications and public relations disaster that BP found itself in following the Gulf of Mexico oil leak. This resulted in high profile vilification by legislators and politicians even forcing executives to appear before the US President Barak Obama and agree to significant multi-billion dollar compensation liabilities. Then during this crisis we see just how much the executives cared about the issue when the chief executive of BP, Tony Hayward, was photographed and filmed in a sailing competition off the Isle of White on his private yacht (Kennedy, 2010). This dissonance in corporate rhetoric and responsibility contributes to stakeholder mistrust and disbelief in some corporate messaging and behaviour relating to social responsibility issues. In 1999, 'greenwash' entered the official lexicon of the English language through its inclusion in the *Oxford English Dictionary*. The *OED* defines greenwash as: 'Disinformation disseminated by an organisation so as to present an environmentally responsible public image'. The watchdog group Green Life has released an annual report since the mid-1990s highlighting the worst offenders for making misleading claims about the environment (Green Life, www. thegreenlifeonline.org). As such the CSR concept must be protected from being inextricably tied to the flawed and much critiscised business model which has negatively affected the business community and particualry the finance communities in the credit crunch with previously discussed traits and behaviours of greed, selfishness and the self-interst of business leaders.

The model of business which saw the financial crisis of 2007 start in the United States may not have happened if alternative views of social responsibility had been in place. Argandona (2009) makes an argument that giving CSR or responsibility an enhanced ethical basis through voluntarily assumed codes of ethics would enable businesses to develop what he calls 'self-generated duties among financial decision makers'.

This brings us back to discussions of trust. Can we trust companies to follow laws? Probably. But law and legislation can only control behaviour so far. Law itself is not enough to ensure we can trust companies to do the right thing. For this we need to trust the executive on a personal level too. Argandona makes a strong case for arguing that personal trust is key. Citing Perez Lopez (1993) he argues personal trust has two components both of which are required for trust in an interpersonal relationship. One is 'functional trust' which is 'technical or skill based' (such as professional knowledge and understanding of the practice) and the second is 'personal' or 'ethical benevolence based' trust. The second is based on ethical reasoning and decision-making influenced by personal conviction or in Argandona's case professional codes (e.g. codes of professional conduct or ethics – think of medical practice codes). In business this is the missing element. Business executives are not medial doctors and bound by Hippocratic oaths. I would argue while this is an element that appears in professional body organisations representing functions within businesses and organisations, there is not a more generic set of codes. This would be an interesting area for exploration and debate from both a theoretical and business practitioner perspective. But the cynic might ask would Enron executives still have ended up in court? Would Goldman Sachs' employees still have appeared before the US senators? And would BP chief executive Tony Hayward repeat his argument that he needed some time off with the family to go sailing? Possibly. But without challenging the behaviour and decision-making of our corporate managers and putting the responsibility for their actions at their own feet we will not get improvements which benefit the wider stakeholders of employees, investors, and society at large.

CONCLUSION

Clearly CSR alone was not to blame for the economic crisis. This responsibility falls at the feet of a range of stakeholders as discussed earlier in this chapter. However would CSR have helped mitigate against some of the culture and behaviour that led to the crisis? Maybe. If managers had taken strategic decisions and choices with a deeper understanding of their corporate *social* responsibility then maybe some of the outcomes would have been different. Certainly they could have been for some of the individuals and firms caught up in the 'crisis' even if it could not have saved the entire marketplace.

So what is the future for CSR? Will CSR emerge unscathed from the economic downturn? Certainly we can identify on going challenges by key stakeholder groups. For instance in the difficult economic times business will want justification possibly through measures including financial performance and return on investment. Also consumers and other stakeholders will challenge companies on the believability of their responsibility activities and actions as well as messages. Then the media in its contemporary guise as discussed can fuel this by breeding cynicism through exposing, tracking and challenging poor ethical behaviour and performance by companies – as examples throughout this book demonstrate these have been too easily identified in recent years.

To respond we need a strategic and refreshing approach. We need to continue working with stakeholders to encourage openness and facilitate stakeholder dialogue. Ultimately this is what Jurgen Habermas (1987) called 'communicative action' initiatives or dialogue. This maybe challenging at the outset but shared mutual understanding of key issues will provide increased support for the organisational objectives, specifically as all groupings in society are experiencing social, political, economic and environmental changes.

So, times are tough. Hard lessons have been learnt. According to the UK media reports we have all been eating more chocolate and taking more Viagra during the credit crunch (Hamilton, 2008)! So will business curb its greed and obesity and control its testosterone fuelled attitude to wealth creation and become more altruistic and paternal? Only time will tell and the next few years – and the next generation of business leaders – are critical. Put simply we can predict that the issues of accountability and responsibility are not going away. Stakeholders still expect and some expect more. Businesses need to keep being responsible.

REFERENCES

Aitken, A. (2008). Local government must lead in a crisis. *PR Week*, 10 October.

Argandona, A. (2009). *Can corporate social responsibility help us understand the credit crisis?* Working Paper, IESE Business School, University of Navarra, Pamplona, Spain, March.

Asda Wal-Mart 'Pulse of the nation'. (2008). Available at http://www.pulse.asda.com/Portal/default.aspx. Last accessed on 10 May 2010.

Baumann, M. (2006). Caught in the Web 2.0. *Information Today*, *23*(8), 38.

BBC News 24. (2010). Voters don't trust politicians. BBC News 24, 18 March. Available at http://www.bbc.co.uk/1/hi/uk_politics/4360597.stm. Last accessed on 12 May.

Beer, D., & Burrows, R. (2007). Sociology and, of and in Web 2.0: Some initial considerations. *Sociological Research Online*, *12*(5).

Bloomberg. (2010). Goldman Sachs Executives Grilled in Senate Hearing. *Bloomberg Business Week* online, 29 April. Available at http://www.businessweek.com/news. Last accessed on 29 April.

Busfield, S. (2010). The Guardian Media Academy. Available at http://www.guardian.co.uk/media-academy. Last accessed on 13 May.

Carrigan, M., & de Pelsmacker, P. (2009). Will ethical consumers sustain their values in the global credit crunch? *International Marketing Review*, *26*(6), 674–687.

Carroll, A. B. (1991). The pyramid of corporate social responsibility: Toward the moral management of organizational stakeholders. *Business Horizons*, *34*(4), 39–48.

Davies, N. (2008). *Flat earth news*. London: Chatto & Windus.

Dicken, P. (2003). *Global shift*. London: Paul Chapman.

Dye, J. (2007). Meet generation C. *EContent*, *30*, 38–48.

Edelman Trust Barometer. (2008, 2009, 2010). Available at http://www.edelman.com/trust/2010/. Last accessed on 7 May 2010.

European Digital Journalism Survey. (2009). © Oriella PR Network MMIX. Available at http://www.europeandigitaljournalism.com/download-report. Accessed on October 06, 2010.

Friedman, M. (1962). *Capitalism and freedom*. Chicago, IL: University of Chicago Press.

Friedman, M. (1970). The social responsibility of business is to increase its profits. *New York Times Magazine*, 13 September, pp. 122–126.

Grayson, D., Zhouying Jin, Z., Lemon, M., Rodriguez, M. A., Slaughter, S., & Tay, S. (2008). A new mindset for corporate responsibility. Cranfield School of Management occasional papers. Available at http://www.dspace.lib.cranfield.ac.uk/bitstream/1826/4161/1/A_new_mindset_for_corporate_sustainability.pdf. Last accessed on 12 May 2010.

Habermas, J. (1987). *The Theory of Communicative Action: Vol 1 Reason and the Rationalization of Society*. Boston, MA: Beacon Press.

Hamilton, J. (2008). Credit crunchie. *The Sun*, 28 November.
Heath, R. M., & Palenchar, M. J. (2009). *Strategic issues management-organizations and public policy challenges.* Thousand Oaks, CA: Sage.
Kennedy, M. (2010). BP chief's weekend sailing trip stokes anger at oil company. *The Guardian*, 2(20 June). Available at http://www.guardian.co.uk/business/2010/jun/20/tony-hayward-bp. Last accessed on 23 June.
Leeper, R. (2001). In search of a metatheory for public relations – An argument for communitarianism. In: R. L. Heath (Ed.), *Handbook of public relations.* Thousand Oaks, CA: Sage.
Lewis, S. (2003). Reputation and corporate social responsibility. *Journal of Communication Management, 7*(4), 356–364.
Perez Lopez, J. A. (1993). *Fundamentos de la direccion de empresas.* Madrid: Rialp.
Tench, R., Bowd, R., & Jones, B. (2007). Perceptions and perspectives: Corporate social responsibility and the media. *Journal of Communication Management, 11*(4), 348–370.
The Economist. (2008). January 19, pp. 3–22.
UN Global Compact. (2008). Corporate Citizenship in the World Economy. Available at http://www.unglobalcompact.org/docs/news.../8/gc_brochure_final.pdf. Last accessed on 1 May 2010.
Zerfass, A., Moreno, A., Tench, R., Verčič, D., & Verhoeven, P. (2008). *European communication monitor 2008. Trends in communication management and public relations – results and implications* (Available at http://www.communicationmonitor.eu). Brussels, Leipzig: EUPRERA, University of Leipzig.
Zerfass, A., Moreno, A., Tench, R., Verčič, D., & Verhoeven, P. (2009). *European communication monitor 2009, 'Trends in communication management and public relations – results of a survey in 34 countries'.* Brussels: EACD, EUPRERA.
Zerfass, A., Van Ruler, B., Rogojinaru, A., Verčič, D., & Hamrefors, S. (2007). *European communication monitor 2007, 'Trends in communication management and public relations – results and implications'* (EUPRERA. Available at http://www.communicationmonitor.eu). Leipzig, Brussels: University of Leipzig.

WEBSITES

ECM. (2008, 2009, 2010). http://www.communicationmonitor.eu
Green Life. http://www.thegreenlifeonline.org
http://www.talkingpointsmemo

CORPORATE SOCIAL IRRESPONSIBILITY: THE ROLE OF GOVERNMENT AND IDEOLOGY

Brian Jones

The focus of this chapter is on the role of government in relation to corporate social responsibility (CSR) and the 2007–2010 financial crises. It argues that the financial crisis was a result of a failure of government. More specifically, it locates the origins of failure, which gave rise to the crisis, in the political and economic changes of the 1980s and after. The UK Thatcher government along with that of the Reagan administration in the United States delivered a new right, neo-liberal, laissez faire economic agenda that has come to be characterised, rightly or wrongly, as market fundamentalism (Soros, 1998; Stiglitz, 2002). The core argument advanced here is that neo-liberalism and market fundamentalism can be equated to government irresponsibility and that the move to free up markets, among other things, ultimately gave rise to the 2007–2010 financial crises.

The chapter begins with a brief background on the financial crisis and a discussion of its possible causes. The key argument advanced is that the move from the post-war tri-partite-based consensus politics to the new right, neo-liberal conviction politics led to loss of public scrutiny and accountability that ushered in increasing levels of irresponsibility. Calculated risk-taking gave way to, at the time unforeseen, reckless irresponsible business procedures and practices that culminated in the 2007–2010 financial

Reframing Corporate Social Responsibility: Lessons from the Global Financial Crisis
Critical Studies on Corporate Responsibility, Governance and Sustainability,
Volume 1, 57–75
ISSN: 2043-9059/doi:10.1108/S2043-9059(2010)0000001009

debacles. The chapter situates the crises in the broad political, societal and economic landscape; in particular, it identifies neo-liberalism as important to an analysis and understanding of the recent events. It draws on and brings together literature in the areas of politics, economics, CSR and irresponsibility. Focusing as it does on the financial crises in relation to the broader political-economic-socio environment and linking this to the debates on corporate responsibility and irresponsibility the chapter is topical, current, context setting and by offering fresh insight it adds value to the existing body of knowledge. The chapter seeks to describe, explain and analyse the background to as well as the impact of the financial crises not just on the economy but also on people's lives. The chapter broadens out analysis of neo-liberal political ideology as it has been applied in practice to the formation, evolution and development of government policies. It teases out and explores some of the links, tensions and contradictions between neo-liberalism as an ideology, government policies and some of the irresponsible actions and behaviours of government and business. Lessons learned and key findings are put forward as a means to theoretically inform and advance the policy agenda and practice of CSR. The chapter seeks to identify, understand and unpick patterns, processes and trends that will shape and influence the ways and means government, through the state, engage with CSR, and it discusses the 2007–2010 financial crises in relation to the concept of corporate social irresponsibility (CSI).

BACKGROUND

In the first decade of the 21st century, the financial crisis of 2007–2010 stands out as a landmark political, societal, business and economic event. Its impact on the financial sector is evident as seen by the collapse of banks such as Lehman Brothers, the sale of Bear Stearns to JP Morgan Chase and by the full or part nationalisation of others such as Northern Rock, Bradford and Bingley, Lloyds (including Halifax Bank of Scotland which they acquired during the crisis) and RBS. Its scope and breadth of impact has spread beyond the financial sector and has affected the broader economy and society. The North American along with a number of European and other economies fell into recession. The UK economy suffered its longest and deepest recession since the Second World War. Government and central banks announced unprecedented policy responses and initiated measures such as record low interest rates and quantitative easing (the printing of money) to stave off a 1930s style depression. Policies such as the car scrappage scheme introduced by the UK and American governments were designed to reduce inventories, stimulate economic recovery and help re-build confidence. Nevertheless, businesses suffered and a number of them collapsed, for example in the United Kingdom, high street retailers Zavvi, Woolworths and among others Borders ceased trading and were put into administration. The story of the financial and economic crisis has been well documented by, among others, Tett (2010), Roubini and Mihm (2010), and Bishop and Green (2010).

Despite a number of initiatives by governments and central banks unemployment in the United States, United Kingdom and Germany and among other places, France increased and economic growth turned negative. Talk of the so-called credit crunch and its consequences were heard and felt across the spectrum of businesses and in wider society. The credit crunch, the drying up of credit, along with the issue of toxic debt, served to fuel fear and sap confidence. On more than one occasion, the Bank of England lent banks emergency funds and that act instead of sating and reassuring markets, served to compound market panic. Central banks across the world co-ordinated and initiated a series of policy initiatives including lowering interest rates and lending and printing money. After one such co-ordinated central bank initiative, one *Guardian* letter writer (Jones, 2007) noted that, 'If £20 billion fails to save one bank, what hope is there of £50 billion saving the world economy? We're doomed'. The sense of doom, financial meltdown and market panic were all pervading and reports of bank collapses; central bank lending and bank takeovers dominated news coverage. At the start of the crisis, the policy response from the authorities was measured. As the crises grew so did the authorities policy response. Financial Armageddon and doom were avoided, but not without casualties. Stock markets plummeted and house prices fell. The Icelandic economy went into meltdown and the country declared bankrupt. It was almost as if a Hollywood script had supplanted reality. The impact on communities, businesses and people's lives was immense.

The financial crisis and its aftermath is a watershed moment, a turning point in economic history as well as being a tipping point (Gladwell, 2000), in economic and business thinking and practice. In terms of financial and economic history, its significance is comparable to the 1929 Wall Street crash and subsequent 1930s depression. It is the historical collective memory of these events that has served to shape and influence recent policy responses. The financial crisis of 2007–2010 has proven to be a major event in terms of its effect on the economy, society, politics and business. The shadow banking system came in for blame, and hedge fund managers, the so-called masters of the universe, fell from grace. Politicians and the media almost in equal measure demonised bankers. Academics, policy makers and commentators put forward, suggested and argued the case for a number of different causes of the 2007–2010 financial crises. Reasons include over indebted consumers, a UK and US savings glut, collapse of the shadow banking system brought about by the forced selling of long-term assets, and among other things, a boom and subsequent collapse in house prices. For those individuals who have seen their business close or have lost jobs, the events of 2007–2010 have been life-changing. Although the crisis was international in origin and nature, its reach and impact has been felt at the local and the personal levels. Business and economic orthodoxy have been called into question, and new ways of thinking, managing and behaving are being sought. To borrow and adapt from Levine, Locke, Searls, and Weinberger (2000) the 2007–2010 financial crises marks the end of business and economics as usual.

ANALYSIS

Neo-Liberalism

In the United Kingdom, the post–Second World War consensus politics based around the idea of full employment, nationalised industries as part of a mixed economy, stable economic growth, a benevolent welfare state and Keynesian demand management of the economy broke down in the 1970s. Unemployment increased, as did inflation and economic growth stagnated as workers went on strike and union might rode high (Gamble, 1994). Stagflation entered the political and economic lexicon as politicians and economists strove to explain the changed landscape. A new breed of politics and economics entered the world stage in 1979 with the election of the UK Thatcher government that advocated and delivered shock therapeutic change. Under the Thatcher government, consensus politics gave way to *conviction politics* and Keynesian economics gave way to *monetarist economics*. The new-right Thatcher government armed with its brand of neo-liberal Anglo Saxon capitalism sought to deliver supply-side economic reforms, put the great back into Britain, punish the work-shy, build an enterprise economy, roll back the frontiers of the state, privatise, de-regulate and limit the size and role of government (Gamble, 1988). Of course what it sought to do and what it actually delivered in terms of public expenditure is not necessarily the same thing (Riddell, 1985, 1989). Nevertheless, in

Britain, in the 1980s, it was apparent that a new political consensus and economic order was being forged. Change was necessary and the consequences of that period are felt today. The 1980s move to free up markets, roll back the frontier of the state and let the market reign supreme have proven to be not without risk as the 2007–2010 financial crises bear testimony.

Theoretical Foundations of Neo-Liberalism

The first wave of the neo-liberal agenda was introduced to the United Kingdom by the Thatcher government, whilst in the United States, a similar programme of political and economic reform was instigated by the Reagan administration. Second and third waves of neo-liberal economic and political reforms were carried out by subsequent UK government administrations throughout the 1990s and the first decade of the 21st century. There are a variety of approaches, interpretations and variations in the uptake and adoption of neo-liberalism. It is not restricted to the United Kingdom and United States but has been interpreted, adapted and applied in different ways throughout the world. The Washington Consensus promulgated its export and adoption as Steger and Roy (2010, pp. 19–20) explain:

> In exchange for much-needed loans and debt-restructuring schemes, governments in the global South were required to adhere to the Washington Consensus by following its ten-point programme:
>
> 1. A guarantee of fiscal discipline, and a curb to budget deficit
> 2. A reduction of public expenditure, particularly in the military and public administration
> 3. Tax reform aiming at the creation of a system with a broad base and with effective enforcement
> 4. Financial liberalization, with interest rates determined by the market
> 5. Competitive exchange rates, to assist export-led growth
> 6. Trade liberalization, coupled with the abolition of import licensing and a reduction of tariffs
> 7. Promotion of foreign direct investment
> 8. Privatization of state enterprises, leading to efficient management and improved performance
> 9. Deregulation of the economy
> 10. Protection of property rights

The theoretical foundations on which this neo-liberal reform programme was based can be traced back to the work of academics such as Hayek (1944, 1960) and Friedman (1962) and think tanks such as the Institute for Economic Affairs and the American Enterprise Institute.

Milton Friedman was awarded, in 1976, the Nobel Prize for economics and is perhaps best known for his theory of monetarism. The focus of Friedman's economic analysis was on the monetary causes of inflation and the need for sound money. In the United Kingdom, in the 1980s, the Thatcher government prioritised the money supply as an important economic target and viewed it as a means to reduce the level of inflation. Friedman was an advocate for free enterprise, competition and self-regulating free markets, and as previously indicated, throughout the 1980s, the Thatcher government privatised a significant number of state-owned industries, many of which represented the commanding heights of the British economy. Friedman argued the case for maintaining a successful business and applauded the use of resources to 'engage in activities designed to increase its profits' (Friedman, 1962, p. 133) over any form of CSR. Friedman believed that the core responsibility of companies is to their shareholders, and in this regard, their remit is to maximise profits; 'few trends could so thoroughly undermine the very foundations of our free society as the acceptance by corporate officials of a social responsibility other than to make as much money for their stockholders as possible' (Friedman, 1962, p. 133). This view on shareholder value theory suggests businesses are first and foremost inward looking and focus only on one stakeholder group – shareholders.

Friedrich A. Hayek was a 1974 Nobel Prize winning economist and political theorist, perhaps best known for *The Road to Serfdom* published in 1944 and *The Constitution of Liberty* published in 1960. Hayek's work warned of the danger socialism/collectivism posed to freedom and was a passionate advocate for the 'free society' with a minimal role for government. As a passionate advocate for libertarianism and the free market, he argued against government intervention in the economy, and in this regard, his worldviews were pitted against those of Keynes (2009). Hayek believed centralised forms of economic planning posed a threat to freedoms.

Both Friedman and Hayek argued that the state should have a minimal role in the economy and that the market mechanism is the most rational, effective and efficient means for the allocation of goods and services. Friedman and Hayek are without doubt key 20th-century neo-liberal economic and political thinkers. They championed the cause of neo-liberalism and played an important role in the world of academia as well as in the real world of politics and economics. Their ideas were taken up, adopted and adapted to varying degrees by politicians such as President Reagan, Prime Minister Thatcher and have even been adopted by the Communist Chinese government. Although Hayek and Friedman both championed freedom and the free market, it would be wrong to conflate their thinking for there are important nuances of difference between them. Undoubtedly, they are ideological bed fellows, but they did nevertheless disagree on a number of issues and for a fuller discussion, see, for example, among others, Gamble (1988, pp. 43–44).

Institute for Economic Affairs is the United Kingdom's leading free market think tank. It seeks to champion the cause of freedom through a research, publication and lecture programme. It argues the case for minimal government, be that in the form of ownership, regulation, legislation or taxation. It analyses and argues the case for the role of the market to help solve social and economic problems. Many of the ideas generated by the Institute have subsequently been taken up as economic and public policy.

American Enterprise Institute is the United States' pre-eminent conservative think tank whose remit covers a wide range of policy areas. However, its core aim is to champion private enterprise, limited government and democratic capitalism. It advocates individual liberty, freedom and responsibility. It stimulates and encourages open debate, and through their work, a number of its scholars have shaped the public policy agenda, particularly throughout the Reagan and Bush years.

The above body of work helped to provide the theoretical rationale and justification for a changed political and economic agenda. The outcome of this work was the new right, neo-liberal social, political and economic policies advocated in the United Kingdom, to greater and lesser extent, among others by the Thatcher–Major and Blair–Brown governments. The neo-liberal agenda has not been without its critics, and the policies pursued have been subject to sustained critique. John Gray's (1998) book, *False Dawn: The Delusions of Global Capitalism*, offered a penetrating analysis of the instability wrought by the neo-liberal political and economic brand of global capitalism. Gray's book served as a warning of the economic instability, uncertainty and economic turbulence that global capitalism could unleash. However, perhaps more than anything, the 2007–2010 financial crises called into doubt the whole neo-liberal agenda. Calls for de-regulation were replaced with calls for more regulation, and arguments for less government intervention in the economy were duly replaced with calls for more. Such calls for change in the economic and policy agenda are likely to be temporary prescriptive fixes, and the neo-liberal agenda will undoubtedly continue anew, albeit with new policy prescriptions. Without it and without new social and economic policies, we will all be the poorer. The market remains the most effective and efficient means for allocating goods and services and for the creation and distribution of wealth.

Defining and Shaping CSR

At the same time as neo-liberalism rose to the fore as the pre-eminent ideology, CSR grew in importance as an area that businesses and management were required to address and expected to engage with. Whether or not there is a connection between these two developments is an open question. There is of course a degree of irony in that while neo-liberalism was advocating less government intervention, many advocates of CSR were calling for more intervention and regulation. It is perhaps worthwhile to look at CSR and the official British government's approach to the concept that is perhaps best captured in the following definitions:

> Corporate Responsibility can be defined as how companies address the social, environmental and economic aspects of their operations and so help to meet our sustainable development goals ... The Government has a role to play in setting standards in areas such as environmental protection, health and safety and employment rights. It can also provide a policy and institutional framework that stimulates companies to raise their performance beyond minimum. The UK Government approach is to encourage and incentivise the adoption of Corporate Responsibility, through best practice guidance, and where appropriate, regulation and fiscal incentives. Specifically, we see CR as the voluntary actions that business can take, over and above compliance with minimum legal requirements, to address both its own competitive interests and the interests of wider society.[1]

Additionally:

> The Government believes that by adopting socially and environmentally responsible behaviour businesses can make a significant contribution to boosting wealth creation and employment, fostering social justice and protecting the environment. Essentially, this means companies taking account of the economic, social and environmental impacts that arise from the way they operate – maximizing the benefits and minimizing the downsides.[2]

The above definitions while useful do of course tell only part of the story. In relation to CSR, the United Kingdom along with other governments (see, e.g., Commission of the European Communities, 2001, 2002; European Commission, 2004) has to meet a number of legal rights, address stakeholder needs (Freeman, 1984; Donaldson & Preston, 1995) and fulfil as best it can a mixture of moral obligations.

The UK government has helped to define, shape and influence CSR.[3] The role of the state and how it interprets CSR is important in understanding the evolving and changing nature of the concept. There is no one universally agreed definition of the concept, and Newell (2005, p. 546) rightly comments:

> Mainstream CSR approaches assume a set of conditions that do not exist in most of the world. CSR can work, for some people, in some places, on some issues, some of the time. The challenge is to identify and specify those conditions in order that inappropriate models of 'best practice' are not universalised, projected and romanticised as if all the world were receptive to one model of CSR.

Governments intervene to regulate, manage and deliver more efficient and effective business societal relationships. It is important to remember that government is not just a regulator of the market but is also a participant in the market. Government plays an important role with regard to defining and shaping the field of CSR. It has the moral authority to intervene to deliver a framework through which businesses can act and behave in a responsible way. Government sets the legal, financial and economic framework by which businesses operate. Operating as it does in the context of the macro- and micro-environment, the business society interface is prone to near constant change. Of course in the midst of all this talk of change, it is important to recognise and state that much carries on as it always has. Continuity and change work together to make CSR an evolving and developing area of business operation and government intervention and is especially interesting given the aforementioned discussion of the rise of neo-liberalism.

The financial crisis of 2007–2010 has forced a reappraisal of the relationship between the state, business and society. This relationship is the base from which CSR stakes its claim to legitimacy as a subject area. The broad macro social, economic, political and technological environment is in a state of continual perpetual change. Macro-environmental change provides the backdrop against which stakeholder expectations about the obligations and responsibilities business has to society are framed and shaped. Government serves as both the conduit and the intermediary in the business society relationship. To set and describe it, as a one-way process is to misread the nature of the relationship for society has obligations, needs and rights with business. Wood (1991, p. 697) argues that

> Businesses are not responsible for solving all social problems. They are, however, responsible for solving problems that they have caused, and they are responsible for helping to solve problems and social issues related to their business operations and interests.

The relationship between business and society is at one and the same time mutually beneficial and mutually destructive. Hence, there is a need and a role for government in CSR, and this is delivered through the machinery of the state. It is however important to broaden out the interpretation of government and to explore the broader political environment in which it operates and the macro policies advocated.

Corporate Social Irresponsibility: The Failure of Government

Much literature on CSR actually describes instances where things have 'failed', not worked as they ought to have done or have simply 'gone wrong', and the financial crisis of 2007–2010 serves as a clear and prime example here. The scale of wealth destruction it wrought is evidence not of CSR but of CSI. Franklin (2008, p. 8) rightly points out that, 'a socially conscious but bankrupt business is no good to anyone'.

Whereas much has been written about CSR (Blowfield & Murray, 2008; Smith & Lenssen, 2009), this is not the case with the issue of CSI, which is an emergent (nascent) and topical subject area. It is emergent insofar as it is a relatively new area of academic study (see, e.g., Frooman, 1997; Bansal & Kandola, 2003; Kotchen & Moon, 2007) and is relatively undeveloped in terms of theory (Jones, Bowd, & Tench, 2009). From societal, political, economic, business practice and practitioner viewpoints, the issue is very topical in that during the 2007–2010 financial crises, politicians, economists and commentators used the word irresponsibility without giving full and due regard to its meaning or how it might be addressed at policy level.

The crisis brought with it much political and media discussion of the irresponsibility of bankers. In the context of 21st-century corporate failings such as Enron and Worldcom, the concept of CSI slowly began to gain credence and credibility as an academic area of study (Mitchell, 2001; Kotchen & Moon, 2007; Wagner, Bicen, & Hall, 2008). The following two newspaper quotes serve to illustrate how the concept of irresponsibility has entered mainstream political and economic lexicon:

> After years of waste, debt and irresponsibility, Britain must live within its means. Mr Osborne said. (Parker, 2010, p. 1)

> while they rely on US demand to make up for their own contradictory policies, they'll lecture us on how irresponsible we're being, running those budget and current account deficits. (Krugman, quoted by Inman, 2010, p. 34)

The financial crisis was born of capital's own making and emerged from the backdrop of neo-liberal ideology. The scale and nature of the financial crisis is without precedent and delivered an economic crisis similar to although nevertheless different from that of the 1930s. Governments' and bankers' response to the crisis has mitigated the worst effects and prevented a slide into a 1930s-type depression. The social impact is still being felt with cutbacks in public spending affecting welfare provision and rising levels of unemployment blighting the lives of the individuals, families and communities affected.

Arguably, the crisis emanated from irresponsible lending in the sub-prime mortgage market of the United States. Politicians have criticised bankers for their irresponsible lending practices, and this has become a much discussed media topic. The 2007–2010 financial crises resulting as it did in the destruction rather than the creation of wealth serve as a prime example of CSI of which, as previously mentioned, there has been increased academic (Wagner et al., 2008; Jones et al., 2009) as well as much political discussion (see, e.g., Parker, 2010). The neo-liberal agenda of a minimal role for government contributed to the financial crisis and serves as an example of CSI. Government failure to act in advance of the crises was subsequently replaced by a requirement to act and deal with the consequences. It is safe to say that as an ideology neo-liberalism has not been spurned or rejected, but recent events inevitably call for a re-appraisal of policies. Such a re-appraisal of policies should address issues that will help renew both neo-liberalism as an ideology and the theoretical foundation for conventional CSR that obviously failed to address the issues of CSI.

DISCUSSION

A Shift Away from Neo-Liberalism

Intervention, regulation, extending state ownership, increasing/stimulating the demand side and restricting or in some cases subjugating market powers have since 2007 been the order of the day. The 2007–2010 financial crises challenged the new right neo-liberal free market orthodoxy. Market fundamentalism was shown wanting. The free market experiment seemed to have run its course, and instead of being rolled back, the state was rolled forward out of the economic necessity to save capitalism from its own excesses. Unfettered free market neo-liberal Anglo-Saxon capitalism is in many ways its own worst enemy. State intervention was born out of economic necessity rather than ideology and ideological persuasion. The state was forced to intervene, albeit on what is perceived to be temporary basis, to prevent economic meltdown born of capital's own making.

The 2007–2010 financial crises are a critical moment in the ordering and structuring of capital, the economy and the operation of the state. Fear was one driver of the financial crisis, and fear of the abyss is what prompted governments to intervene and to stave off financial as well as economic and societal collapse. The idea of minimal state intervention advocated by New Right Neo-liberals (Friedman, 1962; Hayek, 1944, 1960) was replaced with ideas around Keynesian demand style economic intervention. There was increasing recognition that fresh economic thinking was needed. The search for a new economic orthodoxy[4] began before the crisis and sought to replace that which had been criticised and that now lay discredited.

If it has signalled anything, the crisis has signalled a shift away from rampant neo-liberal individualism and a move to *collective responsibility.* Indeed, the ideal of the collective good rather than that of rugged individualism perhaps best exemplify this shift. The state has been forced to intervene in the market. The 2007–2010 financial crises were ushered in by the failings of capital and somewhat ironically were overseen in the United Kingdom by a Labour government. It has delivered an economic crisis for governments and a headache in terms of how to manage public finances (Tett, 2010).

The market failures of 2007–2010 prompted wide-scale government intervention that signalled a move away, albeit temporary, from a free market worldview. The supply-side free market economics of Milton Friedman (1962) were called into question, whereas those of John Maynard Keynes (2009) gained credibility and a new lease of life. Thatcher inspired neo-liberal state orthodoxy that championed minimal government intervention in markets, and a rolling back of the state (Hall & Jaques, 1983; Riddell, 1985; Riddell, 1989) was shown wanting. The core argument advanced here is that in the United Kingdom, the market fundamentalist, new right, neo-liberal Thatcherite reforms of the state and economy of the 1980s ushered in a move towards corporate irresponsibility (see, e.g., scandals that occurred including BCCI and Robert Maxwell, among others, see Blowfield & Murray, 2008, pp. 213–215). Across the globe, the Anglo Saxon neo-liberal free market model of capitalism was challenged, and in part replaced, as a result of increased government ownership of banks, state economic intervention and regulation. This of course posed a challenge to the so-called Washington Consensus (Blowfield & Murray, 2008, p. 50; Steger & Roy, 2010, pp. 19–20).

The crisis serves to demonstrate the enormous power of the state and its ability to martial resources to defend the interests of capital as well as to uphold and champion a particular style and brand of neo-liberal free market capitalism. The scale of the UK, US and other government's intervention in the economy is awesome and in the time frame unprecedented. The economic strategy is not without risk and there has been talk and speculation about the return of inflation as well as new economic bubbles. Risk management lies at the heart of new thinking on corporate governance, financial regulation and economic management. The impact of the crisis on CSR is being felt for example in moves to improve standards of corporate governance through changed regulation and reporting procedures, particularly in the banking and financial services sector. There have, of course, been initiatives and policy changes in the past, but these have not prevented rule or law breaking, mismanagement of corporate governance and ultimately business failure. In the United Kingdom, a number of reports (e.g. Cadbury Report, 1992; Greenbury Report, 1995; Higgs Report, 2003) have been written and codes and procedures to do with standards of corporate governance adopted; yet, still, rules have continued to be broken (for a fuller discussion of these reports and codes, see Solomon, 2010, pp. 45–76).

Challenges Ahead

The outlook for the UK economy is at the time of writing, an uncertain one though, higher unemployment, reductions in public sector headcount, public sector wage control and deflationary policies are all likely scenarios. Looking at the financial prospects and economic outlook for 2010, Somerset Webb (2010, p. 3) wrote,

> All in all, it is getting harder and harder to see anything other than a period in which growth is held back by miserable deleveraging consumers (we are now saving more as a percentage of our disposable incomes than we have for over a decade, for example); rising taxes; a state of semi-crisis in the public finances; and an ongoing scarcity of credit.

The government will have to manage on-going and emerging challenges for UK economic management, and in the near to medium term, it is probable that interest rates will rise. The economic cloud of doom has begun to lift. New rules for corporate governance and finance have yet to be framed and established. The crisis has had a profound effect on the consumer and business psyche, and while this will be restored, it is likely to be a slow process. The down paying of debt will most probably act as a drag on economic growth. More businesses are likely to fail just as new businesses will start. From the crisis and recession, new opportunities will emerge and this will help restore consumer confidence and re-build individual and state finances. The years of public spending excess are at an end, and a cold chill is descending across the public sector as spending is reined back and hard choices made. The need now is to increase productivity and to create new real wealth through enterprise, entrepreneurship and innovation. Risk cannot be eliminated from the market, but it ought to be better managed so as to mitigate the worst of capitalist excess. Calculated risk-taking is critical to effective and efficient market operation and the entrepreneurial process. The neo-liberal model of capitalism needs to be refreshed and injected with a new sense of purpose. One way in which it might be refreshed and given new purpose is to build CSR into its very fabric so that it is *bolted in* rather than bolted on to its every operation and raison d'etre. Although this sounds idealistic, if not cliché ridden, with vision, leadership and commitment, change for the better can be achieved and we will all be richer for it. There does however need to be a collective will and desire for such change, and this change will have to encompass attitudes, behaviours and responsibilities.

Key Findings

A number of key findings can be drawn from the above analysis.

The problems of CSR have undoubtedly been, in part, driven by irresponsible business practices (e.g., the Robert Maxwell scandal – see Blowfield & Murray, 2008) prompting governments of all political persuasions to legislate, regulate and intervene in the market place. In other words, CSI has been a driver of change prompting action that will deliver responsible business behaviours, that is, CSR.

The 2007–2010 financial crises have caused much questioning of the New Right neo-liberals (Gamble, 1988, 1994) untrammelled and unquestioning faith in free market economics. That markets are not always self-correcting, that they are a construct and need to be regulated are lessons that have had to be re-learnt. It is a truism that market failure fails society.

CSR has a role to play in helping to restore public faith in free market capitalism by legitimising what some perceive to be a flawed and failing system and a tarnished, damaged brand of neo-liberal free market capitalism. It is suggested here that from the wreckage of the financial crises will emerge a stronger, differently shaped and more resilient form of capitalism (Brittan, 2010). At times, it will need more as well as less state intervention and regulation. The type of capitalism that emerges will be shaped by political, economic, social and technological imperatives as well as the needs and demands of stakeholders.

The consequences and outcomes of the crisis have yet to be fully played out, but it is clear they are likely to be long lasting and far-reaching. The weaknesses, inadequacies and failings of the existing system for regulating and managing capitalism have been laid bare. The future of capitalism as a regime of accumulation, production and distribution is however not in doubt. It does nevertheless require some fine-tuning, modification, better regulation and varying degrees and types of intervention.

The 2007–2010 financial crises temporarily halted the ascendancy of neo-liberal ideology, but it will re-assert itself in new thinking and new policy guises so as to help make the world anew and make it a better place to live and work and do business. Neo-liberalism is alive and is undergoing a re-birth. The form and shape it takes has yet to be determined. The forward march of neo-liberalism was temporarily halted by the 2007–2010 financial crises but is likely to continue anew on a different route into the future. We can but hope that this new future for neo-liberalism properly and fully addresses the irresponsibility of businesses and governments.

CONCLUSION

The response of government and other authorities to the crisis is ongoing and is as yet unfinished. A new corporate governance and financial regulatory regime of a type and sort yet to be determined is likely although more prescient is the application of the rules. Uncomfortable and difficult decisions have yet to be taken on these issues. The shape and form such decisions take is important in that good rules work and bad rules invariably do not. The danger is that over-regulation stifles innovation, enterprise and entrepreneurship. An additional threat is that too much regulation makes the system difficult to manage and rules hard to implement. Moreover, a further danger is that new rules and regulations change behaviour in lending, managing and risk-taking and could result in moral hazard. A successful regulatory and rule-based regime is one that works for the benefit of the common good and is shown to work at times of stress. Oversight, light touch regulation and factoring true and real (social and environmental) costs into market transactions are a fair and legitimate way to progress and deliver change. How to conceive an alternative future while shackled to the present economic financial system and corresponding modes

of thought is an issue governments and policy makers must surely struggle
to reconcile.

Complexity is a much-discussed topic in the economic and social sciences
(Byrne, 1998), and it is suggested here that it can be used as a mask to hide
untruths. It can be used as a reason to maintain the status quo and leave
structures, processes and rules as they are. The truth is that in this context,
complexity is a chimera. There is a simple, and not a complex need for
people, businesses and organisations of all types to behave in a moral and
ethical way and to structure this practice into the very fabric of their being
and operation. To be successful, meaningful and fit for purpose, a new
corporate governance and financial regulatory regime cannot be imposed
from above but requires buy-in and consent from below. Calls for less, as
well as more, regulation by those at opposing ends of the political economic
spectrum means that the moral compass in this regard is not easy to read.
Corporate governance and CSR can undoubtedly be perceived as
self-serving, virtuous concepts that appease the collective conscience.
Nevertheless, they do have real purpose and meaning and are tools
that can help deliver change and shape a better future. The simple
truth is there is a need for government to set frameworks by which
individuals and businesses are able to change behaviours away from
corporate irresponsibility and towards CSR (Jones et al., 2009). How to
bring about this change in behaviour is a challenge for all. While a new
regime of regulation should be designed to address future issues, it should
draw on and be informed by lessons from history, including the 2007–2010
financial crisis. However, the rules and regulations should not be determined
purely by crises of the past but should be designed so as to prevent and
minimise future crises.

The crisis provides ample evidence and examples of banking rectitude,
mismanagement and CSI. The crisis demonstrates a dereliction of duty by
bankers, regulators and the authorities in general to minimise risk, manage
effectively and to commit fully and realise their wider societal obligations.
A core social responsibility of businesses such as banks is to create rather
than destroy wealth. That the banks lost so much money so spectacularly
simply serves to demonstrate their corporate and financial irresponsibility.
The crisis also heralded the emergence of a new economic and political
thinking. New answers and policy prescriptions are evolving and being
sought for ways for dealing with the crises and its aftermath.

The 2007–2010 financial crises have highlighted the shift in the centre of
economic gravity. The West typified by the United States and United
Kingdom has been shown to be over-indebted (Krugman, 2008, 2010).

China with its record of high economic growth and financial surplus is the US's creditor nation. This shift in the balance of economic and political power will bring about new challenges for businesses wishing to operate an ethical and socially responsible supply chain. How to manage so as to deliver socially responsible goods and services in this new world order requires government to intervene to set a legal and economic framework, but it also requires the strengthening of trust relations throughout the supply chain and across all businesses.

Since the 2007–2010 financial crisis, the world has changed, and there is now a need to imagine a new future and for government to build a new strategy for capital and labour that works for the interests of all and not just the few. Uncritical acceptance and dogmatic adherence to neo-liberal economic orthodoxy is at an end, and a new era of state intervention in the economy has dawned. It calls for a new code of corporate governance that includes and utilises the knowledge and skills of workers, managers, shareholders as well as the wider community. Increased democratic accountability and the spreading of wealth, knowledge and power are necessary steps. An enlightened and informed brand of state-regulated capitalism can build capacity, restore confidence and help economic growth. The 2007–2010 financial crises saw the world change for the worse. The onus on all of us now is to make the world anew and make it a better place to live, work and do business. There is a need to enrich the present and inform the future by learning lessons from the past. History can help guide us to new and better futures. The challenge for government, if not us all, is to change business attitudes, behaviours, processes and practices away from irresponsibility in all its guises and towards CSR. Understanding the broad political and economic environment in which irresponsibility occurs and the role government plays in this is of paramount import for raising standards of governance, practices and behaviours.

NOTES

1. Source from http://www.bis.gov.uk/policies/business-sectors/low-carbon-business-opportunities/sustainable-development/corporate-responsibility
2. Department of Business Enterprise and Regulatory Reform, 2009, p. 2; see http://www.bis.gov.uk/files/file50312.pdf
3. See http://www.bis.gov.uk/Policies/business-sectors/low-carbon-business-opportunities/corporate-responsibility
4. See http://www.neweconomicthinking.org

REFERENCES

Bansal, P., & Kandola, S. (2003). Corporate social irresponsibility: Why good people behave badly in organizations. *Ivey Business Journal* (March/April), 1–5.

Bishop, M., & Green, M. (2010). *The road from ruin: How to revive capitalism and put America back on top*. New York: Crown Business.

Blowfield, M., & Murray, A. (2008). *Corporate responsibility: A critical introduction*. Oxford: Oxford University Press.

Brittan, S. (2010). A credo for a revived capitalism. *The Financial Times*, May 7, p. 13.

Byrne, D. (1998). *Complexity theory and the social sciences: An introduction*. London: Routledge.

Cadbury Report. (1992). *Report of the Committee on the Financial Aspects of Corporate Governance: The code of best practice* (December). London: Gee Professional Publishing.

Commission of the European Communities. (2001). *Promoting a European framework for corporate social responsibility*. Brussels: Commission of the European Communities.

Commission of the European Communities. (2002). *Communication from the commission concerning; Corporate social responsibility: A business contribution to sustainable development*. Brussels: Commission of the European Communities.

Donaldson, T., & Preston, L. E. (1995). Stakeholder theory of the corporation: Concepts, evidence and implications. *The Academy of Management Review*, *20*(1), 65–91.

European Commission. (2004). *European multistakeholder forum on CSR final report*. 29 June. Available at: http://circa.europa.eu/irc/empl/csr_eu_multi_stakeholder_forum/info/data/en/csr%20forum%20final%20report.pdf. Accessed on 8th October 2010.

Franklin, D. (2008). A special report on corporate social responsibility. *The Economist*, January 19, pp. 3–22.

Freeman, R. E. (1984). *Strategic management: A stakeholder approach*. Boston, MA: Pitman.

Friedman, M. (1962). *Capitalism and freedom*. Chicago, IL: Chicago University Press.

Frooman, J. (1997). Socially irresponsible and illegal behaviour and shareholder wealth. *Business and Society*, *36*(3), 221.

Gamble, A. (1988). *The free economy and the strong state: The politics of Thatcherism*. London: Macmillan.

Gamble, A. (1994). *Britain in decline: Economic policy, political strategy and the British state* (4th ed.). London: Macmillan.

Gladwell, M. (2000). *The tipping point: How little things can make a big difference*. London: Little Brown.

Gray, J. (1998). *False dawn: The delusions of global capitalism*. London: Grantna Books.

Greenbury Report. (1995). *Directors' remuneration (report of a study group chaired by Sir Richard Greenbury)* (July). London: Gee Professional Publishing.

Hall, S., & Jaques, M. (1983). *The politics of Thatcherism*. London: Lawrence and Wishart.

Hayek, F. A. (1944). *The road to serfdom*. London: Routledge and Kegan Paul.

Hayek, F. A. (1960). *The constitution of liberty*. London: Routledge and Kegan Paul.

Higgs Report. (2003). Review of the Role and Effectiveness of Non-Executive Directors, Department of Trade and Industry, London, January.

Jones, B. (2007). The guardian letters page. December 14, 45.

Jones, B., Bowd, R., & Tench, R. (2009). Corporate irresponsibility and corporate social responsibility: Competing realities. *Social Responsibility Journal*, *5*(3), 300–310.

Keynes, J. M. (2009). *The general theory of employment, interest and money*. New York: Classic Books America.

Kotchen, M. J., & Moon, J. J. (2007). *Corporate social responsibility for irresponsibility.* [Internet] U.C. Santa Barbara and NBER University of Pennsylvania. Available at http://www2.bren.ucsb.edu/~kotchen/links/CSR9-04-07.pdf. Retrieved on 12 June 2010.

Krugman, P. (2008). *The return of depression economics and the crisis of 2008.* London: Allen Lane.

Krugman, P. (2010). Quoted by Phillip Inman in 'Americans attack European economic hardliners.' *The Guardian*, June 12, p. 34.

Levine, R., Locke, C., Searls, D., & Weinberger, D. (2000). *The Cluetrain Manifesto: The end of business as usual.* Cambridge, MA: Perseus Books.

Mitchell, L. E. (2001). *Corporate irresponsibility: America's newest export.* New Haven: Yale University Press.

Newell, P. (2005). Citizenship, accountability and community: The limits of the CSR agenda. *International Affairs*, *81*(3), 541–557.

Parker, G. (2010). Osborne tells ministers they may be forced to make 15–20% cuts. *Financial Times*, June 9, p. 1.

Riddell, P. (1985). *The Thatcher government.* London: Blackwell Publishers.

Riddell, P. (1989). *The Thatcher decade.* London: Blackwell Publishers.

Roubini, N., & Mihm, S. (2010). *Crisis economics: A crash course in the future of finance.* London: Allen Lane.

Smith, N. C., & Lenssen, G. (2009). *Mainstreaming corporate responsibility.* Chichester: Wiley.

Solomon, J. (2010). *Corporate governance and accountability* (3rd ed.). Chichester: Wiley.

Somerset Webb, M. (2010). Why I'm hoping to be a bull, by the end of the year. *Financial Times*, (Money section), January 9, p. 3.

Soros, G. (1998). *The crisis of global capitalism.* New York: Public Affairs.

Steger, M. B., & Roy, R. K. (2010). *Neoliberalism: A very short introduction.* Oxford: Oxford University Press.

Stiglitz, J. (2002). *Globalization and its discontents.* London: Penguin Books.

Tett, G. (2010). *Fool's gold: How unrestrained greed corrupted a dream, shattered global markets and unleashed a catastrophe.* London: Abacus.

Wagner, T., Bicen, P., & Hall, Z. R. (2008). The dark side of retailing: Towards a scale of corporate social irresponsibility. *International Journal of Retail and Distribution Management*, *36*(2), 124–142.

Wood, D. (1991). Corporate social performance revisited. *Academy of Management Review*, *16*(4), 691–718.

PERFORMANCE MANAGEMENT AND NEO-LIBERAL LABOUR MARKET GOVERNANCE: THE CASE OF THE UK

Alex Nunn

Over the past three decades it has become common place to think of key areas of the economy as being subject to gover*nance* as opposed merely to gover*nment*. This shift is related to the adoption of increasingly neo-liberal approaches to public policy in which key characteristics are the promotion of cost-based efficiency, a preference for contracting and markets and the insulation of key aspects of economic decision-making from democratic and every day political scrutiny. A key cororally of these changes has been the increasing use of private sector management practices in the public sector. Principal among these is the use of performance management. In some respects however, performance management is used not just as a management but as a governance tool, setting 'desirable' social outcomes and aligning public service delivery (either direct or under contract in the market) to the achievement of these. Often performance management approaches are used both to establish high-level policy commitments and at very low levels of implementation and tracking the linkages between these can be very revealing in terms of understanding how balances and tensions in political rhetoric are resolved in the process of delivery. Put simply,

Reframing Corporate Social Responsibility: Lessons from the Global Financial Crisis
Critical Studies on Corporate Responsibility, Governance and Sustainability,
Volume 1, 77–99
Copyright © 2010 by Emerald Group Publishing Limited
All rights of reproduction in any form reserved
ISSN: 2043-9059/doi:10.1108/S2043-9059(2010)0000001010

analysis of performance management can help to differentiate between 'rhetorical' and 'real' policy commitments.

There are clear links here to Corporate Social Responsibility (CSR). Clearly public sector organisations have an obligation to deliver social responsibility at two levels. First, this relates to the delivery of governmental policy objectives. Second, when delivering policy objectives there will often be difficult choices and tradeoffs to be made in how organisations go about these activities. For example, Public Employment Services (PES) will often be charged with the policy objective of reducing the number of welfare benefit recipients, increasing employment and often contributing to the wider objective of combating poverty. They will often also be charged with doing so as efficiently as possible. But what about when delivering this efficiently leads to reducing staff wages or where reducing the welfare role means pushing people into low-paid jobs where the economic and social benefits are questionable? This chapter will deal with some of these core challenges in relation to governance and CSR in relation to a PES. The implications of this discussion have much wider significance for how other public and private organisations might think about their social responsibility and the ways in which it is delivered.

This chapter combines an analysis of performance management to differentiate between real and rhetorical policy commitments in the process providing a commentary on the implications of this for social responsibility. It does so by focusing on the UK labour market policy and is based on a wide range of primary research projects undertaken by the author and collaborators, over the past five years (Johnson & Nunn, 2005, 2006; Nunn, Bickerstaffe, & Mitchell, 2010; Nunn, Bickerstaffe, & Wymer, 2009a; Nunn, Fidler, Wymer, & Kelsey, 2008; Nunn, Johnson, & Bickerstaffe, 2007a; Nunn, Johnson, Kelsey, & Usher, 2007b; Nunn, Johnson, Monro, Bickerstaffe, & Kelsey, 2007c). In particular it focuses on the extent to which the performance management approaches in the PES – Jobcentre Plus – both exhibits the key features of neo-liberal governance and emphasises different aspects of the high-level policy commitments of the New Labour government over the past decade. It suggests that while a consideration of political rhetoric would suggest that there is an equal policy commitment to expand the number of people in work, to increase the skills and productivity of the labour force and to promote social inclusion, in the delivery of public employment services it is the former objective that is to the fore; so much so that the latter two are largely 'crowded out'. This is not to say that initiatives developed in other policy domains – such as the skills system – do not include a focus on these other objectives, just that labour market policy and interventions are the obvious policy domain in which these objectives would be pursued in an integrated way. In addition, at a time of economic crisis the role of performance management may be to 'lock-in' increasingly inappropriate and misaligned objectives into to the delivery of key services.

NEO-LIBERAL GOVERNANCE AND PERFORMANCE MANAGEMENT

The use of performance management in the private sector was prefaced by the establishment of qualitatively new forms of corporate entities in the early years of the twentieth century, particularly in the United States. These vast new corporations involved increasing separation of ownership from control and the establishment of substantial corporate management bureaucracies to organise often technical and geographically diverse tasks and processes. As such, the use of performance management became a key corporate governance tool to extend control to disparate, highly hierarchical and complex organisations and business processes (Drucker, 1955; Kennerley & Neely, 2001, p. 146).

Since the 1970s the neo-liberal revolution in governance and public policy has been accompanied by the transfer of private sector management techniques into the public sector, under the banner of the New Public Management (NPM) practice (Dunleavy, 1994; OECD, 1994; Whitfield, 1992, 2001). Since that time, a large and growing public policy literature on performance measurement and management has emerged (Bouckaert & Peters, 2002; Bourne, 2005; Centre for Business Performance, 2006; Kaplan & Norton, 1992, 2000; Kennerley & Mason, 2008; Kennerley & Neely, 2001; Micheli & Kennerley, 2005; Neely, Gregory, & Platts, 1995; Neely, Marr, Roos, Pike, & Gupta, 2003; Neely, Richards, Mills, Platts, & Bourne, 1997; Paranjape, Rossiter, & Pantano, 2006) and 'how to' type guides have proliferated (e.g. Audit Commission, 2000a, 2000b, 2008; National Audit Office, 2001; Treasury, 2001).

What much of this literature ignores however, is the explicit links between the NPM and performance management on the one hand and neo-liberal policy objectives on the other. In the early phase of implementation neo-liberal policy advocates were particularly concerned to limit the remit of politicised democratic engagement, specifically isolating key aspects of policy-making from popular pressure (Buchanan, 1997). The increasing popularity of central bank independence and rules-based monetary and fiscal policy are examples of attempts to achieve this objective and are closely linked to governance by performance management to the extent that outcome and process measures are used to assess and signal commitment to rules-based economic decision-making.

Other important tenets of neo-liberal governance are focused on reducing the role of the state as a market actor and instead ensuring that it provides a steering and enabling role, with the delivery of services contracted out to private and quasi-market actors (Nunn, 2005). Here performance management performs the role of 'steering' arms-length and contracted-out delivery organisations and at the same time obscuring the establishment of highly political goals in managerial rather than democratic processes which see performance management as a technical function rather than being about determining political and social priorities. In contexts where political rhetoric suggests that important balances in public policy are being held in check, scrutiny of performance management can reveal the real direction of public policy and what the precise trade off between different policy objectives is.

Recent international trends in neo-liberal governance (Nunn, 2005, 2006, 2007) have centralised the core objective of competitiveness (Cammack, 2006). The governance of labour markets is central to these strategies for competitiveness. In particular, labour market policy in pursuit of competitiveness is tailored towards two ultimate objectives: expanding the amount of absolute labour units involved in generating economic output in a given socio-economic-political space (e.g. city, micro-region, country, macro-region) but also the amount of output relative to those units (e.g. per-worker or per-hour worked). As we shall see later, the way in which labour markets are governed is central to the balance struck between these sometimes supportive and sometimes contradictory objectives. Further, political rhetoric and debate means that a third set of commitments to social inclusion also need to be balanced with these concerns with competitiveness. This is formally recognised across the European Union in the widely adopted but ambiguous goal of 'flexicurity' (European Commission, 2007b). This policy 'amalgam' appears to have arisen in the Netherlands but is most frequently associated with welfare reform in Denmark (Wilthagon, 1998, 2008). The idea is that flexible labour markets can be combined with strong levels of social security and that notions of security can be shifted from individual jobs to employment status.

Although the language of 'flexicurity' is much more popular in Europe than it is in the United Kingdom, there has nevertheless been a long-term commitment to balance the apparently contradictory objectives of competitiveness and social protection, and this is explored in more detail in the following sections. On coming to power, the New Labour

Government in the United Kingdom recognised several long-term and structural barriers to competitiveness.

The first was related to the structural exclusion of large sections of the potential workforce from even competition for employment; where industrial restructuring and Thatcherite policies to undermine unionised labour forces in manufacturing and primary industries had left significant spatial and social concentrations of worklessness. These groups were often located at some distance geographically from labour market demand in new service-based industries or in urban centres in increasingly residualised housing estates. In either case deprivation was thought to be having important feedback effects such that whole communities were either benefit dependent or engaged in the informal and criminal economy, or both (Nunn, 2008, pp. 3–5). This 'inactivity' rather than unemployment was so negative not simply because potential workers were not employed and therefore generating output, but because they had no role at all in relation to the labour market.

Second, one consequence of the Thatcherite pursuit of low-cost comparative advantage within the protective barriers of the EU market had been to leave large sections of the employed workforce in often low wage, low productivity and insecure work. As such New Labour faced two interconnected problems: the need to both expand the scope of the labour market to take in previously excluded and inactive groups at the same time as upskilling the lower echelons of the labour force to better position the United Kingdom in the global division of labour, especially in the context of EU enlargement and increasing migration. These objectives were pursued rigorously with a wide variety of initiatives to both widen and upskill the working population (see Nunn, 2005, Chapter 3, 2006, 2007, 2008), though the argument developed in this chapter via an assessment of performance management in the PES is that the implementation of labour market policy has very much focussed on expanding the labour supply as opposed to upskilling. In addition, while policy rhetoric suggests that a politics of social inclusion underpins labour market policy, a consideration of key performance management targets suggests that this is at best a second-order priority.

PERFORMANCE MANAGEMENT, LABOUR MARKET POLICY AND PUBLIC EMPLOYMENT SERVICES

Labour market policy has been one domain in which performance management approaches have been brought to bear and there is a small but significant literature on the use of performance management in managing and governing the delivery of employment services, especially in OECD countries. For example, Mosley and colleagues (Mosley, Schutz, & Breyer, 2001; Mosley, Schütz, & Breyer, 2000) suggest that the use of Management by Objectives (MBO) in PES is widespread across Europe. Grubb's (2004) influential paper identifies mechanisms by which important problems in the use of performance measures in employment services can be overcome. Such problems include the incentive to focus resources on service users who are easy to place into work (known as 'creaming'), while not providing assistance to those facing the most substantial barriers who may actually have more to benefit ('parking') (Bruttel, 2004; Bruttel, 2005; Struyven & Steurs, 2005). Other research projects have included a detailed cross-Europe study (Lehner, Natter, Naylon, & Wagner-Pinter, 2005; Synthesis Forschung and OSB Consulting, 2005, 2007, 2008) in which research has been used to identify and refine a list of benchmark indicators on which participating PES can be measured. The PES benchmarking project is also linked to the European Employment Strategy (EES) Indicators which have been under continual development since 2002 to fit the changing requirements of the EES (European Commission, 2007a, 2008).

Nunn et al. (2010) look at the performance management regime in the PES across Europe, North America and Australia and New Zealand. They establish a typology of performance measures used in PES which groups the types of measures and indicators used according to whether they are output, process or outcome measures, with the latter group being split into intermediate and final outcomes (Table 1). This typology is then used to describe the measures actually in place in the PES reviewed as well as the strengths and weaknesses that each of these measures bring.

NEO-LIBERAL GOVERNANCE BY PERFORMANCE MANAGEMENT IN THE UNITED KINGDOM

Performance Management and High-Level Labour Market Policy Commitments

The management of the UK PES: Jobcentre Plus, performance, under New Labour was set within the wider system of public policy performance measurement established in the Spending Review and Public Service

Table 1. Typology of PES Performance Measures.

Output Measures	Process Measures	Intermediate Outcome Measures	Final Outcome Measures
Vacancy registration	Customer feedback	General off-flows	Employment rate (general and for specific populations)
Activation interviews completed	Qualitative checks on interviews	Specific off-flows	Unemployment rate (general and for specific populations)
Referrals to training/ activation providers	Qualitative checks on plan completions/ documentation	Penetration measures	Productivity
Penetration measures		Benefit duration measures	
Individual plan completion		Vacancy outcomes	
Placement into work trials or subsidized work			
Sanctions			

Source: For a detailed discussion of which countries use which measures see Nunn et al. (2010, pp. 23–32).

Agreement target system and cycle. Three yearly public spending allocations were agreed between the Treasury and spending departments based on the agreement of specific objectives (with associated performance measures and targets) which were intended to reflect agreed cross-government policy objectives. Although it remains to be seen whether this system will be retained by the incoming Conservative-Liberal coalition governance, the Department for Work and Pensions (DWP), the sponsoring government department with responsibility for labour market policy and the UK PES, is currently directly responsible for two PSA targets (Box 1) and contributes to the further nine. The two principle PSAs that are owned by the DWP are: PSA 8: *Maximise employment opportunity for all* and PSA 17: *Tackle poverty and promote greater independence and well-being in later life.* In addition, the DWP is also heavily involved in the delivery agreement for PSA 9 which is a widely shared government objective to reduce Child Poverty. The detail of PSA 8 reveals the need to promote economic inclusion for particular vulnerable groups such as families with children, older people and disabled people.

Box 1. Details of PSA Measures and Targets[1]

PSA 8 – Maximise Employment Opportunity for All

- Indicator 1 – An increase in the overall employment rate, taking account of the economic cycle.
  - Measured as employment on the LFS International Labour Office definition for working age (16–59/64) with an assessment of the economic cycle based on Treasury estimates.
  - The target includes an 'aspirational' 80 per cent employment rate target and a firm target of an improvement of the employment rate over the course of the economic cycle and in excess of sampling variability in the LFS.
- Indicator 2 – A narrowing of the gap between employment rates of specific disadvantaged groups (disabled people, lone parents, ethnic minorities, people aged 50 +, the 15 per cent lowest qualified, people living in the most deprived wards.
  - Measured as employment rate for these groups and the overall employment rate. The most deprived wards are those in the lowest 10 per cent on the Indices of Multiple Deprivation.
  - Targets the PSA does not set out a specific target for each of these indicators, though it does suggest that an improvement on these is required above the level of sampling variability.
- Indicator 3 – Reduction in the number of people on working-age out of work benefits.
  - Measures include the number of people on working age out of work benefits (ESA, IS, IB, JSA).
  - Targets – the PSA does not include any specific targets other than a general improvement in the indicator over the Spending Review period.
- Indicator 4 – Increase the proportion of people who leave benefit who stay off for a sustained period.
  - Measures – tracks those benefit customers who move off benefits and stay off for 6 months using Jobcentre Plus administrative data.
  - Targets – the PSA does not include any specific targets other than a general improvement in the indicator over the Spending Review period.

PSA 17: Tackle poverty and promote greater independence and well-being in later life
- Indicator 1 – The employment rate of those aged 50–69 and difference between this and the overall employment rate
  - Measures – this is measured as the overall employment rate (ILO definition measured through the LFS) of the older age group (50–69) and the overall working age population (aged 16–59/64).
  - Targets – an improvement of the gap between these two rates of at least 1 per cent.
- Indicator 2 – The percentage of pensioners in low income
  - Measures – pensioners who are included in key measures of low income, including 60 per cent of contemporary median income, 50 per cent of contemporary median income and 60 per cent of 1998/1999 median. Income measures are from the Family Resources Survey and are based on an After Housing Costs (AHC) basis.
  - Targets – measurement issues mean that the target for this measure is complex but includes increases above sampling and measurement error.

Source: (HM_Government, 2007, 2008)

Additional PSAs focus on skills and productivity. For example, the preamble to PSA 1: *Raise the Productivity of the UK Economy*, suggests that

> The UK has experienced strong employment performance over recent years, but there is a limit to the number of workers the economy can supply and the number of hours that can be worked. This represents a constraint to the amount that labour can contribute to raising economic growth. Therefore, improving productivity is the primary route to improving long-term standards of living. (HM Government, 2008, p. 3)

This then leads to a number of measurable commitments to increase productivity per-our worked in comparison with competitor countries. PSA 2: *Improve the skills of the population, on the way to ensuring a world-class skills base by 2020*, sets out a range of commitments to improve the skills base of the population, with the objective being 'benefit in terms of higher productivity, greater social mobility and improved overall economic performance' (HM Government, 2007, p. 3).

So these high-level policy commitments, expressed in the performance management system, contain all three core economic policy objectives to secure competitiveness through: (1) expanding the labour market participation; (2) promoting upskilling/productivity and (3) increasing social inclusion for specific social groups, especially families with children. Quite clearly, the labour market was seen as the domain in which these policy objectives were drawn together. It is interesting therefore to consider the extent to which the DWP, as the government department responsible for labour market policy, integrated these three concerns into its own performance management regime. The linkages between departmental activity and these overall policy objectives are established in the DWP's seven Strategic Objectives, several of which are directly relevant to the remit of Jobcentre Plus (Box 2).

What can be seen from these strategic objectives is that widening labour market participation is certainly a key feature. Measures of social inclusion also feature, but the major part of measuring this inclusion is again in relation to labour market participation. What is notable by its absence is any consideration of upskilling to achieve enhanced productivity. Tracing this analysis into implementation then is interesting to consider the extent to which these objectives find their way into the performance management framework for the UK PES: Jobcentre Plus, which is charged with operational delivery of working-age benefits and employment services for the DWP.

Performance Management within Jobcentre Plus

There is a long history of performance measurement, including outcomes measurement in the UK PES, dating back to the former Employment Service (Campbell & Sanderson, 2000; Johnson, 2003). What has been common to all of the different approaches used has been a focus on generating organisational and individual incentives to move unemployed and inactive benefit claimants into work and outcome measures tend to be seen as the most important among the range of headline process targets that the organisation is also subject to.[2] For example, when the new arms-length PES Jobcentre Plus was created out of the merger of the former Employment Service and Benefits Agency in the early part of the past decade it was accompanied by the creation of the Job Entry Target (JET) system. This system allocated points to individual advisors as and when they

Box 2. Department for Work and Pensions Strategic Objectives

1. Reduce the number of children living in poverty
   - The number of children living in workless households.
   - The number of children benefiting from child maintenance, particularly those living in low income households.
2. Maximise employment opportunity for all and reduce the numbers on out-of-work benefits
   - The overall employment rate.
   - The gap between the overall employment rate and the employment rates of disabled people, lone parents, ethnic minorities, the over fifties, those with no qualifications, people living in the most deprived wards and those most likely to be socially excluded.
   - The number of people on out-of-work benefits.
   - The time people spend on out-of-work benefits.
3. Improve health and safety outcomes
   - The incidence of fatal and major injuries in workplaces.
   - The incidence of work-related ill-health.
   - The number of dangerous events in the nuclear industry, and in the offshore and onshore oil and gas sector.
4. Promote independence and well-being in later life, continuing to tackle pensioner poverty and implementing pension reform
   - The employment rate of those aged 50–69 and the difference between this and the overall employment rate.
   - The percentage of pensioners in low income.
   - Setting up a personal account system and implementing automatic enrolment and mandatory employer contributions into qualifying pension schemes.
5. Promote equality of opportunity for disabled people
   - Disabled people's perception of the choice and control they have over their lives.
   - The gap between the overall employment rate and the employment rate of disabled people.
   - Access to goods and services for disabled people.
6. Pay our customers the right benefits at the right time
   - The proportion of benefit expenditure overpaid or underpaid due to fraud and error.

- The time taken to process new claims to benefits, and changes in circumstances, including Housing Benefit and Council Tax Benefit.

7. Make DWP an exemplar of effective service delivery to individuals and employers
   - The proportion of our customers who understand how DWP can help them.
   - The proportion of our customers whose initial contact leads directly to resolution of their needs.
   - The time taken to meet our customers' needs.
   - The proportion of our customers who believe that DWP/ Government is providing them with the help they need.
   - The proportion of our customers who feel respected and valued.
   - Employers' views on the services we provide to them.

Source: (Department for Work and Pensions, 2008a)

could prove that they had in some way helped a benefit claimant into employment. The whole of Jobcentre Plus was tasked with achieving a specific aggregate points total and individual advisers and offices were encouraged to compete to generate as many points as possible. The allocation of points though reflected the policy objective of increasing labour market participation and 'activity' rather than simply increasing employment. Points were allocated using an explicit weights system in which different customer groups were given different points allocations (Table 2). The initial JET system also awarded additional points for job sustainability and after amendment for people living in the most deprived areas.

So there was a clear organisational and individual incentive to bring more people – especially the currently inactive – into employment. On the face of it there was also an incentive to generate sustained job entries; afterall points were allocated on this basis too. However, what is clear from looking at the weighting and criteria for these points is that Job retention points were very much less beneficial (1 point) than getting an unemployed person into work in the first place, and the period which these were measured on – 4 weeks – is hardly evidence of job retention. Moreover, it was actually more beneficial, in terms of the points gained, to be able to help these groups find work that they could not sustain and then try to help them find yet another job, as the combined points total was always at least as beneficial and more often than

Table 2.   Explicit Weighting of Points in the JET Regime.

Client Group	Points
New Deal for Lone Parents and other Lone Parents	12
New Deal for Disabled People and other people with disabilities on inactive benefits	12
Other primary benefit recipients	12
New Deal 50 +	8
New Deal 25 +	8
New Deal for Young People	8
Employment Zones	8
Other people with disabilities	8
Other long-term JSA	8
Short-term unemployed JSA	4
Other jobless non-benefit customers	2
Employed job-entries	1
Additional points	
Retention – for each JSA customer who remains off JSA for 4 weeks after starting a job	1
Area-Based Points – for jobless client job entries in 60 local authority districts	2

Source: Policy Research Institute (2002).

not, more so. Indeed, early evaluations of both JET and the pre-roll out trial concluded that the retention points had little or no impact not just because of these problems but because it was also very difficult for PES staff to influence retention. Although the impact of the differentially weighted points did not have a huge impact on changing organisational emphasis towards the more inactive groups, there was some evidence of managers re-allocating resources as to achieve higher points totals, suggesting that the impact of performance management was to create some degree of behaviour change (Johnson, 2003; Policy Research Institute, 2002).

Later evaluation research was to show however, that the JET system suffered from some significant perverse incentives. 'Claiming' job entries also required proof of a Jobcentre Plus intervention by a particular member of staff. This meant that individual members of staff, despite the weighted points, had an incentive to help those customers who were easiest to get into work, even if they did not strictly do anything to help them to find employment. Indeed, the incentive to help those who were perfectly able to help themselves was so strong that it was widely thought that Jobcentre Plus Advisers would occasionally offer support through the Adviser Discretionary Fund (cash payments to help customers overcome a specific barrier to employment such as transport costs for the first few weeks of work or specialist equipment such as boots or protective clothing) to customers who only visited the Jobcentre to give notification that they had already found work (Johnson & Nunn, 2005, p. 13; 2006). JET therefore had in-built problems which prevented it working correctly in the sense that the incentive structure was perverted. However, what is clear from these evaluation reports is that to expand the scope of the labour market was much more closely aligned with the incentive structure promoted by JET than were either upskilling the population or promoting social inclusion.

The recognition of the flaws in JET led to the piloting and introduction of an alternative organisational performance measure; the Job Outcome Target (JOT) (Johnson & Nunn, 2005, 2006). JOT was intended to resolve the apparent weaknesses in JET in a number of distinct ways. First, it was intended to be more efficient in the way it recorded performance points. Second, the explicit weighting of points in the JOT system was simplified but the emphasis on inactive groups was retained, with for example an employed person moving into different work counting as one point and a Lone Parent claiming Income Support counting as 12. Third, because JOT could not be disaggregated down to the individual Adviser level and because it did not require a Jobcentre Plus intervention to claim 'performance points', it was hoped that JOT would lead to more appropriate staff behaviour, focusing attention on cooperative activity targeted at inactive benefit claimants. Finally, JOT was introduced at the same time as range of measures that aimed to divert those service users most able to find their own employment to the newly established 'self-help' channels such as Jobpoints (computer terminals for undertaking job searches) in Jobcentres, Jobseeker Direct contact centres and the Jobcentre Plus website. Additionally, offices and staffing in them were gradually redesigned to ensure that the only service users able to meet with Advisors had an appointment booked on the grounds of the stage in their benefit claim. As such, it became increasingly difficult for staff to have any contact with claimants unless they were considered to be inactive or relatively long-term unemployed (Nunn et al., 2009b, p. 37).

What these cumulative changes suggest is again that the emphasis of the PES was to be on widening the scope of the labour market – i.e. making the inactive competes for jobs without necessarily doing anything direct to reduce unemployment or to promote upskilling. For sure, services were provided to shorter-term unemployed jobseekers, such as the Fortnightly Job Review interview but these were perfunctory and aimed not so much as delivering any kind of intervention other than to perform conditionality checks (Nunn et al., 2009b, pp. 60–62, 2007a, 2007b). Here the conditionality was the legal obligation of all jobseekers claiming the main unemployment benefit to be 'actively seeking and available for work'. The main intervention provided to these groups therefore was to check that they had searched for work in the previous fortnight and to recommend for sanction (the removal of benefit payments) those assessed as not having done so. The emphasis then was on generating a larger pool of available workers. What is even more persuasive is the fact that when JOT was determined to actually provide an insufficient motivation for individual staff to move inactive and longer-term claimants towards work, other means of individual performance management were introduced to increase this incentive (Nunn et al., 2007c).

Another feature, which perfectly mirrors the characteristics of the NPM, of labour market policy under New Labour has been experiments with the privatisation of employment services, for example through the various New Deal and Pathways to work contracts, the Employment Zone initiative and more latterly the Flexible New Deal. These initiatives have been accompanied also by experiments in performance management with performance measures being combined with payments mechanisms to incentivise results – the achievement of job entries. However, again evaluations have found that even where sustainability points and payments have been in-built into the system, they have been designed to drive little more than labour market 'churn' rather than longer-term transitions from inactivity/unemployment to work. This was so because low-productivity and low-paying employers had little incentive to increase their investment in either labour (skills or retention) or capital because they were constantly supplied by a steady stream of recruits and could export large amounts of their recruitment costs to publicly funded but private sector employment agencies (Policy Research Institute, 2006, p. 95).

Regardless, however, the trend in policy development under New Labour (and doubtless too under the new Conservative-Liberal government (Conservative Party, 2010, section 7)) was to continue to enhance benefit conditionality to reduce inactivity, with employment services increasingly privatised where payments are provided on an outcome basis as judged by performance management data (Department for Work and Pensions, 2008b). Payments are structured according to three sets of performance criteria: 20 per cent is based on the service fee, 50 per cent on short-term job outcomes (13 weeks of continuous employment) and 30 per cent of sustained job outcomes (26 weeks of employment in the last 30 weeks). These payments are staggered with service fees paid monthly and job outcome payments are paid when claimed on a per-unit basis. In the future, the intention is that 'customers' of employment services from private providers will exercise choice, as they do in a constrained way in the current Employment Zone contracts. This choice is to be informed through a Star Rating system similar to that in use in Australia. The Star Rating system is constructed from several datasets including job outcomes, sustained job outcomes, quality and contract compliance. In the case of the first two components, these are relative measures with performance points allocated on the basis of performance against targets in comparison with other contractors (DWP, Undated). Again, what shines through these arrangements is the requirement to increase labour market participation, with productivity enhancing and social inclusion measures less in evidence. That said, the move towards longer-term sustainability payments is at least progress towards the latter, though being introduced at a time when the labour market was in severe crisis as a result of the global economic crisis many providers have questioned whether it is feasible to respond to such incentive measures (Nunn, 2010, forthcoming).

DISCUSSION

It seems clear then that within the PES, the role of performance management has been to resolve the three-way tension in overall government policy commitments decisively in the favour of expanding the workforce as opposed to either social inclusion or upskilling. The emphasis both within the PES and in relation to its contracted service providers is on immediate job outcomes rather than the transitions in work-readiness of individuals or the quality of employment that they may gain. Where there is consideration of the quality of employment outcomes is built-in, this is frequently problematic and less significant than the immediate employment-outcome incentive.

As such, what is notable about the UK labour market policy over the last decade is that it has fed the demand for additional labour during the boom period by gradually reducing the inactive population. Although this is obviously positive from the point of view of public finances, the situation is more complex when considered from the perspective of individual and family well being, and potentially competitiveness also.

There is a great deal of research which suggests that employment has positive health and wellbeing effects (Waddell & Burton, 2006) and the data on poverty clearly shows that being in employment reduces the risk of both individual, family and child poverty (Adams, Johnson, Matejic, Vekaria, & Whately, 2009, p. 6). However, there is a serious concern that because of the way in which the tension between the three policy objectives considered here has been resolved in favour of expanding the labour market, that these benefits may have been undermined. For example, the health and wellbeing benefits of employment may not be realised where inactive people are placed into unsuccessful competition for work, repeated experiences of temporary and insecure work or achieve employment in poor-quality, high-stress and low-paid work (Waddell & Burton, 2006). Equally, it has become widely recognised, even in policy circles, that in-work poverty remains a considerable problem and that parental employment is often not enough, because of low wages, to lift children out of poverty (Harker, 2006; MacInnes, Kenway, & Parekh, 2009; Tripney et al., 2009).

The role of performance management in the expansion of the available labour force in this way may also not benefit competitiveness at all. Clearly, to the extent to which competitiveness is about productivity, it requires improvements in output per unit of labour power (e.g. hour worked); it requires not just an expansion of the available labour force but its upskilling and matching to technological change. As such, it may well be that expanding the available unskilled and relatively low-skilled labour force constitutes a disincentive to investment in productivity enhancing technology, upskilling or simply improving their retention.

Clearly, however, the weaknesses described earlier are not intrinsically related to performance management but to its use. Where there is a problem is that such technical and managerial processes are allowed to resolve political problems without appropriate levels of democratic scrutiny. This is the central problem in strategies of governance by performance management, but it does not necessarily have to be that way. Nunn et al. (2010, p. 33) find that in some countries PES performance targets are the subject of tripartite political debate. However, in the United Kingdom the process of target setting is largely undertaken by specialist teams of researchers and analysts in combination with the relevant Minister. This is a highly technical process whereby statistical models of previous performance are used to forecast possible future performance. There is virtually no external or political discussion of how this process is undertaken. Indeed governance changes over recent years have served to further weaken the connection between this sort of oversight and performance management. Before it was succeeded by the UK Commission for Employment and Skills (UKCES), the National Employment Panel had something of a remit to scrutinise Jobcentre Plus performance, but even then this was largely seen as providing an 'employer voice' on labour market policy. The UKCES does not have the same scrutiny role.

Following this logic, the role of performance management in labour market governance in the United Kingdom suggests that it is characteristic of the neo-liberal commitment to not just to management by objectives but also to the limitation of democratic and political scrutiny of key areas of economic policy. However, despite the frequent popular association of neo-liberal policy commitments with competitiveness it is notable that it is the more socially democratic countries, especially in relation to labour market policy, such as the Scandinavian states that tend to have higher levels of competitiveness. These states tend also to balance the three-way tension between labour market expansion, upskilling and social inclusion towards the latter two (Mailand, 2009). Finally, Nunn et al. (2010) show that it is these countries that also adopt a more open, transparent and negotiated use of performance management in labour market governance, often including social partners.

In the context of the financial crisis, the emphasis in the performance management regime on expanding the available labour force has continued, though it may be that the types of incentive bound up in performance management measures are less important than simply dealing with the workload at this time (Nunn, 2010). However, it is certainly arguable that the role of performance management in the overall 'work first' model of PES delivery in the United Kingdom contributed to a much less resilient labour market during times of recession and also was strongly pro-cyclical during the growth phase. Had employers been forced to overcome labour shortages not simply by taking on cheap labour but by restructuring the organisation of their workforce and the technology involved it is arguable that the competitive base would have been stronger and more resilient? Likewise, the role of performance management in encouraging ever greater numbers of unemployed and inactive people to apply for jobs, which many of them would never get, there may have been pressure placed on their social and mental well-being. To continue, albeit, in constrained form, with the same approach at a time when it is clear that those with barriers to employment will find it the hardest to be successful risks exacerbating such pressures. At such times, it may actually be better to ensure that interventions are not designed to achieve immediate job outcomes but to encourage individuals to move closer to the labour market and the unquestioned benefits that can bring, by gradually overcoming their barriers to employment, including skills, so that they are well placed to take advantage of opportunities when the recovery arrives. However, research suggests that performance management systems are a considerable barrier to this (Nunn, 2010).

CONCLUSIONS

Performance management embodies some of the key features of neo-liberal governance strategies, in the sense that it is suited to arms-length and contracted-out service delivery and it can be used in such a way as to change political and social debate into highly technical and managerial terms. Analysis of performance management can help to resolve ambiguities in political rhetoric which suggest that multiple policy objectives are being pursued simultaneously. In this case, close attention to performance management structures and systems suggests that an equal commitment to expand the labour market, upskilling the workforce and pursuing social inclusion through the labour market, is not carried through in practice and that in reality the former objective is paramount.

However, the issue here is the use to which performance management is put and the context in which it is deployed. In several countries, performance management within the PES is undertaken in a more inclusive, transparent and corporatist fashion, meaning that the agreement and negotiation of targets becomes part of the political rather than managerial process. Used in this way managerial time could be put not into simply agreeing targets but into understanding the causal linkages between actions and outcomes, so as to gradually increase the quality of political debate about the setting of political and social goals. This sort of scrutiny is particularly important at times of crisis where it could help to ensure that rigid and institutionalised performance management processes do not prevent rapid responses to changing external contexts.

The implications of this for CSR are interesting. Clearly, public sector organisations combine a wide range of primary, secondary and tertiary policy objectives. Primary objectives for PES for example often combine reducing welfare payments, increasing employment and combating poverty. Secondary objectives often relate to efficiency – i.e. responsibility in the use of tax payers' money, whereas tertiary objectives relate to the way in which objectives are pursued or services are delivered. For example, it is easy to deliver services cheaply by cutting public sector wages, but this might contribute to poverty. Likewise promoting employment and cutting welfare bills might counteract other attempts to build a high quality economy and combat social exclusion and poverty. To the extent that 'what gets measured gets done' – the very purpose of performance management, then analysis of performance measures can help to show how the tensions and tradeoffs within primary objectives and then between primary, secondary and tertiary objectives are held in balance and resolved. Similar analyses of private sector CSR practices might also help to understand the extent to which CSR objectives are balanced or harmonised with business or profit related ones.

NOTES

1. Indicators which are not relevant to the remit of Jobcentre Plus are not reported.
2. Jobcentre Plus is also subject to headline targets on Employer Engagement, customer service, the completion of interviews, fraud and error and benefit processing times.

REFERENCES

Adams, N., Johnson, G., Matejic, P., Vekaria, R., & Whately, J. (2009). *Households below average income: An analysis of the income distribution 1994/95 – 2007/08*. DWP: London.

Audit Commission. (2000a). *Aiming to improve: The principles of performance measurement*. Audit Commission, 18.

Audit Commission. (2000b). *On target: The practice of performance indicators*. Audit Commission, 26.

Audit Commission. (2008). *In the know – using information to make better decisions: A discussion paper*. Audit Commission, 48.

Bouckaert, G., & Peters, B. G. (2002). Performance measurement and management: The Achilles' heel in administrative modernization. *Public Performance & Management Review, 25*(4), 359–362.

Bourne, M. (2005). Researching performance measurement system implementation: The dynamics of success and failure. *Production Planning & Control, 16*(2), 101–113.

Bruttel, O. (2004). *Contracting-out and governance mechanisms in the public employment service*. TLM.NET conference 'Quality in Labour Market Transitions: A European Challenge'. Royal Netherlands Academy of Arts and Sciences, Amsterdam.

Bruttel, O. (2005). Are employment zones successful? Evidence from the first four years. *Local Economy, 20*(4), 389–403.

Buchanan, J. (1997). *Post-socialist political economy: Selected essays*. Cheltenham: Edward Elgar.

Cammack, P. (2006). The politics of global competitiveness. *Papers in the Politics of Global Competitiveness, 1*, 1–18.

Campbell, M., & Sanderson, I. (2000). *The explicit weighting of APA targets: Rationale, approaches and assessment.* Leeds: Policy Research Institute, Leeds Metropolitan University.

Centre for Business Performance. (2006). Literature review on performance measurement and management. In: I. A. D. Agency (Ed.), *Improvement and development agency* (Vol. 39). Bedford: Cranfield University.

Conservative Party. (2010). *Conservative liberal democrats coalition negotiations agreements reached 11 May 2010.* London: Conservative Party.

Department for Work and Pensions. (2008b). *DWP commissioning strategy.* Norwich: OPSI.

Department for Work and Pensions (Ed.) (2008a). *Department for work and pensions: Three year business plan 2008–2011.* London: DWP.

Drucker, P. (1955). *The practice of management.* London: Heinemann.

Dunleavy, P. A. H. C. (1994). From old public administration to new public management. *Public Money and Management, 14*(3).

DWP. (Undated). *Definitions of star rating key performance indicators.* London: DWP.

European Commission. (2007a). *Employment Guidelines (2005–08) – indicators for monitoring and analysis – endorsed by EMCO 27/06/07.* Brussels: European Commission.

European Commission. (2007b). *Towards common principles of flexicurity: More and better jobs through flexibility and security.* Brussels: European Commission.

European Commission. (2008). *Indicators for monitoring the employment guidelines including indicators for additional employment analysis 2008 compendium.* Brussels: European Commission, DG Employment, Social Affairs and Equal Opportunities.

Grubb, D. (2004). Principles for the performance management of public employment services. *Public Finance & Management, 4*(3), 352–398.

Harker, L. (2006). *Ending child poverty: What would it take? A report for the department for work and pensions.* Norwich: HMSO.

HM Government. (2007). *PSA delivery agreement 2: Improve the skills of the population, on the way to ensuring a world-class skills base by 2020,* London.

HM Government. (2008). *PSA delivery agreement 1: Raise the productivity of the UK economy.* Norwich: HMSO.

HM_Government. (2007). Tackle poverty and promote greater independence and wellbeing in later life. In: H. Treasury (Ed.). London: HM Treasury.

HM_Government. (2008). PSA delivery agreement 8: Maximise employment opportunity for all. In: Treasury, H. (Ed.). London: HM Treasury.

Johnson, S. (2003). *Jobcentre plus performance targets: A review of the evidence, 2000–2002.* Leeds: DWP Corporate Document Services.

Johnson, S., & Nunn, A. (2005). *Evaluation of the job outcome target pilots: Findings from the qualitative study.* Leeds: Corporate Document Services.

Johnson, S., & Nunn, A. (2006). *Evaluation of the job outcome target pilots: Synthesis report.* Leeds: Corporate Document Services.

Kaplan, R. S., & Norton, D. P. (1992). The balanced scorecard – measures that drive performance. *Harvard Business Review, 70*(1), 71–79.

Kaplan, R. S., & Norton, D. P. (2000). Having trouble with your strategy? Then map it. *Harvard Business Review, 78*(5), 167–176.

Kennerley, M., & Mason, S. (2008). *The use of information in decision making: Literature review for the audit commission.* Audit Commission, 53.

Kennerley, M., & Neely, A. (2001). Performance measurements frameworks: A review. In: A. Neely (Ed.), *Business performance measurement: Theory and practice*. Cambridge: Cambridge University Press.

Lehner, U., Natter, M., Naylon, I., & Wagner-Pinter, M. (2005). Mutual learning-benchmarking among public employment services (PES). *PES Benchmarking Project Report*. Vienna: Austria.

MacInnes, T., Kenway, P., & Parekh, A. (2009). *Monitoring poverty and social exclusion*. York: Joseph Rowntree Foundation.

Mailand, M. (2009). Corporatism in Denmark and Norway – yet another century of Scandinavian corporatism? *Monatszeitshrift des Wirtscharfts- und Sozialwissenschaftlichen Instituts in der Hans-Böckler-Stiftung*, 1/2009.

Micheli, P., & Kennerley, M. (2005). Performance measurement frameworks in public and non-profit sectors. *Production Planning & Control*, 16(2), 125–134.

Mosley, H., Schütz, H., & Breyer, N. (2000). *Operational objectives and performance indicators in European public employment services*. Berlin: Wissenschaftszentrum Berlin für Sozialforschung (Research Unit Labour Market Policy and Employment).

Mosley, H., Schutz, H., & Breyer, N. (2001). *Management by objectives in European public employment services*. Discussion Paper, Berlin, Wissenschaftszentrum Berlin fur Sozialforschung, 164.

National Audit Office. (2001). *Measuring the performance of government departments report by the comptroller and auditor general*. The Stationary Office.

Neely, A., Gregory, M., & Platts, K. (1995). Performance measurement system design a literature review and research agenda. *International Journal of Operations & Production Management*, 15, 80–116.

Neely, A., Marr, B., Roos, G., Pike, S., & Gupta, O. (2003). Towards the third generation of performance measurement. *Controlling*, 15(3/4), 129–135.

Neely, A., Richards, H., Mills, J., Platts, K., & Bourne, M. (1997). Designing performance measures: A structured approach. *International Journal of Operations & Production Management*, 17(11), 1131–1152.

Nunn, A. (2005). The political economy of crisis and global governance: A thesis submitted to the University of Manchester for the degree of Doctor of Philosophy in the Faculty of Humanities. University of Manchester, Manchester.

Nunn, A. (2006). What next for the new labour project after Blair? *State of Nature*. Nov/Dec 2006.

Nunn, A. (2007). Competitiveness and the new labour project. *Papers in the Politics of Global Competitiveness*, 8, 1–32.

Nunn, A. (2008). Restructuring the English working class for global competitiveness. *Papers in the Politics of Global Competitiveness*, 9, 1–29.

Nunn, A. (2010). Early effects of the economic downturn on the welfare to work system in deprived areas (forthcoming).

Nunn, A., Bickerstaffe, T., & Mitchell, B. (2010). *International review of performance management systems in public employment services*. Norwich: HMSO.

Nunn, A., Bickerstaffe, T., & Wymer, P. (2009a). Explaining levels of customer satisfaction with first contact with jobcentre plus: Results of qualitative research with jobcentre plus staff. *Department for Work and Pensions, Research Report, 567*. Norwich: The Stationary Office.

Nunn, A., Fidler, Y., Wymer, P., & Kelsey, S. (2008). *Customers' experiences of first contact with jobcentre plus: Findings from the quantitative survey*. DWP Research Report No 504. Norwich: HMSO.

Nunn, A., Jassi, S., & Walton, F. (2009b). A qualitative study of satisfaction and dissatisfaction with jobcentre plus; an exploration of issues identified in the 2007 Customer Satisfaction Survey with a particular focus on those most likely to be dissatisfied. *DWP Research Report, 575.*

Nunn, A., Johnson, S., & Bickerstaffe, T. (2007a). Working with JOT 18 months on: Qualitative research in former option 1 pilot districts. *DWP Research Report 409*, Leeds, DWP Corporate Document Services.

Nunn, A., Johnson, S., Kelsey, S., & Usher, D. (2007b). Job outcome target national evaluation. *DWP Research Report 462*, Leeds, DWP Corporate Document Services.

Nunn, A., Johnson, S., Monro, S., Bickerstaffe, T., & Kelsey, S. (2007c). *Factors influencing social mobility: Department for work and pensions research report 450.* Leeds: Department for Work and Pensions.

OECD. (1994). *Performance management in government: Performance measurement and results orientated management.* Public Management Occasional Paper OECD.

Paranjape, B., Rossiter, M., & Pantano, V. (2006). Insights from the balanced scorecard performance measurement systems: Successes, failures and future – a review. *Measuring Business Excellence, 10*(3), 4–14.

Policy Research Institute. (2002). *Review of the job entry target.* Leeds: DWP Corporate Document Services.

Policy Research Institute. (2006). Phase 2 evaluation of multiple provider employment zones: Qualitative study. *DWP Research Report, 399.*

Struyven, L., & Steurs, G. (2005). Design and redesign of a quasi-market for the reintegration of jobseekers: Empirical evidence from Australia and the Netherlands. pp. 211–229.

Synthesis Forschung and OSB Consulting. (2005). *PES-performance indicators good practice.* PES Benchmarking Project Report.

Synthesis Forschung and OSB Consulting. (2007). Rporting the benchmarking results to the Head of PES: A tentative proposal in the Austrian context. *PES Benchmarking Project Report.*

Synthesis Forschung and OSB Consulting. (2008). Context variables. *Blue Paper 03*, Vienna, Synthesis Forschung.

Treasury, H. (2001). Choosing the right fabric: A framework for performance information. In: H. Treasury (Ed.), HM Treasury, Audit Commission, Cabinet Office, National Statistics, National Audit Office, 40.

Tripney, J., Newman, M., Bangpan, M., Hempel-Jorgensen, A., Mackintosh, M., Tucker, H., & Sinclair, J. (2009). *In-work poverty: A systematic review.* Norwich: HMSO.

Waddell, G., & Burton, A. (2006). *Is work good for your health and well being?* London: The Stationery Office.

Whitfield, D. (1992). *The welfare state: Privatisation, deregulation and commercialisation of the public services: Alternative strategies for the 1990s.* London: Pluto Press.

Whitfield, D. (2001). *Public services or corporate welfare: Re-thinking the nation state in the global economy.* London: Pluto.

Wilthagon, T. (1998). Flexicurity: A new paradigm for labour market policy reform? *Flexicurity Research Programme FXPaper, 1.*

Wilthagon, T. (2008). Mapping out flexicurity pathways in the European Union. *Flexicurity Research Programme FXPaper.*

WHO IS RESPONSIBLE FOR THE FINANCIAL CRISIS? LESSONS FROM A SEPARATION THESIS

William Sun and Lawrence Bellamy

The global financial crisis lasting from 2007 to 2010 has affected virtually everyone in the world. People wonder why the crisis occurred and how to prevent a similar crisis in future. Media and commentators have quickly pointed to Wall Street greed as the main cause of the financial crisis, because it was argued that greed motivated banks, financial corporations and their executives to take huge risks, speculate in the markets and gamble on the entire economy. Indeed, this explanation is somewhat reasonable, as we have observed 'a culture of greed embedded in the DNA of the company and the financial markets' (Visser, this volume). However, this convenient explanation is too simplistic and superficial because it assumes greed as pre-given, as if bankers, executives and other market participants were naturally born with greed and possessed with an intention to harm society and destroy economy. It isolates greed from societal environments in which the seed of greed has grown and fails to understand why greed has grown up from there. Greed, in the German root of the word, means having a sickness or disease (see Visser, this volume). Disease is acquired and is externally and internally linked to the living environment and the weak defence system of our body. The greed explanation does not address how greed has been

---

Reframing Corporate Social Responsibility: Lessons from the Global Financial Crisis
Critical Studies on Corporate Responsibility, Governance and Sustainability,
Volume 1, 101–124
Copyright © 2010 by Emerald Group Publishing Limited
ISSN: 2043-9059/doi:10.1108/S2043-9059(2010)0000001011

produced in the socio-cultural environment and functioned in the economic system and why people are not immune from the greed disease.

This chapter is not aimed to simply discuss greed. Instead, it goes further to understand the man-made corporate and social reality where greed is only a by-product or derivative of social constructions represented by a separation thesis. What we concern is that the business-related reality has been artificially constructed into a split world where all shareholding and other stakeholding groups participating in business are perceived and conceived as being naturally separate and isolated with their own identities, objectives, values, and vested and desired interests. The separate entity paradigm encourages pursuit of a specific agenda to serve a particular stakeholder group. Yet, in doing so, it ignores its possible conflicting interests with other stakeholder groups; it justifies excessive self-interest, even at the expense of others; it rationalises transfer of risks to others and externalisation of social costs, regardless of social and environmental consequences; it presupposes managerial power taken for granted to coordinate the separate entities and tolerates managerial dominance and hegemony.

The separation thesis represents a particular set of underlying assumptions in business and economy, which are developed and reinforced through the dominant discourse in society. For example, mainstream economics from classical to neoclassical economics is grounded on the basic assumption that economic man is a self-contained, unitary, independent and self-interested entity, with a full desire to possess wealth and a rational calculus to maximise his utility and minimise his costs. Accordingly, for economists (and some jurisprudents), the corporation is only the extension, aggregation or nexus of individual entities and is formed to serve the interests of its owners; namely, shareholders (see Barker, 1958; Arthur, 1987; Mayson, French, & Ryan, 1994).

It is worth noting that the separation thesis in business management and economics is in fact informed by a much broader separation thesis dominated in the western intellectual tradition (Carr, 1994, 2003; Glenn, 2006). In Glenn's definition, the separation thesis is 'the idea that true separation, of concepts, things, people or peoples, is possible and even necessary' (Glenn, 2006, p. 223). The separation thesis is a mode of thinking, with the key idea of atomistic entity, dichotomisation and mutual exclusion originated in ancient Greek philosophies, such as in Parmenides' being cosmology, Democritus' atomism (see Sun, 2009) and Aristotle's formal logic (see Glenn, 2006). It is also a way of organising society and the world by, for example, claiming the superiority of a social group against others

(Pinxten, 2006). It is also a principle of theorising the world in a dichotomised and polarised way. For instance, Freeman (1994) identifies the separation thesis in business ethics literature, that is, the discourse of business and the discourse of ethics can be separated so that business and ethics are mutually exclusive (see also Driver, 2006).

Surely, the separation thesis does not reflect a naturally given reality in its first place, but is a social construct (Glenn, 2006; Pinxten, 2006; Pierik, 2006; Sun, 2009). Unlike Berger and Luckmann's (1966) version of social construction theory that regards social reality as objective, purely resulted from social interactions and negotiations, we see the social construction of separate entity as an intended ideological instrument to serve and justify a certain purpose and particular interests (Sun, 2009). Whereas the separation thesis is constructed through dominant discourse, it is subject to changing social conditions (particularly in social and economic crises) and can be changed and transformed through strategies of discourse formation.

It is argued in this chapter that the separation thesis was explicitly or implicitly beneath the entire subprime mortgage-lending and transaction processes and largely responsible for the resulting crisis. As the global financial crisis started from the subprime mortgage crisis in the United States of America in its earlier stage, a deep examination of the subprime mortgage crisis and its underlying thesis would help us understand the fundamental problems with the financial crisis. This chapter examines how the long-constructed separation thesis was reinforced and developed before and during the subprime mortgage crisis. Whereas the separate entity thesis has been embedded in the whole corporate and social system, the subprime mortgage crisis serves as a vivid example to illustrate what the separation thesis is, how the separation thesis took shape in the business process, how the financial crisis was related to the separation thesis, what consequences of the separation thesis has produced and what lessons can be learned from the crisis.

SUBPRIME LENDING FOR AMERICAN HOMEOWNERSHIP DREAM

Subprime mortgage was a kind of high-risk and high-interest lending, especially targeted at low-income and minority borrowers. The majority of subprime mortgage loans were made to non-affluent, low-income and poor borrowers who were previously unable to buy properties and might have poor credit histories (Pitcoff, 2003; Schwarcz, 2009). Why did mortgage lenders compromise their lending standards and dare to take obviously huge risks in mortgage lending? It is clear that the origin of the aggressive subprime mortgage practices were linked to the US Government's policy for increasing national homeownership and encouraging lenders to provide mortgage loans and other credits to low-income and minority borrowers, as a specific stakeholder group.

Evidence shows that the US government from Clinton's administration in the mid-1990s to Bush's administration in the early 2000s had laid down clear and straightforward policies, strategies and methods to promote American homeownership. The Clinton's national homeownership policy started in 1994[1] (Coy, 2008) with a goal to raise the national homeownership rate to 67.5% by the end of the 1990s (Pitcoff, 2003) compared with 43.6% in 1940, and 64.2% in 1990 (US Census Bureau, 2004). The implementation plan formulated by the Department of Housing & Urban Development in a 'historical meeting' with private and public housing-industry organisations in August 1994 set financing strategies to address financial barriers to low-income people by encouraging creative measures in the home mortgage markets (Coy, 2008).[2]

The Bush administration continued Clinton's homeownership policy with a more ambitious plan announced in June 2002. It targeted increasing minority homeownership by 5.5 million families before the end of that decade (HUD, 2003). The Department of Housing and Urban Development (HUD) set a national homeownership goal of 70% by 2006. Then President George W. Bush urged the public and private sectors to work together to reach or exceed that goal (Pitcoff, 2003). In the historical document 'Blueprint for the American Dream' produced by HUD, one of the key action plans was to improve mortgage lending by increasing funds for affordable loans and redoubling efforts to eliminate discrimination against low-income and minority borrowers (HUD, 2003).

IMPLICATIONS OF THE HOMEOWNERSHIP POLICY FOR MORTGAGE LENDERS

Traditionally, the mortgage finance industry had conservative lending standards and set severe boundaries between high-income and low-income borrowers and between good credit records and poor credit histories. Restricted lending policies were formulated to prevent or limit lending mortgage loans to those borrowers with low-income and poor credit records. This was all done in the name of shareholder value, as all companies are supposed to be owned by shareholders and thus have legal and moral duties to serve the interests of shareholders.

However, after the US government's homeownership policy actively promoted the interests of low-income and minority families and attempted to boost national economic growth, the mortgage finance industry at least in the beginning was pressured to adapt to the government's policy orientation towards serving the interests of non-shareholders by compromising their lending standards. The key stakeholders that the financial companies had to care about were not just poor and minority families, but also the US government. The government's policies, strategies and regulations exerted huge power and influence on financial companies. As the key official document 'Blueprint for the American Dream' showed, conventional mortgage lenders were attacked as 'predators' and mortgage barriers to low-income borrowers set by the mortgage finance industry were charged as 'predatory' and 'discriminatory' by the Bush administration. The US government took concrete measures to remove the mortgage barriers to low-income and minority families by 'targeting enforcement activities to stop predatory lenders from preying on uneducated homebuyers' and 'aggressively developing new mortgage products so that conventional market alternatives are available to combat the predatory loan products that are disproportionately targeted to minorities' (HUD, 2003). The mortgage lenders were 'encouraged' to follow the government policy and join in partnership with the government to promote homeownership. Other stakeholder groups like the media, pressure groups and local communities all influenced by government policy, also played on the frontline and joined in the ideological construction. Then mortgage companies and other financial institutions quickly moved on, not just to follow government policy and meet government targets but also to take advantage of opportunities created by the government policy to prosper from it.

As a result, mortgage lenders loaned aggressively to low-income homebuyers. From 1993 to 1999, mortgage loans to low-income borrowers increased by 94%. In 2001, in part due to record low mortgage rates, mortgage volume was much higher than before, and more than $2 trillion loans were borrowed and 59% of the loans for mortgage refinancing (Pitcoff, 2003). Subprime mortgage loans amounted to $35 billion (5% of total origination) in 1994 and $600 billion (20% of total origination) in 2006 (Federal Reserve, 2008). Mortgage-lending standards were rather low, as no qualifications of employment and proof of income and asset ownership guarantees were required for mortgage borrowing. Loans with zero-down payments were made widely available in the late 1990s and early 2000s. In 2005, 43% of first-time home buyers made no down payments, and the median down payment for those buyers was 2% (Knox, 2006). This is compared with 40% down payments in the 1930s and 15% down payments in the 1970s and 1980s. More aggressive mortgage policy was that some mortgage companies offered mortgage loans more than the equity value of the house and provided cash to borrowers to cover their transaction and moving costs (Pitcoff, 2003). With such available money offered to home buyers, home values appreciated dramatically, by 16% a year from 2002 to 2006, in contrast to only 3% annually in the prior 55 years (Zuckerman, 2008).

'SECURITISATION': RISK TRANSFER AND REDISTRIBUTION

While following the US government's homeownership policy, mortgage companies faced a greatly increased risk of credit default from the low-income mortgage borrowers. Obviously, the traditional mortgage model where a mortgage lender originates a loan to the borrower, holds it to maturity and retains the credit default risk was no longer workable, as the mortgage companies were not willing to take risks. The 'ideal' solution seemed to be finding an 'innovative' way of transferring subprime mortgage risks to others, while still retaining profits from subprime lending at the mortgage companies. With the support of the US government, mortgage lenders were able to find an 'ideal' solution, that is, subprime mortgage 'securitisation'.

Subprime mortgage securitisation was a process of issuing securities backed by subprime mortgages. Mortgage lenders[3] sold their mortgage loans to a special-purpose vehicle or entity (i.e. SPV or SPE).[4] In such transactions, rights to payment from subprime mortgage loans (including principal and interests) were transferred to a SPV. The entire mortgage loans sold to a SPV were then assembled into a mortgage pool, from which mortgage-backed securities (MBS, usually, bonds) were issued and sold to financial market investors. The SPV used the proceeds from investors to pay for the mortgage loans. Investors bought those securities based on assessments of the mortgage loan values (actually relying on the credit rating agencies' ratings) and were repaid from collections of mortgage loans with different expected rates of returns in correspondence to different risks of derivatives. MBS was the most basic form of subprime mortgage securitisation. Other complex forms included collateralised debt obligation (CDO) securities (in which payment derived directly from a mixed pool of mortgage loans and sometimes from other financial assets owned by the SPV) and 'ABS CDO' securities (in which payment derived from MBS and CDO securities owned by the SPV and thus indirectly from the mortgage loans and other financial assets underlying those owned securities, see Schwarcz, 2008).

This new mortgage approach was called 'originate to distribute' model. Mortgage lenders no longer held mortgage loans to maturity nor bore any risk from mortgage loans. By selling the mortgages to investors, they transferred and redistributed the risks to investors around the world and replenished their funds that enabled them to issue more mortgage loans to homebuyers. What mortgage lenders gained from the securitisation transaction were huge mortgage fees. The fees were generated in each lending and transaction ensuring that mortgage lenders could gain more fees from more mortgage issuing and transactions.

The credit default risk of the subprime mortgages was hidden when house prices appreciated,[5] as borrowers could refinance for their mortgage payments based on the increased values of their houses. Once house prices stalled and started to decline, refinancing would become more difficult, and as a consequence, defaults and foreclosures would increase sharply. This was exactly what happened in the United States in 2006 when house prices peaked and the housing 'bubble' burst. The large number of foreclosures started in late 2006 in the United States drained wealth from consumers and eroded the financial strength of banks and other financial institutions. The subprime mortgage crisis was what occurred.

A SEPARATION THESIS UNDERLYING THE SUBPRIME MORTGAGE CRISIS

Whereas huge risks were externalised by the mortgage-lending companies to protect themselves, other stakeholder groups ultimately took over these to their detriment. The subprime mortgage crisis produced many victims, including mainly poor homebuyers in the United States who lost income from house value depreciation and then lost their homes; then, the investors, mainly, banks, institutional investors and foreign governments who bought a large amount of the MBSs and other financial derivatives based on rosy ratings by the credit rating agencies; shareholders, who lost their fortunes in the stock markets; and employees, taxpayers and the general public, as they had to assume the consequences of the financial crisis.

But risk transfer in the subprime mortgage lending was supported by the US government to pursue its political agenda and justified by the mortgage industry and other related financial companies to serve the interests of both shareholders and particular stakeholder groups (i.e. in this case, the US government and a special customer group – low-income and minority families who were encouraged to pursue the American homeownership dream). Under the US government's homeownership policy, the mortgage finance industry faced a dilemma. On one side, those companies in the private sector were established with the conventionally justified aim to serve shareholder interests through profit maximisation. On the other side, however, they had to serve other stakeholder interests by providing mortgage loans to very risky borrowers. The question for those private companies was how to serve both sides' interests that were seemingly separate and conflicting with each other. Shareholders' value could be significantly undermined by the risk of satisfying the stakeholders who pursued a different agenda from that of the companies. It seems that securitisation (and the resulted risk transfer) was their 'witty' solution to mitigate the huge subprime mortgage risks for themselves in facing the conflicts and dilemma between the two sides' interests.

Thus, on the surface, the private companies had two different but parallel objectives to simultaneously serve: shareholder value and stakeholder interest, instead of a traditionally assumed one. Surely, there is nothing wrong for private companies to consider both shareholder and stakeholder interests, as this is completely justifiable in business ethics. For over three decades, the stakeholder movement and promotion of corporate social responsibility in the West have requested private companies to rethink their traditional business model with a single bottom line (e.g. Carroll, 1979, 2000; Freeman, 1984; Elkington, 1997). What was problematic in the subprime mortgage crisis was that the two different objectives were pursued with an individualistic and self-contained mentality; a dualistic mode of thinking and an artificially split world with the shareholding world on one side and the stakeholding world on the other. Both realities seemed to have opposite objectives and were competing for their own interests: one wins at the loss of the other and only one winner emerges. The shareholder and stakeholder groups were each perceived to be homogenous with their own distinguished and fixed identities. Both shareholders and stakeholders as economic actors were supposed to be outside the boundary of the firm. They were external resources (capital, material and human) and forces (power and influence) and thus could provide opportunities as well as threats to the firm.

Sun (2009, pp. 40–42) observes that the individualistic conception of the corporation, which gives rise to the separation thesis, is dominant in mainstream economics and the theoretical foundation of Anglo-American corporate governance model. There are several prevalent assumptions within the individualistic mentality. For example, individual economic actors are viewed as self-contained, rationalised and atomistic units. Self-interest is the nature of human behaviour. Possession of wealth is a human natural desire. The maximisation of self-interest and individual wealth will automatically lead to the maximisation of national wealth and the efficient allocation of corporate resources. Shareholders as members of the corporation are individually independent entities, unrelated to each other, except for economic relationships formed through contracts. The corporation is an extension and aggregation of individual entities, and thus individual rights and obligations, and is formed to serve the interest of shareholders through profit maximisation. Sun (2009, p. 199) also notes that the individualistic mentality of the corporation is largely influenced by the ideology of individualism first emerged in England in the 15th and the 16th centuries and then spread throughout the English colonised world. Three primary conceptions underpinned individualism; namely, individual separation (with self-confidence, self-awareness and self-help), freedom (free mobility, free exchange and free competition) and autonomy (private interest, self-determination and self-regulation) (Macfarlane, 1978). Individualism was later justified in classical and neo-classical economics and the individualistic mentality becomes a foundation for modern economics. There are three ideological pillars underpinning individualism in contemporary capitalism: 'utility as the basis of value, self-interest as the basis of rational behaviour, and free market competition as the basis of social efficiency' (Oliga, 1996, pp. 45–46).

Such a separate paradigm is also evidenced in recent debate between the shareholder and the stakeholder models (e.g. Friedman, 1970; Evan & Freeman, 1993; Hutton, 1995; Sternberg, 1998, 2000), as the debate by scholars, policy makers and business practitioners has often been preoccupied with a separate and split view of corporate reality in which shareholding and stakeholding, and in a broad sense, business and ethics, and profit and responsibility, seem to be mutually exclusive. A broader separation thesis in business and management ensued (e.g. Freeman, 1994; Wicks, 1996;

Abela, 2002; Letza, Sun, & Kirkbride, 2004; Sandberg, 2008; Sun, 2009), with its root in the western intellectual tradition as mentioned previously.

The separation thesis has been constructed with some paradoxical assumptions on both sides of shareholders and stakeholders. For example, the pursuit of short-term profit maximisation by the mortgage companies and other financial companies was acted in the name of shareholder interests and based on the assumption that shareholders demand short-term profit maximisation. It was for shareholder value[6] (in terms of share price and dividends) that justified managerial motives on short-term profit and risk transfer and externalisation. However, this assumption is too simplistic and does not necessarily reflect the complex reality. It is arguable that short-term profit maximisation is actually not ultimately beneficial for shareholders, as it could be detrimental to long-term shareholder value (Kolstad, 2007). Normally, shareholders' long-term value would be larger than any short-term value. Evidence shows that apart from some speculators in the stock markets, many shareholders prefer long-term stability and growth of the companies where they hold shares. This is particularly so for institutional shareholders, as they are hard to exit the stock markets in a short term (e.g. Solomon & Solomon, 2002).

On the other side, the separation thesis presupposes a homogeneous stakeholder group with a strong demand for their own entrenched interests. Aggressive mortgage lending to traditionally unqualified borrowers was grounded on the assumption that those poor and minority people in the United States desperately needed their homeownership and genuinely demanded homeownership beyond their affordable incomes. It was such strong demands from those people that justified low-standard supply of, or even unconditional offer for, mortgage loans. However, evidence shows that such an assumption was only constructed by the politicians (the Clinton and Bush administrations and the Congress) that promoted the 'national homeownership' or 'ownership society' to serve their political agenda (see, e.g., Pitcoff, 2003; Coy, 2008; Zuckerman, 2008) such as boosting the economy to win elections. Even with such strong political and financial promotions and encouragement for homeownership, national homeownership only increased from 64% in 1994 to 69.2% in 2004, with a net increase by 5.2% over 10 years (US Census Bureau, 2007). This indicates that there was in fact no huge eagerness for homeownership. Furthermore, many home purchases were not genuinely for residence, but for speculative investment. In 2005, 28% of homes purchased were for investment only and 12% of home purchased for vacation homes. In 2006, the figures were 22% and 14% respectively. That means that about 40% of homes purchased were not for primary residences (Christie, 2007). Therefore, it is clear that the homeownership demand assumption did not match the dynamic and complex reality and was hardly more than an ideological construction and promotion.

Surely, the separation thesis in the subprime mortgage crisis was not just reflected in the artificially constructed split world between shareholding and stakeholding groups as discussed previously, but also among all stakeholder groups. It is easily seen that in the subprime mortgage lending and transaction processes, each stakeholder group had their own objective, agenda and desired interests. For example, the government had a political agenda, the mortgage finance industry had its profit targets, the homebuyers had their homeownership dreams, the market investors had their desired ratio of return on investment and the shareholders had their preferred share price and dividends. With the existence of conflicting and seemingly incompatible interests, those separate entities had to compete for their own interests and protect themselves. Even though they did not necessarily want to fight each other, they had been influenced by the separation paradigm constructed in the dominant discourse and had thus interpreted the reality in an always competing and conflicting way and had been 'obliged' to fight for themselves. This exacerbated and accelerated the subprime mortgage crisis.

MANAGERIAL POWER, DOMINANCE AND IRRESPONSIBILITY

While the business world is split into separate entities and interest parties, mediators are needed to coordinate conflicting interests and enable business to survive and grow. Thus, managerial responsibility with power and dominance is presupposed and justified. The theoretical logic is that it is because of the separation in the first place, then, integration and coordination are needed to enable business to be normally run and to meet social acceptance and expectation (Wicks, 1996). Such a dualistic reality is conceived as 'rational' in its origin, as if it were naturally given rather than artificially created. Hence, governance and management is logically thought as a necessary tool and process to prioritise one side of the separate reality or to coordinate all functional parts of corporate business. Power is justified as what the term 'corporate governance' intrinsically refers to and also legitimated in the hands of professional governors, that is, directors and managers. The dominant functionalistic perspective on power in organisation studies has long taken managerial power and dominancy embedded in organisational hierarchical structure for granted, rather than views it as socially constructed (see Hardy & Clegg, 1999). In economics, the assumed separation of ownership from control and the prevalence of managerialism since the Great Depression also justify the power and dominance of professional managers (see Sun, 2009).

What should be concerned is that the separation thesis creates room and opportunity for management to take advantage of the separated interest parties, with limited and asymmetrical information of the firm, to behave irresponsibly and serve their own interests. In the subprime mortgage crisis, risk transfer and externalisation represents a typical example of managerial irresponsibility, and neither shareholders nor key stakeholders (e.g. investors, borrowers, government and employees) had clear information of the innovative and complex financial products created by the mortgage companies and other financial institutions (Schwarcz, 2010). Scholars have pointed out that the 'originate to distribute' model created a 'moral hazard' (e.g. Lewis, 2007; Schwarcz, 2008), as the mortgage lenders who originated the mortgage loans did not need to bear any risk and consequence for such loans. Mortgage underwriting standards were put aside, because mortgage lenders could make more money from the greater volume of loans originated. In 2007, for example, 40% of subprime loans were made through automated underwriting approvals that allowed loans to be approved without appropriate review and documentation (Browning, 2007). Mortgage fraud was also spread during the house booming period, as some mortgage lenders manipulated borrowers' income and some borrowers lied about their income to qualify for loans (Frieden, 2004; Bajaj, 2007).

Manager's own interests were particularly served with a huge amount of compensations obtained from enormous fees generated from mortgage loans and securitisation. It was estimated that Wall Street executives received $23.9 billion of bonuses in 2006 alone (Nocera, 2009). The bonuses were largely cash rather than stocks, which were not linked to the performance of their products and corporate profits over time and did not subject to 'claw-back' (recovery) of the bonuses if their financial products were under-performed. While most of executives did not understand their investments in financial derivatives, they took extremely short-term (a quarter or a year) gains and ignored long-term obligations (Story, 2008).

The separation entity paradigm could facilitate managers to manipulate the dualistic mode of thinking on shareholding and stakeholding to entrench their power dominance and self-interest. If active shareholders attempted to challenge managerial power, managers would simply reject shareholder intervention by claiming that they have to ethically consider stakeholder interests rather than shareholder value alone. In the takeover movement in the 1980s, for example, management used such an excuse to resist hostile takeovers (Allen, 1992). Conversely, corporate managers may simply dismiss stakeholders' reasonable requirements and pressures by reclaiming the conventional assumption that only shareholders, as owners, have legal rights and legitimate interests to monitor corporations. The separation thesis can be easily employed by managers as a tool to serve their own interests.

Surely, there has been a long-term concern about the abuse of managerial power and corporate irresponsibility. Shareholder activism and the stakeholder movement since the 1990s have been aimed to address managerial irresponsibility issues and ensure good governance. But shareholders and other stakeholder groups have been acting in isolation without recognition of their common objectives and interests in corporate governance and responsibility. Hence, the effects of both sides' pressures on corporations have been very limited and the failings of corporate governance and corporate social responsibility as one of the major causes of the financial crisis were evidenced everywhere (Sun, Stewart, & Pollard, forthcoming). It seems that in reality, shareholders and stakeholders have been mentally trapped by their conscious, subconscious or unconscious underlying assumptions that give rise to the separation thesis. They 'naturally' set their distinguished identities, objectives and agenda, fenced their circles without leaving or creating a common place for each other. Sometimes, coalitions may be formed between separate entities, but tend to be very pragmatic and temporary, rather than a radical change of their identities, objectives and interests. With conflicting interests between shareholders and stakeholders perceived as taken for granted, managers are viewed as independent agents and mediators (a third party) to sit in the middle of both sides to coordinate the conflicts. With such a privileged and advantageous position, management find it easy to control and manipulate other parties. Therefore, we must be aware that while the separation thesis has some limited validity here, the influence and consequence of such a paradigmatic and ideological construction should never be underestimated.

INSEPARABILITY OF THE SEPARATE WORLD

Whereas the separation thesis is artificially constructed by politicians, scholars and business practitioners for certain purposes, the conceptual and abstract 'separate' world is actually inseparable in logic and in business practice.

The separation thesis is logically flawed. The term 'shareholding' only has complete meanings with the conjoined (or opposite) term 'stakeholding'. Separating and isolating them could result in the loss of their meanings. Corporate dualism always privileges one side over the other, as if the privileged side could have a 'closure of meaning' independency of its opposite (Knights, 1997).

Under the separation thesis, the world is split into two poles and only one side seems to be superior and important, and the other is inferior and less important, who are often neglected or marginalised. The two poles are often represented as shareholding versus stakeholding (see Prabhaker, 1998; Friedman & Miles, 2002; Letza et al., 2004; Sun, 2009), or one stakeholder group versus another stakeholder group. The separation thesis, therefore, justifies that corporate policy and business strategy should give priority to one side of the split world for effective governance and efficient business operations. In the subprime mortgage business before the credit crunch, the priority of their business services was given to the low-income mortgage borrowers under the governmental homeownership policy. Investors who bought the subprime MBSs assumed the mortgage default risks and their interests were simply ignored and marginalised. Although risk transfer to investors was in the name of shareholder value, shareholders were also victims of the subprime mortgage crisis because they lost their share values in stock markets and from corporate bankruptcies.

The separation thesis ignores the fact that shareholders and stakeholders are in reality interdependent and inseparable, as shareholder value needs the support of stakeholders and stakeholder interests need the support of shareholders. There is no pre-born superiority and priority on either side (superiority is of our own ideological making). Both shareholders and stakeholders are important for business. A firm cannot exist without the support of its participants, wider network and social environment. As Post, Frederick, Lawrence, and James (1996) pointed out, the world is a systematic whole in which business, government and other elements of society are entwined and interacting, particularly in the new age of globalisation. 'The boundary line between the two is blurred and indistinct' (Post et al., 1996, p. 8). Unfortunately, in the subprime mortgage case, the interconnectedness of shareholders and stakeholders was ignored, and the interest of one side was served simply at the expense of others.

There is also an identity problem with the separation thesis in corporate reality. A shareholder may be simultaneously an employee, a manager, a consumer and a creditor, to name a few. Similarly, stakeholders can also be shareholders. The scheme of the ownership share by managers and employees in many companies is a typical example. In 1996, 90% of publicly held companies in the United States had employee stock-option programmes. Of 200 of the largest US companies, 15 had from 24% to 91% of their shares set aside for employee options and other stock awards (see Clarke, 1998). When a person is mixed with multiple identities and multiple interests and preference, the separation of identities would mean to divide the person into parts. Thus, the separation thesis can be easily constructed in theory, but is less workable in practice. Moreover, business practice is not fixed, but completely changeable, and thus, the status of shareholders and stakeholders is quickly transformable. In stock markets, for example, a shareholder's status in a particular firm may only be held for a few minutes, because he/she might only buy and sell shares based on speculation, rather than governance. Thus, inserting a boundary between shareholders and stakeholders is often meaningless in corporate governance.

The debate between the shareholder model and the stakeholder model is often based on the claim that only one model is superior and ideal in terms of efficient or effective business operation and corporate governance. In the subprime mortgage case, it seems that the stakeholder model (in service of the interest of subprime mortgage borrowers) would be ideal for business prosperity and economic growth. However, the business boom came at the huge expense of a housing 'bubble' bursting and the subsequent global financial crisis. Therefore, it is not merely a philosophical argument that the search for an ideal model is naïve and utopian. The very limitation of human capacity to know any perfection and truth is also well acknowledged in economics by the notions of 'bounded rationality' (Simon, 1957; Williamson, 1975, 1985) and 'information asymmetry' (Stigler, 1961, 1967; Stiglitz, 1982, 2000). Corporate history has shown that there are no perfect shareholder models and perfect stakeholder models anywhere. There is not even a perfect combination of both. The choice is only between imperfect alternatives, as a matter of emphasis and degree. Yet, the differences of choices may have enormous effects on the performance of economic and social systems (Wolf, 1988, p. 152). In the subprime mortgage case, ideological bias and paradigmatic impact had a heavy weight towards the selection of an 'ideal' model. Whereas emphasis was on the interest of low-income and minority people without careful consideration of balanced interests among all the participants, the consequences have been disastrous. If the interests of mortgage loan borrowers, investors and shareholders were carefully coordinated and well balanced with a prudent rather than aggressive mortgage policy, the subprime mortgage crisis could have been prevented. Interest coordination and balance would be very possible in reality, as most shareholders and investors prefer long-term stability, safety and reasonable return of their investments rather than highly risky short-term profit maximisation. Most low-income and minority people actually do not prefer to borrow money they cannot afford to pay back. High-level family debts in the West were a result of misleading governmental policy and encouragement as well as business promotion, influenced by the separation thesis.

CONCLUDING REMARKS

The subprime mortgage crisis was both a real estate crisis and financial crisis initially occurred in the United States, characterised by a sharp rise in mortgage delinquencies and foreclosures, a dramatic decline in the market value of subprime MBSs and a large drop in the capital and liquidity of many banks and financial institutions and widespread tightening credit. The trigger of the subprime mortgage crisis was the bursting of a house bubble in the United States in late 2006. Who created the house bubble? It has been shown in this chapter that the US homeownership policy beginning in the 1990s along with a lower interest rate policy was the origin. Although the governmental policy created conditions for a possible housing bubble, however, it was financial manipulators and market speculators who directly blew the bubble and then burst it in the US housing markets. Policy makers, financial manipulators and market speculators should share responsibilities for the subprime mortgage crisis.

However, the questions are why the policy makers created the conditions for the financial crisis, why the bankers and mortgage lenders and brokers manipulated the homeownership and mortgage policy and why market investors speculated in the house markets and eventually destroyed the markets. The popular greed explanation is too simplistic, as it does not explain why greed was present in the first place. This chapter has examined that a separation thesis was underlying the homeownership policy and mortgage-lending and transaction processes. It has been artificially and widely constructed that people involved in business are naturally separate entities with their own identities, objectives and vested interests, as if they were born with separation, boundary and conflicts, truly different, independent and untrustworthy, and incompatible with each other's values and interests. Aggressive and irresponsible mortgage lending was undertaken in the name of pursuing the interest of low-income borrowers, and the securitisation was in the interests of particular shareholder groups. Yet, all those were done at the expense of market investors and other stakeholders, and ultimately, the public in general. But the problem is that it was not seen as a problem. The separate entity paradigm has been taken for granted by many market participants, business practitioners, media, scholars and policy makers.

Under the separation thesis, it seems to be quite reasonable and rational that policy makers merely needed to pursue their own political agenda such as national homeownership or economic growth for their own interests such as winning a general election in a short term and did not need to care about any possible negative consequences in a longer term or for next generations. When they gave advantage and priority to a specific stakeholder group, it seems that policy makers did not need to care about whether the political agenda could at the same time cost and damage other stakeholder groups. The separation thesis justified that financial managers and market speculators were free to take advantage of the homeownership policy (or any other governmental policy) to pursue their own interests, even risking huge costs to others. It justified the separation of benefits from risks, private profits from social costs, and rationalised retaining benefits and profits for themselves, transferring and redistributing risks and costs to others. It believed that in business, there is one winner only and all others are inevitably losers, and businesses must fight to win.

Thus, it implicitly encouraged speculation and gambling in the markets to blow and burst one bubble following another, which then created one crisis after another. The separation thesis regarded managerial power and dominance as taken for granted, because managers were not just agents to serve their principals, but also mediators to coordinate the separate entities. By living in a split world, for over two decades, we have placed the hope of corporate social responsibility on managers rather than ourselves, believing that only managers as powerful people could really change themselves to change the landscape of corporate social responsibility. It turned out to be naïve. When we are living in an ideologically constructed world and trapped in a false mode of thinking, we could not expect people would automatically get out of the trap (Morgan, 1986). By turning a blind eye to greed and even believing that 'greed is good' for innovation and creation, how could we expect people would get rid of greed?

Therefore, it is the separation thesis, rather than any individual, that is largely responsible for the financial crisis. The separation thesis is a social construct, inherited in the capitalist culture and tradition (Abela, 2002). It is beyond the scope of this chapter to examine the cultural, ideological and philosophical root (Carr, 2003) of the separation thesis, but a more general separation paradigm can be found in capitalism itself, that is, the separation of private interest and public interest, the separation of economic interest and social interest and the separation of principal's interest and agent's interest (Sun, 2009). Those separations have created fundamental conflicts and dilemmas in capitalism, which have proved to be difficult to resolve. However, as Jackson and Carter (1995, p. 883) pointed out, capitalism itself does not change much, yet,

> As an inherently amoral system, concerned only with money making money, capitalism is, always has been, and must be, extremely efficient at responding to, and adapting to, changes in the general values of its context.

Hence, the sustainability of capitalist society relies on its quick response and adapting to the changes of societal values and social tolerance and acceptance. This is particularly so in the wake of a major event like the current global financial and sovereign debt crisis. It therefore opens many potential and possible avenues and chances for continuous construction and reconstruction of the social reality in general and corporate reality in particular through discourse formation (Sun, 2009). One of the lessons we have learned from the financial crisis is that what is particularly needed today is the advancement of management education. This is not just an urgent demand for better business ethics and responsibility education, such as the reform of MBA education for responsible management (e.g. Windsor, 2008; Podolny, 2009). It is more about management education for critical thinking. Many people are unaware of the separation thesis as socially constructed in nature, because social construction always turns to be apparently 'objective' as if it was independent of human subjectivity (Berger & Luckmann, 1966). When managers are trapped by their unconscious underlying assumptions shaped by the dominant discourse of capitalism, the need for the development of critical thinking skills in managers is critical, as it would enable managers to be aware of the artificiality of social reality and to identify and challenge the dominant discourse.

This chapter has shown that while the separation thesis has been artificially and ideologically constructed, its consequences are rather destructive, and its negative impacts on people's mindsets cannot be underestimated. Furthermore, the separation thesis is logically and empirically flawed. The world has not been split fundamentally and does not need to be artificially split forever. The opposite of the separation assumption is true: the world is inherently interconnected, particularly in the age of globalisation. The subprime mortgage crisis occurred in the United States and turned out to be a global financial crisis indicating strong evidence of interconnectedness instead of separation. Excessive self-interest at the expense of others will inevitably damage self. One winner at the losses of others cannot be sustainable. The general value we could commonly share is a harmonised, coordinated and mutually interested society as a whole where a double win, multiple win or even everyone's win is not impossible, rather than a manipulated world broken into separate pieces.

In summary, what lessons can be learned from the subprime mortgage and financial crisis?

Lesson one: Whereas the business-related reality is underpinned by a separation thesis, the tacit permission or explicit encouragement of excessive self-interest and self-regulation would inevitably trigger financial and economic crises. The key issue with the separation thesis is that the thesis assumes a natural-like and pre-given separate boundary of social and stakeholder groups, each of which is ruthlessly fighting to pursue their own objectives, agenda and vested and desired interests, regardless of the interest of others. If we stick to such an artificially and ideologically constructed reality, our demand for social justice and for a sustainable and crisis-free business reality would only be an out-of-reach dream.

Lesson two: If a political agenda takes over a business agenda to serve political and ideological interests, it reinforces the separation thesis and encourages excessive self-interested behaviour. In the subprime mortgage-lending and transaction processes, financial manipulators and market speculators were at least implicitly allowed to take advantage of the government's national homeownership policy to serve their own interests. For example, the US government encouraged the mortgage finance industry to lend mortgage loans to low-income and minority people by low lending standards and financial product innovations.

Lesson three: The separation thesis justifies the handover of power to professional managers to mediate conflicting interests in the split business world and encourages strategic business priority given to some specific stakeholder groups at the cost of others. When professional managers dominate the business world without appropriate monitoring and regulation, then, abuse of power, irresponsible lobbying, corruption and plundering in the financial markets are all inevitable. Under the dominance and influence of the separation thesis, we cannot automatically rely on managers to voluntarily change their own irresponsible behaviours to make the world better and sustainable.

Lesson four: We often forget the fact that the separation thesis is only a social and ideological construct and many people tend to take the artificial world for granted. Over the last five decades, numbers of interest and pressure groups have more than tripled to fight for their own interests and demand corporate social responsibility. That is not necessarily wrong, but quite demanded, as long as the separation thesis dominates our society and everyone's mindsets. However, we must realise that the separate boundaries in a business society were not pre-existent in their origins and should never be fixed forever; they are our own making and construction. Now that we have collectively constructed it as it was and is, we can reconstruct it as it should be and will be, all based on changes in social expectations and acceptance.

Lesson five: We should never abandon genuine hopes and beliefs for a better society and business reality, even if the severe financial crisis has damaged our trust and confidence. Indeed, our distrust and lack of confidence in the business world have proved the bankruptcy of the separation thesis. It is time to change our preoccupied mindsets and trapped modes of thinking. In the underlying processes of business reality, we are deeply interconnected and inseparable. The separation thesis often deceives us as if we were inevitably living in a split world. As discussed previously, many assumptions made by the separation thesis were paradoxical and imaginary and did not necessarily map the territory, but actually imposed the ideas on the reality. In recent years, the fast-growing ethical investment, corporate social responsibility initiatives and programmes, green economy, the enlightened shareholder model (see Gamble & Kelly, 2001) and enlightened stakeholder model (Jensen, 2001) all have ignited our hopes for building *a connection thesis* to replace the separation thesis. A connection thesis may or may not be related to the idea of integration, as sometimes integration is not necessarily needed or is unrealistic to achieve. It is more related to interrelationship, interdependence, mutual understanding and appreciation, and reciprocity. If we take a holistic view and a balanced approach to interconnecting and coordinating the interests of all business participants with a mindset of double-win and everyone's win, then, common values and objectives could be built and shared, and conflicts and fighting could be minimised and avoided. As a result, our trust and confidence in the business world could return, and any similar financial crisis could be prevented.

NOTES

1. This policy was largely reflected in the landmark document 'The National Homeownership Strategy: Partners in the American Dream' produced by the US Department of Housing & Urban Development (HUD). See Coy (2008).

2. An excerpt of the plan reads:

> For many potential homebuyers, the lack of cash available to accumulate the required downpayment and closing costs is the major impediment to purchasing a home. Other households do not have sufficient available income to make the monthly payments on mortgages financed at market interest rates for standard loan terms. Financing strategies, fueled by the creativity and resources of the private and public sectors, should address both of these financial barriers to homeownership. (Coy, 2008)

3. In subprime mortgage securitisation, mortgage lenders are called 'originators', including mortgage companies, banks and other originators.

4. In the United States, most MBS's were issued by US government-sponsored enterprises: the Federal National Mortgage Association (Fannie Mae) and the Federal Home Loan Mortgage Corporation (Freddie Mac). Ginnie Mae, backed by the full faith and credit of the US government, guaranteed that investors would receive timely payments. Fannie Mae and Freddie Mac also provide certain guarantees, not backed by the full faith and credit of the US government, but by special authority to borrow from the US Treasury. Some private institutions like brokerage firms, banks and homebuilders also securitise mortgages, known as 'private-label' mortgage securities. (*Source:* Wikipedia, http://en.wikipedia.org/wiki/Mortgage-backed_security, accessed on 18 May 2010).

5. Nobel laureate Dr. A. Michael Spence pointed out: 'Financial innovation, intended to redistribute and reduce risk, appears mainly to have hidden it from view. An important challenge going forward is to better understand these dynamics as the analytical underpinning of an early warning system with respect to financial instability' (Spence, 2008).

6. The term 'shareholder value' became popular in the 1980s and is particularly associated with the former CEO of General Electric Jack Welch. In 1981, Jack Welch made a speech 'Growing fast in a slow-growth economy' in Hotel Pierre, New York City. He stated that GE's aim was to be the biggest or second biggest market player and to return maximum value to stockholders. However, in March 2009, Welch openly dumped the concept, calling shareholder value 'the dumbest idea in the world' (*Source:* Wikipedia, http://en.wikipedia.org/wiki/Shareholder_value, accessed on 15 May 2010).

REFERENCES

Abela, A. (2002). Adam Smith and the separation thesis. *Business and Society Review, 106*(3), 187–199.

Allen, W. T. (1992). Our schizophrenic conception of the business corporation. *Cardozo Law Review, 14*(2), 261–281.

Arthur, E. E. (1987). The ethics of corporate governance. *Journal of Business Ethics, 6*, 59–70.

Bajaj, V. (2007). A cross-country blame game. *New York Times*, May 8.

Barker, E. (1958). Introduction. In: O. Gierke (Ed.), *Natural law and the theory of society: 1500 to 1800*. E. Barker (Trans.). Cambridge: Cambridge University Press.

Berger, P. L., & Luckmann, T. (1966). *The social construction of reality: A treatise in the sociology of knowledge*. Garden City, NY: Anchor Books.

Browning, L. (2007). The subprime loan machine. nytimes.com, March 23. Available at http://www.nytimes.com/2007/03/23/business/23speed.html?_r = 1&partner = rssnyt&emc = rss&oref = slogin. Retrieved on 18 May 2010.

Carr, A. (1994). For self or others? The quest for narcissism and the ego-ideal in work organisations. *Administrative Theory and Praxis, 16*(2), 208–222.

Carr, A. N. (2003). The "separation thesis" of self and other: Metatheorizing a dialectical alternative. *Theory & Psychology, 13*(1), 117–138.

Carroll, A. (1979). Three-dimensional conceptual model of corporate performance? *Academy of Management Review, 4*(4), 497–505.

Carroll, A. (2000). Ethical challenges for business in the new millennium: Corporate social responsibility and models of management morality. *Business Ethics Quarterly, 10*(1), 33–42.

Christie, L. (2007). Homes: Big drop in speculation. CNNMoney.com, April 30. Available at http://www.money.cnn.com/2007/04/30/real_estate/speculators_fleeing_housing_markets. Retrieved on 16 May 2010.

Clarke, T. (1998). The stakeholder corporation: A business philosophy for the information age. *Long Range Planning, 31*(2), 182–194.

Coy, P. (2008). Bill Clinton's drive to increase homeownership went way too far. *BusinessWeek*, February 27.

Driver, M. (2006). Beyond the stalemate of economics versus ethics: Corporate social responsibility and the discourse of the organizational self. *Journal of Business Ethics, 66*, 337–356.

Elkington, J. (1997). *Cannibals with forks: The triple bottom line of 21st century business*. Oxford: Capstone.

Evan, W. M., & Freeman, R. E. (1993). Stakeholder theory of the modern corporation: Kantian capitalism. In: T. Beauchamp & N. Bowie (Eds), *Ethical theory and business* (pp. 75–84). Englewood Cliffs, NJ: Prentice-Hall.

Federal Reserve. (2008). FRB: Speech-Bernanke, fostering sustainable homeownership, 14 March. Available at http://www.federalreserve.gov.

Freeman, R. E. (1984). *Strategic management: A stakeholder approach*. Boston: Pitman.

Freeman, R. E. (1994). The politics of stakeholder theory; some future direction. *Business Ethics Quarterly, 4*(4), 409–421.

Frieden, T. (2004). FBI warns of mortgage fraud "epidemic". CNN.com, September 17. Available at http://www.edition.cnn.com/2004/LAW/09/17/mortgage.fraud. Retrieved on 19 May 2010.

Friedman, A., & Miles, S. (2002). Developing stakeholder theory. *Journal of Management Studies, 39*(1), 1–21.

Friedman, M. (1970). The social responsibility of business is to increase its profits. *New York Times Magazine*, September 13, pp. 32–33, 122, 124, 126.

Gamble, A., & Kelly, G. (2001). Shareholder value and the stakeholder debate in the UK. *Corporate Governance: An International Review, 9*(2), 110–117.

Glenn, H. P. (2006). Legal traditions and the separation thesis. *Nederlands Tijdschrift voor Rechtsfilosofie & Rechtstheorie, 35*(3), 222–240.

Hardy, C., & Clegg, S. R. (1999). Some dare call it power. In: S. R. Clegg & C. Hardy (Eds), *Studying organization: Theory & method* (pp. 368–387). London: Sage.

HUD (Department of Housing and Urban Development). (2003). Blueprint for the American Dream. White House. Available at http://archives.hud.gov/initiatives/blueprint/blueprint.pdf

Hutton, W. (1995). *The state we're in.* London: Jonathan Cape.

Jackson, N., & Carter, P. (1995). Organisational chiaroscuro: Throwing light on the concept of corporate governance. *Human Relations, 48*(8), 875–889.

Jensen, M. C. (2001). Value maximisation, stakeholder theory, and the corporate objective function. *European Financial Management, 7*(3), 297–317.

Knights, D. (1997). Organization theory in the age of deconstruction: Dualism, gender, and postmodernism revisited. *Organization Studies, 18*, 1–19.

Knox, N. (2006). 43% of first-time home buyers put no money down. *USA Today*, January 17.

Kolstad, I. (2007). Why firms should not always maximize profits. *Journal of Business Ethics, 76*(2), 137–145.

Letza, S., Sun, X., & Kirkbride, J. (2004). Shareholding versus stakeholding: A critical review of corporate governance. *Corporate Governance: An International Review, 12*(3), 242–246.

Lewis, H. (2007). "Moral hazard" helps shape mortgage mess. Bankrate.com, 18 April. Available at http://www.bankrate.com/brm/news/mortgages/20070418_subprime_mortgage_morality_a1.asp?caret = 3c. Retrieved on 15 May 2010.

Macfarlane, A. (1978). *The origins of English individualism: The family, property and social transition.* Oxford: Blackwell.

Mayson, S. W., French, D., & Ryan, C. L. (1994). *Company law.* London: Blackstone Press.

Morgan, G. (1986). *Images of organizations.* Beverly Hills: Sage.

Nocera, J. (2009). Talking business: First, let's fix the bonuses. *The New York Times*, February 20.

Oliga, J. C. (1996). *Power, ideology, and control.* New York: Plenum.

Pierik, R. (2006). The necessity of categories and the inevitability of separation, reply to Glenn. *Nederlands Tijdschrift voor Rechtsfilosofie & Rechtstheorie, 35*(3), 252–262.

Pinxten, R. (2006). Separation, integration and citizenship, reply to Glenn. *Nederlands Tijdschrift voor Rechtsfilosofie & Rechtstheorie, 35*(3), 241–251.

Pitcoff, W. (2003). Has homeownership been oversold? National Housing Institute: *Shelterforce Online*, Issue 127, January/February.

Podolny, J. M. (2009). The buck stops (and starts) at business school. *Harvard Business Review, 87*(6), 62–67.

Post, J. E., Frederick, W. C., Lawrence, A. T., & James, W. (1996). *Business and society: Corporate strategy, public policy, ethics* (8th ed.). New York: McGraw-Hill.

Prabhaker, S. (1998). Governance and stakeholding. *New Economy, 5*(2), 119–122.

Sandberg, J. (2008). Understanding the separation thesis. *Business Ethics Quarterly, 18*(2), 213–232.

Schwarcz, S. L. (2008). Protecting financial markets: Lessons from the subprime mortgage meltdown. *Minnesota Law Review, 93*, 373–382.

Schwarcz, S. L. (2009). Understanding the "subprime" financial crisis. *South Carolina Law Review, 60*, 549.

Schwarcz, S. L. (2010). Regulating complexity in financial markets. *Washington University Law Review, 87*(2), 211–268.

124   WILLIAM SUN AND LAWRENCE BELLAMY

Simon, H. A. (1957). *Models of man: Social and rational.* New York: Random House.
Solomon, A., & Solomon, J. (2002). Empirical evidence of long-termism and shareholder activism in UK unit trusts. *Corporate Governance: An International Review, 7*(3), 288–300.
Spence, A. M. (2008). Lessons from the crisis. PIMCO, November. Available at http://www.pimco.com/LeftNav/Viewpoints/2008/Viewpoints + Lessons + from + the + Crisis + Spence + November + 2008.htm. Retrieved on 16 May 2010.
Sternberg, E. (1998). *Corporate governance: Accountability in the marketplace.* London: The Institute of Economic Affairs.
Sternberg, E. (2000). The defects of stakeholder theory. *Corporate Governance, 5*(1), 3–10.
Stigler, G. J. (1961). The economics of information. *Journal of Political Economy, 69,* 213–225.
Stigler, G. J. (1967). Imperfections in the capital market. *Journal of Political Economy, 75,* 287–292.
Stiglitz, J. E. (1982). The inefficiency of the stock market equilibrium. *Review of Economic Studies, 49,* 241–261.
Stiglitz, J. E. (2000). The contributions of the economics of information to twentieth century economics. *The Quarterly Journal of Economics* (November), 1441–1478.
Story, L. (2008). The reckoning on Wall Street, bonuses, not profits, were real. *The New York Times,* December 17.
Sun, W. (2009). *How to govern corporations so they serve the public good: A theory of corporate governance emergence.* New York: Edwin Mellen.
Sun, W., Stewart, J., & Pollard, D. (Eds.), (forthcoming). *Corporate governance and the global financial crisis: International perspectives.* Cambridge: Cambridge University Press.
U.S. Census Bureau. (2004). Housing and household economic statistics division. Available at http://www.census.gov/hhes/www/housing/census/historic/owner.html. Retrieved on 2004.
U.S. Census Bureau. (2007). Census Bureau reports on residential vacancies and homeownership. 26 October. Available at http://www.census.gov/hhes/www/housing/hvs/qtr307/q307press.pdf
Wicks, A. C. (1996). Overcoming the separation thesis: the need for a reconsideration of business and society research. *Business Society, 35*(1), 89–118.
Williamson, O. E. (1975). *Markets and hierarchies: Analysis and antitrust implications.* New York: The Free Press.
Williamson, O. E. (1985). *The economic institutions of capitalism: Firms, markets, relational contracting.* New York: The Free Press.
Windsor, D. (2008). Education for responsible management. In: A. Crane, A. McWilliams, D. Matten, J. Moon & D. S. Siegel (Eds), *The Oxford handbook of corporate social responsibility* (pp. 503–521). Oxford: Oxford University Press.
Wolf, C., Jr. (1988). *Markets and governments.* Cambridge: MIT Press.
Zuckerman, M. B. (2008). We deserve a better bailout. *U.S. News and World Report,* October 3.

PART III
IMPLEMENTATION OF CSR: REGULATORY MODELS AND MANAGERIAL FRAMEWORKS

CRISIS, RESCUE, AND CORPORATE SOCIAL RESPONSIBILITY UNDER AMERICAN CORPORATE LAW

Robert J. Rhee

This chapter discusses the legal issues of corporate governance raised by the unique events surrounding the Bank of America – Merrill Lynch merger in the fourth quarter of 2008. It is substantially based on the author's previous article on a corporate board's fiduciary duty related to the management of a public crisis and the provision of aid to government and the public (Rhee, 2010).[1] The thesis is that American corporate law adequately provides corporate boards authority to assume broad principles of corporate social responsibility, and that during a public crisis this authority is specially recognized in the enabling statutes of corporate law and should be broadened even further to pursue the public good in exigent circumstances. No situation calls from a greater sensitivity to corporate social responsibility than during a crisis when great detriment to the social wealth and welfare are at stake.

Since the financial crisis of 2008–2009 and the financial industry provide the context for the discussion here, a little background is in order. In the past 20 years, the investment banking industry underwent a fundamental transformation. Before the 1999 repeal of the Glass–Steagall Act, which had separated commercial and investment banking, investment banks merged among themselves, and after the regulatory wall came down investment banks were acquired by larger commercial banks. By 2007, there were only

Reframing Corporate Social Responsibility: Lessons from the Global Financial Crisis
Critical Studies on Corporate Responsibility, Governance and Sustainability,
Volume 1, 127–144
ISSN: 2043-9059/doi:10.1108/S2043-9059(2010)0000001012

five independent pure investment banks of significant size and operational scale: Goldman Sachs, Morgan Stanley, Merrill Lynch, Lehman Brothers, and Bear Stearns. Their activities in the post-9/11 years precipitated the financial crisis of 2008–2009. In 2008, the unthinkable happened: three of the five banks collapsed or were sold under duress. In March, Bear Stearns became insolvent and it was rescued by JPMorgan Chase and the federal government. In September, Lehman Brothers filed for bankruptcy on the same day that Bank of America announced the acquisition of an increasingly troubled Merrill Lynch. The fall of three major investment banks, the bulk of old Wall Street, within a few months confirmed a systemic crisis.

The events unique to the Bank of America – Merrill Lynch merger, which gave rise to the author's contemplation of these issues, are briefly summarized. As the financial crisis was deepening in the fourth quarter of 2008, Merrill Lynch was losing money at an astonishing rate (ultimately $15 billion in the fourth quarter). This prompted Bank of America to consider terminating the pending merger under the merger agreement's material adverse change clause. The deal ultimately closed, but only after the government threatened to fire Bank of America's management and board if the company attempted to terminate the deal. The government feared that a broken deal would continue a domino effect on other financial institutions resulting in a systemic financial market meltdown. In fact, Bank of America did not have a contractual right to terminate the merger. As defined in the merger agreement, material adverse change did not encompass Merrill Lynch's astonishing losses. The government was correct to coerce a reluctant Bank of America management and board to do the right thing. However, suppose hypothetically Bank of America had a sound contractual right to terminate the merger, thereby cutting Merrill Lynch loose for the sake of avoiding the assumption of its losses. All would agree that a broken deal would have resulted in the collapse of Merrill Lynch as an independent firm, thus exacerbating the financial crisis with unknown consequences on other financial institutions, the capital markets, and the greater society. Consider, then, the counterfactual: Bank of America had a legally viable option to terminate the merger and the cost–benefit based on private gain or loss to the firm weighed in favor of termination.

This history and counterfactual contextualize an analysis of important, unresolved theoretical issues at the intersection of corporate governance and public crisis management:

1. What is the nature and scope of its fiduciary duty under American corporate law during a public crisis?

2. Should the board have specific authority and discretion to advance the
   public welfare at the direct cost of the shareholder wealth?

There will always be public crises that entangle the government and
corporations in a complex relationship. These questions continue the
longstanding academic debate on the purpose of the corporation and
the manager's duty to stakeholders (Berle, 1931; Dodd, 1932).

Here, a brief explanation of the US corporate law system is needed. The
reference to "American corporate law" is a misnomer to the extent that it
connotes a single body of law. In the United States, corporate law is the set
of rules governing the internal affairs and management of the corporation.
It is not unified under federal law, but is primarily based on individual state
law. The Delaware General Corporation Law ("DGCL") and the judicial
opinions of the Delaware courts are prominent. In addition to Delaware
law, many other states have substantially adopted the Model Business
Corporation Act (the "Model Act"), an influential model statute prepared
by a committee of the American Bar Association. American corporate law is
thus composed of many sets of corporate law. However, Delaware law can
be seen as a quasi-national body of corporate law simply because so many
public companies are incorporated in Delaware. For this reason, this
chapter focuses on Delaware law.

This chapter discusses the board's fiduciary obligation during a public
crisis. Even without a grant of power specific to the management of a public
crisis, corporate boards have broad power as managers of the corporation
to incorporate principles of corporate social responsibility in the pursuit of
business enterprise, and such decisions are protected by the business
judgment rule. As a positive thesis, this chapter shows that the board has the
specific power to nationalize corporate purpose per public necessity, which
is authorized by section 122(12) of the DGCL and section 3.02(14) of the
Model Act. As a normative thesis, this chapter argues that these statutes
provide a framework for courts to recognize a fiduciary exemption based on
the board's determination that the firm, being uniquely situated to avert or
mitigate the public crisis, should provide aid. Public necessity, a well
established concept in Anglo-American tort law, excuses the destruction of
private property. When the board perceives that the threat to the public
welfare is great enough, the shareholder primacy norm can and sometimes
does fail the stress test of a crisis. The thesis depends on a fundamental
assumption, which is explicitly stated: the situation examined here is where a
corporation is uniquely situated to avert or mitigate a public crisis at a
substantial private cost to the firm, but where the cost–benefit calculation

from a societal perspective overwhelmingly weighs in favor of such action. This is the nature of a public necessity.

CORPORATE SOCIAL RESPONSIBILITY AND BUSINESS JUDGMENT

When a board is faced with a choice of aiding the public or government during a crisis, or more generally any corporate social responsibility initiative, well established doctrines of American corporate law can protect directors from legal liability in a shareholder derivative lawsuit. A hallmark trait of the public corporation is a separation of ownership and control (Berle & Means, 1932). Accordingly, managers have great authority over corporate assets. Delaware corporate law provides that "[t]he business and affairs of every corporation organized under this chapter shall be managed by or under the direction of a board of directors."[2] The board has the authority to manage the "business and affairs" of the corporation, which in the judgment of the board may include corporate social responsibility initiatives and decisions based thereon.

To serve the end of manager prerogative, American courts have developed the business judgment rule, which gives great deference to the business decisions of managers. The rule is a rebuttable presumption that in making a business decision the board acted on an informed basis, in good faith and in the honest belief that the action taken was in the best interests of the company.[3] The rule applies when four conditions are met: (1) a judgment must have been made; (2) a reasonable decision making process was used; (3) the decisions must have been made in subjective good faith; and (4) the decision was not tainted by self-interest. The conditions boil down to two questions: Did the board reach its decision in good faith pursuant to a legitimate corporate interest? Did the board do so advisedly?[4] The first question concerns the loyalty of directors to the best interest of the corporation, and the second question concerns a reasonable use of procedure in making a decision.

The business judgment rule is a presumption operating in favor of the propriety of the board's intent and decision, and an objecting shareholder must rebut the presumption of good faith and reasonable process with particular facts demonstrating the contrary. If a board decides to aid the public or government during a public crisis, the most important point is that it must do so advisedly. It must use a reasonable decision-making process characterized by adequate information gathering and deliberation. When the procedural requirement of the business judgment rule has been met, courts will only review the decision under the waste standard, which is met when the board's decision is so disadvantageous to the firm that no reasonable person could deem it fair.[5]

Even when a board decision appears to injure the corporation, courts avoid active scrutiny of the decision's merit by invoking the elision that a board's decision may have a "long-term" benefit,[6] however abstract or unarticulated this benefit may be so long as there is no evidence of bad faith against the corporation. Injury to and bad faith against the corporation are not coterminous. For example, a corporate gift and provision of public aid, being transactions without consideration, financially injure the corporation, and yet such actions are clearly permitted. Courts routinely invoke the Potemkin explanation of a "long-term" corporate benefit to shield business judgments from active judicial scrutiny of merit even when it appears they have injured the corporation. This is not a judicial wink and a nod to managers who are pursuing some illicit goal, though one must add that with such deference managers sometimes do follow illicit goals as courts abide by a restricted standard of liability. Instead, the Potemkin explanation is really an acknowledgment that the road to a successful corporate enterprise can take many routes. One such route is the incorporation of robust principles of corporate social responsibility into the corporate mission. Would any court admonish the rejection of child labor even though its use may prove to be highly profitable? Would any court admonish the use of corporate resources to actively fight child labor as IKEA did (Bartlett, Dessain, & Sjdman, 2006)? Another example, a board's decision to assume enormous financial loss by voluntarily rescuing another firm during the financial crisis may be valid on the ground that the long-term interest of a stable financial market is in the best interest of the corporation and shareholders. Much of the legitimacy of corporate law, which gives managers great authority over corporate assets, depends on plausible good faith that precludes substantive review of the board's decision.

An important caveat must be noted. The decision rationale should not be explicitly stated as the pure benefit of a third-party or the social good in a situation where such benefit is not specifically authorized. In other words, the nexus between the long-term benefit of the corporation and the board decision must not be broken with an explicit avowal to the contrary. In *Dodge v. Ford*, Henry Ford testified that "the Ford Motor Company has made too much money, has had too large profits, and that, although large profits might be still earned, a sharing of them with the public, by reducing the price of the output of the company, ought to be undertaken."[7] The Michigan Supreme Court rebuked Ford and ruled against his company with respect to the decision to withhold dividends from the company's minority shareholders. In so doing, the court added the famous passage that a "business corporation is organized and carried on primarily for the profit of the stockholders. The powers of the directors are to be employed for that end."[8]

Since this 1919 Michigan case, few jurisdictions have adopted an unconditional rule of shareholder primacy. Outside of the context of a cash buyout of a target in the takeover context where the board is required to maximize shareholder profit,[9] Delaware courts have eschewed a legal requirement to maximize shareholder profit in favor of manager's prerogative to set the corporate agenda, which may include principles of corporate social responsibility, with the understanding that market forces will influence that agenda significantly. The Delaware Supreme Court has gone so far as to state that a board "is not under any per se duty to maximize shareholder value."[10] The unique aspect of *Dodge v. Ford* is that Ford explicitly rejected the nexus between profit and his purported social ambition. Whether Ford believed this or it was a part of an ill-advised litigation strategy, he chose this black-and-white characterization. In truth, the two ends were closely linked. It is well known now that Ford's social initiative was tied to his production process, which resulted in increased profit, productivity, labor wage, and enhanced social welfare.[11] Few situations are as stark as Ford seemed to portray. Corporate social responsibility is often positively correlated to profit and enterprise sustainability. Moreover, the author has previously argued that the board can and should reject profit when it believes that a reasonable shareholder would do so given full information as to the choice of profit and moral imperative. Since soliciting actual shareholder preferences is infeasible, managers should abide by what they guess a reasonable shareholder would prefer in a morally complex situation (Rhee, 2008). Profit maximization may be a default principle, but it is always conditional. Again, under American corporate law, moral deliberation and resulting corporate action are the manager's prerogative. To the extent that *Dodge v. Ford* has doctrinal authority beyond its unique facts, the lesson is this: if the board's decision is informed and in good faith, and the decision appears to have some nexus to a corporate benefit, however abstract or unformulated it may be, the probability of judicial scrutiny is minimized.

Another caveat is that the decision must meet the standard of rationality.[12] The board's decision does not constitute waste of corporate assets. A claim of waste will arise only in the rare, unconscionable case when a board irrationally squander or give away corporate assets.[13] This is a corollary to the business judgment rule, which embodies the concept that the board has the power to manage the corporation. In the context of the provision of public aid, the board cannot endanger the corporation as a going concern. No principle of corporate law can support this end. In all other circumstances, the board's decision to use corporate assets and resources in aid of the government or the public good will be protected by the business judgment rule so long as the board used a reasonable procedural process to make the decision.

In summary, the current framework for determining liability allows a board great discretion to pursue business enterprise in a socially responsible way. This is consistent with the entity theory of the corporation, which is the view that the corporation is an entity distinct from its managers and capital providers. Prominent Delaware jurists have suggested that Delaware law leans toward the entity theory (Strine, 2002; Allen, Jacobs, & Strine, 2002). Accordingly, corporate entities, like natural persons, can be expected to assume basic social responsibilities. Courts understand that the profit motive and corporate social responsibility of the corporation are not mutually exclusive, and that the board acting on behalf of the corporation may lean toward the latter if there is an irreconcilable conflict. In fact, however, the two ends are more aligned than divergent and the long-term sustainability of the corporate enterprise may depend on how responsible it is. Responsible people tend to do well in our society, irresponsible ones do not, and corporations probably track this trend as well. Misbehavior and shirking social responsibility increase the risk to the going concern.

POWER TO AID GOVERNMENT

The legal framework based on the business judgment rule would allow a board to provide enormous economic resources during a public crisis. But there remains the possibility of liability if an objecting shareholder can prove that the use of corporate resources had no rational nexus to a corporate objective. A real possibility of liability for waste or bad faith introduces significant legal uncertainty, which may paralyze the decision-making process during a national crisis, precisely when such paralysis could cause great harm.

Assume that a board intentionally provided large corporate assets where the cost–benefit against the action, net of all short- and long-term, direct and indirect factors. Deliberate conduct to injure a corporation would normally violate the duty of loyalty.[14] But the board took this action to avert public harm during a national crisis with the understanding that there would be a net loss, perhaps a large one, to the corporation. The board would have intentionally inflicted financial harm, but would there have been a foul? American corporate law has a mechanism that addresses this problem. In the case of a public crisis, no nexus between the provision of corporate resources and corporate purpose is needed. A board need not disingenuously obfuscate the rationale for a decision to rescue the public under the cover a "long-term benefit of the corporation and shareholders."

First of all, the provision of corporate assets to third-parties without any consideration has long been a part of corporate law. Corporate philanthropy is authorized by section 122(9) of the DGCL, which provides that a corporation has the power to "make donations for the public welfare or for charitable, scientific or educational purposes, and in time of war or other national emergency in aid thereof."[15] Gifts need not be justified by some benefit to the corporation, else it would not be a gift but an economic transaction. For instance, the New York corporation statute makes explicit that gifts can be made "irrespective of corporate benefit."[16] The authority to provide corporate gifts as a part of a broader corporate social responsibility agenda has long been established. For instance, the New Jersey Supreme Court wrote in the well-known case, *A.P. Smith Manufacturing Company v. Barlow*: "It seems to us that just as the conditions prevailing when corporations were originally created required that they serve public as well as private interests, modern conditions require that corporations acknowledge and discharge social as well as private responsibilities as members of the communities within which they operate."[17] The power to distribute corporate assets free of consideration toward the public welfare in an appropriate and responsible manner is the most direct evidence that corporate law allows managers broad discretion to incorporate principles of corporate social responsibility in the management of the firm.

There is also a specific statute addressing the board's authority to provide resources in furtherance of the social good during a public crisis. Section 122(12) of the DGCL empowers a corporation to "transact any lawful business which the corporation's board of directors shall find to be in aid of government authority."[18] Surprisingly, no Delaware court has cited or analyzed section 122(12) and scholarly attention has been scant, presumably because the circumstance required to invoke this power would be most unusual.

This provision is a broad grant of authority. The board has the authority to "transact *any* lawful business ... in aid of government authority." The dictionary definition of aid is "help given ... tangible means of assistance (as money or supplies)."[19] The historical definition is a "subsidy or tax granted to the king for an extraordinary purpose" as well as a "benevolence or tribute (i.e., a sum of money) granted by the tenant to his lord in times of difficulty and distress" (Garner, 2009). This etymology is obviously meaningful.

The Bank of America – Merrill Lynch episode shows the potential utility of section 122(12). Even if Bank of America had the option to terminate the transaction, the board should not be held liable for choosing to assume Merrill Lynch's $15 billion loss, as long as it did so to aid government and rescue the public welfare. The statute has application beyond the financial crisis since crises are a part of the human condition. Consider the following hypothetical. There is a full-blown global pandemic, and a pharmaceutical company has the only treatment for this particular disease. In light of a global pandemic, the board decides to sell the treatment at cost to wealthy countries and give it away to poorer countries at a direct cost. Can the board sacrifice an enormous profit opportunity by coming to the aid of government and society? Boards are authorized to do so under American corporate law so long as the action was done so advisedly and it does not impair the corporation as a going concern. Any question of waste would be dispelled by a powerful cocktail of the business judgment rule and the evocation of the "long-term" benefit to the corporation and shareholders to be gotten from the goodwill gesture.

FIDUCIARY EXEMPTION

The board has the authority, but there remains the question: Is such authority bound by a legal limit? Since no court has spoken on section 122(12) or similar provisions found in other state statutes, this question remains open. In this subsection, an argument for unbounded authority is advanced.

The plain text of the statute suggests the boundary is very broad at least. Since the government is the primary beneficiary, one may infer that the legislature intended to grant the board great discretion in providing private aid to a public cause. Delaware courts could import into section 122(12) a limit based on some formulation of the rationality standard. If there is to be limiting principle, such principle should be the foundation of the business judgment rule, specifically an appropriate ex ante procedure leading to an informed, good faith decision with the limit of rationality as the outer boundary. During a national crisis, the limit of rationality would be the point at which the board's decision could be said ex ante to have financially endangered or impaired the corporation as a going concern. Corporate endangerment, self-mutilation or suicide is not an aspirational end of corporate law. The risk of such event occurring is sufficiently great from the acts of the unfortunate, negligent or corrupt manager, and the law need not add to this burden. Therefore, a reasonable limiting principle may be that the board would be irrational when it takes action knowing ex ante that its action would impair the corporation's long-term financial health as a going concern.

However, there are countervailing considerations. A legal limit would be problematic. The waste standard could be inadequate during a public crisis, which is always some large, exigent social problem. The standard must be malleable to the circumstances. The standard applicable to corporate gifts to hospitals or museums may be meaningless in the context of a public crisis. Recall that Bank of America assumed Merrill Lynch's $15 billion fourth-quarter loss; this loss may be so breathtaking that it constitutes clear waste from the standpoint of an ordinary corporate gift. One expects that any meaningful aid during a public crisis may be substantial, thus automatically creating a potential legal liability for the board if the provision of resources are commensurate with the enormity of the stake involved. There is a potential Catch-22 absurdity: the exigency of the situation creates a real legal risk when a board exercises the very authority granted by statute.

The existence of legal risk suggests that the board's authority should be absolute, and not qualified even under the lenient standard of rationality, which would always open the door to the possibility of liability. Although there is a strong argument for a limiting principle, an argument is advanced here that there should be a fiduciary exemption when a board acts under section 122(12) to "aid of government authority" or when it otherwise provides aid in response to a public crisis. A fiduciary safe-harbour is better because it removes legal risk from the board's decision involving a public necessity.

The experiences in tort law and public catastrophes have shown that the paralyzing effect of litigation risk is real during a public crisis and can lead to very poor outcomes. The Pennsylvania Supreme Court's reflection on history is informative: "We find, indeed, a memorable instance of folly recorded in the 3 Vol. of Clarendon's History, where it is mentioned that the Lord Mayor of London, in 1666, when that city was on fire, would not give directions for, or content to, the pulling down forty wooden houses ... for fear he should be answerable for a trespass; and in consequence of this conduct half that great city was burnt."[20] A small probability of liability would not be reassuring for a board. Public crises may require consequential decisions with large sums of resources at stake. A low probability, high magnitude liability payout may still result in a significant expected value of the legal risk. Exposure to such litigation risk may be sufficiently high to deter potentially beneficial motive and action.

Authority without legal limit, which is another way to view a fiduciary safe-harbor, would be novel. The basic assumption bears repeating that the cost–benefit of providing aid during a public crisis would be clear. No *legal* limit on authority is not equivalent to no limitation at all. First of all, few boards are irrational, and fewer boards still have been found to have acted irrationally with corporate assets. Because the rationality standard is so lenient, it does not result in much liability; but the threat of liability may pose a real risk of hesitation and inaction at a time when such a response can prove to be most unhelpful. Also, self-preservation is a powerful instinct even when a board is acting as an agent for the legal entity. The moral sentiment of a good Samaritan is limited by the perceived economic and moral obligations to the various constituents of the corporation, including shareholders, creditors, employees, and communities. Board members are also bound by their own reputational interests, and a good deed at a ruinous cost to the corporation would not assure a board member's reputation or standing in the corporate ballot box. The instinct for self-preservation and self-interest are powerful constraints on a desire to provide overly generous provision of aid to the impairment of the corporate enterprise.

Moreover, the circumstances of a crisis provide the necessary constraint. Just because there is a public crisis, corporate boards would not be lining up to provide large resources in amounts that would trigger the threat of litigation. The situational context dictates that for a firm to consider a rescue at all, it would have to be uniquely situated in relation to the crisis. One would not expect Pfizer to rescue financial institutions during a crisis in the financial markets, and likewise we would not expect JPMorgan Chase to rescue the public during a global pandemic. A direct causality would connect corporate munificence. The uniqueness of a firm's situation in relation to the public crisis provides a natural, extra-legal constraint on board action.

There is also a pragmatic political reason for fiduciary exemption. In the American scheme, the primary threat to state control of corporate law is federal preemption of the field, which is constitutionally permissible. States, and particularly Delaware, are always wary of this potential of federal intervention into their corporation laws. If state corporate law undermined federal policy by deterring corporate cooperation with government policy or punishing corporate boards with liability for providing public aid when the dust settles, there would be a real risk of federal preemption of corporate law or some aspects of it. States would not want this result. Corporate law is primarily state law only upon the implicit approval of the federal government.

Based on the above reasons, a rule of fiduciary exemption is more sensible. The proposed rule is simply stated: *upon a public necessity, a board of a firm that is uniquely situated to avert or mitigate a public crisis is exempt from its ordinary fiduciary duty to the corporation insofar as it distributes corporate assets with the intent to aid the government or the public.*

PUBLIC NECESSITY AND COST–BENEFIT

The theoretical justification for fiduciary exemption can be found in a well established doctrine of tort law dealing with public crisis and necessity. Corporate law borrows much of its concepts of duty and standard of liability from tort law. The analogy to tort law is a natural one. The most obvious application of tort law principles is a director's duty of care, which defined in terms of a cause of action for negligence. The tort analogy does not stop at the concept of negligence. The duty of loyalty resembles the concept of an intentional tort. Theft of corporate assets is a breach of the duty of loyalty, as is bad faith conduct resulting in harm to the corporation.[21] The influence of tort law is seen even in the realm of takeover law. The law of self-defense informs Delaware's standard for reviewing the appropriateness of a board's adoption of antitakeover defenses. Under *Unocal Corp. v. Mesa Petroleum*, the target has the burden to establish that the board reasonably perceived that the hostile takeover bid was a threat to the corporation, and the takeover defensive measure adopted was reasonable in response to the threat.[22] This standard is analogous to the tort standard, which provides that self-defense measures cannot be "in excess of that which the actor correctly or reasonably believes to be necessary for his protection."[23]

Tort law informs the liability scheme of corporate law as the two bodies of law fundamentally concern wrongful conduct and liability there from, though obviously applications and policies may differ, perhaps substantially so, in the details of the liability scheme. Tort law proves useful in analyzing a board's liability for financial harm arising from a private sacrifice of corporate profit or assets. Specifically, the tort doctrine of public necessity provides a theoretical justification for fiduciary exemption.

In tort law, public necessity creates a complete defense against an intentional tort to property. A public necessity is a situation when there is a broader threat to the public wealth or welfare. The common law has long recognized this defense, which dates back as far as 1609 to *Mouse's Case*,[24] and it states that an actor who harms the property of another in response to a public emergency is not liable to the property owner. The efficiency consideration of public necessity is apparent: the cost–benefit analysis always weighs in favor of preserving the public welfare or wealth over private property. This rule clearly satisfies the cost–benefit criterion. Nevertheless, the question is: why not impose the imperfect privilege and require compensation? The simple answer is that the cost–benefit always works in favor of mitigating a public crisis and the risk is too great from the moment's hesitation by an actor who is in a position to rescue based on the calculation of the risk of liability.

The thesis advanced here is consistent with the animating principle of corporate law – that is, corporate law is founded on the principle of social wealth maximization. This principle is not the same as shareholder profit maximization, which at its essential level is a distributive concern. Shareholder primacy is a default norm only, and it can be subjugated to the interests of other constituents. Many states have constituency statutes that permit the board to consider the stakeholder interests. Shareholder primacy is subjugated to the specific power of the board to provide both gifts and government aid under sections 122(9) and 122(12).

Shareholder primacy is based on efficiency consideration, but maximizing profit is not ipso facto a superior proposition. The proposition fails, for example, when the shareholders' claim is viewed as an out-of-the-money call option, as is the case in insolvency. Intrinsic in the concept is a distributive quality. Stated simply, it is fairly obvious that shareholder wealth can increase in only three distinct ways: (1) the total size of the wealth created by the enterprise increases, thus leaving a greater residual claim for the shareholders; (2) the economic pie remains the same, but shareholders take a greater portion than other claimants; and (3) shareholders increase their wealth by taking action that reduces the size to the economic pie, thus diminishing the aggregate returns to other claimants.

Only the first proposition increases social wealth and is thus a normatively superior outcome. The second proposition is neutral as to social wealth, and the matter concerns only the equity of distribution. In these circumstances, the law generally does not interfere in the contractual relationships establishing the distribution of the economic pie. It is said that enterprise law provides a set of default contract terms among factors of production.

Absent fraud or some other bad motive, the contract terms govern and market forces primarily provide the pricing mechanism for these commercial relationships, including the market for corporate control if the shareholder slice is less than it should be. The third proposition is a clearly inferior proposition. The notion that shareholders are made wealthy by reducing the social wealth cannot be a desired goal. To be sure, this effect is seen, perhaps frequently, as is the case when limited liability is used as an ex ante liability avoidance scheme. Would any efficient or just society provide a shield against liability if it had perfect information and knew beforehand that a firm would impart social cost for which its assets cannot pay? Such a society would be economically and morally bankrupt. A rule promoting a reduction in the aggregate social wealth is inefficient and can be justified only on the illicit premise that a specific class of capital providers has an inalienable entitlement to their wealth maximization.

The criterion used to determine corporate law's efficiency is important. Efficiency is based on the Kaldor–Hicks criterion, which is distinguished from the Pareto superior efficiency. The Pareto superior criterion states that a change is efficient if at least one person is made better off and no person is made worse off. This criterion has few practical applications because transactions often have third-party effects and the cost of bringing about compensation may often exceed the net surplus. Kaldor–Hicks efficiency provides that a change is efficient if gainers gain more than the losers lose. The important concept is that in principle the gainers could compensate the losers and still enjoy a surplus, but compensation is not required. This is essentially a cost–benefit analysis.

A cost–benefit analysis is the governing principle of corporate law. Society has a normative preference for greater aggregate wealth and welfare. The distributive principle of shareholder primacy is not the end of corporate law, but is instead a default setting because in most cases profit maximization nicely correlates to increased social wealth and welfare. The default setting can change when the social cost–benefit calculus changes. In the face of clear evidence of the threat of abnormally large social harm associated with a national crisis, the board can subjugate shareholder primacy, which even in normal times is an unenforceable norm, to directly advance the societal interest preventing or mitigating such harm.

The financial crisis of 2008 teaches that the cost–benefit analysis does not always weigh in favor of private financial gain. Much of its causality can be explained by the pursuit of short-term private gain by employees, managers, and vicariously passive shareholders of the many firms responsible for the crisis. In ordinary circumstances, the framing of shareholder primacy is not at issue, and we correctly assume that the profit-maximizing firm with its embedded distributive principle generally tends to enhance social wealth and welfare because the legal process is ill-suited to engage in an individualized assessment of the cost–benefit and distribution of surplus to the various participants and constituents. The rising tide of shareholder wealth lifts all boats, it is correctly assumed as the default aspiration. The incentive structure underlying profit maximization works most of the time in ordinary circumstances. This default setting, however, should not diminish society's greater interest in the protection of the financial markets and the national economy, or the public good more generally in time of great crises. These interests can outweigh the narrow financial interests of any single firm since a sound economy and market are preconditions to the long-term health of the company.

Although Delaware law cannot mandate the pursuit of the public welfare, just as it cannot mandate shareholder profit maximization, without encroaching on the board's prerogative to manage the corporation, it leaves the board with great leeway to do precisely that. The business judgment rule protects board action within the bounds of rationality, and the board can rely on such half-fictional, abstractized reasoning as pursuing the "long-term" interest of the corporation and shareholders. Additionally, Delaware law provides broad flexibility in terms of the provision of corporate assets in times of national crisis through sections 122(9) and 122(12) of the DGCL. In crisis, fiduciary duty and board authority are elastic concepts sufficient to encompass the promotion of the public welfare as the primary objective of action.

The Bank of America – Merrill Lynch episode is instructive. Bank of America's board had many things to consider before determining whether to complete the merger with Merrill Lynch, including the potential harm to the financial markets and the public welfare in time of great crisis. This is no small consideration, and a systemically important financial institution should have important obligations toward the soundness of the financial system. Moreover, shareholder primacy has little role in the government's policy decision making. Even when the government is an investor in a bailout, it is myopic to believe that such public funds are deployed for the primary benefit of the shareholders in the firm. Any benefit to shareholders from government action was incidental toward the larger goal of stabilizing a collapsing economy. In a crisis, larger issues can be at stake than the wealth of shareholders. The board of a financial institution could also legitimately take a similar view. A board would have been well within its authority to consider the public welfare as the primary, albeit temporary, end of corporate action.

CONCLUSIONS

While not perfect, American corporate law is ingenious in the flexibility it provides managers. Intrinsic in the business judgment rule is a judicial recognition that managing a complex economic organization in an even more complex economy is quite challenging. A corporation operates not in the abstract vacuum of a nexus of contracts among its factors of production, but in the greater web of social and political relationships to which that nexus forms a vital part. Under Delaware law, at least, a corporation is an entity distinct from its capital providers and managers. This suggests that the corporation as served by the board has social responsibilities it should meet while conducting its business and affairs. These obligations, like the obligation to achieve profit, cannot be legally mandated, but are instead mandated by moral and economic duties to various constituents and factors of production. Establishing the judicial decision standard for either goal is illusory. Instead, the board has the discretion to calibrate this balance, including the deliberation of the ethics of the action and principles of corporate social responsibility.

No situation calls for sensitivity to corporate social responsibility more than when a public crisis strikes. The stakes are the greatest. In time of crisis, corporate activity can take the form of public–private activity, or at least it can impart significantly greater effects on social wealth and public welfare. American corporate law is flexible enough to provide for this contingency. The combination of the business judgment rule and section 122(12) – together, embodying the principle that managers shall have the authority to manage the corporation – provides the board with sufficient authority to act in the interest of the public welfare at the sacrifice of corporate resources. However, there still remains a real possibility of legal liability, simply because the amount of any meaningful resources in a rescue can be extraordinary. No American court has ruled on this issue. This ambiguity in the liability scheme is problematic.

In these situations, the normal rules do not apply. There should be a fiduciary safe-harbor where a board acts in the public interest during a public crisis. Given an unavoidable Hobson's choice, it would be inefficient to uphold a norm or legal rule requiring a board to pursue private economic gain at a tremendous direct cost to society when a board can avoid such cost through the provision of aid. A norm or legal rule that jeopardizes or deters a voluntary rescue would also be morally suspect. If the cost–benefit analysis on a broader level is obvious, a board should be allowed to provide aid to the public without legal risk overhanging its decision.

The animating principle of corporate law is the maximization of social wealth and welfare, and not the more narrow interest of shareholder profit, which is essentially a distributive principle. In time of crisis, the benefit to the public may be so large and obvious that the presumptive social benefit of shareholder primacy is clearly rebutted by the potential harm. The cost–benefit analysis may permit a primary obligation to consider the public good. Despite the sometimes ideological nature of the defense of shareholder primacy, corporate decision making is much more complex than can be served by unconditional, bright-line rules or canons of economic or political philosophy. A board should be allowed to act explicitly on behalf of the public good without resort to such disingenuous elision as the "long-term interest of the corporation and shareholders." Such honesty recognizes that the corporate enterprise is integrated into the fabric of society rather than a separate, discrete nexus of contracts removed from the surrounding context and designed solely to maximize value for shareholders as residual claimants. The financial crisis of 2008 will not be the only national crisis. When crises strike, the public welfare should not be sacrificed upon the altar of shareholder primacy. Faith therein has its limits.

NOTES

1. Portions of this chapter are adapted from an earlier published article with permission from the *George Mason Law Review*.
2. Del. Code Ann. tit. 8 § 141(a). *See* Mod. Bus. Corp. Act § 8.01(b) (1984).
3. Aronson v. Lewis, 473 A.2d 805, 812 (Del. 1984).
4. Gantler v. Stephens, 965 A.2d 695, 706 (Del. 2009).
5. Brem v. Eisner, 746 A.2d 244, 262-64 (Del. 2000).
6. See, e.g., Shlensky v. Wrigley, 237 N.E.2d 776, 780 (Ill. App. Ct. 1968); Paramount Communications, Inc. v. Time, Inc., 571 A.2d 1140, 1151-55 (Del. 1989); Katz v. Oak Indus., 508 A.2d 873, 879 (Del. Ch. 1986).
7. 170 N.W. 668, 683-84 (Mich. 1919).
8. *Ibid* at 684.
9. Revlon, Inc. v. MacAndrews & Forbes Holdings, Inc., 506 A.2d 173, 182 (Del. 1986).
10. Paramount Commc'ns, Inc. v. Time, Inc., 571 A.2d 1140, 1150 (Del. 1989).
11. http://www.ford.com/
12. Sinclair Oil Corp. v. Levien, 280 A.2d 717, 720 (Del. 1971).
13. In re Walt Disney Co. Derivative Litigation, 906 A.2d 27, 74 (Del. 2006).
14. *Ibid* at 67 ("[W]here the fiduciary intentionally fails to act in the face of a known duty to act, demonstrating a conscious disregard for his duties ...").
15. Del. Code Ann. tit. 8 § 122(9). See Model Bus. Corp. Act § 3.02(13) (corporation has the power "to make donations for the public welfare or for

charitable, scientific, or educational purposes") and § 3.02(15) (corporation has the power "to make payments or donations, or do any other act, not inconsistent with law, that furthers the business and affairs of the corporation").

16. N.Y Bus. Corp. Law § 202(12) (McKinney 2009).

17. A.P. Smith Mfg. Co. v. Barlow, 98 A.2d 581, 586 (N.J. 1953).

18. Del. Code ann. tit. 8 § 122(12) (2009). See Model Bus. Corp. Act § 3.02(14) (containing a similar provision: "[T]o transact any lawful business that will aid governmental policy").

19. *Webster's Ninth New Collegiate Dictionary* (1985).

20. Respublica v. Sparhawk, 1 Dall. 357, 362 (Pa. 1788).

21. Stone v. Ritter, 911 A.2d 362, 370 (Del. 2006).

22. 493 A.2d 946, 954-55 (Del. 1985).

23. Restatement (Second) of Torts § 70(1) (1965).

24. (1609) 77 Eng. Rep. 1341 (K.B.) (holding that "it is lawful for any passenger to cast the things out of the barge [upon a sudden storm] ... everyone ought to bear his loss for the safeguard and life of a man").

REFERENCES

Allen, W. T., Jacobs, J. B., & Strine, L. E. (2002). The great takeover debate: A mediation on bridging the conceptual divide. *University of Chicago Law Review, 69*, 1067–1100.

Bartlett, C.A, Dessain, V., & Sjdman, A. (2006). IKEA's global sourcing challenge: Indian rugs and child labor (B). *Harvard Business School,* 14 November.

Berle, A. A. (1931). Corporate powers as powers in trust. *Harvard Law Review, 44*, 1049–1074.

Berle, A. A., & Means, G. C. (1932). *The modern corporation and private property.* New Brunswick, NJ: Transaction Publishers.

Dodd, E. M. (1932). For whom are corporate managers trustees? *Harvard Law Review, 45*, 1145–1163.

Garner, B. A. (2009). *Black's law dictionary* (9th ed). St. Paul, MN: West Group.

Rhee, R. J. (2008). Corporate ethics, agency, and the theory of the firm. *Journal of Business & Technology Law, 3*, 309–332.

Rhee, R. J. (2010). Fiduciary exemption for public necessity: Shareholder profit, public good, and the Hobson's choice during a national crisis. *George Mason Law Review, 17*, 661–736. Portions of this chapter are adapted from this article with permission from the George Mason Law Review.

Strine, L. E. (2002). The social responsibility of boards of directors and stockholders in change of control transactions: is there any "there" there? *Southern California Law Review, 79*, 1179–1187.

Webster's Ninth New Collegiate Dictionary. (9th ed.). (1985). Springfield, MA: G. & C. Merriam Co.

INSTITUTIONALISATION OF CORPORATE SOCIAL RESPONSIBILITY IN THE CORPORATE GOVERNANCE CODE: THE NEW TREND OF THE DUTCH MODEL

Tineke Lambooy

The past decade can be characterised by an increasing awareness about the limits to growth. Many voices have been heard pointing to the fact that the planet does not support an unlimited economic growth and increasing consumption patterns by more and more people (Club of Rome, 2009). Food, fresh water and biodiversity crises are pending on a near-by horizon (Berendsen, 2009; UNEP & WCMC, 2010; FAO, 2003; World Bank, 2008). Besides these pending crises, the financial crisis still continues today. Apparently, people in general, including the decision-makers in business and politics, tend to have short-term horizons. A frequently heard point of criticism is that the contemporary financial crisis can be to an important extent attributed to failures and weaknesses in corporate governance arrangements (OECD Report: Kirkpatrick, 2009, pp. 1–2; Eumedion, 2010, p. 1).

Reframing Corporate Social Responsibility: Lessons from the Global Financial Crisis
Critical Studies on Corporate Responsibility, Governance and Sustainability,
Volume 1, 145–179
Copyright © 2010 by Emerald Group Publishing Limited
All rights of reproduction in any form reserved
ISSN: 2043-9059/doi:10.1108/S2043-9059(2010)0000001013

Another view has been expressed by Cheffins (2009), who argued that corporate governance did not fail. However, the 'Report of the high-level group on financial supervision in the EU' (EU, 2009, pp. 29–30) is very critical and marked corporate governance as 'one of the most important failures of the present crisis'. It states,

> procedural progress has no doubt been achieved, [e.g.] establishment of board committees, (...) but looking back at the causes of the crisis, it is clear that the financial system at large did not carry out its tasks with enough consideration for the long-term interest of its stakeholders. Most of the incentives (...) [and] the new accounting rules were systematically biased towards short-term performance.

The past decade has also seen the resurgence of the notion of corporate social responsibility (CSR). The Social and Economic Council of the Netherlands (*Sociaal Economische Raad*, SER) defines CSR as 'the concern for the social impact of the company's operations'. It describes CSR as 'deliberately focusing the business activities to create value in three dimensions – people, profit, planet – and therefore also contributing to longer-term prosperity and welfare in society; maintaining relations with the various stakeholders on the basis of transparency and dialogue, answering justified questions that are raised in society' (SER, 2000, p. 86). Transparency and accountability from a CSR perspective regards the environmental, social and governance (ESG) aspects of the business activities, including attributing value to natural assets such as ecosystem services and biodiversity, thereby internalising external costs (TEEB, 2008, 2009a, 2009b). Companies, governments and civil society have embraced the idea that the business sector has an important role to play in 'saving' the planet.

As many international and industry codes of conduct have been drafted and accepted over the past decade, and the GRI third generation Sustainability Reporting Guidelines (GRI G3) have been put into practice by companies from many parts of the world, one could say that CSR has been seriously acknowledged. Some countries have incorporated CSR as a concept in their legislation (Articles 1 and 74 Indonesian New Company Law No. 40/2007), others have imposed a duty on certain large companies to publish an annual sustainability report (i.e. Denmark and Sweden; Lambooy & Rancourt, 2009), and in the Netherlands, CSR has been recognised in the revised Dutch corporate governance code, effective as of 2009 (Frijns Code). This Code states that the directors shall adopt a policy on the CSR subjects that are material to the company's business. This implies that CSR is considered to belong to the core of corporate strategy. The United Kingdom has included similar concerns in the directors' duties description in Section 172 of the Company Code. Overall, on paper, the progress seems enormous. The logical next step is to embed CSR in a company's activities and to make its employees aware of what is expected from them from a perspective of making the company's activities sustainable. Corporate governance is very instrumental in this respect and can constitute a powerful instrument.

How will good corporate governance based on CSR and with a long-term view be achieved? Corporate law professor Charlotte Villiers of Bristol University insists that it is through law, possibly a combination of soft law and hard law, that the triple-bottom-line basis of CSR will be made a reality. Although she acknowledges the successes of UN initiatives and concedes that there have been improvements on the part of many companies, she points out that there is no consistency in responsible behaviour (Villiers, 2009; Boeger, Murray, & Villiers, 2008).

As a case study, the institutionalisation of CSR in the Dutch corporate governance model, which constitutes a combination of hard law and soft law, is examined in this chapter. The next section briefly describes the theoretical foundation of the model. Next, it will be described how CSR elements have entered into the Frijns Code. The relevant provisions will be analysed. Subsequently, the role of shareholders, in particular the corporate governance commission's decision *not* to include a CSR-related obligation for institutional investors in the Frijns Code will be elaborated. Following that, commentaries regarding the introduction of the Frijns Code and subsequent developments in practice and legislation are evaluated. Then, an overview of the 2010 Dutch status quo on corporate governance linked with CSR will be provided. The chapter ends with concluding remarks. The perspective in this chapter is the Dutch corporate governance code and corporate law. The research method is theoretical.

THE 2004 FOUNDATION OF THE DUTCH CORPORATE GOVERNANCE MODEL

In the Netherlands, the 'Tabaksblat Code' (the Dutch corporate governance code of December) was a semi-private regulation instigated by the Dutch government, the stock exchange and industry associations to restore trust in the public equity markets. The aim was 'to put the relationship between listed companies and providers of capital under the microscope' in order to establish a new balance with a larger role for the shareholders (Tabaksblat, 2003, p. 59).

The subject of CSR was contemplated at the time but rejected. The explanatory notes expressed that CSR concerned a different subject matter and that various CSR codes of conduct had been or were being developed; hence, it would not be necessary to include the subject (Tabaksblat, 2003, pp. 66–67). At the same time, however, it should be noted that the Tabaksblat Code stated that it was based on the stakeholders' model, which in the author's view also constitutes a base for CSR. Stakeholders were defined as 'the groups and individuals who directly or indirectly influence (or are influenced by) the achievement of the aims of the company. In other words, employees, shareholders and other providers of capital, suppliers and customers, but also government and civil society' (Tabaksblat, 2003, p. 3; slightly different: Frijns, 2008, p. 6).

The Tabaksblat Code contains 'Principles' that reflect the general views on good corporate governance and enjoy wide support. The principles have been elaborated in the form of specific 'Best Practices' provisions, which create a set of standards on recommended corporate conduct. The principles and best practice provisions regulate relations between the management board, the supervisory board and the shareholders.

Through the application of the 'comply or explain' mechanism, introduced in the Article 2:391(5) Dutch Civil Code (hereafter: DCC) in 2004, the Tabaksblat Code acquired a public regulatory aspect. This Article states that more detailed prescriptions concerning the content of the annual report may be imposed on companies, and more specifically, obligations regarding compliance with a designated code of conduct. The Tabaksblat Code was designated (Decree, 2004); hence, since 1 January 2004, listed companies have been obliged to report on their compliance with the Tabaksblat Code in their annual report, and in case of a deviation to provide an explanation. It is up to the shareholders to call the management and the supervisory boards to account for this. Pursuant to Article 5:86 of the Dutch Financial Supervision Act (*Wet Financieel Toezicht*), Dutch institutional investors have also been obliged from 1 January 2007 to include in their annual report, or on their websites, a statement about their compliance with the Tabaksblat Code's provisions to the extent applicable to them.

The new pro-equity balance was further strengthened by amendments to Dutch corporate law (*Structuurwet*, 2004), among others empowering shareholders of listed companies to propose subjects for the general meeting (i.e. shareholders possessing 1 or more per cent of the voting rights or representing €50 million; Article 2:114a(2) DCC; for proposed changes see Parl.Doc. 32014).[1] Another amendment granted an approval right to shareholders in respect of strategic board decisions concerning the identity or character of the company or the enterprise run by the company (Article 2:107a DCC). The termination of protective anti-takeover measures had already started in the Netherlands at the end of the 1990s. Other statutory changes in 2004 regarded the supervisory board of certain large companies, the so-called two-tier companies: the shareholders meeting appoints members of the supervisory board and can dismiss them (Articles 2:158(4)/268(4) DCC).[2] Previously, supervisory board members in such companies were elected by co-optation.

CSR ENTERING THE DUTCH CORPORATE GOVERNANCE MODEL

When the Tabaksblat Code entered into force, a 'Corporate Governance Code Monitoring Committee' (Monitoring Committee) was appointed to evaluate compliance with the Code. Annually, this Committee published a report. In 2008, it was decided that various observations by the Monitoring Committee merited an attempt by the Monitoring Committee to update the Tabaksblat Code.[3]

Over the years, various arguments had been put forward for extending the Code to cover new themes. For this chapter, the most notable ones are the position of women in board composition, diversity and CSR (e.g. VBDO, 2003). As regards CSR, two options were suggested: to include provisions on CSR in an updated corporate governance code or to draft a separate CSR code and subject it to a 'comply or explain' mechanism (Koelemeijer, 2005; Douma, 2006; Lambooy, 2007).

The new text of Section 172 of the UK Company Act (2006) also provided ideas. It requires boards to employ a broader and long-term perspective in their management, including the *long-term consequence* of the decisions as well as the interests of the employees; the relationships with suppliers and customers; the impact of the decision on the community and environment; the desirability of maintaining a reputation for high standards of business conduct and the need to act fairly as between members of the company (DTI; Chivers, 2007). The difference with the Dutch stakeholder model remains that a UK director's duty developed from the fiduciary duty of good faith to act in the company's best interest (Hicks and Goo, 2008; Bytestart, 2007).

In May 2008, a study was commissioned by the Dutch State Secretary for Economic Affairs, to be carried out by a committee under the chairmanship of Anthony Burgmans, the former CEO of Unilever (a Netherlands based multinational company), into the relationship between CSR and corporate governance (Burgmans Committee).[4] The resulting report contained two specific recommendations for supplementing the Tabaksblat Code with provisions on CSR (Burgmans Report; Burgmans, 2008, pp. 41–42):

I.   to urge the management and supervisory boards to consider the material concerns for the company of societal aspects of its business and to communicate those; and
II. to encourage institutional investors to bring more clarity about ESG considerations.

The Monitoring Committee subsequently decided to follow the first recommendation and to reject the second recommendation as it considered the latter 'beyond the scope of the Code' (Frijns, 2008, p. 50).

A proposal for the amended code was released for comments in June 2008. The Monitoring Committee also held consultations with special interest groups and experts about the Burgmans Committee's recommendations. On 10 December 2008, the Monitoring Committee published the final revised corporate governance code, that is, the 'Frijns Code' named after the chairman of the Monitoring Committee, Jean Frijns. The Frijns Code became applicable as of 1 January 2009 to listed companies with a registered office in the Netherlands (Frijns, 2008, p. 45; Decree, 2009).[5]

DISCUSSION ON THE CSR PROVISIONS IN THE FRIJNS CODE

Stakeholder Model, Conflict Resolution, Dialogue and Participation

Similar to the Tabaksblat Code, the core perspective of the Frijns Code is 'that a company is a long-term alliance between the various parties involved in the company'. The Frijns Code states that the management board and the supervisory board have the overall responsibility for taking into account the various interests. This aligns with the common Dutch perception of the role of a company in society, that is, that corporate activities are embedded in a stakeholder model (as opposed to the shareholder model usually explained in the Anglo-Saxon legal literature from the concept of agency theories).[6]

Besides ensuring the continuity of the enterprise, and trying to create long-term shareholder value, the Frijns Code advocates that the management board and the supervisory board should take account of the interests of the various stakeholders, including *CSR* issues that are relevant to the enterprise. If stakeholders are to cooperate *within and with* the company, it is essential for them to be confident that their interests are represented. It was stipulated that the two pillars on which good governance is founded and which are essential conditions for stakeholder confidence are (i) good entrepreneurship, which includes integrity and the transparency of the management board's actions, and (ii) effective supervision of their actions and accountability for such supervision. Moreover, it was argued that good relations between the various stakeholders are of great importance, particularly through a continuous and constructive dialogue (Frijns, 2008, pp. 5–8).

In the consultation phase, one respondent drew attention to 'the inherent tension in the stakeholder model between, on the one hand, the rule that when taking decisions the management and supervisory boards should be guided by the interests of the company and its stakeholders and, on the other hand, the fact that these boards are accountable for their actions to shareholders, who are themselves entitled to put their own interests first' (Frijns, 2008, p. 51). The Frijns Code indicates that this tension is particularly relevant in takeover situations, but that the solution will differ from case to case. For example, shareholders can give priority to their own interests with due regard for the principle of reasonableness and fairness. The greater the interest which the shareholder has in a company, the greater is his responsibility towards the company, the minority shareholders and other stakeholders. The Code points at general rules of conduct which are supposed to ensure the careful handling of the processes involving the various bodies that constitute the company. These are designed to help the management and the supervisory board to 'weigh up the different interests correctly' (Frijns, 2008, pp. 5–8).

Whereas the Frijns Code specifically addresses the issue of the tension between shareholders and directors in takeover situations, the author regrets that it does not elaborate on how to solve conflicts with other stakeholders, for example, concerning the company's CSR strategies. This is unfortunate because CSR conflicts frequently occur, and it seems that a company's management does not always know how to deal with them constructively (Van Tulder & Van der Zwart, 2006; Lambooy & Rancourt, 2008;

Lambooy, 2009). The Frijns Code could have proposed procedural and substantive ways to deal with them, for example, to create a platform for complaints or how to take remedial measures.

Another CSR and corporate governance subject regards *stakeholder participation* (OECD MNE Guidelines, pp. 5, 7; 2004 OECD Principles of Corporate Governance, Part IV). In the view of the author, a stakeholder dialogue is a first step, and stakeholder participation constitutes the next step. The Frijns Code explicitly maintains that the directors take into consideration the concerns of in-company *and* outside stakeholders and that they engage in the dialogue with them.

Stakeholder participation in the decision-making process is however not framed in the Frijns Code. The participation of the employees as one of the stakeholder groups is regulated elsewhere, that is, in the Dutch Works Councils Act (DWCA; *Wet op de Ondernemingsraden*). Nonetheless, the Frijns Code stipulates that the supervisory board's terms of reference are to include a paragraph on how it would maintain a relationship with the central works council or works council (provision III.4.1.g). Pursuant to a bill, the works councils will acquire some rights to express their opinion in the general meeting (Parl.Doc. 31877; see below 'Developments in Legislation and Practice'). Scholars have argued however that the drawbacks of shareholder activism pursuing short-term financial returns while disregarding the interests of the other stakeholders call for a reinforcement of the participation and position of the works council by granting it the right of investigation, that is, the right to start an enquiry procedure (*enquête*; Articles 2:344–359 DCC) (Sprengers, 2009). Enquiry proceedings are aimed at halting mismanagement or an adrift situation.

Management Board and CSR

Dutch law lays down the task and duty of the management board, i.e. 'to manage the company' (Article 2:129 DCC). Many books have been produced about the role of the directors in corporate governance. Defining the strategy, organising the business and the creation of value are the themes that usually emerge (Huse, 2007). The Frijns Code (Principle II.1) states,

> The role of the management board is to manage the company, which means, among other things, that it is responsible for achieving the company's aims, the strategy and associated risk profile, the development of results and *corporate social responsibility issues that are relevant to the enterprise*. [emphasis added]

Compared to the Tabaksblat Code, the inclusion of the CSR theme is new here. According to the author, the Frijns Code could have gone one step further, e.g. by requiring the management board to annually define tangible CSR ambitions in its annual report or on the company's website. Only then, stakeholders can test whether CSR ambitions have been achieved. This would also have been in line with the Dutch Accounting Guideline 400 as will be explained below.

To support Principle II.1, best practice provision II.1.3(b) requires that a code of conduct be published on the company's website as an instrument of internal risk management and control systems. The Tabaksblat Code had a similar provision (provision II.1.3). As the Frijns Code does not further explain this provision, it must probably be understood as only relating to the company's risk and control systems (compare SOX [Sections 406/407-6] and NYSE 2004, which also require companies to disclose a code of ethics). In the author's view, the Frijns Code has missed an opportunity here to affirm the best practice that many companies have endorsed an international or an industry CSR code of conduct. The Frijns Code could have obliged the management board to publish on the company's website any applicable CSR codes of conduct. This would have enhanced transparency concerning what type of conduct might be expected from the company.

The Frijns Code imposes that the management board shall submit certain subjects to the supervisory board for approval (provision II.1.2(d)), including *'corporate social responsibility issues that are relevant to the enterprise'*. Clearly, times have changed since the introduction of the Tabaksblat Code: CSR issues are now considered part of management strategy and are believed to be sufficiently important to require the supervisory board's consent (compare Articles 2:164/274 DCC which also oblige the management board of certain large 'two-tier' companies to obtain supervisory board approval regarding important decisions).

Furthermore, the Frijns Code states that the management board is also accountable for its performance to the general meeting and that it must mention the main elements of the CSR strategy in the annual report (provision II.1.2). This provision aligns with Dutch corporate law and accounting guidelines. Pursuant to the EU Modernisation Directive (Modernisation Directive, 2003), Article 2:391(1) DCC requires of large companies to include *extra-financial information* in their annual reports, such as information regarding environmental and employee matters (Lambooy & Van Vliet, 2008). Furthermore, the Dutch Accounting Standard Board has issued Accounting Guideline 400, which recommends to provide in the annual report ample information on the CSR strategy, policies and results (Kamp-Roelands & Lambooy, 2008; DASB, 2003). Consequently, best practice provision II.1.2 did not introduce a new topic in Dutch corporate practice. However, because the provision does not refer to the DCC, Accounting Guideline 400 or the GRI G3 sustainability reporting guidelines, it has been considered unclear (Parl.Doc. 31083). In the opinion of the author, the provision does not affirm best practices as many internationally operating companies already follow the more detailed and sector-specific GRI G3 framework in their sustainability reports and the instructions of Accounting Guideline 400 in their annual reports. The Frijns Code could have positioned this best practice more distinctively by including a reference or recommendation to the GRI G3 and/or Accounting Guideline 400.

Supervisory Board and CSR

Dutch law describes the supervisory board's task as follows: 'The supervisory board shall supervise the management, and the general affairs of the company and the related enterprise. The supervisory board shall support the management board with advice. In the fulfilment of their duties, the supervisory board members shall focus on the interest of the company and the connected enterprise' (Article 2:140(2) DCC; De Bos & Lückerath-Rovers, 2009). For an overview of the various opinions in the Netherlands about the role of the supervisory board regarding CSR, see the study of Dick de Waard, 2008).

Principle III.1 of the Frijns Code, concerning the role of the supervisory board, follows more or less the above-cited DCC text (as did the Tabaksblat Code). In addition thereto, this Principle determines that 'the supervisory board shall also have due regard for *corporate social responsibility issues* that are relevant to the enterprise' [emphasis added]. It also states that the supervisory board 'shall take into account the relevant interests of the company's stakeholders'.

This Principle is elaborated in best practice provisions. Provision III.1.6 highlights the most important matters that require the supervision by the supervisory board: '(a) achievement of the company's objectives; (b) corporate strategy and the risks inherent in the business activities; (c) the design and effectiveness of the internal risk management and control systems; (d) the financial reporting process; (e) compliance with primary and secondary legislation; (f) the company-shareholder relationship; and (g) *corporate social responsibility issues that are relevant to the enterprise'* [emphasis added]. The part under (g) is new compared to the Tabaksblat Code. Part (g) concurs with provision II.1.2(d) discussed above in 'Management Board and CSR'.

Provision III.1.1 stipulates that the division of duties within the supervisory board and the procedure of the supervisory board shall be laid down in 'terms of reference', which shall be posted on the company's website. They shall include a paragraph outlining how the supervisory board's relations with the management board, the general meeting and the (central) works council will be maintained. As the Frijns Code assigns significant responsibility to the supervisory board, it was considered desirable that a form of structured consultation be set up to enable the members to exchange ideas and information and to serve as a point of contact for *third* parties. The supervisory board members are expected to develop initiatives in this respect (Frijns, 2008, p. 48). This is exemplified by provision III.4.1(g), which obliges the chairman to ensure that the supervisory board has proper contact with the management board and the (central) works council. From a CSR perspective, especially the instruction to maintain a good relationship with *third* parties is interesting as this can stimulate stakeholder participation. However, in the author's view this provision could have included more concrete instructions, e.g. by requiring supervisory boards to include in their terms of reference the appointment of a 'CSR-Committee' or 'CSR-supervisory director' among them. This practice had been suggested (e.g. by VBDO, 2003). There are pros and cons to be mentioned about this idea: (pro) because it would clearly lay down CSR responsibilities with one or more persons, and (con) because CSR now remains a collective duty of the supervisory board, which concurs with the idea that CSR concerns all core activities of the enterprise.

Another best practice provision asserts that 'the supervisory board and its individual members each shall have their own responsibility for obtaining all information from the management board and the external auditor that the supervisory board needs in order to be able to carry out its duties properly'. The board may obtain information from company officers and external advisers and require that they attend its meetings (provision III.1.9). This provision thus allows the supervisory board to invite experts in the field of People and Planet to provide their opinion on the company's CSR strategy and policies, which would contribute to taking care of stakeholder interests (i.e. stakeholders inside and outside the company).

Principle III.3 on 'Expertise and Composition' evidently stipulates that 'each supervisory board member shall be capable of assessing the broad outline of the overall policy' and 'the specific expertise required for the fulfilment' of his or her duties. Noteworthy from a CSR perspective is that this Principle also lays a new foundation in terms of *gender*. It states that the supervisory board 'shall aim for a diverse composition in terms of such factors as gender and age'. Best practice provision III.3.1 elaborates on this by stating that the supervisory board 'shall prepare a profile of its size and composition', which profile 'shall deal with the aspects of diversity' and 'state what specific objective is pursued' in that respect. In so far as the existing situation differs from the intended situation, the supervisory board 'shall account for this in its report and shall indicate how and within what period it expects to achieve this aim'. The profile will be made generally available and be posted on the company's website. Provision III.1.2 states that the annual statements[7] shall include a report by the supervisory board, in which the board describes its activities in the financial year, including certain specific information about each supervisory board member, such as *gender*, age and profession (provision III.1.3). Annually, the supervisory board shall discuss the desired profile, composition and competence of the supervisory board, and the conclusions that must be drawn on the basis thereof (provision III.1.7).

In the consultations preceding the adoption of the Frijns Code, some respondents had advocated the inclusion of a target figure for female board representation in the Code. In response, the Monitoring Committee pointed at the 'explicit provision that companies are expected to apply and disclose a specific objective in relation to diversity' (i.e. provision III.3.1) and stated that 'there is wide support for this amendment' (Frijns, 2008, p. 55). From a CSR perspective, the provision would have been stronger had it included target figures for female members on both supervisory and management board. This will be elaborated below.

Gender Concerns in Board Composition

The above-mentioned principles and provisions seem to indicate that the gender representation issue only concerns the supervisory board composition. However, reflecting on the above-cited response of the Monitoring Committee, and referring to the content of provision III.5.14, one understands that the gender issue in the board composition also relates to the management board. See provision III.5.14:

> The selection and appointment committee [of the supervisory board] shall in any event focus on: (a) drawing up selection criteria and appointment procedures for supervisory board members *and management board members*; (b) periodically assessing the size and

composition of the supervisory board *and the management board,* and making a proposal for a composition profile of the supervisory board. [emphasis added]

The author considers it a missed opportunity that the Frijns Code does not contain a specific provision on management board composition and its desired profile.

It is interesting to note that gender has entered the corporate governance discussions about board composition. A fair representation of women in company boards is certainly a CSR theme. It would help to abolish discrimination based on sex, which in many places in the world is still more of a rule than an exception in work and income situations (Worldconnectors, 2010). For example, in the Netherlands, listed companies' boards comprise, on average, 7 per cent female board members, whereas the European average stagnates at 11 per cent (Lückerath-Rovers, 2008, 2009a, 2009b). The same research indicated that the support by large listed Dutch companies for greater gender diversity in the board still only seems to be words and no deeds. Together with Belgium, Italy and Spain, the Netherlands sits in the lowest European echelon (Kalma, 2008).

On an international level, a 2007 McKinsey study offers fact-based insights into the importance for companies of fostering the development of women in the business arena, so that a greater number attain positions of high responsibility (Desvaux, Devillard-Hoellinger, & Baumgarten, 2007). The study suggests that the companies where women are most strongly represented at board or top-management level are also the companies that perform best. The same outcome can be found in a Finnish study demonstrating a 48 per cent higher profitability of companies with women 'on board' (Kotiranta, Kovalaine, & Rouvinen, 2007). The reasons are that without females on board, a board lacks half of the talents, misses the voice that brings into the decision-making process the concerns and interest of women with regard to the products and services offered by the company, and it appears that decisions might be taken better, quicker, in a more nuanced manner, and generally with a stronger long-term perspective.

In her case study 'Boardroom composition and gender parity,' Villiers (2009) compared the effectiveness of approaches chosen by different European countries. As gender discrimination is embedded in long-established cultural patterns, she concluded that imposing an obligation or the threat of sanctions is the only effective tool to avoid it. For example, the UK voluntary approach proved to be unsuccessful: the female board member figure still lags behind (15 per cent in 2009). Norway, on the contrary, regulated that a company would be dissolved unless it complies with the gender quotas for company boardrooms laid down in the Law on Public Companies.[8] This measure turned out to be effective: by 2007, over 90 per cent of the 460 listed Norwegian companies complied with the new norm, and by 2009, boards had 44 per cent females (Villiers, 2009; Kalma, 2008).

Gender is not a criterion that, as yet, can be found in Dutch law or case law regarding board composition. In that light, Principle III.3 of the Frijns Code is welcomed. Subsequently, a bill that intends to force a change in traditional role models and to encourage companies to actively scout for and coach female talents has been adopted by the Dutch Lower House in 2009 and submitted to the Upper House (Parl.Doc. 31763). It reads that a board of a large company (>250 employees) should be composed of at least 30 per cent female and 30 per cent male members, in so far as it comprises natural persons. It will be applicable to all large privately and publicly held Dutch companies (BVs and NVs), both in a one-tier system and in a two-tier system. Non-compliance is to be explained in the annual report.

With a same view, a bill submitted to the French Parliament in January 2010 requires – with a gradual implementation – of all companies listed on the Paris stock exchange that they ensure that female employees make up 50 per cent of their board members by 2015. The proposal also applies to state-owned companies and non-listed firms with supervisory boards. The approval of both Houses of Parliament must still be obtained (*The Guardian*, 2009).

Summary Evaluation – CSR Provisions for Boards in the Frijns Code

According to Dutch tradition, the Frijns Code is embedded in a *stakeholder model*, in which the interests of in-company and outside stakeholders are to be taken into account and weighed against one another when taking corporate decisions. CSR aligns well with this tradition and additionally makes the Planet concerns and outside stakeholders' interests more explicit and tends to embrace a wider stakeholders group. The Frijns Code institutionalises CSR and requires of managing directors – in general wording – that they 'manage CSR issues that are relevant to the enterprise' and that they submit CSR issues to the supervisory board for approval. Unfortunately, the provisions fail to encourage setting *conduct standards and defining tangible ambitions*. The general idea is that making CSR part of corporate governance will enhance *accountability*. However, accountability would definitively be improved if applicable codes of conduct and concrete ambitions were to be disclosed. In respect of *remedies*, the Frijns Code does not address how to deal with CSR stakeholder complaints or conflicts. It would have been a plus point if the Frijns Code had included language on how to resolve CSR conflicts with external stakeholders. Regarding the *transparency of business activities*, the Frijns Code requires to mention the main elements of the company's CSR strategy in the annual report. The pertinent provision is considered unclear. It could be improved by referencing the Accounting Guideline 400 or the GRI G3 sustainability reporting guidelines and by additionally recommending verification by independent auditors, in order to generate comparable and reliable information.

Concerning the subject of *participation of external stakeholders in the decision-making process*, it seems that the authors of the Frijns Code did not intend to further institutionalise this. The author considers this a next step in the development of corporate governance based on CSR. The participation of stakeholders is necessary to create legitimacy of business decisions. Establishing a special 'company CSR committee' could be of assistance. Propositions to this end were also recorded by the Burgmans Committee (Burgmans, 2008, p. 41). *Board composition* has to do with expertise but can also link up with stakeholder participation as shareholders and works councils have a say in the appointment of directors in Dutch companies. Interestingly, the Frijns Code pays attention to gender and diversity considerations concerning the board composition. Equal gender representation of boards is also part of a new bill that prescribes clear targets. The Frijns Code could have elected this approach, which would be better in line with best practices in the international arena.

DISCUSSION ON THE LACK OF CSR PROVISIONS FOR INVESTORS IN THE FRIJNS CODE

Shareholders – No CSR Provisions

Principle IV.1 of the Frijns Code concerns the role of the shareholders. It states, 'Good corporate governance requires the full-fledged participation of shareholders in the decision-making in the general meeting'. And: [to play its role] 'in the system of checks and balances in the company. Management board resolutions on a major change in the identity or character of the company or the enterprise shall be subject to the approval of the general meeting'. The last sentence concurs with Article 2:107a DCC (discussed supra in 'The 2004 Foundation').

According to the Frijns Code, the increase of the general meeting's powers as promoted by the Tabaksblat Code had been prompted by the need to strengthen the checks and balances within the company aimed at improving the quality of corporate governance. However, the increase in shareholder rights has also resulted in greater emphasis being put on the interests of shareholders both individually and collectively. To neutralise the power pendant swinging too far to the shareholders' side (Frijns, 2008, p. 47 and 56),[9] the Frijns Code requires shareholders to act in accordance with the principle of *reasonableness and fairness*. Principle IV.4 expresses this. The same phrasing can be found in a key provision of the DCC, Article 2:8, stipulating that a company and those who, pursuant to the law or the articles of association, are involved with its organisation must behave towards each other in accordance with the principle of reasonableness and fairness.

The Frijns Code explains that in the case of conflicts, shareholders should demonstrate their willingness to enter into a dialogue with the company and fellow shareholders. If the dialogue fails to produce a result, shareholders are entitled to exercise their statutory rights to express their views they have on the strategy, including the right to put items on the agenda and the right to call an extraordinary meeting of shareholders (Frijns, 2008, p. 56; Parl.Doc. 32014).[10] It has been regretted that the Frijns Code does not provide more 'guidance' as to how a constructive dialogue is to be conducted, for example, how should the media and other means of pressure be dealt with and how should parties organise their normal exchange of views (Raaijmakers, 2009, p. 39)?

Institutional Investors – No CSR Provisions

Principle IV.4 of the Frijns Code defines institutional investors such as pension funds, insurers, investment institutions and asset managers as a special category of shareholders (Frijns, 2008, p. 56; Maatman, 2004a, 2004b), because they 'shall act primarily in the interests of the ultimate beneficiaries or investors'. For that reason, they shall 'have a responsibility to the ultimate beneficiaries or investors and the companies in which they invest, to decide, in a careful and transparent way, whether they wish to exercise their rights as shareholder of listed companies'. Owing to this special position, provisions from IV.4.1 to IV.4.3 instruct institutional investors to publish annually, in any event on their website, their policy on the exercise of the voting rights, the implementation of their policy in the year under review, and at least once a quarter whether and, if so, how they have voted as shareholders at the general meeting.

CSR does not play a role here despite the recommendation in the Burgmans Report to add to Principe IV.4 the phrase: [to publish annually] *whether and to which extent they take into account ESG factors* (Burgmans, 2008, p. 42). If this text had been included, institutional investors would have to disclose to which extent they consider extra-financial information regarding ESG aspects in their decision-making process. However, the Monitoring Committee decided that this matter was beyond the scope of the Code. The author regrets this as will be explained below.

Integrating ESG Factors: The Freshfields Report

Traditionally, many ESG factors have not been incorporated into financial analysis. This is beginning to change as institutional investors see the connection between the long-term interests of their beneficiaries and the medium-term to long-term risk of issues such as climate change, dependence on biodiversity and ecosystem services like water provision and the function of bees, HIV/AIDS, corporate governance and employee relations. For a long time, pension funds contended that their fiduciary duties only allowed them to strive for profit maximalisation and that they were not allowed to consider ESG factors in their investment decisions or to promote socially responsible investment (SRI) (Mercer, 2006; Maatman, 2007; Bauer, 2008). The UN Environment Programme – Finance Initiative, Asset Management Working Group (UNEP FI)[11] – commissioned a study on this dilemma. The main question was,

> Is the integration of environmental, social and governance issues into investment policy (including asset allocation, portfolio construction and stock-picking or bond-picking) voluntarily permitted, legally required or hampered by law and regulation; primarily as regards public and private pension funds, secondarily as regards insurance company reserves and mutual funds?

In 2005, a report entitled 'A legal framework for the integration of environmental, social and governance issues into institutional investment' was released by UNEP (hereinafter: the Freshfields Report) (Freshfields, 2005). The concept of fiduciary duties was therein defined as: 'duties that common law jurisdictions impose upon a person who undertakes to exercise some discretionary power in the interests of another person in circumstances that give rise to a relationship of trust and confidence'. The UNEP FI question was analysed in several major capital markets' jurisdictions: (i) the common law jurisdictions of the United States, the United Kingdom, Australia and Canada, and (ii) the civil law systems of Germany, France, Italy, Spain and Japan. The Freshfields Report remarked that none of these jurisdictions had rules prescribing how ESG factors should be integrated and that investment decision-makers retain some degree of discretion as to how they invest the funds under their control. One common legal element for all the examined jurisdictions is the requirement that decision-makers follow the 'correct process' in reaching their investment decisions. For common law jurisdictions, this requirement stems from the fiduciary duties of prudence and, in the civil law jurisdictions, the duty to seek profitability and otherwise manage investments conscientiously in the interests of beneficiaries. To be a 'prudent fiduciary', ESG factors should be considered where there is the potential for a material, financial impact from those factors. For example, climate change was mentioned as an example of an environmental consideration that is recognised as affecting value. Consequently, the Report clears the fact that there are limitations on the integration of ESG factors in the investment decision-making process; on the contrary, the law not only allows it but also requires to do ESG due diligence in certain circumstances (Freshfields, 2005, p. 7, 10–11; SDI, 2005; Baue, 2005). According to the Freshfields Report:

> Decision-makers are required to have regard (at some level) to ESG-considerations in every decision they make. This is because there is a body of credible evidence demonstrating that such considerations often have a role to play in the proper analysis of investment value. As such they cannot be ignored, because doing so may result in investments being given an inappropriate value.

One remaining controversial question relates to the interests of beneficiaries: does this regard the immediate future or their long-term interest? For example, the question was posed: 'If what you do now is very likely to create a world 30 years from now that's far more polluted, is that in the beneficiaries' best interest or not?' (Baue, 2005). The Freshfields Report does not provide an answer to this question as it merely states that the term 'interests' can have different meanings in different jurisdictions.

Launch of PRI
Since the publication of the Freshfields Report, there has been more innovation and evolution in the field of ESG integration. The launch of the Principles for Responsible Investment (PRI) in 2006 by then UN

Secretary-General Kofi Annan was a significant development. The PRI considers itself 'an investor initiative in partnership with UNEP FI and the UN Global Compact' and 'a framework to help investors achieve better long-term investment returns and sustainable markets through better analysis of environmental, social and governance issues in the investment process and the exercise of responsible ownership practices'. With over 550 signatories from the institutional investment community, including many of the world's largest pension funds, collectively representing approximately USD 18 trillion in assets under management, the PRI is helping to identify best practices among investors.[12]

Fiduciary II Report

In 2009, UNEP FI published a sequel to the Freshfields Report, entitled 'Fiduciary responsibility. Legal and practical aspects of integrating environmental, social and governance issues into institutional investment' (Fiduciary II). It updates the legal ramifications of ESG criteria in investment management (for a critical analysis, see Richardson, 2010). Fiduciary II states that professional investment advisors and service providers to institutional investors – such as investment consultants and asset managers – may have a far greater legal obligation to incorporate ESG issues into their investment services or face 'a very real risk that they will be sued for negligence' if they do not (Fiduciary II, p. 16). The report also provides indicative legal language that can be used to embed ESG considerations in the investment management agreements and related legal contracts between institutional investors and their asset managers.

Eumedion Position Paper

In March 2010, Eumedion, the Dutch corporate governance forum, issued a position paper on engaged shareholdership (Eumedion, 2010). Eumedion remarked 'that the debate on the role of shareholders in the system of corporate governance had taken a new direction'. Whereas in 2004, the emphasis was on encouraging shareholders to make use of their new rights, today 'following the actions of some reputedly activist shareholders involving a number of Dutch listed companies, the discussion is now mainly concerned with the manner in which shareholders use their rights. Shareholders are presently being increasingly reminded of their obligations'. In a vote at a seminar in 2009, 49 per cent of the participants indicated that the financial crisis had undermined the reliance in the shareholder model of corporate governance. The paper pointed to the Monitoring Committee's reference to the 'citizenship' of the shareholder (Monitoring, 2009) and affirmed that greater responsibility is expected from institutional investors in particular, because they hold the majority of the shares in Dutch listed companies and manage other people's money (Eumedion, 2010, p. 1).

Eumedion's recommendations to institutional investors included: (i) substantial investments in personnel and training or to mandate – based on its own ESG policy – an external asset manager to act as an engaged shareholder; (ii) integration of ESG factors into the investment process; (iii) willingness to cooperate with other institutional investors; (iv) remuneration of fund managers that is more strongly linked to the long term and to the interests of the client and the ultimate beneficiaries; (v) a mandate to asset managers that covers a longer period and addresses engaged shareholdership; (vi) the drafting of internal rules on dealing with a number of different interests; (vii) the recall of lent shares when there are important matters on the agenda for the shareholders' meeting and openness on the subject of control positions during dialogue with enterprises (based on research by Kemna and Van de Loo, 2009). Of listed companies, Eumedion expects a good corporate governance structure and a high degree of transparency and willingness on the part of the management board and the supervisory board to enter into dialogue with institutional investors. Finally, Eumedion itself will undertake research into (i) the increase of the involvement of major shareholders in the selection of supervisory directors and (ii) the added value of drafting a Dutch code for institutional investors (Eumedion, 2010, p. 3).

Summary Evaluation – Lack of CSR Provisions for Investors in the Frijns Code

The Freshfields Report analysed that it is not only permissible for institutional investors to consider ESG factors, but that their fiduciary duty requires that these factors be considered for possible material financial impact. It may even be a breach of a fiduciary duty to ignore those issues, given the link between ESG and financial performance. The same line was followed in Fiduciary II and affirmed for the Netherlands by Eumedion, which promotes training of institutional investors and their asset managers in order that they will be able to integrate ESG factors into the investment process. Consequently, according to the author, the Burgmans Report pointed in the right direction by advising to include in the Frijns Code that institutional investors decide, in a careful and transparent way, whether they wish to exercise their rights as shareholder of listed companies *and whether and to which extent they take into account ESG factors*. It is regrettable that the Frijns Code has not included this last phrase. However, we may perhaps anticipate – as announced by Eumedion – a new Dutch code for institutional investors covering such issue. Also, CSR would be supported if investors show a stronger loyalty and engage more actively in ESG issues with the companies in which they invest.

DEVELOPMENTS IN LEGISLATION AND PRACTICE

Commentaries to the Frijns Code and Subsequent Developments

Regarding the inclusion of CSR as a subject in the Frijns Code, various developments are interesting to record.

The first one is positive: various leading Dutch companies have set up a CSR commission.[13] This shows an increasing awareness of the importance of the role of CSR. Even more so, it demonstrates that these companies consider CSR a strategic issue.

The second development is a disappointing one. Not only is the lack of a CSR definition reiterated as a manifest problem, but interviewed supervisory board members indicated their concern that the new CSR provisions may only be followed in a 'tick-the-box' way (Havelaar, 2010). Furthermore, informal consultations with Dutch listed companies indicated that corporate secretaries of boards often express a legalistic approach. They wonder whether the new CSR provisions pertain to strategic decisions only or also to decisions at the operational level that relate to CSR.

The third development is an interesting one. As the Frijns Code provision II.1.2, which requires the management board to report on the main elements of the company's CSR strategy in the annual report, was considered unclear (see supra 'Management Board and CSR'), Dutch MP Kalma has put questions to the Dutch Cabinet. The answers did not clarify the point (Parl.Doc. 31083). Consequently, he decided to prepare an initiative bill, which amends Article 2:391(1) DCC to align it with the Frijns Code, that is, to require large Dutch companies to account in their annual reports on CSR aspects which are important for the enterprise: 'report or explain'.[14] Noticeable is also the Practitioner's Guide launched by the GRI on 'Embedding Gender in Sustainability Reporting' (GRI and IFC, 2009).

Another development that will be mentioned here is not a new one that relates to the Frijns Code, but it affirms the decision to consider CSR as a principle of corporate governance. Since a few years, there have been shareholders of listed companies who have called for a more sustainable board strategy. See, for example, the resolution of Shell shareholders submitted to the general meeting 2006 (ECCR, 2006).[15] The resolution indicated concerns about three projects: Corrib Gas in Ireland, Bayelsa State in the Niger Delta and Sakhalin in Russia. It requested that 'in the interests of the good reputation of the Company, and the avoidance of costly delay to, or interruption of, production', the directors undertake greater action on environmental sustainability to ensure the peace, safety, environment and prosperity of local communities directly affected by the company's operations. The resolution also called upon the directors to report to the shareholders by the 2007 general meeting how the company has implemented the measures. The resolution was defeated (83 per cent voted against, 6 per cent for and 11 per cent abstained).[16]

In 2010, another resolution was presented requiring Shell to perform further research as to how the intended oil exploration of the tar (oil) sands in Canada can be performed in a sustainable way (FairPensions, 2010; *Het Financieele Dagblad*, 2010).[17] Eleven per cent of the shareholders voted for the resolution or abstained (ECCR, 2010). A similar resolution was submitted to the British Petroleum (BP) 2010 general meeting. A number of institutional investors communicated the intention to vote for these shareholder resolutions (ECCR, 2010).[18] From a responsible corporate governance perspective, reflecting with hindsight on the BP disaster in the Gulf of Mexico and the fact that BP had successfully lobbied with the US Minerals Management Services for an exemption from performing a detailed environmental impact analysis (*Washington Post*, 2010), those shareholder resolutions seem to have been on the spot.

New Revisions of the Dutch Company Code
Impacting Corporate Governance

In December 2009, the Dutch Lower House adopted various important proposals to amend corporate law in the field of corporate governance.[19] They are expected to be adopted by the Upper House in the course of 2010.

Among other subjects, they aim at modernisation and creating flexibility in the structure of Dutch companies (Parl.Doc. 29752(2)). One bill introduces the permissibility of a 'one-tier board', that is, one corporate body that includes executive directors and non-executive directors (Parl.Doc. 31763). Many Anglo-American legal systems allow this model. The same bill determines that the division of seats between men and women within the company must be balanced (discussed supra in 'Gender Concerns in Board Composition').

Another bill provides for a change in the provisions regarding the convening and registration of shareholders' meetings, thereby implementing the European Directive concerning the exercising of certain rights of shareholders in listed companies (Parl.Doc. 31746). This Directive is aimed at strengthening the cross-border exercise of shareholders' rights in listed companies including voting and proxy voting.

Worthy of note is the bill that introduces certain new rights for the works councils of Dutch public limited companies (Parl.Doc. 31877). The bill declares that a works council can express its opinion about (i) key board resolutions as referred to in Article 2:107a DCC submitted for shareholder approval (supra in 'The 2004 Foundation'), (ii) resolutions to appoint, suspend and dismiss managing directors and supervisory directors and (iii) the remuneration policy, that is, concerning management salaries and bonuses. The bill also entails the right for the works council to communicate its view regarding any proposal for the appointment of supervisory board members (Article 2:158(4) DCC). This applies to works councils of holding companies and works councils of subsidiary companies (provided that the majority of the employees of the company and the group companies work within the Netherlands). The new rights are in addition to the works council's advisory rights pursuant to Articles 25 and 30 Dutch Works Council Act and are meant to reinforce codetermination at such a time that the works council's view can play a role in the decision-making process in the general meeting.

OVERVIEW OF THE 2010 DUTCH STATUS QUO ON CORPORATE GOVERNANCE AND CSR

Resuming, the previous sections elaborated on the current Dutch corporate governance and CSR situation. A compact overview is presented in Box 1.

Box 1. Dutch Corporate Governance and CSR

CSR POLICIES

The Frijns Code acknowledges CSR as belonging to the core corporate strategy. It indicates that the management board is expected to formulate a CSR policy and to submit their CSR policy to the supervisory board for approval.

The Frijns Code explicitly records that the supervisory board's responsibilities include the supervision and approval of the management's CSR policy.

Both the DCC and the Frijns Code prescribe that the main elements of the company's CSR strategy are to be included in the annual report, thereby informing the shareholders and other stakeholders. It is however unclear to which reporting standard the Frijns Code refers. Dutch Accounting Guideline 400 offers a guideline on how to include CSR aspects in the annual report.

An initiative bill is currently under preparation requiring large companies to include full information on their CSR policies and conduct in their annual report ('report or explain'). Furthermore, a proposal is considered to designate the GRI G3 reporting guidelines as a code of conduct for large companies ('comply or explain'). Both initiatives aim to make information published by companies on CSR more complete, uniform and comparable, thereby enhancing the usefulness of ESG information for outside stakeholders including banks and institutional investors.

GENDER AS AN ISSUE IN THE BOARD'S COMPOSITION

The Frijns Code prescribes that the supervisory board's composition should be well balanced, also from a gender perspective. In a more indirect way, the composition of the management board is also considered a concern of the supervisory board.

A bill has been adopted in the Lower House requiring that the composition of the management board and the supervisory board of large companies (>250 employees) reflects a gender balance, that is, comprising at least 30 per cent females and 30 per cent males.

The works council can exert an influence on the board's composition because it will have a right to communicate its position in the general meeting regarding the appointment of directors; it already has a right to propose candidates in certain large companies (Article 2:158/268 concerning large two-tier companies), and it is entitled to advise on proposals for new managing directors (Article 30 DWCA).

DISPUTES

The Frijns Code states that the supervisory board has the duty to maintain relations between the company and its stakeholders such as the shareholders, the works council and others.

According to the Frijns Code and the DCC, the supervisory board shall be guided by the interests of the company and the enterprise and shall take into account the relevant interests of the company's stakeholders. It might be assumed that interests refer to long-term interests. In the case of conflicts, the supervisory board must weigh the interests of the different stakeholders against each other.

A new bill proposes that a request made by shareholders to place an item on the agenda must be substantiated and may no longer be refused by the management board because of 'important company interests'. Disputes need to be solved using the standard of 'reasonableness and fairness', which guidance is already provided for in Article 2:8 DCC. The same standard was suggested in the Frijns Code for solving disputes with shareholders.

NEW SHAREHOLDERS' RIGHTS AND DUTIES

A new bill will improve the cross-border exercise of shareholders' rights in listed companies including voting and proxy voting.

The Frijns Code stipulates that the fact that shareholders are bound by the principle of reasonableness and fairness includes the willingness to enter into a dialogue with the company and fellow shareholders.

Transparency will be increased concerning the voting policies of institutional investors as the Frijns Code stipulates that – as an obligation to their beneficiaries and to the listed companies in which they invest – institutional investors must decide in a careful and transparent manner whether they wish to exercise their voting rights, and if so, how they have voted.

Despite the Freshfields Report, the Frijns Code did not follow the suggestion of the Burgmans Report to require institutional investors to be transparent as to whether and to which extent they take ESG factors into account. Eumedion, the Dutch corporate governance forum, recommends institutional investors to integrate ESG factors into the investment process and explores whether a Dutch code for institutional investors should be drafted.

WORKS COUNCILS' RIGHTS

Pursuant to a new bill that introduces new rights for works councils, they will be involved in the decision-making process in the general meeting. The works council will be able to share its opinion and to speak at the general meeting on (i) key board resolutions that need shareholder approval as referred to in Article 2:107a DCC, (ii) resolutions to appoint, suspend and dismiss managing directors and supervisory directors and (iii) the directors' remuneration policy.

The works councils in certain large companies were already entitled to propose supervisory board candidates (Article 2:158/268 DCC concerning large 'two-tier' companies).

For a long time, the works council has had the right to advise on strategic decisions as listed in Article 25 DWCA and on proposals for director appointments pursuant to Article 30 DWCA.

CONCLUDING REMARKS

Much progress has been made during the past decade in improving CSR. Nonetheless, it remains a challenge for boards to employ strategies with a long-term focus on sustainability. New types of shareholders, such as hedge funds and private equity parties, have attempted to influence corporate strategy. Their acts sometimes caused conflicts with boards on corporate strategy. These conflicts as well as the financial crisis sparked the debate about short-termism in corporate governance (Pruijm, 2008; Kirkpatrick, 2009; EU, 2009). To counter the contemporary crises and to avoid new crises, the author contends that we need a true reorientation of our economy and business methods towards a model that encourages a value increase in three dimensions: People, Planet and Profit, that is, a fusion of interests.

The supporting corporate governance model can enhance this by requiring company boards (i) to adopt a CSR code of conduct, preferably a specialised sector code or a detailed company code, and publish the same on the company's website; (ii) to annually define tangible ambitions and publish those; (iii) to create transparency of business activities by publication of an annual CSR report, which preferably follows the GRI G3 sustainability reporting standards or – in case of Dutch companies, if so desired – the Dutch Accounting Guideline 400, and which report has been externally audited. As gender is one of the CSR concerns, a corporate governance model can (iv) support CSR by requiring that company boards reflect diversity. As has been demonstrated in Norway, this can be best achieved by imposing strict quota and sanctions for non-compliance. In the Netherlands, a bill imposing quota is pending with the Upper House. To implement stakeholder participation, the corporate governance model should (v) make explicit how stakeholders can participate in the decision-making process. The boards will have a clear role here and can formulate guidelines and programmes for consultation. Dutch law provides a co-determination role to works councils. Embedding outside stakeholder participation in corporate decision-making has not been made part of the Frijns Code. Thoughts about this probably have to develop further. As regards investors, the corporate governance model can (vi) stimulate them to take ESG factors into account in their decision-making process. This will be aided by requiring institutional investors to disclose to what extent they take into account ESG factors when deciding on an investment. A last aspect of CSR which can be embedded in the corporate governance framework is (vii) to stimulate accountability for corporate conduct by providing instructions and guidance on how to remedy problems.

Concluding, making CSR part of the Dutch corporate governance code is an interesting step. It can assist boards to guide the company towards sustainable business with a long-term view. However, as explained in this chapter, there is still room for improvement of the Frijns Code. Corporate governance will undoubtedly develop further as a tool supporting CSR.

NOTES

1. At the end of 2009, a legislative proposal was presented to change the required percentage from 1 to 3 per cent and another proposal to lower the major shareholder disclosure threshold from 5 to 3 per cent as prescribed in Article 538 Financial

Supervision Act. They have not yet been adopted by the Lower House (Parl.Doc. 32014).

2. In other companies, supervisory board members are also appointed by the general meeting. Pursuant to the Articles 2:132/242, 162/264 DCC, managing directors are also appointed by the general meeting or, in the case of certain large 'two-tier' companies, by the supervisory board.

3. Pursuant to the request submitted in the spring of 2008 by the Dutch National Federation of Christian Trade Unions (CNV), corporate governance forum Eumedion, the Federation of Dutch Trade Unions (FNV), the Netherlands Centre of Executive and Supervisory Directors (NCD), NYSE Euronext, the Association of Stockholders (VEB), the Association of Securities-Issuing Companies (VEUO) and the Confederation of Netherlands Industry and Employers (VNO-NCW). The government endorsed the request.

4. As interviewee of the Burgmans study, the author had recommended to include CSR in the new corporate governance code or to draft a separate CSR code subject to the same mandatory comply or explain mechanism.

5. 'Whose shares or depositary receipts for shares have been admitted to listing on a stock exchange, or more specifically to trading on a regulated market or a comparable system', and large companies with a registered office in the Netherlands (i.e. balance sheet value > €500 million) 'whose shares or depositary receipts for shares have been admitted to trading on a multilateral trading facility or a comparable system'.

6. Articles 2:140/250 DCC require of supervisory directors to consider the interest of the company and the enterprise. Van Schilfgaarde (2006, pp. 11–15, 35) argues that this norm also applies to managing directors. He points to Supreme Court 13 September 2002 (JOR 2002/186); Slagter (2006, pp. 4–20, 135–137, 140) claims that this norm also applies to shareholders.

7. The 'annual statements' comprise the entire annual report referred to in Article 2:391 DCC, the financial statements referred to in Article 2:361 DCC, the other information referred to in Article 2:392 DCC, the report of the supervisory board, key figures, multi-year figures, shareholder information and so forth (provision III.1.2).

8. Private firms were given until July 2005 to increase female representation on their boards. However, these voluntary measures failed; by the deadline, the number of women had increased, but had only reached about 25 per cent. In response, the government introduced official legislation in that same year. This time, the penalties for non-compliance were severe: as of 1 January 2008, firms were penalised first with fines, then with deregistration from the Oslo Stock Exchange and finally with dissolution. See: http://www.mba.unisg.ch/org/es/mba.nsf/SysWebRessources/March-April/$FILE/Norway.pdf (accessed on 26 January 2010).

9. The Frijns Code refers to the activities of some shareholders and the foreign takeovers of leading Dutch companies that have prompted social debate. It stated that since 2004, Dutch listed companies have increasingly come under the influence of the market for corporate control (mergers and acquisitions).

10. For example, a request made by shareholders to the management board to place an item on the agenda (Article 114a DCC) may no longer be refused based on the argument that weighty interests of the company dictate otherwise (Parl.Doc. 32014 and see note 1, supra). The request, however, must be substantiated.

In addition, the item to be put on the agenda can be tested against the standard of 'reasonableness and fairness'.

11. UNEP FI is a strategic public–private partnership between UNEP and the global financial sector. UNEP FI works with over 180 banks, insurers and investment firms, and a range of partner organisations, to understand the impacts of ESG on financial performance and sustainable development (http://www. unep.org/Documents.Multilingual/Default.Print.asp?DocumentID = 593&ArticleID = 6247&l = en; accessed on 23 April 2010).

12. See www.unep.org/Documents.Multilingual/Default.Print.asp?DocumentID = 593&ArticleID = 6247&l and www.unpri.org (accessed on 23 April 2010).

13. Discussed as an option in the Burgmans Report, p. 41. Furthermore, for example, Shell's supervisory board has a CSR Committee chaired by former Dutch Prime Minister Mr Wim Kok; www.shell.com/home/content/aboutshell/ who_we_are/leadership/the_board/board_of_directors_09112006.html; TNT has a 'CR Council'; see www.TNT.com; Rabo bank has a Young Rabo CSR Committee comprising employees from all levels of the organisation; http://www.jongrabo. nl/index.php?option = com_content&view = article&id = 134:spetterende-aftrap-mvo-commissie&catid = 22:verslagen&Itemid = 43; Heineken has installed a 'CSR Advisory Board'. The most important task is to define the main areas of focus for the corporate responsibility agenda and to develop interventions that will lead to improved company performance in these areas. Measuring, benchmarking and stakeholder dialogue all help the CSR Advisory Board to determine their priorities; http://www.heinekeninternational.com/VISION.aspx (all sites accessed on 30 March 2010).

14. This would apply to all large companies including non-listed companies. Kalma also contemplated to propose a Decree as meant in Article 2:391(5) DCC to designate the GRI G3 guidelines as a code of conduct with which large companies have to comply in their annual reporting or in a separate sustainability report ('comply or explain'). So far, the Cabinet has responded negatively to his suggestion. In February 2010, the Cabinet fell. New elections were held in June 2010. It is unclear what will happen to these legislative proposals.

15. Resolution by the Ecumenical Council for Corporate Responsibility, supported by the World Council of Churches and 130 other shareholders.

16. At that time, the Shell directors issued a recommendation to the general meeting to reject the resolution arguing that it was not necessary to adopt the resolution as the Shell board already acted responsibly. The value of the shares that day that did not follow the board recommendation was over £10 billion (ECCR, 2006).

17. The major Dutch pension asset manager APG has indicated that it considers to withhold its vote or to vote for the resolution, depending on whether the critical questions that it submitted to Shell will be answered satisfactorily (*Het Financieele Dagblad*, 2010).

18. Behind the resolutions is a coalition of major investors, NGOs and trade unions, including Co-operative Asset Management, CCLA, Rathbone Greenbank, FairPensions, ECCR, WWF, Greenpeace, Platform and Unison (ECCR, 2010).

19. Legislative proposals of 8, 10 and 15 December 2009. The revision originates from the 2004 Memorandum of Amendments on the modernisation of the corporate law proposed by Minister Donner, the then Minister of Justice (Parl.Doc. 29752(2)).

REFERENCES

Baue, W. (2005). Fiduciary duty redefined to allow (and sometimes require) environmental, social and governance considerations. *SRI News Item*, November 3. Available at http://www.sri-adviser.com/article.mpl?sfArticleId = 1851. Retrieved on 21 March 2010.

Bauer, R. (2008). Verantwoord beleggen: de hype voorbij? [SRI: A hype?] Introductory lecture Faculty of Economics and Business Administration, Maastricht University. Available at http://www.arno.unimaas.nl/show.cgi?fid = 13645. Retrieved on 20 March 2010.

Berendsen, B. (Ed.) (2009). *Emerging global scarcities and powershifts*. Amsterdam: KIT Publishers.

Boeger, N., Murray, R., & Villiers, C. (Eds). (2008). *Perspectives on corporate social responsibility*. Cheltenham, UK: Edward Elgar Publishing. Reviewal by Kasey Lowe (2009). Available at http://www.webjcli.ncl.ac.uk/2009/issue4/pdf/lowe4.pdf. Retrieved on 21 January 2010.

Burgmans. (2008). Commissie Burgmans, *Onderzoeksrapport Geborgd of verborgen, Maatschappelijk Verantwoord Ondernemen in Corporate Governance* [Report on CSR in corporate governance]. Dutch Ministry for Economic Affairs. Available at http://www.ez.nl/Actueel/Kamerbrieven/Kamerbrieven_2008/November_2008/Maatschappelijk_Verantwoord_Ondernemen/Brief_advies_commissie_Brugmans/Advies_Commissie_Burgmans. Retrieved on 15 March 2010.

Bytestart. (2007). Companies Act 2006 and directors duties. Overview. At Bytestart. Available at http://www.bytestart.co.uk/content/legal/35_2/companies-act-directors-duties.shtml. Retrieved on 6 March 2010.

Cheffins, B. R. (2009). Did corporate governance 'fail' during the 2008 stock market meltdown? The case of the S&P 500. Available at http://ssrn.com, May 2009. Retrieved on 7 April 2010.

Chivers, D. (2007). The companies act 2006: Directors' duties guidance. The Corporate Responsibility (CORE) Coalition. Available at http://www.corporateresponsibility.org/wp/wpcontent/uploads/2009/09/directors_guidance_final.pdf. Retrieved on 15 June 2010.

Club of Rome. (2009). *Club of Rome global assembly Amsterdam 2009*. Conference Proceedings. Available at http://www.clubofrome.at/2009/amsterdam/index.html. Retrieved on 31 March 2010.

DASB. (2003). Guide to sustainability reporting (version 2003). Available at www.rjnet.nl/readfile.aspx?ContentID = 51535&ObjectID = 492464&Type = 1&File = 0000025166_HandreikingMVO_Engels.pdf; and DASB, International Visitors. Available at http://www.rjnet.nl/RJ/RJ + Meta/International + visitors/default.aspx. Retrieved on 15 June 2010.

De Bos, A., & Lückerath-Rovers, M. (2009). *Gedragscode voor Commissarissen en Toezichthouders. Discussiedocument* [draft code of conduct for supervisory board members for discussion purposes], Erasmus Instituut Toezicht & Compliance, [Erasmus University Institute for Supervision and Compliance], No. 10.

Decree. (2004). Royal Decree of 23 December 2004. *The Netherlands Bulletin of Acts and Decrees*, 2004/747.

Decree. (2009). Royal Decree of 10 December 2009. *The Netherlands Bulletin of Acts and Decrees*, 2009/545.

Desvaux, G., Devillard-Hoellinger, S., & Baumgarten, P. (2007). *Women matter-gender diversity, a corporate performance driver* (28pp.). Paris: McKinsey & Company, Inc.

de Waard, D. (2008). *Toezicht op Maatschappelijk Verantwoord Ondernemen [supervision on CSR]*. Assen: Van Gorcum.

Douma, K. (2006). Overheid, onderneem eens wat [government: take action]. In: T. Lambooy (Ed.), *Een wereld te winnen. Zestien visies op maatschappelijk verantwoord ondernemen* [16 views on CSR] (p. 52). Alphen a/d Rijn: Kluwer.

DTI. UK Department of Trade and Industry (DTI) guidance on the Bill. Available at http://www.dti.co.uk. Retrieved on 6 March 2010.

ECCR. (2006). Shell shareholder resolution. The Ecumenical Council for Corporate Responsibility. Available at http://www.eccr.org.uk/dcs/ShellShareholderResolution.pdf; and information on http://www.eccr.org.uk/dcs/CoracleShellHague_Aug06.pdf. Retrieved on 2 April 2010.

ECCR. (2010). ECCR to support BP and Shell shareholder resolution on tar sands. News ECCR. Available at http://www.eccr.org.uk/News-article-sid-179.html. Retrieved on 2 April 2010. *ECCR newsletter June 2010*, Available at http://www.eccr.org.uk/dcs/ECCRNewsletter_June10.pdf. Retrieved on 15 June 2010.

EU. (2009). Report of the high-level group on financial supervision in the EU of 25 February. Available at http://www.ec.europa.eu/economyfinance/publications/publication14527_en.pdf. Retrieved on 31 March 2010.

Eumedion. (2010). Position paper on engaged shareholdership. Adopted on 12 March 2010. Available at http://www.eumedion.nl/page/downloads/Position_Paper_Engaged_shareholdership_DEF.pdf. Retrieved on 2 April 2010.

FairPensions. (2010). What FairPensions is doing about tar sands. *News Item*. Available at http://www.fairpensions.org.uk/tarsands. Retrieved on 2 August 2010.

FAO. (2003). *The state of food insecurity in the world 2003* (Available at ftp://ftp.fao.org/docrep/fao/006/j0083e/j0083e00.pdf. Retrieved on 31 March 2010.). Fiduciary II (2009). FAO.

Fiduciary II. (2009). UNEP FI, *Fiduciary responsibility: Legal and practical aspects of integrating environmental, social and governance issues into institutional investment* (Available at http://www.unepfi.org/fileadmin/documents/fiduciaryII.pdf. Retrieved on 23 April 2010).

Freshfields. (2005). *A legal framework for the integration of environmental, social and governance issues into institutional investment* (Available at http://www.unepfi.org/fileadmin/documents/freshfields_legal_resp_2005.pdf. Retrieved on 30 March 2010.). USA: UNEP FI.

Frijns. (2008). Dutch corporate governance code 2008. Available at www.commissiecorporategovernance.nl/page/downloads/DEC_2008_UK_Code_DEF_uk_.pdf. Retrieved on 3 January 2010.

GRI and IFC. (2009). *Embedding gender in sustainability reporting – A practitioner's guide* (Available at http://www.globalreporting.org. Retrieved on 15 June 2010.). Amsterdam, the Netherlands: GRI and IFC.

Havelaar, R. (2010). Commissarissen; zie toe en daag uit. Evaluatieonderzoek naar invoegen Maatschappelijk Verantwoord Ondernemen in Code Corporate Governance. Rol van commissarissen: toezichthouders, adviseurs en aanjagers voor MVO bij beursgenoteerde bedrijven' [research regarding the role of supervisory board members in relation to the incorporation of CSR in the corporate governance code]. Triple Value. Available at http://www.triple-value.com/upload/docs/Zie_toe_en_daag_uit_SAMENVATTING_MASTER_THESIS.pdf. Retrieved on 30 March 2010.

Het Financieele Dagblad [Dutch Financial Times]. (2010). Kritiek APG op Shell Canada. Pensioenbelegger eist duurzame oplossing voor omstreden oliewinning uit teerzanden [critical comments APG on Shell Canada. Pension fund asset manager demands sustainable solution for disputed oil operations concerning tar sands]. *Het Financieele Dagblad*, 19 January 2010.

Hicks, A., & Goo, S. H. (2008). *Cases and materials on company law* (p. 385). Oxford: Oxford University Press.

Huse, M. (2007). *Boards, governance and value creation: The human side of corporate governance*. Cambridge: Cambridge University Press.

Kalma, P. (2008). Voorkeursbeleid: voor of tegen? (2). Ter overname: glazen plafond' [Preferential treatment: In favour or against? Glass ceiling for sale]. S & D, Wiarda Beckman Stichting, The Netherlands, *12*, 48–52.

Kamp-Roelands, N., & Lambooy, T. E. (2008). Maatschappelijk verantwoord ondernemen [CSR]. In: *Het jaar 2007 verslagen. Onderzoek jaarverslaggeving ondernemingen* [the reporting year 2007. Research into corporate annual reporting], NIVRA-No. 78 (pp. 115–143). Deventer: Kluwer.

Kemna, A. G. Z., & Van de Loo, E. L. H. M. (2009). Role of institutional investors in relation to management boards and supervisory directors: A triangular survey. Available at http://www.eumedion.nl/page/downloads/Onderzoeksrapport_DEF_III.pdf. Retrieved on 2 April 2010.

Kirkpatrick, G. (2009). The corporate governance lessons from the financial crisis. OECD Report, *Financial Market Trends*. Available at http://www.oecd.org/dataoecd/32/1/42229620.pdf. Retrieved on 31 March 2010.

Koelemeijer, M. (2005). Naar een Nederlandse gedragscode maatschappelijk verantwoord ondernemen? [Towards a Dutch code of conduct for CSR?]. In: J. J. A. Hamers, et al. (Eds), *Maatschappelijk Verantwoord Ondernemen: Corporate social responsibility in a transnational perspective* (pp. 105–124). Antwerp: Intersentia.

Kotiranta, A., Kovalaine, A., & Rouvinen, P. (2007). Female leadership and firm profitability. *EVA Analysis*, (3). Available at www.eva.fi. Retrieved on 15 June 2010.

Lambooy, T. (2009). Case study: The international CSR conflict and mediation. *Nederlands-Vlaams Tijdschrift voor Mediation en Conflictmanagement [Dutch-Flemish Journal for Mediation and Conflict Management]*, *13*(2), 5–46 and *14*(1), 59–61.

Lambooy, T. E. (2007). Een gedragscode voor maatschappelijk verantwoord ondernemen zoals de Code Tabaksblat voor corporate governance? [A CSR code of conduct like the Tabaksblat Code?]. *INS Web Publication*. Available at http://www.insnet.org/nl/insnl_observations.rxml?id = 3918&photo = 61. Retrieved on 7 March 2010.

Lambooy, T. E., & Rancourt, M. E. (2008). Shell in Nigeria: From human rights abuse to corporate social responsibility. *Human Rights and International Legal Discourse*, *2*(2), 255–259.

Lambooy, T. E., & Rancourt, M. E. (2009). Private regulation: Indispensable for responsible conduct in a globalizing world? In: *Law and globalisation* (pp. 108–110). Saarbrücken: Bocconi School of Law, Milano and VDM Publishing.

Lambooy, T. E., & Van Vliet, N. (2008). Transparency on corporate social responsibility in annual reports. *European Company Law*, *2008*(4), 127–135.

Lückerath-Rovers, M. (2008). *De Nederlandse 'Female board index,' 2007*. Rotterdam: Erasmus Instituut Toezicht en Compliance.

Lückerath-Rovers, M. (2009a). *The Dutch 'Female board index,' 2008*. Rotterdam: Erasmus Instituut Toezicht en Compliance.

Lückerath-Rovers, M. (2009b). *The Dutch 'Female board index' 2009* (Available at http://www.mluckerath.nl/uploads/FemaleBoardIndex2009.pdf. Retrieved on 15 June 2010.). Rotterdam: Erasmus Instituut Toezicht en Compliance.

Maatman, R. H. (2004a). *Het pensioenfonds als vermogensbeheerder.* Deventer: Kluwer.

Maatman, R. H. (2004b). Tabaksblat en de botsende doelstellingen. *Ondernemingsrecht [Corporate Law Journal],* 4, 116–120.

Maatman, R. H. (2007). Prudent-person-regel en verantwoord beleggingsbeleid. *Tijdschrift voor Ondernemingsbestuur [Journal on Company Management],* 6, 177–187.

Mercer. (2006). *Mercer investment consulting. Universal ownership: Exploring opportunities and challenges,* April. Conference Report. Saint Mary's College of California, Canada/USA, pp. 10–11.

Modernisation Directive. (2003). Directive 2003/51/EC of the European Parliament and of the Council of 18 June 2003 amending Directives 78/660/EEC, 83/349/EEC, 86/635/EEC and 91/674/EEC on the annual and consolidated accounts of certain types of companies, banks and other financial institutions and insurance undertakings.

Monitoring. (2009). *First report on compliance with the Dutch corporate governance code.* Corporate Governance Code Monitoring Committee, December 2009. Available at www.commissiecorporategovernance.nl/Information%20in%20English. Retrieved on 2 April 2010.

Parl.Doc. 31083, *Parliamentary Documents II 2009/10,* 31 083 (32)8, (35)6, (83)5 and (88)8, questions MP Paul Kalma to the Dutch Cabinet regarding 'Corporate governance, hedgefondsen en private equity'.

Parl.Doc. 29752(2), *Parliamentary Documents II 2003/04,* 29 752(2).

Parl.Doc. 31763, *Parliamentary Documents II 2008/09,* 31 763.

Parl.Doc. 31746, *Parliamentary Documents II 2008/09,* 31 746.

Parl.Doc. 31877, *Parliamentary Documents II 2008/09,* 31 877.

Parl.Doc. 32014, *Parliamentary Documents II 2008/09,* 32 014.

Pruijm, R. A. M. (2008). Evenwichtig Ondernemingsbestuur: een wensdroom? [Balanced Corporate Governance: A Dream?]. *Introductory lecture Hogeschool Fontys Financieel Management,* pp. 53–58.

Raaijmakers, G. T. M. J. (2009). De financiële markt en het ondernemingsrecht. De behoefte aan lange termijn-waarborgen in het ondernemingsrecht [Financial market and corporate law. The need for long-term guarantees in corporate law]. Introductory lecture Vrije Universiteit Amsterdam. Available at http://www.nautadutilh.com/publicationfiles/16_06_09_Geert%20Raaijmakers_De%20financiele%20markt%20en%20het%20ondernemingsrecht.pdf. Retrieved on 16 March 2010.

Richardson, B. (2010). From fiduciary duties to fiduciary relationships for socially responsible investment. Paper presented at PRI Academic Conference, Copenhagen, 5–7 May 2010. Available at http://www.unpri.org/academic10/Paper_2_Benjamin_Richardson_From%20Fiduciary%20Duties%20to%20Fiduciary%20Relationships%20for%20Socially%20Responsible%20Investment.pdf. Retrieved on 13 June 2010.

SDI. (2005). Sustainable development international. *SDI news item,* November 9. Available at http://www.sustdev.org/index.php?option = com_content&task = view&id = 977&Itemid = 34. Retrieved on 21 March 2010.

SER. (2000). SER advisory report on corporate social responsibility: A Dutch approach' (*De winst van waarden*) of 15 December. Available at http://www.SER.nl. Retrieved on 21 March 2010.

Slagter. (2006). *Ondernemingsrecht*. Deventer: Kluwer.
SOX and NYSE. (2004). US Sarbanes-Oxley Act (Sections 406/407-6) and the 'New York Stock Exchange, NYSE Final Corporate Governance Listing Standards, approved by the Securities and Exchange Commission on 4 November 2003 and amended on 3 November 2004 (Section 303A.10 'Corporate Governance Rules'. Available at www.nyse.com/pdfs/finalcorpgovrules.pdf. Retrieved on 7 April 2010.
Sprengers. (2009). *De toekomst van de medezeggenschap. Aanbevelingen aan de wetgever.* [The Future of Co-Determination. Recommendations to the Legislator]. Deventer: Kluwer.
Structuurwet. (2004). The act on the Dutch large, two-tier board companies of 9 July 2004. *The Netherlands Bulletin of Acts and Decrees*, 2004/370.
Tabaksblat. (2003). Tabaksblat code. Available at http://www.commissiecorporategovernance.nl/page/downloads/CODE%20DEF%20ENGELS%20COMPLEET%20III.pdf. Retrieved on 21 March 2010.
TEEB. (2008). The economics of ecosystem and biodiversity (TEEB): An interim report, 2008. European Communities. Available at http://www.ec.europa.eu/environment/nature/biodiversity/economics/pdf/teeb_report.pdf. Retrieved on 22 May 2010.
TEEB. (2009a). The economics of ecosystem and biodiversity (TEEB): Climate issues update. Available at http://www.teebweb.org/InformationMaterial/TEEBReports/tabid/1278/language/en-US/Default.aspx. Retrieved on 14 June 2010.
TEEB. (2009b). The economics of ecosystem and biodiversity (TEEB): Report for national and international policy makers, 2009. Available at http://www.teebweb.org/ForPolicymakers/tabid/1019/language/en-US/Default.aspx. Retrieved on 2 May 2010.
The Guardian. (2009). French government gender equality plan. *The Guardian*, December 2. Available at http://www.guardian.co.uk/world/2009/dec/02/french-government-gender-equality-plan. Retrieved on 26 January 2010.
UNEP & WCMC. (2010). Global biodiversity outlook, 3rd edn, 10 May 2010 (GBO-3). Available at http://www.unep-wcmc.org/latenews/PressReleaseGeo3.htm. Retrived on 29 October 2010.
Van Schilfgaarde. (2006). *Van de BV en de NV*. Deventer: Kluwer.
Van Tulder, R., & Van der Zwart, A. (2006). *International business-society management: Linking corporate responsibility and globalisation.* London: Routledge Publishing.
VBDO. (2003). Recommendations to the Tabaksblat Committee of 4 September 2003. Vereniging van Beleggers voor Duurzame Ontwikkeling (Association of stockholders for sustainable development). Available at http://www.corpgov.nl/page/downloads/Vereniging%20van%20Beleggers%20voor%20Duurzame%20Ontwikkeling.pdf. Retrieved on 30 March 2010.
Villiers, C. (2009). Enforcement of CSR standards with incentives or sanctions? Paper presented at HiiL law of the future conference. Globalisation, the nation-state and private actors: rethinking public-private cooperation in shaping law and governance. The Hague, 8 and 9 October, Conference Report. Available at http://www.hill.org. Retrieved on 31 March 2010.
Washington Post. (2010). U.S. exempted BP's Gulf of Mexico drilling from environmental impact study. *Washington Post*. May 5. Available at http://www.washingtonpost.com/wp-dyn/content/article/2010/05/04/AR2010050404118.html. Retrieved on 15 June 2010.
World Bank. (2008). Action, resources and results needed now for food crisis, Zoellick says. *World Bank Press release*, June 4. Available at http://www.web.worldbank.org/WBSITE/EXTERNAL/COUNTRIES/LACEXT/EXTLACREGTOPECOPOL/0,.contentMDK:21790151~menuPK:832562~pagePK:34004173~piPK:34003707~theSitePK:832499,00.html. Retrieved on 31 March 2010.

Worldconnectors. (2010). Statement on gender and diversity: Justice and solutions for all: Through gender and diversity. Worldconnectors, March 2010. Available at http://www.worldconnectors.nl/upload/cms/617_NCDO_statement_gender.pdf. Retrieved on 15 June 2010.

WEBSITES

http://www.globalreporting.org. Retrieved on 31 March 2010.

http://www.IUCN.org. Retrieved on 7 April 2010.

http://www.heinekeninternational.com/VISION.aspx. Retrieved on 31 March 2010.

http://www.jongrabo.nl/index.php?option = com_content&view = article&id = 134:spetterende-aftrap-mvo-commissie&catid = 22:verslagen&Itemid = 43. Retrieved on 31 March 2010.

http://www.shell.com/home/content/aboutshell/who_we_are/leadership/the_board/board_of_directors_09112006.html. Retrieved on 31 March 2010.

http://www.tnt.com.

http://www.unep.org/Documents.Multilingual/Default.Print.asp?DocumentID = 593&ArticleID = 6247&l. Retrieved on 31 March 2010.

http://www.unpri.org. Retrieved on 23 April 2010.

WHEN SHOULD COMPANIES VOLUNTARILY AGREE TO STOP DOING THINGS THAT ARE LEGAL AND PROFITABLE BUT 'SOCIALLY USELESS'; AND WOULD THEY EVER?

Colin Fisher

All companies now claim to practice corporate social responsibility (CSR). Different companies quite legitimately justify their claim in different ways. In the absence of a consensus definition of CSR companies can take a pick and mix approach. They may choose any one of, or any combination of, or give varying priority to, the following:

- charitable donations and philanthropy,
- adopting socially responsible business practices,
- avoiding environmental damage and pollution and acting in a sustainable manner,
- engaging in community projects and development,
- involving stakeholders' perspectives in their decision-making and

Reframing Corporate Social Responsibility: Lessons from the Global Financial Crisis
Critical Studies on Corporate Responsibility, Governance and Sustainability,
Volume 1, 181–205
Copyright © 2010 by Emerald Group Publishing Limited
All rights of reproduction in any form reserved
ISSN: 2043-9059/doi:10.1108/S2043-9059(2010)0000001014

- having their activities audited for a responsible approach to social, environmental and ethical issues by signing up to an appropriate assurance standards

Quazi and O'Brien (2000) have produced a two-by-two model that identifies the range of choices for implementing CSR that are logically available to a company. Each option represents a different combination of items from the list shown above. Using the two dimensions of, firstly, whether a company sees CSR as a source of profitability or cost; and secondly whether a company takes a broad or narrow view of its ethical, social and environmental obligations, they identified four broad approaches. The first of these is the classical view which takes a minimalist view of CSR. The second, philanthropic, view accepts that companies have a responsibility to the wider society and that this will create costs for them. The socio-economic approach is the third stance that assumes that by taking some action on social, ethical and environmental issues the company can save costs and prevent damage to intangible assets such as brand reputation. The fourth position that is termed the modern view is that by accepting its broad CSR responsibilities and company will prosper both financially and in terms of enhancing its reputation.

The factor analysis carried out by Quazi and O'Brien (2000, pp. 48–49) suggested that generally only two positions, the classical or the modern, were actually taken by managers in companies. The choice made in a company between these two options reflects, inter alia, the extent to which they either seek to embed social and ethical considerations into their decision-making and operations or see CSR as a defensive legal and public relations activity.

In Quazi and O'Brien's work the two positions on CSR are identified from a factor analysis of an attitude survey of managers. This is helpful, but a test that uses a company's strategic decisions to identify which of these two positions is taken would also be beneficial. Such a test for a corporation could be similar to the 'career anchors' test that Schein (1992) proposes for an individual's core values. Schein argues that it is difficult for a person to decide which of the values they hold in daily life are truly important to them. Such a core value, or career anchor, is one for which a person would rather sacrifice their job, or suffer some other serious disadvantage, than offend against. He further argues that a person only finds out what their careers anchors are when faced by a challenging dilemma that forces then to chose their core values. A similar test would propose that a company takes ethical and social responsibility seriously when it is prepared to suffer some loss or disadvantage rather than offend against some ethical principle or standard. Faced by serious social or ethical harm would a company see its financial performance as its anchor or would it be prepared to accept lower profits in order to limit the harms being done. In the terms that will be used in this chapter the test would be whether a company was willing to change its core business model because of ethical or social considerations. The more it is willing to do so the more could it be said to be corporately socially responsible.

Three levels of response can be identified to gauge how far a company is willing to change its business model. These levels are conventional in that they represent a simplification of the many nuances of position that a company could adopt when its business model comes under social or ethical criticism. The three levels are:

- If a company is willing to adjust or even begin to abandon, its business model because the model creates or makes worse social or ethical harms, even though this might reduce profitability in the short term, then such a company can be said to exhibit an embedded sense of corporate responsibility.
- If it is not prepared to change it business model but is willing to take actions to limit the harms or wrongs caused by it basic business activity then it may be said to practice palliative social responsibility.
- If it is not prepared to either adjust its business model or to ameliorate its effects then it cannot be said to be socially responsible, no matter what other good works or care it takes.

In this chapter I have proposed a normative debating scheme that a company could use when deciding how to respond to ethical and social challenges to its business model. In doing so I am making a major assumption that companies do, or would wish to, use open and transparent discussion and debate when making such decisions. The literature on discourse ethics of course says that they should do (Zakhem, 2008). The notion that decisions are best made by debate between proponents of opposing views, who use their rhetorical skills to win a debate, stems from the classical world. Modern philosophers such as Habermas (Outhwaite, 1994) have considered how discourse can set a framework of standards and values within which issues can be resolved. However, the normative demands of philosophy are in contrast to sociologists' empirical findings that decisions may be made heuristically, intuitively, politically, self-interestedly and by a closed caucus. A preliminary test of whether a company has embedded CSR in its decision-making would be whether it was prepared to openly debate the issues; irrespective of whether the debate did or did not lead to change in its business model.

This chapter proposes a normative model and use two case studies to show how it might be applied. One of the case studies will be the industry that manufactures and sells alcoholic drinks. There have been two recent challenges to its business models that have arisen out of concern about the rates of alcoholism and binge drinking in the United Kingdom. One challenge is that the industry should stop advertising, much as in the way that tobacco advertising has been banned. The second challenge has been the demand for minimum pricing for alcohol. The way that the industry has responded to these challenges will be considered. The second case will be the structured financial products (STPs), which were at the root of the global financial crisis, and which Lord Turner (BBC, 2009a) called 'socially useless products'. He demanded that banks should voluntarily cease trading in these products even though they were legal and could be very profitable.

CORE BUSINESS MODELS

The term business model is a phrase that is loosely used but in this chapter it will be given a temporarily fixed definition. Magretta (2002) likens a business model to a story that explains what a company does to make a profit. The plot of the story is how all the characters in the story, the employees, the customers, the suppliers interact to produce a product or service that the customers are willing to pay for at a price that is profitable. Like a good short story a good business model has a 'twist' or an unexpected sting in the tail. Johnson, Christensen, and Kagermann (2008) illustrate this by the way that Apple's business model for the iPod involved providing cheap downloads in order to lock customers into purchasing the hardware. In other market sectors, such as white goods, the twist is the reverse, the products are sold cheaply in order to realise profit on adjunct services such as insurance and maintenance contracts.

Just as a story has several components, such as characters, plot, scene, so a business model has its constituent parts. Schweizer (2005, pp. 41–42) identifies four elements:

• The network of organisations involved in the flow of activities that generate the service or the product; this is the narrative stream of the business model story.

- The relationship between the organisations and entities in the network in relation to innovation and ownership of intellectual property rights: this is the plot of the story.
- The revenue generating model, how is revenue to be generated; this is the conclusion of the story.
- The people and resources needed to operate the business model; these are the characters in the story.

The business model is therefore fundamental to the functioning of an organisation. It is what it does and why it does it.

THE DEBATING SCHEME

What questions should companies ask themselves when debating whether they should modify their business models to respond to social and ethical issues? A debating scheme is proposed in this chapter that would provide a framework for managers to discuss the ethical issues that surround this issue. The debating scheme is presented as a flow chart (Fig. 1). First the structure and nature of the scheme will be explained and secondly it will be used to explore the two case studies.

Academics frequently recommend dialogue as a way of business decision-making (Ungvari-Zrinyi, 2003). There is a rather more restricted record of such techniques actually being used in organisations. There are some examples however. Steinmann and Lohr (quoted in Preuss, 1999, p. 414) applied forms of debates based on impartiality, non-coercion, non-persuasiveness and expertise in some German companies. Levi-Strauss has trained its managers in a dialogue process designed by Toulmin and Brown to help in resolving ethical dilemmas. This process begins by indentifying principles shared by all the parties to the issue and using these agreed norms to reach a new position on the problem (French & Albright, 1998, p. 192). Hamilton, Knousse, and Hill (2009) developed a model for aiding decision-making in cases of inter-cultural conflicts of values. This model was based around six questions and was a development of an earlier four question model. They reported that the earlier model (Hamilton et al. 2009, p. 145) had been used for ethical decision-making in a number of companies.

The scheme presented in this model shares with these other decision-making tools a heuristic purpose. It is not intended to lead a manager algorithmically to a definitive and authoritative solution to an issue but

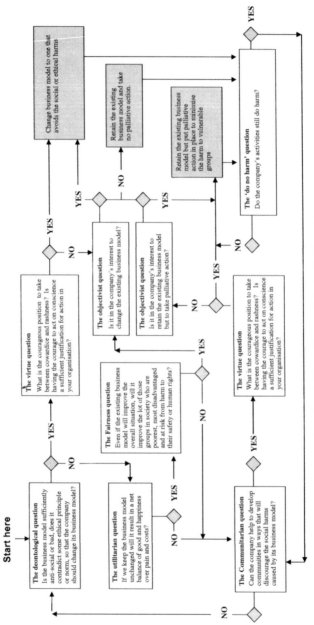

Fig. 1. A Flow Chart of the Debating Scheme.

rather to act as an aide memoire that prods the user into looking at the issue from a number of different perspectives.

The existence of different standpoints from which ethical issues can be viewed is at the heart of the problem of creating aids or tools for ethical decision-making. It is often pointed out that there are a range of different ethical theories that can be brought to bear on a problem and that they do not all necessarily lead to the same conclusion (Petrick & Quinn, 1997). The cynical response to this situation might be to just pick the one set of theories that it is hoped will lead to the solution that is intuitively wished for. This might lead to a 'fanatical rush to judgement' to use Petrick and Quinn's phrase (1997, p. 63). Such an approach might well meet the internal organisational demand for decisiveness but, if the issue is both fundamental and important it will not silence the voices of critical stakeholder groups who might see the issue from contrary ethical points of view. A scheme for guiding ethical debate should therefore seek to incorporate a breadth of ethical perspectives and try to bring the different approaches into some kind of commonality.

The scheme proposed in this chapter tries to do this in two ways. First, it assumes that all of the ethical perspectives have some contribution that they can bring to the debate and that they can be ordered in a sequence, such that some perspectives are adjuncts or supplementary to others. The different ethical perspectives are not seen as independent of each other but are connected in a logical sequence of linked questions. The second way in which the potential for contradiction between ethical viewpoints is handled is to create a scheme which has no definitive conclusion but one in which a provisional resolution of an issue simply acts as a starting point for further rounds of debate. This reflects the situation in many organisations in which periods of decision and action are followed by periods of aporia and uncertainty. I will consider this second point first.

Acceptance of ethical ambiguity is unusual in organisations. Organisational leaders often prefer to present ethical issues as clear cut choices between right and wrong, and to diminish the perception of moral grey areas between such extremes. Bruhn (2008, p. 211) proposes instead that,

> learning to live with gray areas and having dialogue about them opens up leaders and their organizations to new opportunities.

This argument points out that moral uncertainty is inevitable and it should not be hidden behind a façade of take it or leave it options. Rather managers should learn that recognising grey areas, and managing them well, can be beneficial for organisations. Mounce (1997, pp. 185–189) noted, the importance of keeping the conversation going. If there is no definitive solution to be discovered then it is necessary to keep the debate going and not to lapse into cynicism. As Gustafson (2000, pp. 652–654) expresses it people thinking about ethical problems need to conduct a 'tempered quest' that continually strives, regardless of the knowledge that the quest is indefinite.

Let us return to the matter of the sequencing of the ethical perspectives. In the debating scheme the discussion begins with a deontological question that asks whether 'the business model is sufficiently anti-social or bad that the company should change its business model'. This question implies a principled position from which the morality of a situation should be judged against fixed principles; and then, as in the Roman law maxim used by Lord Mansfield in 1772 'let justice be done though the heavens fall'. Principled approaches are unbending and whether the question results in a positive or a negative answer there are follow-up questions that emerge that set the principled answer in some kind of real life context.

If it is decided that a company's business model is socially or ethically unacceptable then it is necessary to ask whether the managers of that company have the courage to act according to principle even though the heavens may then fall, in the form of a loss of profitability. This question is a matter of virtue ethics as courage is one of the classical virtues. Like all virtues courage is a mean position between extremes, in this case of rashness and cowardice. So the virtue ethics question asks people to consider whether to refuse to act on principle is simply a result of cowardice or whether a rush to change the offending businesses model would be rash. If the managers within the organisation are courageous enough to act on principle then they would proceed to modify the business model.

It would be quite likely however that arguments of virtue would not determine a company's strategy or business model. In this case it is necessary to ask whether it would be in the company's interest to change the business model; in short could a business case be made for change? This question comes from an ethical position known as objectivism. This is the philosophy of the American novelist Ayn Rand. Her thinking is perhaps more influential in the United States than it is in the United Kingdom or in Europe. Her view was that people are rational and objective beings who know what their best interests are and should be encouraged and allowed to follow their own best interests as long as they do not harm the interests of others. If transposed from individuals to corporations (a move Rand would probably disapprove of) this approach encourages them to concentrate on their corporate best interests, or perhaps for managers to see corporations as vehicles for attaining their personal best interests. If the business model is one that generates good rates of return then it might seem foolish to change the model. Except, if the social or ethical harm that flows from the business model has a high public profile it might damage the value of the company's brand image. Reputations, and brands, are seen as important intangible contributors to the value of a company and any damage to them might be seen as a threat to long-term profitability.

An alternative sequence of questions develops if the answer to the initial deontological question is negative. This new sequence begins with a question based on utilitarian ethics. This asks whether in aggregate the company's business model creates more pleasure than pain, more good than harm. Good in this context is not taken simply to mean what is good for the company in the short term. The evaluation of pleasures and pains has to take into account the external impact of the company on the wider society and environment and to consider these effects over the long term.

The question subsequent to a positive answer to the utilitarian question is based on Rawls' (1999) theory of justice, which can be viewed as an adjunct of utilitarianism (Wolff, 2006). Wolff defines 'unfortunate circumstances' which includes situations in which 'true odds' do not hold, so that certain groups in society (the poor for instance) lose out in society more often than others (the educated for example). In such a circumstance he argues that policy should be assessed in two waves. The first wave is utilitarian to identify the greatest overall good and if the overall assessment is positive, the second wave is Rawlsian that checks to see if the worst off in society are being further damaged. This is what the debating scheme does.

Rawls focuses on a concern, not just for the balance of the total harms and goods caused by an action, but also with the distribution of those consequences between different groups in the population. In particular he proposes a principle that inequalities in society are only justified if removing them would *not* improve the position of the most disadvantaged in society; or indeed would make it worse. If we use the example of structured financial products then their continued use would only be justified by Rawls' difference principle if their abolition would not improve the lot of the worst off in society.

If the business model is thought to do harm, either in aggregate or to particular disadvantaged groups then a question based on communitarian ethics has to be asked – Can the company help to develop communities in ways that will discourage or diminish the social harms caused by its business model. A negative answer to this question returns the debate to the starting point to enquire whether the business model is unethical and therefore causes the company to reconsider its business model. A positive answer to the communitarian question then leads to a now familiar sequence of questions. First it is asked whether the company has the courage to act, simply because something is the right thing to do (the virtue ethics question) and if not, then to ask whether there is a business case for taking those same actions (the objectivist question).

The sequence of questions in the debating scheme leads to one of the three options.

- Change the company's business model so that no social or ethical harms are caused.
- Keep the business model but take palliative actions that are designed to diminish or mitigate the harms caused by the business plan.
- Keep the business model and take no palliative action.

Whichever action is recommended it cannot be the end of the debate. Each action then raises what I have called the 'do no harm question'. This is an ancient ethical principle – in Latin, *primum non nocere* – firstly do no harm, which requires that even if they cannot do good people have a minimum responsibility to do no harm. Whichever action a company has taken therefore it should consider whether as a result it is doing harm. Like all ethical questions the answer given depends on resolving supplementary questions. Does, for example, the question only concern harm directly caused by the company's actions or does it include indirect harm; is, for example, a cigarette manufacturer responsible for the indirect harm caused by passive smoking when people freely choose to smoke their products? If the answer to the 'do no harm' question is 'yes' than the debating scheme directs the discussion back to the starting place.

The debating scheme will now be applied to the two case studies and an attempt will be made to surmise how those in the industries would respond to the questions it poses.

ADVERTISING BANS AND MINIMUM PRICING IN RELATION TO ALCOHOLIC BEVERAGES

The social problems that can arise from excessive and binge drinking of alcohol are currently a matter of public debate. There is no question that the social harms are significant in terms of the damage to individuals' health, the consequent costs to the National Health Service and the problems of anti-social behaviour that drunkenness can cause. In one survey (BBC, n.d.) nearly 40% of men and 15% of women said they binge drank on at least one night a week; although consumption of alcohol in excess of the recommended guidelines diminishes as people grow older. The number of hospital admissions where alcohol was diagnosed as a cause increased from 147,659 in 2003–2004 to 193,637 in 2006–2007. A Cabinet Office (2003) report estimated the costs of alcohol misuse in 2001, the year studied, as between £18 billion and £20 billion.

Few call for prohibition and abstinence. There is a recognition that much pleasure and social benefit can be had from alcohol. It is also generally accepted that an individual has a choice about whether to drink to excess and that it would be wrong to punish the majority, by prohibition, because of the choices of a minority. One expression of this position arose when McDonalds were sued in a New York court by two obese teenagers who claimed that they were fat because they had eaten too many of McDonalds' products. The judge stated that as long as the company provided sufficient nutritional information and did nothing to encourage people to eat excessively then it was not liable for the consequences of customers' personal choices. Only if the company encouraged customers to eat more than was sensible would there be 'proximate cause' to sue the company for damages (United States District Court, Southern District of New York, 2003).

There is a debate about whether the companies that manufacture and retail alcoholic beverages encourage consumers to consume alcohol excessively and irrationally through their business models. Although it is wrong to assume that all the companies in the industry have the same business model there are some commonalities in those adopted by many companies. The key is sales volume growth achieved by a number of means.

- Expanding the volume of channels, as seen in the relaxing of licensing regulations and the expansion of supermarket sales.
- Advertising of the products. The 2006 advertising campaign for Magners cider for instance led to an increase in sales of 225%. (Though sales dropped the following year as bad weather and competition from cheaper ciders had an impact (Ruddock & Siburn, 2008)). A report (Ofcom, 2007) identified that there had been a large increase in TV advertising slots for cider and that the popularity of cider amongst young people had increased.
- Developing new products that are sweeter and hence more palatable to those as yet unused to alcohol. Some companies however have voluntarily

ceased selling some drinks that were too sweet or too strong (Smithers, 2008; McGuiness, 2008).
- Competitive pricing and up-selling (large glass of wine for the price of a small one for example) promotions.

Such business models are claimed by some to make the problems of alcohol abuse and binge drinking worse. These concerns for instance have led to the British Medical Association calling for a ban on advertising of alcoholic beverages (Triggle, 2009) and the government's Medical Officer, among others, (BBC, 2009b) calling for a minimum price for alcohol that is intended to discourage excessive drinking. Such demands challenge the basic business model of many alcohol producing and retailing companies. The particular demands of an end to advertising and a minimum price for a unit of alcohol are probably matters of public policy and could only be implemented through legislation. Nevertheless the question arises therefore whether companies within the industry should decide to modify their business models that currently emphasise competitive advantage through pricing and advertising.

How might companies in the alcoholic beverage manufacturing and retail businesses debate these issues about advertising and minimum pricing, using the debating scheme? They would mostly answer the starting, deontological question by saying 'No', the business model does not transgress any ethical principle and so it is not necessary to change its business models by adopting a minimum price or banning advertising. They would support this position by pointing out that the decision to drink excessively is an individual decision made by consumers. To punish the many responsible consumers of alcohol for the foolish decisions of the few would be improper. Although they might not invoke Kant's categorical imperative its two provisions might lie behind their arguments. To base their business model on the wrong-headedness of some individuals would contradict the maxim that an ethical decision should be based on a principle that applies universally. Actions designed to deal with the particular circumstances of an unconventional minority are not universalisable. They would also claim that their actions do not break Kant's other maxim that people should be treated as persons in themselves and not simply as means to others' ends, which would be the case if they encouraged customers to drink excessively. They would argue that they encourage consumers to enjoy alcoholic drinks responsibly. They would also argue, as does Diageo (2009, pp. 7–8), that it runs campaigns to encourage responsible drinking. To complaints that its marketing encourages excessive alcohol consumption it argues that its advertising is only intended to encourage people to buy Diageo brands rather than competitors' brands and to encourage the people to buy more expensive, higher margin products. It does not, they claim, encourage people to drink more or to drink to excess. They also point out that they adhere to a number of external standards about alcohol advertising such as the Portman group (2008) voluntary code that prohibits, inter alia, appealing to the under 18s, associating alcoholic beverages with bravado, dangerous behaviour, anti-social behaviour and sexual success. The company also has to comply with the Advertising Standards Authority's rules (ASA, 2005) for broadcast advertising of alcoholic drinks. The social harms to the minority of its customers, the industry argues are the consequence of many social and individual factors and are not the simple result of alcohol availability. It follows therefore that the responsibility for dealing with the problems are shared between private companies, public organisations and local communities.

If the answer to the deontological question is 'No' then the debating schemes brings us to the utilitarian question. This is a tough one to answer with any certainty. As we have seen from the Cabinet Office Report (2003) the social and economic cost of alcohol are between £18 billion and £20 billion. This has to be offset against the turnover of the industry of about £30 billion in 2001 (Institute of Alcohol Studies, n.d.). Of course utilitarian ethics are not simply concerned with financial costs and benefits. It is concerned with pleasure and pain and therefore to the financially measurable items in the balance sheet have to be added the individual pleasures and agonies that drink can bring. Bentham (1982) argued that the intensity of pleasure or pain should be part of the felicific calculus. It is a calculation, impossible to make, where small amounts of pleasure by a large minority may outweigh the intense pains of a minority. Even taking into account that alcoholism and alcohol related illness may be more intense than the pleasures of social drinking it may be that the answer to the utilitarian question is 'yes'. Another weakness of utilitarian thinking is that it is based on forecasts of what the consequences of a particular action might be. And forecasts are often wrong. There is a debate between the health professionals and the drinks industry as to whether raising the price of a unit of alcohol does lead to a reduction in binge drinking amongst those groups most prone to it (BBC, 2010). The industry can therefore mount an argument that changing their business models would not, of itself, reduce the pains that arise from excessive drinking.

A positive answer to the utilitarian question identifies one of the criticisms made of this consequentialist approach to ethics. The criticism is that utilitarianism pays no regard to the equity of the distribution of pleasures and pains between different groups in society; it is only concerned with the aggregate balance between them. The next question to be asked therefore is the fairness question. Does the industry's business model improve the lot of the worst off groups in society? The answer to this question is probably 'no'. The poorest and the most vulnerable groups in society tend to have higher rates of alcoholism than other classes. One study found that amongst men the less well educated and those in unskilled occupations were up to three times more likely than those with higher qualifications and professional jobs to binge drink up to early middle age. The pattern was different amongst women. Better educated professional women in the early twenties were more likely to binge drink than their less well educated and occupied contemporaries. The pattern changed as women reached their 30s and those in unskilled manual jobs were more likely to binge drink. Generally the young binge drink more often than older people (Institute of Alcohol Studies n.d., pp. 7–8). Those too young to drink legally sometimes binge drink. In one survey a quarter of children in year 8 reported binge drinking within the past 4 weeks (Communities that Care, 2002).

It can be argued that competition in the alcoholic beverages market is based on price and this has tended to drive the prices of drinks down. The bar and pub companies have laid much of the blame for this on the supermarkets who often use cheap alcohol as a loss leader. An argument can be made that cheap alcohol makes alcohol more affordable to the most vulnerable groups in society, the less well educated, the young and those in unskilled jobs, who have the greatest propensities to binge drink. This indeed is the rationale behind the demands for a minimum price for alcohol. It might appear to be a paternalistic response; and indeed it may be so, because there has always been an element of authoritarianism, requiring a strong state to force people to behave better, in consequentialist ethical approaches such as utilitarianism (Fisher & Lovell, 2009, p. 137). The answer to the fairness question is likely to be 'Yes'.

This then raises an interesting problem for companies in the industry. Overall their activities may do more good than harm but certain disadvantaged groups suffer from them. It might be excessive in such a situation to expect a company to radically change its business model; for example by ceasing to trade in alcohol and develop other products. But palliative action that diminishes the harms to the vulnerable groups might be an option.

The next question therefore is the communitarian one; can the company take actions that will support and develop communities and thereby reduce the harms that arise from excessive alcohol consumption. The answer to this question is positive because many companies in the industry do take such action. Wetherspoon for example is part of the Portman group which is an industry body set up to promote responsible drinking and it encourages all its pub managers to join a local Pubwatch scheme, and if there is not one in existence then to form one. PubWatch is groups of licensees who band together to identify and take action against people who cause or threaten damage, disorder, violence, use or deal in drugs in their premises or are a general nuisance. They normally use a communication system to keep each other informed so that a person who is ejected from one pub cannot simply go to the pub next door and get served. Wetherspoon also implements the 'Challenge 21' programme to discourage under age drinking by asking those who might look to be under age to provide identification. Though Tim Martin the chairman of Wetherspoon has argued that the Police's habit of using school children as agents provocateurs to entrap pub staff into selling them alcohol, and the Government's policy of removing the license of pubs that had been caught selling drinks to those too young to drink, is unethical and excessive (Martin, 2010).

A company may decide to adopt palliative actions because they wish to behave in a virtuous manner. They would do this by asking themselves whether their conscience about the harm caused is enough to decide it to take palliative action. Put into a more typical virtue ethic form the company would have to decide where the sensible mean position exists between the extremes of recklessness (threatening the viability of the company in an attempt to minimise harms) and timidity (not willing to take any action to mitigate the mal-effects of its actions). Wetherspoon has on one occasion has almost been reckless in its concern for behaving in a socially responsible manner. Before the ban on smoking in pubs began the company unilaterally declared 49 of its pubs smoke zones. It consequently saw a loss of sales in those pubs and stopped its programme of rolling out the ban to all its pubs (Blitz, 2006). By that time it was known that the government was going to make smoking in pubs illegal and so it was sensible to wait until there would be no competitive disadvantage to having a smoking ban in its pubs. Indeed this is one of the problems faced when companies considering acting virtuously by, for example, deciding to cease advertising its products. If an alcoholic drinks manufacturer or retailer decided that advertising was encouraging people to binge drink and decided to cease advertising then they would be at an immediate competitive disadvantage because its competitors would in all likelihood continue to advertise. The alternative would be an agreement between all the companies in the industry to cease advertising, or to apply a minimum price to alcoholic beverages, but this would be cartel like behaviour and would be illegal under competition law.

A company, or more accurately a sufficient number of managers within it, do not need courage to undertake the same level and type of palliative actions that all the other companies in the industry take. A similar range of palliative actions is in fact taken by nearly all the companies in the industry. The virtue of courage is only needed to do more than the norm for the industry. Of course when a company decides to act virtuously this does not exclude the possibility that there may be an advantage to the company of so acting. In some cases they may adopt palliative actions because they believe it is in the self-interest of the company to do so. This brings us to the objectivist question in the debating scheme.

The objectivist question is presented in two forms in the debating scheme, one asks whether the introduction of palliative measures is the company's best interest but the other, reached through a positive response to the 'deontological question', is whether it would be in a company's best interest to change its core business model. There are a number of reasons why a company might see changing its business model to remove ethical or social harms as in it own best interests. The most obvious one would be the 'business case' that it will result in greater profitability, especially in the long run; other reasons might be more defensive. They might consider that the potential harm to company's reputation and brands may be sufficient to damage its income.

It is hard without having detailed case study evidence to know why a company changes its core business model but there is at least one possible instance of a company changing a business model that was ethically suspect. Whitbread was founded by Samuel Whitbread who began brewing beer in 1742. By the end of the nineteenth century it had become a major brand with a large brewery in Chiswell Street, London. In the 1990s it began to change its business model through diversification and acquisition. It became a leisure and hospitality company as well as a brewer and pub chain. The mainstays of the conglomerate were the budget hotels business and the Costa coffee retailer. It then moved out of the beer business entirely by selling the brewery in 2000 and the pubs in 2001. It still retained pub restaurants and with the disposal of a number of its businesses such as the David Lloyd gyms its business model became a location with a budget hotel alongside one of its pub restaurants (Stevenson & Groves, 2005; Sharkey, 2008; Whitbread, n.d.). The changes in the model were associated with the Chief Executive Alan Parker who took over the role in 2004. Whitbread moved out of the alcoholic beverage business. It would seem that the change was based on a business case rather than a concern for the social and ethical harms arising from manufacturing and retailing beer. Certainly Parker made it clear that his strategy was designed to improve returns to shareholders (Stevenson & Groves, 2005) and he was ruthless in selling off businesses within the group that were under-performing. It was probable that the long-term decline in beer sales and in the habit of drinking in pubs that led to Whitbread's change in business model.

SELLING STRUCTURED FINANCIAL PRODUCTS (SFPS)

The debating scheme will now be used to consider the second case study. As we have seen Lord Turner has suggested that structured financial products are anti-social and that the banks should consider changing their business models and cease trading in them. But before we use the debating scheme to consider this proposal it is necessary to explain why the products might be considered anti-social.

The technique underlying structured financial products is asset securitisation which is used to create a liquid, saleable asset from future streams of revenue. Some rock bands for example have securitised the future earnings from their songs. Two examples of SFPs are asset backed securities (ABS) and mortgage backed securities (MBS). ABS are based on income streams other than mortgage repayments, it could be rental income for example. I will however explain the technique of securitisation using MBS. Let us imagine a bank makes a number of mortgage loans. It's not content just to collect the income from those mortgages; it wants to raise more money to sell more mortgages. So it sets up a special investment vehicle (SIV) and it sells a pool of the mortgages to the SIV. If the transfer can be accounted for as a sale of the assets to the SIV then the transfers are taken off the balance sheet of the originating company. This protects the mortgage assets from bankruptcy claims; if the originating bank goes bust then their creditors cannot claim on the mortgage assets in the SIV. This makes the pooled mortgages safer for investors. The SIV raises the money to buy the mortgages by issuing securities based on the mortgages. These securities are credit rated by the rating companies. Now here comes the magic. By credit enhancement the securities achieve a higher credit rating than that of the original mortgages. How is this achieved? It is basically done by pooling risk and using complex mathematical models to calculate the subsequent level of risk. Let us assume the probability of a loan default is 10%. If I loan someone £100 k I have a 10% chance of losing it all. But If I buy a £100 k share in a £1,000 k pool of mortgages when 10% of that large pool defaults I will only lose a tenth of my investment of £100 instead of all of it. Some securitisations add to the credit enhancement by third party guarantees. Anyway the upshot is that the rating agencies will give these securities a higher credit rating than that of the underlying mortgages taken individually. The constructors of the structured product then make it more sophisticated by dividing the pools into tranches. There are normally three tranches, a senior tranche, which gets the lowest return but also has the lowest risk, a mezzanine and a junior (or equity) tranche. The equity tranche gets the highest return but the entire investment has a higher risk of being lost. Again this means that the senior tranche get an even higher credit rating. The banks can also take out, what is in effect, an insurance policy to protect against default on the underlying assets. Another way of hedging against credit default risk is 'pure' credit derivatives such as a Credit Default Swop (CDS). In a CDS the originator of the loan retains their relationship with the borrower and collects the regular income from the debt; but they get rid of the associated credit risk by paying the protection seller periodic premium payments and in return the protection seller bears the risk of a default.

A collateralised debt obligation (CDO) is a method of asset securitisation, similar to ABS and MBS. But a CDO is one step up the pyramid because it is constructed from other financial derivatives. So CDOs can be based on ABS, MBS or CDS. There are also CLOs based on loans and CBOs based on bonds. It is worth noting that the pool of instruments that the CDO is based on is actively managed and there are parameters that the manager of the CDO has to work within. Synthetic CDOs are based on the premiums that come in from the sale of credit protection (CDS) on a set of reference assets (but not from the assets themselves). You can then have a further step up the pyramid when you have 'pools of pools' i.e. CDOs of CDOs. These are CDOs squared and there can even be CDOs cubed.

The danger inherent in these products became clear during the financial crisis of 2008. The mortgage assets on which the structured financial products were based were sub-prime which means that the risk of default was great. The construction of the CDOs appeared to reduce and minimise the risk. Risk was apparently reduced by spreading, pooling and insuring the risk; but these techniques only worked if the underlying mortgage assets were independent of each other; so that default on one mortgage did not increase the risk of default on all the others. In fact the risks of default on sub-prime mortgages were highly interrelated. If one mortgage defaulted it was likely that many others would; so that pooling, or slicing and dicing, would not protect against the risk. This problem was exacerbated by the pyramidal structure of the products in the market. As we have seen new levels of CDOs could be built on existing ones. A failure of CDOs at the base level of the pyramid of SFPs would have knock on effects for the multiplicity of CDOs built on it.

From this discussion the key elements of the banks' business models for structured financial products can be discerned. They are:

- rapid product innovation, with;
- the new products based on complex mathematical models and algorithms;
- and the exploitation of the information and data flows available through companies trading and client information systems and
- complex cross interests between the banks' roles as constructors of SFPs, sellers of SFPs, adviser to its clients and a trader with its own and its clients' money.

When the bubble burst in the first quarter of 2008/2009 the level of losses suffered by the banks and the impact of these on the banks' balance sheets nearly brought a collapse to the global banking system. The social danger was that the losses of the investment and trading activities of the banks threatened the survival of the day-to-day banking services (payments and money transfer, personal loans, loans to businesses and so on) that all societies need to function.

How would the discussions go if the banks were to use the debating scheme to argue about whether they should change their business models to exclude structured financial products? The first question to ask is the deontological one. Whether selling structured financial products broke some ethical principle partly depended upon whether those who constructed and sold them were being honest. The as yet untested allegations against Goldman Sachs, that it knowingly sold purchasers products that they knew would fail and indeed thought it would be in the best interests of other clients if they did fail, suggest that in some cases at least the vendors of the financial products were deceiving their customers. If this was so then this would be a clear breach of moral standards. If there was no deception then no ethical principle is transgressed and it is simply a matter of the purchasers accepting the maxim of caveat emptor, buyer beware, especially where the purchasers were banks and investment companies who might be considered 'sophisticated' purchasers.

Let us assume for the moment that banks considered that there was a potential conflict of interest when they used their own money to speculate on markets and products that could benefit some of their clients and disadvantage others. This would lead to a positive answer to the deontological question. They would then have to consider the virtue question and decide whether as a matter of principle they should cease proprietary trading. However, thinking in such a virtuous manner would require moral imagination and this may not be a feature of the financial industry. Werhane (1999) proposed a series of necessary elements for the practice of moral imagination. First an individual needs to have a particular concern over some issue or harm. However, traders in structured financial products tended to assume that their customers are sophisticated players well aware of the risks in the markets and so if they were suffering it must be their own faults. The trader need have no conscience if other traders lose from a deal. Secondly a sympathetic understanding of the views, values and emotions of others is required. Within markets such sympathy would take the form of schadenfreude and others failures would simply reinforce the traders' sense of their own infallibility. Consequently the third requirement of moral imagination, surfacing the assumptions and mental models that trading behaviours are based upon would be superfluous. If the financial collapse was not their fault why would traders and financial managers have to challenge these assumptions? Indeed financial managers seem to be resisting challenges such as the idea of a Tobin tax or separating utility and speculative banking. As the initial stages of moral imagination are not present within the industry then also absents must be the final stages of envisioning, imaging, new behaviours being enacted and finally creating a new social consensus. Bankers just want the situation to return to normal and so are pleased with the recent large profitability of the investment arms of banks. It would seem unlikely therefore that thinking virtuously will lead bankers to drop socially dangerous products from their business models.

Assuming that moral imagination is lacking within the financial industry the answer to the virtue question would probably be 'No'. In which case the next question is the objectivist one. This would cause the debate to move to whether it was in the best interests of a bank to cease trading in structured financial products. This would be a hard decision for banks to make as, since the crisis, they have to rebuild their balance sheets; and the profits they are currently making from their investment arms are required for that task. This route through the debating scheme would in all likelihood lead to a retention of existing business models.

If we revert to the point in the discussion where we were considering the deontological question; a negative answer to it would lead to the utilitarian question. Does trading in structured financial products overall do more good than harm? It is clear that for a time this market increased wealth particularly in financial centres such as London. The traders and bankers did well from bonuses and the UK Treasury benefited from increased tax revenues. But the calculation of utility does not just focus on the short term and whilst bubbles create wealth while they expand this is more than countered by the costs when the bubble bursts. What is more these costs were not just borne by the banks, the bulk of them were borne by governments. Which in turn means higher tax burdens on all in a country and public service cuts that harm the disadvantaged most. From a long-term perspective therefore it might be considered that the markets for structured financial products do not result in a net balance of good and happiness over pain and cost.

This negative answer would lead, in the debating scheme, to the communitarian question. The financial services industry can, and does, like the alcoholic beverages industry act philanthropically and support all kinds of community development initiatives. Yet the banks, in their service functions already discussed, have a more fundamental role in supporting communities and society in general. They provide basic financial functions that are necessary to keep society functioning. It was this irreplaceability that meant that governments could not allow banks to fail during the financial crisis. Since the crisis it has been argued that the utility, retail banking function, and the investment functions should be separated so that if in future investment banks fail then the retail banks are not also dragged into failure. In the terms used in the debating scheme the separation of retail and speculative banking might be viewed as palliative action. The markets for structured financial products would remain (although probably they would be more tightly regulated) but the threat to the continuance of the utility functions of banks would be much diminished. The business model would not be radically changed. Of course, whether the banks would decide on their own account to divest themselves of their investment banking arms would depend on whether they had the moral courage to do so or whether they believed it was in their best interests. It has already been argued that those in the financial sector probably lack moral imagination and banks without their investment arms would look financially unattractive to the markets.

CONCLUSIONS

The questions in the debating scheme are of two types. Some questions seek to identify whether there is an ethical issue and what its nature might be.

Two questions however focus on whether, if there is a moral issue, the company should do anything about it? These two questions are the virtue question and the objectivist question. Essentially they fix the two motivations a company might have for acting decently, either because it is the right thing to do or because it is in the company's interests to do so, or of course a combination of the two. Companies seldom have a single motivation; virtue and interests make a powerful combination. This may be illustrated by Dunhill. Originally best known as a cigarette manufacturer the company sold its cigarette business and brand to Rothman International in 1981. No doubt an astute move given the long-term prospects for the cigarette market; but the chairman's statement that the company that now deals in luxury goods is 'a bit embarrassed' (Dunhill, 2000) by its association with tobacco suggest also a virtuous motive.

The two case studies in this chapter suggest that a powerful combination of motives is necessary for a company to change its core business model. Although some companies in the alcoholic beverage industry have changed their business models most have continued with using advertising and price to increase turnover. This does not mean that they have not responded to the social and ethical harms that are consequent on their business model. Their response is in the form of palliative measures; measures that allow them to continue their business model whilst also trying to limit the problems that customers' misuse of their products might occasion. By stressing that it is the customers who decide whether to drink responsibly or not the companies can both advertise price deals and upsising promotions whilst simultaneously supporting a 'Drink responsibly' campaign. In the first case study most of the companies involved have kept their core business model but have taken palliative action. In the second case study in the aftermath of the global financial collapse the financial services companies are both unwilling to change their business models and unwilling to adopt palliative changes to the structure of the industry.

If companies are unwilling for the most part to fit their business models to ethical and social imperatives is there any role within companies for debating schemes such as the one presented in this chapter? Probably not might be an initial conclusion; to hold internal debates on ethical and social issues, if desirable changes are likely to be blocked by the company's financial self-interest, might be counterproductive, especially if the debates were leaked to the media. However companies' refusal to engage in open and transparent debate does not mean that the debate does not take place. It does, only not within the corporate structure but within the public arena. It takes place in people's conversations, in the media, within lobby groups and NGOs and within the forums of government policy. Those involved in these debates will be interested to know whether a company's commitment to CSR was simply a PR led defensive commitment or whether they were trying to embed CSR in their decision-making. A company's willingness to hold such debates in a transparent manner, at least internally, would be a marker of that company's commitment to corporate social responsibility, more so if the debates were transparent enough to be reported to, or even involve, external stakeholders.

REFERENCES

ASA (Advertising Standards Authority). (2005). TV advertising standards codes. Available at http://www.bcap.org.uk/The-Code/BCAP-Code.aspx. Retrieved on 28 May 2010.

BBC. (2009a). FSA argues for 'radical change'. *BBC News Online*. Available at http://www.news.bbc.co.uk/1/hi/business/8270340.stm. Retrieved on 30 October.

BBC. (2009b). Plans for minimum alcohol price. *BBC News Online*. Available at http://www.news.bbc.co.uk/go/pr/fr/-/hi/health/7944334.stm. Retrieved on 28 April.

BBC. (2010). Watchdog backs a minimum price for alcohol. *BBC News Online*. Available at http://www.news.bbc.co.uk/hi/health/10207827.stm. Retrieved on 2 June.

BBC. (n.d.) In detail: Drinking in the UK. Available at http://www.news.bbc.co.uk/1/shared/spl/hi/pop_ups/05/uk_drinking_in_the_uk/html/4.stm.

Bentham, J. (1982). An introduction to the principles of morals and legislation. Original Edition in 1781, In: J. H. Burns, & H. L. A. Hart (Eds.), London: Methuen.

Blitz, R. (2006). Wetherspoon halts plans to curb smoking. *The Financial Times*, Companies section, 4 March, p. 16.

Bruhn, J. G. (2008). The functionality of gray area ethics in organizations. *Journal of Business Ethics, 89*, 205–214.

Cabinet Office. (2003). *Alcohol misuses: How much does it cost?* London: Cabinet Office. Available at http://www.cabinetoffice.gov.uk/upload/assets/www.cabinetoffice.gov.uk/strategy/econ.pdf. Retrieved on 3 March 2008.

Communities that Care. (2002). *Youth at risk: A national survey of risk factors, protective factors and problem behavior among young people in England, Scotland and Wales.*

Diageo. (2009). Corporate citizenship report 2009. Available at http://www.annualreview2009.diageoreports.com/library/diageo_cr09.pdf. Retrieved on 12 July.

Dunhill, R. (2000). Interview with Richard Dunhill. Available at http://www.exero.com/mastergate/secured/fashion/dunhill. Retrieved on 10 May 2010.

Fisher, C. M., & Lovell, A. T. (2009). *Business ethics and values: Individual, corporate and international perspectives* (3rd ed.). Marlow: FT Prentice Hall.

French, W., & Albright, D. (1998). Resolving a moral conflict through discourse. *Journal of Business Ethics, 17*, 177–194.

Gustafson, A. (2000). Making sense of postmodern business ethics. *Business Ethics Quarterly, 10*(3), 645–658.

Hamilton, J. B., Knousse, S. B., & Hill, V. (2009). Google in China: A manager-friendly heuristic model for resolving cross-cultural ethical conflicts. *Journal of Business Ethics, 86*, 143–157.

Institute of Alcohol Studies. (n.d.) Economic costs and benefits: IAS factsheet. Available at http://www.ias.org.uk/resources/factsheets/economic_costs_benefits.pdf. Retrieved on 8 May 2010.

Johnson, M. W., Christensen, C. M., & Kagermann, H. (2008). Reinventing your business model. *Harvard Business Review, 86*(December), 51–59.

Magretta, J. (2002). Why business models matter. *Harvard Business Review, 80*(5), 86–92.

Martin, T. (2010). The war on pubs. Available at http://www.jdwetherspoon.co.uk/home/discover-jdw/our-responsibilities/chairmans-message-for-face-book.pdf. Retrieved on 8 May.

McGuiness. (2008). Tesco may lead ban on super-strength drinks. *Metro*, 25 February, p. 5.

Mounce, H. O. (1997). *The two pragmatisms: From Peirce to Rorty.* London: Routledge.

Ofcom (Office of Communication). (2007). *Young people and alcohol advertising: An investigation of alcohol advertising following the changes to the advertising code.* London: Ofcom.

Outhwaite, W. (1994). *Habermas: A critical introduction.* Cambridge: Polity Press.

Petrick, J. A., & Quinn, J. F. (1997). *Management ethics: Integrity at work.* London: Sage.

Portman Group. (2008). *Code of practice on the naming packaging and promotion of alcoholic drinks.* 4th ed., Available at http://www.portmangroup.org.uk/assets/documents/4th%20Ed%20of%20Code.pdf. Retrieved on 12 July 2009.

Preuss, L. (1999). Ethical theory in German business ethics research. *Journal of Business Ethics, 18*, 407–419.

Quazi, A. M., & O'Brien, D. (2000). An empirical test of a cross-national model of corporate social responsibility. *Journal of Business Ethics, 25*, 33–51.

Rawls, J. (1999). *A theory of justice* (Revised edition). Oxford: Oxford University Press.

Ruddock, G., & Siburn, J. (2008). Bad weather sees Magners cider sales go flat. *Telegraph.co.uk*, 12/07/2008. Available at http://www.telegraph.co.uk/finance/newsbysector/retailandconsumer/2793103/Bad-weather-sees-magners-cider-sales-go-flat. Retrieved on 27 May 2010.

Schein, E. (1992). *Career anchors: Discovering your real values* (Revised edition). San Diego: Pfeiffer.

Schweizer, L. (2005). Concept and evolution of business models. *Journal of General Management, 31*(2), 37–56. Available at http://www.annualreview2009.diageoreports.com/respopnsiblity. Retrieved on 12 October 2009.

Sharkey, G. (2008). Alan Parker: Bringing Whitbread into focus. *Caterer and Hotelkeeper, 198*(4539), 10.

Smithers, R. (2008). Asda bans shooters to deter binges. *The Guardian*, 26 February, news section, 5.

Stevenson, R., & Groves, E. (2005). Business analysis: Whitbread disposes of its past but its future is far from guaranteed. *The Independent*, 7 September.

Triggle, N. (2009). The power of alcohol marketing. *BBC News Online*, Available at http://www.news.bbc.co.uk/go/pr/fr/-/1/hi/health/8244194.stm.html. Retrieved on 7 May.

Ungvari-Zrinyi, I. (2003). Dialogic ethics for business. *Society and Economy, 25*(2), 235–248.

United States District Court: Southern District of New York. (2003). *Opinion in the case of Pelman and Bradley against McDonald's Corporation*. Available at http://www.tajnedokumenty. com/MDpelmandismissal. Retrieved on 29 September 2004.

Werhane, P. H. (1999). *Moral imagination and management decision making*. New York: Oxford University Press.

Whitbread. (n.d.) *Whitbread key dates*. Available at http://www.whitbread.co.uk/about_us. cfm?id = Whitbread_key_dates. Retrieved on 28 April 2010.

Wolff, J. (2006). Making the world safe for utilitarianism. *Royal Institute of Philosophy Supplement, 81*, 1–22.

Zakhem, A. (2008). Stakeholder management capability: A discourse-theoretical approach. *Journal of Business Ethics, 79*, 395–405.

THE DARK SIDE OF SOCIAL CAPITAL: LESSONS FROM THE MADOFF CASE

Paul Manning

In the wake of the recent financial crisis, J. K. Galbraith's classic account of 'The Great Crash 1929' has once again become a best seller. One can speculate that readers are curious to examine the previous global financial meltdown for insights that it can provide on the contemporary crisis, and one of the most interesting sections in this study of greed and folly is Galbraith's analysis of larceny. In Galbraith's view, the business cycle affects levels of fraud, with booms and crashes causing an exaggeration of the norms of trust based relations:

> In good times, people are relaxed, trusting and money is plentiful ... Under these circumstances the rate of embezzlement grows, the rate of discovery falls off, and the bezzle increases rapidly. In depression all this is reversed. Money is watched with a narrow, suspicious eye. The man who handles it is assumed to be dishonest until he proves himself otherwise. Audits are penetrating and meticulous. Commercial morality is enormously improved ... Just as the (stock market boom) accelerated the rate of growth (of embezzlement), so the crash enormously advanced the rate of discovery. (Galbraith, 1954, pp. 152–153)

Galbraith argued that in the boom phase of the business cycle, embezzlement increased rapidly, based on high levels of trust and a plentiful supply of money. In contrast in the ensuing crash, low levels of trust would expose

Reframing Corporate Social Responsibility: Lessons from the Global Financial Crisis
Critical Studies on Corporate Responsibility, Governance and Sustainability,
Volume 1, 207–228
Copyright © 2010 by Emerald Group Publishing Limited
ISSN: 2043-9059/doi:10.1108/S2043-9059(2010)0000001015

the extent of corporate larceny. Galbraith described the swiftness of the collapse in trust:

> Within a few days, something close to universal trust turned into something akin to universal suspicion. Audits were ordered. Strained or preoccupied behaviour was noticed. Most important the collapse of stock values made irredeemable the position of the employee who had embezzled to play the market. (*ibid.*)

Galbraith's analysis on trust and fraud remains pertinent today. For example, one of the few positive outcomes of the recent financial crisis has been the exposure of a number of egregious frauds and fraudsters, or as Warren Buffet put it: 'You only find out who is swimming naked when the tide goes out'.

The purpose of this chapter is to examine the most significant example of fraud that the recent financial crisis has exposed. There is lamentably a long list of examples that this chapter could examine to illustrate contemporary cases of large scale fraud. For example, Enron and Parmalat are cases from both sides of the Atlantic of large-scale corporate larceny. However, in terms of scale, both have been over-shadowed by biggest fraud yet to be uncovered by the crash, which has even led to the coining of a new verb: 'To be Madoffed', meaning to be cheated. This chapter's aim is to examine the fraud perpetrated by Bernard Lawrence Madoff, who it could be argued personified the limitations of the self-regulating market hypothesis and the general de-regulated economic hubris that characterised the financial boom that preceded the 'Credit Crunch'.

Furthermore, this chapter examines Madoff's fraud with reference to sociological and humanistic phenomena, which Galbraith refers to as 'trust', 'being relaxed' and 'suspicion', and thus will complement orthodox accounting and legal approaches to understanding fraud. This chapter's perspective is that an analysis of the sociological or humanistic character-istic of Madoff is vital for understanding his nature and substance of his crimes. For example, Harry Markopolis, a certified fraud examiner, was asked by his employers, 'Rampart Investment Management', to reverse engineer Madoff's strategy. Markopolis claims: 'When I saw the return stream, I knew it was a fraud in five minutes'. He also claimed it took him only 20 minutes to prove it was a fraud: 'His performance line went up at a 45-degree angle; that only exists in geometry class. It was clearly impossible'. Another banker, Rob Picard of 'The Royal Bank of Canada', reckons it took him 15 minutes talking to Madoff to realise it was all a fraud (Arvedlund, 2009, p. 90). However, Madoff continued to prosper, despite

Markopolis' best efforts to stop him, including reporting Madoff to the financial authorities:

> Countless times over eight-and-a-half years – meetings, written submissions, e-mails, phone calls. [What I provided] went from six red flags to 30 red flags, and any one of them was enough to stop Madoff.

Thus, the fraud was easy for an industry expert to unravel, and furthermore, Markopolos and others were determined to expose Madoff for being a swindler.

> I thought, this is so unbelievable, is it really true? I went to the CEO of a major financial modelling firm who worked across the street from us. He has the best financial mind. He checked my math and said this is definitely a fraud. That's when I knew I had to turn him in to the SEC. I never told my bosses. I thought I might get fired if I kept pursuing this. But I knew I had to stop him from going forward.[1]

Yet, Madoff continued to prosper until market conditions forced the fraud to unravel in public. This chapter argues that the continued success of the fraud was based on Madoff's ability to create closed bonding networks and to develop trust-based social relations and that these resources were adroitly used by the swindler to stifle investigations and assuage doubters. Thus, Madoff was a highly effective manipulator of social capital.

The chapter makes two sequential theoretical contributions. First, the chapter considers the dark side of social capital, which is under-reported in theoretical literature. Second, and related to the first theoretical contribution, this chapter examines Madoff's structural and relational interactions to demonstrate that sociability is morally neutral. This chapter therefore adds to the developing literature that challenges the 'sociological bias to see good things emerging out of sociability' (Portes, 1998, p. 15). For example, the seminal social capital scholars, the neo-Marxist Pierre Bourdieu, the neo-capital and rational choice theorist James Coleman and the neo-Tocquevillian Robert Putnam all stress the advantages of social capital and pay scant attention to its drawbacks. In Field's words, they all represent social capital, 'as largely benign, at least for those who possess high volumes of it' (2003, p. 141). In consequence, the negative aspects of sociability are under-reported in social capital literature. This chapter therefore seeks to rebalance this bias and adds to a developing literature stream that includes, 'The nature and logic of bad social capital' (Warren, 2008). This chapter also builds on Portes' observations on the negative aspects of social capital, which he describes as the exclusion of outsiders; excess claims on group members; restrictions on individual freedom; and downward levelling of norms (1998, p. 15).

In addition, from a socio-economic perspective, Granovetter's broad view of rationality, which acknowledges economic goals, as well as the significance of social influences and social structure (1985, p. 505), will further frame the analysis. In Granovetter's view, personal relations engender trust, which in turn creates vulnerability and 'enhanced opportunity for malfeasance', as reflected in the saying about personal relations that 'you always hurt the one you love' (*ibid*, p. 491).

In sum, this case analysis of Madoff will expand the social capital and socio-economic perspective by explicitly examining the negative side of structural and relational social interaction. This chapter also endeavours to offer a theoretically informed investigation to demonstrate that a social capital and socio-economic analysis adds original and significant insights into the understanding of fraud. The research illustrates the crucial role that 'getting the social relations right', played in Madoff's crimes. Ultimately, the chapter highlights the significance of social interactions, for creating the social capital and embedded trust and shared ways of viewing the world that enabled Madoff to accomplish his fraud.

The chapter is organised as follows. Following the introduction, the chapter examines the economic significance of social capital and the socio-economic embedded perspective, which are related but distinct approaches to framing economic actions. This section discusses the meaning of social capital as it relevant to fraud and argues that the economic form of social capital has background assumptions taken from Coleman's rational choice theoretical treatment (1988, 1990). The relationship between social capital and notions of rationality is significant for fraud: Madoff can be understood as an extreme rationalist who was unencumbered with any irrational notions of morality in his approach to social interactions. This section then develops the social capital perspective by the addition of the notion of socio-economic embeddedness, which again is significant because Madoff was an arch manipulator of bonding socially connected people to his financial schemes.

The subsequent section elucidates a theoretically informed framework for analysing Madoff from a social capital and socio-economic perspective. The chapter then introduces Madoff and proceeds to examine the swindle with reference to Granovetter's structural and relational dimensions (1992). The case describes how Madoff committed his crimes using an obscure 'index option', 'split-strike' conversion strategy that was convincing enough to gull Securities and Exchange Commission (SEC) investigators. However, the analysis also argues that to succeed for as long as he did, Madoff also needed the right embedded social networks and inter-subjective social relations. The fraud therefore was based on Madoff exploiting his social networks and social relationships, for instance, to generate high levels of trust so that it became difficult to question the fraudster's integrity, after all it was well known that Madoff was a highly respected self-made trader, philanthropist and IT innovator. The chapter then describes its theoretical contribution and concludes with reflections and lessons to be learnt from the case as well as suggestions for future research.

THE ECONOMIC SIGNIFICANCE OF SOCIAL CAPITAL

The contemporary social capital discourse is 'probably less than twenty or so years old' (Castiglione, 2008, p. 1), and its meaning remains elusive and contested (Castiglione, Van Deth, & Wolleb, 2008, pp. 2–21). However, this section develops the view that the returns of social capital can be understood in terms of two sets of intangible assets. First, intangible assets concerned with identity intangibles such as credibility, goodwill and reputation, and second, in terms of intangible assets to do with knowledge management. This section also contends that social capital is context dependent and in its economic context is framed by background assumptions taken from Coleman's rationalist theoretical treatment (1988, 1990). Furthermore, the relevance of the socio-economic perspective is discussed in terms of fraudster's exploitation of the socially embedded nature of all economic activity, including that of the market.

In more detail, the chapter understands social capital (SC) as situational, in Coleman's words: 'A given form of social capital that is valuable in facilitating certain actions may be useless or even harmful for others' (1990, p. 302). Thus, there are different forms of SC, which Woolcock has argued, '… coalesced around studies in (at least) seven fields-(1) families and youth behaviour problems; (2) schooling and education; (3) community life ('virtual and civic'); (4) work and organisations; (5) democracy and governance; (6) general case of collective action problems; and (7) economic development' (2001, p. 194). In consequence, this chapter offers an understanding of SC that is relevant for the research focus into economic fraud, but conversely is not appropriate in other contexts, such as for health or education research. This reflects Sandefur and Laumann's (1988, p. 69) view that 'Different types of social capital are useful for attaining different goals'.

The chapter also takes the view that the economic form of SC is concerned with intangible assets. Thus, SC is understood as integral to the processes that create and develop intangible assets that are termed as image, social esteem, prestige, goodwill or reputation, which can be classified as referring to the general standing of individuals and organisations among their stakeholders. For example, SC's embedded social relations facilitate transactions in terms of raising confidence and levels of trust that contracts and negotiated agreements will be honoured. Coleman's vignettes on the wholesale New York diamond market (see later) and on the Kahn El Khalili market in Cairo are examples of this function of SC facilitating economic activity (1988, pp. 20–22). Furthermore, in SC literature, it is argued that rational self-interest dictates that the short-term benefits of breaking an agreement will be balanced by the longer term cost of negative gossip and sanctions levied by social networks (Burt, 2005, pp. 93–111).Therefore, one of the economic returns of SC is reduced 'transaction costs' based on SC networks of reciprocity engendering trust: a vital economic and cultural asset that lubricates the smooth operation of the market (Fukuyama, 1995). It is also significant that SC's facility to lower 'transaction costs' also complements insights from exchange economics (Williamson, 1985, 1993).

Furthermore, SC's relational nature is also concerned with knowledge management. This characteristic of the economic form of SC, for instance, refers how economic agents 'learn the ropes'; that is, in reference to how they gain accesses to the difficult to codify information or the skills of their business and context. This is an important function as it has been argued that the contemporary knowledge society places increasing significance on social relations and intangibles as competitive resources (Bueno, Salmador, & Rodriguez, 2004, p. 557). Moreover, this function can be thought of as complementary to Cohen and Levinthal's 'absorptive capacity', which describes the ability of organisations to recognise, assimilate and commercially exploit knowledge (1990).

The economic form of SC also provides reassurance that agreements are more likely to be honoured as 'closure' (Coleman, 1990; Burt, 2005) can work to enforce obligations by providing sanctions against wrongdoers. SC further provides access to valuable contemporary and context-specific information, including referrals, leads and openings for business opportunities as well as facilitating more favourable trading terms and resource pooling. Moreover, 'Seen in economic terms, social capital is an input of the production function, and the sole criterion of its utility is its efficiency, its capacity to enhance total factor productivity' (Castiglione et al., 2008, p. 70).

Further definitions that are relevant for the economic form of SC include Lin's functionalist treatment that avers that SC is 'Investment in social relations with expected returns in the market-place' (Lin, 2001, p. 19). Moreover, according to Lin, 'an elementary exchange, evoking a relationship between two actors and a transaction of resource(s), contains both social and economic elements' (*ibid.*, p. 144).

However, this chapter argues that although social capital has become a catch all theory, in its economic form, it is framed by assumptions taken from orthodox economics and its rational optimisation modelling. These assumptions take social interaction as a process of social exchange and derive from the most influential social capital theorist in the economic context (James Coleman, 1988, 1990). In Coleman's rational action treatment, social capital can be viewed as a version of methodological individualism, or individual-level utilitarianism, based on the pursuit of utility maximisation. It is also worth noting that Coleman (1990, p. 18) took a broad understanding of methodological individualism to contend, 'much of what is ordinarily described as non-rational or irrational is merely so because the observer has not discovered the point of view of the actor, from which the action is rational'. Thus, from this 'present aims theory' of rationality, any behaviour can be interpreted as rational as the outcome of the individuals' preferences.

Thus, a recurring characteristic and limitation of extant literature into social capital is a reliance on assumptions drawn from rational action theory, which in turn depend on an exchange theory view of social interaction. Flavio Commin, for instance, has commented on social capital literature's focus on the 'instrumentalisation of social relations' (2008, p. 629). A typical illustration of this instrumentalisation is in Robert Putnam's seminal '*Bowling alone*', which used a plethora of statistics to support a calculative, 'means to an end' perspective on why business interactions are formed. For illustration, 'social contacts affect the productivity of individuals and groups' (Putnam, 2000, p. 19). The pervasiveness of these rational action inspired theoretical understandings can be gauged by the following understandings of leading social capital scholars (Table 1).

In sum, from this perspective, social capital offers greater productivity returns or provides greater ends-means rationality. Therefore, it is taken as desirable to develop and nurture interactions and a collective social structure, as these will lead to positive utility outcomes. It follows that it is rational to develop social capital for its utility returns: an understanding that chimes with the utility maximising 'homo economicus' of the 'formalist school'. However, there are numerous criticisms of end-means rationality,[2]

Table 1. Summary of Rational Choice Understanding of Social Capital.

Scholar	Rational Choice Understanding of Social Capital	Key Features
James Coleman	'aspects of social structure that enhance opportunities of actors within that structure' (1990, p. 302)	Instrumental view of social structures
Robert Putnam	In terms of generalised reciprocity quotes approvingly of de Tocqueville's: 'Self interest rightly understood' (2000, p. 135)	Ends-means rationality
Nan Lin	'the notion of social capital-capital captured through social relations. In this approach, capital is seen as a social asset by virtue of actors' connections and access to resources in the network or group of which they are members' (2001, p. 19).	Instrumental view of social relations and structures
	Investment in social relations with expected returns in the market-place' (Lin, 2001, p. 19)	Self-interested rationality
	'investment by individuals in interpersonal relations useful in the markets' (2001, p. 25)	
Ron Burt	To provide, 'access, timing and referrals' (1990, p. 62)	Economic notions of social relations to maximise returns
	'The advantage created by a person's location in a structure of relationships is known as social capital ... Social capital is the contextual complement to human capital in explaining advantage ... social structure defines a kind of capital that can create for individuals or groups an advantage in pursuing their end. People and groups who do better are somehow better connected' (2005, pp. 4–5)	
Henry Flap	'an entity consisting of all future benefits from connections with other persons' (2002, p. 136)	Resource maximisation
Ben Fine	'Essentially social capital is nepotism-you have to use the ones you know, but at least you know them' (2001, p. 157)	Maximising returns on social interactions
Portes describes Coleman's and Putnam's social capital treatment as	'An approach closer to the under-socialised view of human nature in modern economics sees social capital as primarily the accumulation of obligations from others according to the norms of reciprocity' (1998, pp. 48–49)	Utility maximisation in terms of creating and accumulating social credits

but in terms of fraud, its relevance is obvious: Madoff can be understood as an extreme rationalist who ruthlessly pursued his own economic utility, unencumbered with any moral or legal constraints. Thus, if 'social capital consists of relations between people' (Coleman, 1990, p. 316), Madoff was amoral enough to instrumentalise these relations ruthlessly for his own gain.

This chapter also contends that the social capital perspective can be expanded with the addition of a socio-economic viewpoint, which will allow for a more in-depth examination of the arational factors that were significant in the fraud, including the importance of developing a closed network of investors and for the significance of sociological factors in enhancing trust among regulators and investors. In more detail, socio-economics is predicated on the understanding at the macro level that the economy is embedded in wider society, whereas at the micro level, economic relations are viewed as being embedded in social relations. Thus, the socio-economic perspective applies a sociological/humanistic perspective to the economy. This understanding is rooted in the key texts of the social sciences (Smelser & Swedberg, 1994). However, the most obvious originator of this understanding is Karl Polanyi's (1944/1981, p. 60) embedded notion of the economy, which in the author's words aimed to reinstate the 'human and natural substance of society'. This approach was subsequently developed by the social network theorist Mark Granovetter (1973, 1985, 1992, 2005). It is also significant that Granovetter has never claimed allegiance with the burgeoning social capital discourse, which suggests that he regards his social network theory as separate and belonging to a different, one could speculate, 'embedded' theoretical literature.[3] Polanyi's 'embeddedness' is his most influential contribution to social theory and his theory has two main strands. First in Polanyi's view, classical economics made a radical break with every previous society in that the market instead of being embedded in wider society would dominate and be the organising principal for wider society. However, the second part of Polanyi's embedded argument (which is less commented upon) is that the disembedding of markets, for example, the self-regulating, laissez-faire markets, is an impossibility, or chimera. For example, in Polanyi's view, markets have to be expensively rescued by civil society (government) at crisis points, which are unpredictable, but recurring. For this research, the significance of the second strand of Polanyi's embedded argument is Polanyi's emphasis on embedded social relations in the market. It is worth stating unambiguously that Polanyi was arguing that although markets were idealised as being dismebedded, the reality was that this was impossible: markets were and had always been embedded in broader society. This view was subsequently developed in socio-economic literature, most notably by Granovetter in an article entitled: 'Economic action and social structure: The problem of embeddedness' (1985). For this case, the significance of this insight is that the Madoff's fraud was embedded in his social relations, a reality he knew and exploited. Finally, it is significant that Granovetter has commented on the deviousness and subtlety of 'Economic Man' to question the rational choice notion that

> one's economic interest is pursued only by comparatively gentlemanly means. The Hobbesian question-how can it be that those who pursue their own interests do not so mainly by force and fraud-is finessed by this conception. Yet as Hobbes saw so clearly there is nothing in the intrinsic meaning of 'self-interest' that excludes force of fraud. (Granovetter, 1985, p. 488)

In Madoff's case, self-interest meant fraud.

ANALYTICAL FRAMEWORK

Nahapiet and Ghoshal's (1998) de-composition is the most influential in recent social capital research. For instance, Edelman, Bresnen, Newell, Scarbrough, and Swan (2004) and Liao and Welsch (2005) have adopted this three-fold decomposition in conducting recent research into the economic significance of social capital. Furthermore, Napahiet and Ghoshal acknowledged that they based their decomposition on Coleman's theoretical treatment (they quote him extensively in their article) and also drew inspiration from Granovetter's discussion of structural and relational embeddedness (1992). It is further worth mentioning that they also introduced a third 'cognitive' dimension, which they stress is of particular importance for their study into intellectual capital (*ibid.*, p. 123).[4] However, this chapter analyses the case with reference to the Granovetter sourced dimensions, as the cognitive dimension is more specific to research into intellectual capital, and furthermore, the phenomena captured in this dimension can be accommodated in Granovetter's two cross-cutting categories. Thus, for this case study, the two dimensions that will be used as a theoretical framework for discussing and analysing Madoff are as follows:

- Structural dimension: 'refers to the overall pattern of connections between actors that is who you reach and how you reach them' (Nahapiet & Ghoshal, 1998, p. 244). This dimension comprises network ties, network configuration and appropriable organisation, meaning how easily social capital can be transferred from one context to another, that is, its fungibility (1998, p. 251).

- Relational dimension: 'describes the kind of personal relationships people have developed with each other through a history of interaction ... It is through these ongoing personal relationships that people fulfil such social motives as sociability, approval and prestige' (*ibid.*, p. 244). This dimension comprises trust, norms, obligations and identification (*ibid.*, p. 251).

Halpern's vitamin metaphor (2005, pp. 35–37) is also relevant, as it indicates that social capital requires a consideration of the blend of the two dimensions to be effective. Thus, the cross-cutting nature of dimensions means that any research has to be guided by an appreciation that the two dimensions are interwoven. This approach is also consistent with the ontology of SC, which is understood as situational (Coleman, 1990, p. 302) and self-generating, that is, antecedent and consequent and inter-woven (Cohen & Prusak, 2001).

The case is presented with an introduction offering an overview of Madoff's criminality, followed by a structural and relational examination of the fraud.

OVERVIEW OF THE MADDOF CASE

Had the stock market in the US not collapsed, Madoff's scam would probably have continued. (Arvedlund, 2009, p. 263)

On March 2009, the previously highly respected financier and pioneer of electronic trading, credited with turning the NASDAQ into one of the leading trading exchanges, pleaded guilty to a $65 billion 'Ponzi' scheme. Madoff admitted all of the charges, including securities fraud, mail fraud, wire fraud, money laundering, making false statements and perjury and was sentenced to the maximum terms allowed, 150 years. Apart from his close associate David Frihling, Madoff's longtime lawyer, no other perpetrator of the fraud has yet to face justice. Many interested observers are convinced that Madoff's family who worked closely with the fraudster, including his wife Ruth, his brother Peter, his nephew Charles, his niece Shana and his sons Mark and Andrew, have therefore escaped justice. It is also worth noting that the preceding judge Chin commented that Madoff had not been helpful in recovering assets.

Madoff was a 'self-made' man. He had founded Bernard L. Madoff Investment Securities in 1960 and boasted that he had earned his initial investment stake by working as a lifeguard at city beaches. Madoff's firm prospered and established itself as one of the largest independent trading operations in the securities industry. For example, the company had around $300 million in assets in 2000 at the height of the Internet bubble and was ranked among the top trading and securities firms in the world.

Madoff was unique in the industry for the consistency of his returns and for his firm low fee charging. Industry insiders had long puzzled over the success of Madoff and not everyone was surprised when the truth emerged that he had been running the biggest 'Ponzi' scheme in history. One view is that Madoff initially had a trading strategy that failed and that he had made very few, if any, stock or option trades for clients over the years. Instead his operation consisted of taking money in from new clients and paying it out to existing clients. Thus, Madoff was running a giant pyramid scheme, which collapsed when depositors started withdrawing their money faster than deposits could cover. In the end, the scheme collapsed because large investors wanted to take their money out, not because they had lost faith in Madoff but rather because they needed cash to cover other bad investments exposed in the downturn.

STRUCTURAL EMBEDDEDNESS: SWINDLER'S LIST

The first dimension researched the Madoff's patterns of relations from a relational sociology viewpoint that takes networks as influencing the actions of those in the networks. This section examines Madoff's structural embeddedness with reference to social capital and socio-economic literature, which in part will highlight aspects of these literature streams that are hitherto under-discussed.

The most transparent connection with Madoff in social capital literature is Coleman's view that 'Reputation cannot arise in an open structure' (1988, p. 28), which he illustrated with a number of vignettes, the most relevant for this case is the form of social capital described in the New York wholesale diamond market. In Coleman's account, this market is based on high trust closed networks in which merchants will hand over stones to be inspected by traders in private, even though the diamonds are highly valuable and can be easily substituted or stolen. In Coleman's view, this efficient practice was based on a closed network, with a Jewish community, living in Brooklyn, going to the same synagogues and intermarrying. Thus, 'If any member of this community defected through substituting other stones or stealing stones in his temporary possession, he would lose family, religious, and community ties' (*ibid.*, pp. 21–22).[5]

This is a vignette that is relevant for understanding Madoff's fraud in that Madoff exploited his network ties first in terms of his primary reference group. Tamotsu Shibutani describes reference groups as providing comparisons or contrasts that are used in forming judgements about oneself. 'A second referent of the concept is that group in which the actor aspires to gain or maintain acceptance: hence, a group whose claims are paramount in situations requiring choice' (1955, p. 109). In consequence, the New York and then whole US Jewish community was disproportionately swindled.

39% of American Jews said they were affected in some way, either because an organization or charity they supported had been affected by the Madoff crimes (29%) or because someone they knew had been affected (17%). (Arvedlund, 2009, pp. 272–273)

Furthermore, this focus on Madoff's primary reference group supports Lin's view that there is a preference for homophilious interactions in networks, that is, 'birds of a feather will flock together' (2001, p. 46–54). Thus, at one level, Madoff cultivated network ties based on shared sociological and humanistic characteristics. For example, Madoff's first victims were Jewish 'friends' who the swindler met while vacating in the Catskills[6] (Arvedlund, 2009, pp. 25–26), including many retired professionals who were more comfortable than rich.

However, as the swindle developed, Madoff's victims were to be found in a broad spectrum of ethnic groups and classes; he was in the words of one of his victims, 'an equal opportunities destroyer' (Arvedlund, 2009, p. 276). The pattern is once Madoff established his bonded networks in the Jewish community, he sought to extend his network reach to ensnare further victims. It is therefore worth examining how Madoff cultivated these networks to understand further the mechanics of the fraud.

First, being invited to join Madoff investment was presented as a privileged opportunity. In social capital literature, this corresponds to Putnam's bonding social capital (2000, pp. 22–24); Coleman's network closure functions (1988, p. 22; 1990, pp. 318–320); Lin's homophilious interactions (2001, pp. 46–52) and Burt's conclusions on network closure reinforcing pre-dispositions (2005, p. 168).

A significant part of this networking was also outsourced in the sense that referrals were actively encouraged: satisfied clients became an active sales force. Further because an investment opportunity with Madoff was presented as a privilege, (becoming a Madoff client often required a personal referral), few of this select group were prepared risking the opportunity by questioning the firm's investment strategy. One can speculate that investors must have thought well after all how could this be a fraud, this is – in theory at least – one of the most heavily regulated industries in the United States. However, the reality was that being invited to join Madoff's scheme was not a privilege: on the contrary, it was open to anyone foolish enough to invest. For example, Harry Markopolos has recounted his concerns over the dangers of exposing Madoff because:

> It was apparent that some of the investors were tax cheats in their home nations; [some] were in organized crime. He was stealing from the Russian mob and from drug cartels. If those people found out he was stealing from them, they would kill him. We were lucky we weren't killed by Madoff, who had a lot to protect. We took too many risks along the way but you couldn't undo what you'd already done. It was safer to go forward. (Interview in *AARP Bulletin*)

Second, Madoff made extensive use of feeder networks. These feeder networks can be understood in terms of Granovetter's weak ties (Granovetter, 1973, 1983). 'More novel information flows through weak ties than strong ties' (Granovetter, 2005, p. 34).

These networks comprised individuals who would take a commission for gaining new investment for Madoff's schemes. In Granovetter's perspective, these were weak ties that brought novel information, information about potential investors to Madoff. For instance, Robert Jaffe, a noted philanthropist like Madoff, 'worked' the 'Palm Beach Country Club' to the extent that over 30% of its members eventually invested with Madoff. However, Jaffe failed to tell his 'golf buddies' about the commission he charged or the fact that they were investing their funds with Madoff. In return for this deception, Jaffe became extremely wealthy, and the fraud continued apace. This deception also meant that a considerable number of investors in Madoff had no idea that they were connected to the fraud until they received news that the Ponzi scheme had collapsed and that they had lost their investments.

Third, Madoff developed networks exploiting his philanthropic activities. This approach fitted in with Madoff's preferred sales pitch of avoiding financial or 'capital introduction' parties, which would be full of financially savvy investors; instead, he targeted 'friends' and fellow philanthropists by word of mouth recommendations. Madoff and other members of his family assiduously targeted the charity circuit, sitting on the boards of many charities and donating money to many others. This networking gave Madoff two main paybacks. First, it allowed him access to high society, which added lustre to the Madoff brand: it made him more respectable. Second, it allowed him to aggressively market his products to gullible charity commissioners and hence provided a lucrative source of investors.

Fourth, Madoff enhanced his network reputation by cultivating highly respected network ties that could serve as a conduit to channel further victims into the fraud. In social capital literature, Lin has noted that reputation is promoted by; 'recruiting actors with a reputation established elsewhere in society' (1999, p. 154), and Madoff fully understood the value of these network ties for facilitating his fraud. For example, Madoff developed a close commercial relationship with Micheal Engler who ran a brokerage firm and enjoyed high status in his suburban community based on his exemplary war record. Engler recommended many veterans to invest with Madoff, and these military ties also served to ensnare an extensive network of unsuspecting investors who were connected to these veterans. Thus, Madoff targeted the respectable – and gullible – to form close bonding ties, to enhance exposure to lucrative investor networks.

Fifth, 'not all connections connect us to resources that matter' (Briggs, 2004, p. 152), and Madoff was calculating enough to target the most significant networks for facilitating the fraud. For example, Madoff courted high society politicians and other opinion formers, which perhaps confirms the view that 'Higher socio-economic status was found to be associated with higher levels of social capital' (Cairns, Van Til, & Williamson, 2004, p. 4). Further he targeted regulatory bodies. For example, he developed close ties with the SEC by training their newly appointed lawyers in the hard to codify context-specific insider knowledge of Wall Street (Arvedlund, 2009, p. 195). Thus, Madoff's networking insulated him from the concentrated gaze of investigators because he was so deeply structurally and relationally embedded that the charges made by Markopolos and others lacked creditability.

In sum, Madoff was a skilled networker from an extreme rationalist perspective of ends-means utility. Social network and network connections were instrumentalised without recourse to any social and moral considerations, exclusively to make Madoff money.

RELATIONAL DIMENSION: 'IT WAS TOO GOOD TO BE TRUE'

The relational embeddedness dimension of Madoff's fraud concerns the significance of beliefs, attitudes, values and norms of behaviour, as well as business ethics, or in Madoff's case, lack of business ethics. This section explicates the significance of this relational dimension in five sub-headings.

First, Granovetter has noted from a social network perspective that victim/offender relationships in financial scams were based on a surprising level of intimacy (1992, pp. 43–44). In Madoff's case, it has been claimed that this intimacy extended to a shared set of beliefs. For example,

> To stay in Madoff' game, they agreed to cooperate with his deceptions. They honored his request to not talk about him or to tell others that he was managing their money. They didn't do due diligence. (Arvedlund, 2009, p. 220)

Thus, one view is that many investors knew that something was amiss due to criminal activity, that is, they 'sort-of knew', as how otherwise could Madoff consistently produce such stellar returns? Instead, investors, blinded by greed, chose to passively go along with the fraud. Thus, a significant number of investors were aware that Madoff was cheating in some way, but they were the ones gaining from this cheating; therefore, they chose not to delve too deeply into Madoff's activities. One can speculate that they thought to conduct a proper audit would damage their prospect of a fat return on their investment.

Second, Madoff cultivated a brand identity that was conservative and reassuring, always immaculately presented, a committed family man and vigorous philanthropist who did not live an ostentatious lifestyle. The Madoff's were smart, educated, admired and respected (*ibid.*, p. 53). In short, he was a pillar of his community, a model American as well as being admired on Wall Street. The Madoff's were also noted for their conservative values and paradoxically were associated with low risk investment strategies: to his conservative investors, he appeared anti-risk. Furthermore, his returns were good, but remained within the realms of what a skilful and lucky trader could achieve in a good year 8–12% per annum – except Madoff uniquely achieved these returns every year. Thus, the fraud was facilitated by Madoff apparent conservatism, which gave him the persona opposite to that of a 'get rich quick' 'shady' operator. From social capital literature, this approach reflects Lin's homophily principle, that is, 'birds of a feather will stick together' (2001, pp. 46–52) and one can speculate that Madoff's fraud was facilitated because he appeared to embody values and behaviours that his investors shared, respected and wished to emulate.

Third, 'Madoff was an expert at gaining trust without giving up a lot of information' (Arvedlund, 2009, p. 93). This was significant for the fraud as malfeasance requires high trust: in low-trust environment, transactions are scrutinised in detail and economic actors are wary of being cheated. Therefore, although high-trust transactions create economic advantages, for instance, in terms of reduced transaction costs (Fukuyama, 1995), at the same time high level of trust also created opportunities for fraud. For example, Madoff followed a typical scam in claiming to have privileged 'insider knowledge' based on his network connections. Thus, it was 'understood' that Madoff possessed exclusive bridging capital or network brokerage opportunities that offered the privileged investors access to highly lucrative investment opportunities. This high level of trust can be observed in the loyalty of Madoff's investors, with widows recounting how their spouses had implored them, often on their deathbed 'to never sell their Madoff holdings' (Arvedlund, 2009, p. 50). In social capital literature, the significance of trust is emphasised for success in the marketplace. Fukuyama, for instance, had discussed at length the advantages that cultural values and trust have for economic success at macro, state level and at the micro, individual level (1995), and as already stated, Granovetter has also commented on the significance of engendering trust to perpetrate fraud (1985, p. 491). Thus, theoretical literature highlights that trust is a critical economic asset, and this case demonstrates that Madoff was an expert at facilitating and then exploiting this critical resource to enhance his fraud.

Fourth, Madoff was skilled at targeting investors when they were at their most trusting. For instance, Judge Chin who sentenced Madoff admitted to being swayed in the severity of this verdict by a victim statement of a widow. The widow wrote that she had gone to see Madoff following her husband's heart attack. Madoff put his arm around her to express his condolences and said, 'Don't worry your money is safe with me'. The widow subsequently lost all of her savings (Granovetter, 1996, p. 275). Madoff's technique was to interact or approach investors in non-financial settings. Thus, he would ingratiate himself in social and religious settings as he knew that these environments fostered an ambience of trust. Thus, potential investors would be more likely to see Madoff as 'one of us', and in consequence let their guard down. These trusting environments included country clubs in Palm Beach and the Hamptons and places of worship such as churches and synagogues in Florida, New York, Minnesota and Los Angeles (*ibid.*, p. 26). In theoretical literature, these manoeuvres also correspond to the insight that: 'Higher socio-economic status was found to be associated with higher levels of social capital' (Cairns, Van Til, & Williamson, 2004, p. 4). Furthermore, Granovetter has also noted that personal relations in business develop over time (1985, p. 496), that is, these relationships are influenced by maturing shared experiences and narratives. In sum, Madoff targeted the affluent away from an explicit economic setting to exploit their trust and social capital a task that he realised would only reap dividends over the long term.

Fifth, Madoff developed special status that was reflected in his special reputation. In part, this status/reputation was built on genuine business ability. For instance, Madoff had proven himself a mould-breaking innovator in terms of pioneering the introduction of electronic stock trading. The fact that Madoff was also a former chairman of the NASDAQ stock market further increased his credibility. However, this special status/ reputation was also based on Madoff understanding the importance of nurturing relations over time for cementing his reputation for integrity as Madoff developed an image of being reliable and in it for the long term, that is, he was consistent in his scam (Granovetter, 1985, p. 496). In social capital literature, Burt (2005) and Fukuyama (1995) confirm Granovetter's observations that norms are created over time and thus have a path dependency nature: it is a two-way process, needing both the trusting and the trustworthy. From this social capital perspective, reputation is built over a series of encounters, in which the parties establish levels of reciprocity. Thus, reputation has path-dependency characteristics that develop chronologically, influenced in shared experiences and narratives. To achieve this objective, Madoff worked on his 'good guy' persona. For example, most people loved working for the Madoff's and many stayed with them till the bitter end. For illustration, in 2002, a rookie trader was seriously injured when he was hit by a car while training for the New York City marathon. 'I passed out and woke up in the emergency room', the trader remembers. When he came to me, 'I looked to one side of my bed, and my mom and dad were there. On the other side was Bernie'.

THEORETICAL CONTRIBUTION

This chapter has examined what Putnam terms 'The dark side of social capital' (2000, pp. 350–362).[7] The chapter has established two theoretical contributions. First, the chapter's view is that social capital is too often taken as a 'honeyed term' or as an unalloyed force for good, and this over-optimistic perspective on structural and relational interaction has led to an imbalance in theoretical literature. In consequence, this chapter has endeavoured to offer a more accurate view of social capital as it is in reality, by examining one case that highlights what economists refer to as 'dis-utilities'. The first theoretical contribution is therefore to contribute to a re-gauging of the social capital scale to include its less desirable aspects.

Second, the chapter has contributed to a developing literature examining the under-reported ethical component of social capital. The Madoff case demonstrates the significance of ethics in structural and relational interaction. In Madoff's case, the absence of morality in his manipulation of his social capital is integral to understanding the fraud. Furthermore, the ethical aspects of social capital have been described as 'under-conceptualised' (Preuss, 2004, pp. 154–164), and the explicit literature examining the social capital/ethical interface is limited (Spence & Schmidpeter, 2003; Spence, Schmidpeter, & Habisch, 2003). This chapter's view is that in terms of ethics, SC is not a double-edged sword, as suggested by Woolcock (2001, p. 195), but rather should be thought of as morally neutral. Therefore, social capital can just as easily facilitate positive as well as negative ethical outcomes: it is contingent on context and on the behaviour of individuals. In theoretical terms, SC can be conceptualised as existing on a continuum, as opposed to having Manichean qualities, and therefore, the divide between positive and negative SC as sometimes proposed in theoretical literature (Warren, 2008, pp. 122–149) is inaccurate.

CONCLUSION: DO DE-REGULATED, 'FREE MARKETS' UNDERMINE MORAL LIFE?

In supposedly the most numbers dominated part of the economy, with investors increasingly taken as sophisticated and well informed, Madoff was able to perpetrate the biggest fraud in American history undetected for over a decade. This chapter has argued that Madoff perfected his nefarious scheme by being an exemplary manipulator of social capital, who approached interaction with a morality free, self-serving rationality. Furthermore, this chapter has described how social capital and supporting and inter-related concepts, such as trust, can be understood as being morally neutral. Thus, social capital can be used for moral and immoral purposes, just as trust can result in ethical as well as unethical outcomes. This view accords with Fukuyama conclusions on the ethical drawbacks in: 'Networks, understood as informal ethical relationships, (which) are therefore associated with phenomena like nepotism, favouritism, intolerance, in-breeding, and non-transparent, personalistic arrangements' (2000, p. 202). Fukuyama illustrates these observations with an example of another financial scandal, 'Barings', which he characterises as a network structure that allowed Nick Leason to 'bet the firm' (2000, p. 225). For this chapter, Madoff's 'personalistic' relations were the embedded networks and social relations that the fraudster cultivated over time, which sustained the 'Ponzi' scheme.

In sum, Madoff can be taken to illustrate the danger posed by a financial criminal, cunning enough to cultivate and manipulate social capital. It is also worth considering who the victims were not: they were not the major Wall Street financial institutions who were immune to the attractions of Madoff's social capital; they had their own structural and relational resources that gave them sufficient insider knowledge to avoid Madoff investments.

There is also an emerging consensus that one cause of the credit crunch was an over-reliance on self-regulation and a concomitant under-appreciation that markets are human constructions. In Madoff's case, the human construction of the market was revealed in the central role that greed played in the fraud. Thus, to a significant extent, the fraud was driven by naked self-interest, in which too many people looked the other way when they had more than an inkling that it was all too good to be true. This conclusion also suggests a puzzle over whether Madoff was merely an egregious criminal, or more significantly did he personify the excesses of (casino) capitalism, with a tendency to promote self-interest at the expense of morality? Only time will tell if Madoff emerges as the emblematic figure of the credit crunch.

Finally, further research based on this case could investigate Madoff's social capital in more detail, with the aim to develop a deeper understanding of fraud in terms of constructing frameworks for identifying the characteristics of legitimate economic actions, as opposed to criminally focussed social capital interactions. This investigation into Madoff indicates that one approach to increasing understanding of fraud is to forensically examine how networking and ongoing embedded relations facilitated the biggest swindle so far uncovered by the credit crash.

NOTES

1. Carole Fleck, *AARP Bulletin Today* senior editor, talked with Markopolos about his journey to expose Madoff, published in 2010 'No one would listen: A true financial thriller'.

2. For a criticism of the limits of rational choice theory, see Bohmam (1992). Also see, Friedman (1995).

3. Granovetter's CV is available at http://sociology.stanford.edu/people/mgrano vetter/, and a list of his extensive publications reveals he has never published anything with social capital in the title.

4. There is another 'cognitive' dimension, designed for their research purposes into intellectual capital, and for this research, this dimension was not considered appropriate.

5. Curiously, the role of De-Beers is not mentioned in this relationship.

6. As made famous in the film 'Dirty Dancing'.

7. There is a limited literature stream that considers the dis-utilities associated with social capital. This approach is based on the notion that social relations and shared values can be exploitative and downward levelling (Portes, 1998; Field, 2003; Dasgupta, 2005). For example, being too tightly embedded within a network can lead to inertia and absence of the competitive abrasion necessary for entrepreneurial drive. Uzzi (1996), for example, has cautioned about the danger of being over-embedded in a network in the context garment manufacturers in New York.

REFERENCES

Arvedlund, E. (2009). *Madoff, the man who stole $65 billion*. London: Penguin.

Bohmam, J. (1992). The limits of rational choice explanation. In: J. S. Coleman & T. S. Farraro (Eds), *Rational choice theory, advocacy and critique* (pp. 207–227). London: Sage.

Briggs, X. (2004). Social capital: Easy beauty or meaningful resource. In: J. Hutchinson & A. C. Vidal (Eds), Using social capital to help integrate planning theory, research and practice (pp. 151–158). *Journal of American Planning Association, 70*(2), 142–192.

Bueno, E., Salmador, M. P., & Rodriguez, O. (2004). The role of social capital in today's economy. *Journal of Intellectual Capital, 5*(4), 1469–1930.

Burt, R. S. (2005). *Brokerage and closure*. Oxford: Oxford University Press.

Cairns, E., Van Til, J., & Williamson, A. (2004). *Collectivism-individualism and community background in Northern Ireland*. The Office of the First Minister and Deputy First Minister and Head of the Voluntary and Community Unit of the Department for Social Development, March.

Castiglione, D. (2008). Social capital as a research programme. In: D. Castiglione, J. W. Van Deth & G. Wolleb (Eds), *The handbook of social capital*. Oxford: Oxford University Press.

Castiglione, J. W., Van Deth, J. W., & Wolleb, G. (Eds). (2008). *The handbook of social capital*. Oxford: Oxford University Press.

Cohen, W. M., & Levinthal, D. A. (1990). Absorptive capacity: A new perspective on learning and innovation. *Administrative Science Quarterly, 35*(1), 128–152.

Cohen, D., & Prusak, L. (2001). *In good company: How social capital makes organizations work*. Boston: Harvard Business School Press.

Coleman, J. S. (1988). Social capital in the creation of human capital. In: E. L. Lesser (Ed.), *Knowledge and social capital: Foundations and applications* (pp. 17–41). Oxford: Butterworth and Heinemann.

Coleman, J. S. (1990). *Foundations of social theory*. Cambridge: Bellknap Press.

Commin, F. (2008). Social capital and the capability approach. In: D. Castiglione, J. W. Van Deth & G. Wolleb (Eds), *The handbook of social capital* (pp. 624–651). Oxford: Oxford University Press.

Edelman, L. F., Bresnen, M., Newell, S., Scarbrough, H., & Swan, J. (2004). The benefits and pitfalls of social capital: Empirical evidence from two organisations in the United Kingdom. *British Academy Journal of Management, 15*, 59–69.

Field, J. (2003). *Social capital*. London: Routledge.

Fine, B. (2001). *Social capital versus social theory*. London: Routledge.

Flap, H. D. (2002). No man is an island. In: E. Lazega & O. Favereau (Eds), *Conventions and structures*. Oxford: Oxford University Press.

Fukuyama, F. (1995). *Trust: The social virtues and the creation of prosperity*. New York: Simon Schuster & Press.

Fukuyama, F. (2000). *The great disruption*. New York: Touchstone.

Galbraith, J. K. (1954). *The great crash*. London: Penguin Books.

Granovetter, M. (1973). The strength of weak ties. *American Journal of Sociology, 78*, 1360–1380.

Granovetter, M. (1985). Economic action and social structure: The problem of embeddedness. *American Journal of Sociology, 91*(3), 481–510.

Granovetter, M. (1992). Problems of explanation in economic sociology. In: N. Nitin & R. G. Eccles (Eds), *Networks and organisations; structure, form, and action*. Boston, MA: Harvard Business School Press.

Granovetter, M. (2005). The impact of social structure on economic outcomes. *Journal of Economic Perspectives, 19*(1), 33–55.

Halpern, D. (2005). *Social capital*. Cambridge: Polity Press.

Liao, J., & Welsch, H. (2005). Roles of social capital in venture creation: Key dimensions and research implications. *Journal of Small Business Management, 43*(4), 345–362.

Lin, N. (1999). Social networks and status attainment. *Annual Review of Sociology, 25*, 467–487.

Lin, N. (2001). *Social capital: A theory of social structure and action*. Cambridge: Cambridge University Press.

Nahapiet, J., & Ghoshal, S. (1998). Social capital, intellectual capital and the organizational advantage. *Academy of Management Review, 23*(2), 242–266.

Polanyi, K. (1944/1981). *The great transformation* (2nd ed.). Boston: Beacon Press.

Portes, A. (1998). Social capital: Its origins and applications in modern sociology. *Annual Review of Sociology, 24*, 1–24.

Preuss, L. (2004). Aristotle in your local garage: Enlarging social capital with an ethics test. In: L. J. Spence, A. Habisch & R. Schmidpeter (Eds), *Responsibility and social capital: The world of small and medium enterprises* (pp. 154–164). New York: Palgrave Macmillan.

Putnam, R. D. (2000). *Bowling alone*. New York: Simon Schuster.

Sandefur, R. L., & Laumann, E. D. (1988). *A Paradigm for Social Capital, Rationality and Society, 10*(4), 481–501. In: E. L. Lesser (Ed.) (2000) *Knowledge and Social Capital*. Oxford: Butterworth Heinemann, pp. 69–88.

Smelser, N. J., & Swedberg, R. (1994). The sociological perspective on the economy. In: N. Smelser & R. Richard Swedberg (Eds), *The handbook of economic sociology* (pp. 3–26). New York: Russell Sage Foundation.

Spence, L. J., & Schmidpeter, R. (2003). SMEs, social capital and the common good. *Journal of Business Ethics, 45*, 93–108.

Spence, L. J., Schmidpeter, R., & Habisch, A. (2003). Assessing social capital: Small and medium sized enterprises in Germany and the UK. *Journal of Business Ethics, 4*, 17–29.

Uzzi, B. (1996). The sources and consequences of economic embeddedness for the economic performance of organisations: The network effect. *American Sociological Review, 61*(4), 94–289.

Warren, M. E. (2008). The nature and logic of bad social capital. In: D. Castiglione, J. W. Van Deth & G. Wolleb (Eds), *The handbook of social capital* (pp. 122–149). Oxford: Oxford University Press.

Williamson, O. E. (1985). *The Economic Institutions of Capitalism*. Free Press.

Williamson, O. E. (1993). Calculativeness, trust and economic organization. *Journal of Law and Economics, 36*(2), 453–486.

Woolcock, M. (2001). Microenterprise and social capital: A framework for theory, research, and policy. *Journal of Socio-Economics, 30*, 193–198.

PART IV
THE FUTURE OF CSR:
A POST-CRISIS AGENDA

CSR 2.0: FROM THE AGE OF GREED TO THE AGE OF RESPONSIBILITY [*]

Wayne Visser

> The point is, ladies and gentleman, that greed, for lack of a better word, is good. Greed is right, greed works. Greed clarifies, cuts through, and captures the essence of the evolutionary spirit. Greed, in all of its forms; greed for life, for money, for love, for knowledge has marked the upward surge of mankind.
>
> – Gordon Gekko, Wall Street (the movie)

> Responsibility is literally what it says – our ability to respond. To be responsible is to be proactive in the world, to be sensitive to the interconnections, and to be willing to do something constructive as a way of giving back. Responsibility is the footprints we leave in the sand, the mark of our passage. What tracks will you leave?
>
> – Wayne Visser, Business Frontiers (the book)

The 1987 movie *Wall Street* and our recent global financial crisis (GFC), despite one being fictional and the other painfully real, tell a common story. Over the past few decades, we have been living through an Age of Greed, characterised by a colossal failure of corporate responsibility and corruption of individual morality. This Crisis of Responsibility has had catastrophic consequences for the global economy, bankrupting whole economies (like Iceland) and wreaking havoc with the lives of ordinary citizens around the world, many of whom are now without a job and without a roof over their heads.

[*] This chapter is based on the book *The Age of Responsibility* by Wayne Visser (Wiley, 2011).

Reframing Corporate Social Responsibility: Lessons from the Global Financial Crisis
Critical Studies on Corporate Responsibility, Governance and Sustainability,
Volume 1, 231–251
ISSN: 2043-9059/doi:10.1108/S2043-9059(2010)0000001016

In this chapter, I explore the ways in which the GFC represents a multi-level failure of responsibility – from the individual and corporate level to the finance sector and entire capitalist system. I also examine the impact of the GFC on what is traditionally viewed as corporate social responsibility (CSR). To conclude, I set out my conviction that unless CSR itself is fundamentally transformed, into CSR 2.0, it will do nothing to prevent an equally (if not more) devastating Crisis of Responsibility from recurring in future.

THE AGE OF GREED

Gordon Gekko's words, although spoken by a fictitious Hollywood character, captures the spirit of a very real age: the Age of Greed. This was an age that, in my view, began when the first financial derivatives were traded on the Chicago Mercantile Exchange in 1972 and ended (we hope) with Lehman Brothers' collapse in 2008. It was a time when 'greed is good' and 'bigger is better' were the dual-mottos that seemed to underpin the American Dream. The invisible hand of the market went unquestioned. Incentives – like Wall Street profits and traders' bonuses – were perverse, leading not only to unbelievable wealth in the hands of a few speculators, but ultimately to global financial catastrophe.

The story of Gordon Gekko (and his modern day real-life equivalents like Richard Fuld, the captain of the titanic Lehmans before it hit the iceberg) gets to the heart of the nature of greed. The word 'greed' – from the old English *grædig* – has etymological roots that relate to 'hunger' and 'eagerness'. This is similar to the older word, *avarice*, coming from Old French and Latin (*avere*), meaning 'to crave or long for'. Those are characteristics that Gekko and Fuld had in spades. The Greek word for greed – *philargyros*, literally 'money-loving' – also has a familiar echo in their stories. The trouble is that capitalism in general, and the American Dream in particular, has tended to interpret greed as a healthy trait. Gekko and Fuld did not believe that they were being unethical, or doing anything wrong. Each was playing the capitalism game – extremely well – and being rewarded handsomely.

Perhaps we would do well to recall the German root of the word for greed (*habsüchtig*), which means 'to have a sickness or disease'. Greed acts like a cancer in society – whereby an essentially healthy cell in the body becomes selfish and ends up destroying its host. As important as the greedy cell itself is the environment which enables it to live and prosper. A certain measure of selfishness is natural, but it needs to be moderated by norms, rules and cultural taboos that keep its destructive tendencies in check.

The Age of Greed was not something 'out there'. It was not the preserve of a few rogue traders or evil moguls. We were all caught up in its web. It is in fact a multi-level phenomenon, incorporating executive greed, banking greed, financial market greed, corporate greed and ultimately the greed embedded in the capitalist system. These different facets of greed are each explored in turn below, before considering what the alternatives might be.

Executive Greed

The most convenient explanation for the financial crisis is to point a finger at the greed and irresponsibility of a few individual executives, like Enron's former CEO Jeffrey K. Skilling and Lehman's Fuld. It is an argument with significant weight.

In 2000, Enron was the 7th largest company in America, with revenues of $111 billion and over 20,000 staff. When the company collapsed in 2001, due to various fraudulent activities fuelled by a culture of greed, the average severance payment was $45,000, while executives received bonuses of $55 million in the company's last year. Employees lost $1.2 billion in pensions and retirees lost $2 billion, but executives cashed in $116 million in stocks.

At the end of 2007, when the GFC writing was already writ large on the wall, in large part due to the greed-hyped activities of Lehman's and other financial institutions, CEO Fuld and president Joseph Gregory paid themselves stock bonuses of $35 million and $29 million respectively. Fuld lived in an enormous Greenwich mansion, over 9,000 square feet, valued at $10 million. He had four other homes and an art collection valued at $200 million. Hardly a picture of responsible restraint.

Taken on their own, these executive pay packages are outrageous enough. But the extent of creeping executive greed comes into even sharper focus when we look at trends in relative pay. In 1965, the U.S. CEOs in major companies earned 24 times more than a typical worker, a ratio that grew to 35 in 1978 and to 71 in 1989. By 2000, it had hit 298, and despite falling to 143 in 2002 (after the post-Enron stock market slump), it bounced back again and has continued rising through the 'noughties' (2000s).

According to Fair Economy, in 2007, despite the looming economic recession, CEOs of the largest 500 companies in America (S&P 500) earned an average of US$10.5 million, 344 times the pay of typical American workers and 866 times as much as minimum wage employees. The same year, the top 50 hedge and private equity fund managers earned an average of $588 million, according to *Alpha magazine* – more than 19,000 times as much as average worker pay. And in 2008, while the financial crisis was beginning to bite for ordinary citizens, average CEO pay went up to US$10.9 million, while CEO perks averaged US$365,000 – or nearly 10 times the median salary of a full-time worker.

It is easy to go cross-eyed or brain-fried when confronted by a barrage of numbers like that. And yet, there is one particular number that shocked me so much at the time (in 1997) that it has stuck in my conscience. I believe I read it in Anita Roddick's book, *Body and Soul*. She claimed that it would take one Haitian worker producing Disney clothes and dolls *166 years* to earn as much as Disney's then president, Michael Eisner, earned in *one day*. Reflecting on this, I wrote in my book *Beyond Reasonable Greed*: 'rather than spreading around the wealth for the common good, it seems that Adam Smith's invisible hand has a compulsive habit of feeding itself'.

Banking Greed

As horrific as these trends in executive greed are – and they certainly represent a responsibility train-wreck – I do not believe that the GFC can be adequately explained by 'bad apples' (as the media liked to characterise these now-disgraced captains of industry). In addition to those leaders who were driven by personal greed, the sub-prime crisis was also a story of institutional greed, aided and abetted by deregulation of the financial sector since the 1980s.

Aside from this general trend of deregulation, we can point to a number of poor U.S. policy decisions that were to have disastrous consequences. The first was Bill Clinton's campaign promise to increase home ownership in poor and minority communities – a noble cause, to be sure, but one which put pressure on the banks to make riskier loans: two million of them between 1993 and 1999. The folly of this policy, while obvious in retrospect, did not pose any immediate concerns, as the housing market was strong and prices continued to rise.

Over the same period, Clinton was coming under increasing pressure by the banking lobby to repeal the Glass-Steagall Act of 1933, a piece of post-Wall Street crash legislation that prevented commercial banks from merging with investment banks. The law was specifically put in place to prevent another global financial crisis and ensuing depression. At first, Clinton resisted. But the banks were relentless. In 1998, one of them, Citicorp, decided to flaunt the law, announcing a $70 billion merger with Travellers

Insurance. Clinton tried to block it but failed in the Senate, despite the fact that the merger was technically illegal.

A year later, Clinton bowed to rising pressure and repealed the Glass–Steagall Act. This single action proved to be the 'butterfly effect' that would bring the world financial system to its knees. With the stroke of a pen, and bullied by the greed of the banks, Clinton had given permission for speculative financial traders to start gambling with the hard-earned deposits of ordinary Americans. Soon, all manner of financial instruments exploded onto the market – from CDOs (collaterised debt obligations) and CLOs (collaterised loan obligations) to CMBSs (commercial mortgage-backed securities) and CDSs (credit default swaps).

For a year or two, it seemed like the party may have ended before it had begun. Saddled with $65 billion in unpayable debt, Enron spiralled to their death at the hands of the financial markets, with their share price falling from US$90 to just a few cents. In the months that followed, a spate of bankruptcies rocked the world, all of companies which had issued convertible bonds: Global Crossing, Qwest, NTL, Adelphia Communications and WorldCom. The 9/11 tragedy and Dotcom crash happened around the same time, and some measure of caution returned to the markets, but not for long.

Alan Greenspan took an action that, like Clinton's repeal of Glass–Steagall, would cause another 'butterfly effect'. Between December 2000 and June 2003, he cut interest rates from 6% to 1%, and kept them there. Suddenly, not only was the housing market growing, but money was almost free. With the help of the newly invented financial voodoo instruments, the sub-prime party bonanza really got going.

Preposterous loans like the NINJA mortgage were invented – that stands for No Income, No Job, No Assets. It did not matter that you were poor and had no collateral. Not only would you get a mortgage, the broker would pay you 10% more than you needed to buy the house. The initial interest rate (what the brokers called the 'teaser rate') would also be next to nothing, although it would increase 5 or 10 fold in the years to come. The infallible logic behind this – if that is not an inappropriate use of the term – was that house market prices would continue to rise steadily, and everyone would be a winner.

The result was that, according to the Mortgage Bankers' Association, the number of sub-prime loans offered to borrowers with below average credit ratings increased nearly 15 times between 1998 and 2007, from 421,330 to 6.2 million. And the banks were in a feeding frenzy, leveraging themselves to the hilt, so that they could make obscene profits from the market boom. Historically, a leverage of 10 times EBITDA[1] (i.e. where the company has debts of 10 times its actual value) was considered very high. But by the time it hit the iceberg, Lehman Brothers was well on the way to being leveraged to 44 times its value, owing more than $700 billion. The face of banking greed was unmasked.

Financial Market Greed

Many GFC analysts would stop there, satisfied that the combination of executive greed and banking greed provide sufficient explanation for the Crisis of Responsibility. And while they certainly represent the most obvious signal failures that caused the mother-of-all meltdowns, I still do not believe that these two factors tell the whole story. To understand banking greed, we need to look at the nature of the broader financial markets – how they are designed, how they operate and the behaviours that they incentivise.

In order to understand what 'greed is good' really means – in terms of hard numbers – we must wrap our heads around the concept of financial derivatives. Larry McDonald (2009), a Lehman's insider who called the collapse 'a colossal failure of common sense', refers to derivatives as 'the Wall Street neutron'. They are essentially speculative bets on changes in various market indicators (like currencies and interest rates) and they have been growing exponentially since their introduction in 1972. By the turn of the century, these wizz-kid invented, esoteric financial instruments were just hitting their stride, growing at around 25% per year over the last decade. Today, according to some accounts, the derivatives market is worth over US$1,000 trillion (that's 15 zeros!).

Why this is so significant is that most of this 'trade' is not happening in the 'real economy'; it is a casino economy. Take trade in currencies, for example. In 1998, around US$1.5 trillion (that's 12 zeros) in currency was traded *daily* on the global markets, up 46% from 1994. But only 2.5% was linked to 'real economy' transactions such as trade, tourism, loans or genuine investment on stock markets. The other 97.5% (up from 20% in the 1970s) was pure speculation – a casino economy in which financial traders were making eye-popping truckloads of money, without actually contributing anything tangible to the products and services that give us quality of life.

One of the more modern varieties of derivatives is the credit default swap (CDS). Larry McDonald reflects that 'in the merry month of May 2006, Wall Street took hold of this gambling concept and decided to transform itself into something between a Las Vegas casino and an off-track betting parlour'. Early in 2006, there were $26 trillion of CDS bets outstanding in the market. By the beginning of 2008, it was $70 trillion, with just 17 banks carrying that risk. And there was another $15 to $18 trillion in other derivatives and fancy instruments (an alphabet soup of CDOs, RMBSs, CMBSs, CLOs and ABSs).

This was all well and good when it was just a high-stakes game for rich kids to play. But as we have seen, with the repeal of the Glass–Steagall Act and the introduction of the Financial Services Modernisation Act in 1999, the greed-infused, short-term obsessed gambling habits of Wall Street traders can have (and have had) very real and devastating effects on very real economies and very real people. And even today, in the aftermath of the GFC, very few of these financial market agents have taken responsibility, or been made accountable, nor have the financial market rules been significantly changed.

As it happens, that great post-Depression economist, John Maynard Keynes, had foreseen this and warned: 'Speculators may do no harm as bubbles on a steady stream of enterprise. But the position is serious when enterprise becomes the bubble on a whirlpool of speculation. When the capital development of a country becomes a by-product of the activities of a casino, the job is likely to be ill-done'. And ill-done it has been, woefully ill-done. No wonder billionaire investor Warren Buffet first described derivatives as 'weeds priced as flowers', and later as 'financial weapons of mass destruction'. If Kenyes were here today, standing with us on financial 'ground zero ', gazing at the post-apocalyptic debris of our once gleaming citadels of commerce, he might quite justifiably shake his head and mutter, 'I told you so!'

Corporate Greed

Even financial market greed may not be ultimate cause. Could it be that unbridled greed is, by design, the unavoidable consequence the corporation? We often forget that when corporations were originally introduced in America in the mid-1800s, it was with the explicit purpose of serving the public good (enshrined in a charter), with liable shareholders. But the nature of the corporation changed when the US Supreme Court ruled that a corporation should have the same rights as individuals, thus making it a legal person. The problem, according to critics, is that the corporation is a 'person' with no moral conscience and an exclusive focus on the benefits of shareholders. This results in a pattern of social costs imposed by business in exchange for private gains for its executives and owners.

In his controversial, yet hugely influential book and documentary, *The Corporation*, Canadian legal academic Joel Bakan, suggests that corporations are, by their legal constitution, pathological in nature: 'The corporation has a legally defined mandate to relentlessly pursue – without exception – its own self-interest regardless of the often harmful consequences it might cause to others. Lying, stealing and killing are not rare aberrations but the duty of the corporation when it serves the interests of its shareholders to do so'. This, according to Bakan, means that corporations have all the characteristics of a psychopath, as defined by the World Health Organisation.

Not everyone – even among those concerned about business responsibility – would go this far in their diagnosis. But there is certainly little doubt about the in-built greed of the modern corporation. David Korten, author of *When Corporations Rule the World*, is among the many critics that remind us of the power of modern business, in which more than half of the top 100 'economies' in the world are in fact multinational corporations. With such power comes responsibility, but left their own devices, many corporations are cost externalisation machines – meaning that they will naturally try to avoid paying for any negative human, community or environmental costs that they impose on society.

In an interview I did with Korten in 2008, he told me that the problem is even more fundamental than the corporations themselves: 'If I were to rewrite the book now, I would probably put the title *When Corporations Rule the World* with a slash through 'Corporations' and a little carrot pointing to 'Money'. It's actually *When Money Rules the World*. This has become so much more obvious, so much stronger and so much more disruptive as we've seen the rampant speculation in the financial markets. That very structure drives a predatory dynamic in the corporate system that you really can't do very much about at the level of the individual corporation. You can do a little tinkering around the edges, but those are pretty limited relative to the depth of the changes that we need to navigate'.

Capitalist Greed

So this begs the question: is capitalism itself fundamentally flawed? Will capitalism – with its short-term, cost-externalisation, shareholder-value focus – always tend towards greed, at the expense of people and the planet? Will the scenario of 'overshoot and collapse' that was computer modelled in the 1972 *Limits to Growth* report (and confirmed in revisions 20 and 30 years later) still come to pass? Has Karl Marx been vindicated in his critique (if not his solution) that by design, capitalism causes wealth and power to accumulate in fewer and fewer hands?

To answer these quintessential questions, we need to look at the facts. According to WWF, humanity's Ecological Footprint, driven by the spread of capitalism globally, has more than tripled since 1961. Since the late 1980s, we have been in overshoot – meaning that the world's Ecological Footprint has exceeded the Earth's biocapacity. Between 1970 and 2003, WWF's Living Planet Index, which tracks over 6,000 populations of 1,313 species, fell by 29%. By their estimates, we would need three planets if everyone on earth were to adopt the energy intensive, consumptive lifestyle of the capitalist Western world.

The UN Millennium Ecosystem Assessment, issued in 2005, reaches similar conclusions: 60% of world ecosystem services have been degraded; of 24 evaluated ecosystems, 15 are being damaged; water withdrawals have doubled over the past 40 years; over a quarter of all fish stocks are overharvested; since 1980, about 35% of mangroves have been lost; about 20% of corals were lost in just 20 years and 20% more have been degraded; and species extinction rates are now 100–1,000 times above the background rate. So, by all accounts, capitalism is failing spectacularly to control the environmental impacts of the economic activities that it is so successful at stimulating.

The social impacts of capitalism are more ambiguous. On the one hand, critics like Naomi Klein (author of *No Logo* and *The Shock Doctrine*) argue that 'Gucci capitalism' results in labour exploitation and a 'race to the bottom'. In other words, capital flows to wherever the social or environmental standards are lowest. Not only this, but capitalism is designed to create the instability that we have seen in the markets and those that suffer the most from this volatility are always the most vulnerable, namely the poor of the world.

On the other hand, largely thanks to its adoption of capitalism, China has enjoyed economic growth of more than 9% a year over the past 30 years and as a result, between 1981 and 2005, their poverty rate fell from 85% to 16%, or by over 600 million people. That represents real positive impacts on real people. But at what cost? Some estimate that environmental damage robs China of 5.8% of its GDP every year. What's more, the gaps between rich and poor in China are growing.

Perhaps the trillion-dollar question is not whether capitalism *per se* acts like a cancer gene of greed in society, but whether there are different types of capitalism, some of which are more benign than others? To date, the world has by and large been following the American model of shareholder-driven capitalism, and perhaps this is the version that is morally bankrupt and systemically flawed? Management guru, Charles Handy, seems to agree. In an interview I conducted with him in 2008, he confessed: 'I've always had my doubts about shareholder capitalism, because we keep talking about the shareholders as being owners of the business, but most of them haven't a clue what business they're in. They are basically punters with no particular interest in the horse that they're backing, as long as it wins'.

THE AGE OF RESPONSIBILITY

What then is the alternative version of capitalism? Can there be an economic system that is not fuelled by greed? The jury is still out on this, but at least we are starting to explore the idea. We hear Bill Gates talking about 'creative capitalism' which combines the 'two great focuses of human nature – self-interest and caring for others'. Jonathon Porritt calls for 'capitalism as if the world matters' and Paul Hawkens, Amory Lovins and Hunter Lovins propose 'natural capitalism'.

Whichever version we ultimately go for, I am convinced it will have to be a more regulated capitalism. We sometimes forget that Adam Smith was a moral philosopher and always assumed that markets would take place within a rules-based system of norms and controls. Having witnessed the disaster of unregulated capitalism and deregulated financial markets, it is time for the pendulum to swing back to greater government involvement. History has taught us that, without a strong policy framework, we will not get responsible markets or sustainable products at the scale and with the urgency that we need them.

The Rise and Fall of CSR

One of the proposed antidotes to the Age of Greed is corporate social responsibility (CSR), which has been debated and practiced in one form or another for more than 4,000 years. For example, the ancient *Vedic* and *Sutra* texts of Hinduism and the *Jatakas* of Buddhism include ethical admonitions on usury (the charging of excessive interest) and Islam has long advocated *Zakat*, or a wealth tax (Visser & McIntosh, 1998).

The modern concept of CSR can be more clearly traced to the mid-to-late 1800s, with industrialists like John H. Patterson of National Cash Register seeding the industrial welfare movement and philanthropists like John D. Rockerfeller setting a charitable precedent that we see echoed more than a hundred years later with the likes of Bill Gates (Carroll, 2008).

Despite these early variations, CSR only entered the popular lexicon in the 1950s with Howard Bowen's (1953) landmark book, *Social Responsibilities of the Businessman*. The concept was challenged and strengthened in the 1960s with the birth of the environmental movement, following Rachel Carson's (1962) critique of the chemicals industry in *Silent Spring* and the consumer movement off the back of Ralph Nader's (1965) social activism, most famously over General Motors's safety record.

The 1970s saw the first widely accepted definition of CSR emerge – Archie Carroll's (1979) 4-part concept of economic, legal, ethical and philanthropic responsibilities, later depicted as a CSR pyramid (Carroll, 1991) – as well as the first CSR code, the Sullivan Principles. The 1980s brought the application of quality management to occupational health and safety and the introduction of CSR codes like Responsible Care.

In the 1990s, CSR was institutionalised with standards like ISO 14001 and SA 8000, guidelines like the Global Reporting Initiative and corporate governance codes like Cadbury and King. The 21st century has been mostly more of the same, spawning a plethora of CSR guidelines, codes and standards (there are more than 100 listed in *The A to Z of Corporate Social Responsibility* (Visser, Matten, Pohl, & Tolhurst, 2010)), with industry sector and climate change variations on the theme.

Why is all this potted history of CSR important in a discussion about the future? Well, first, we must realise that CSR is a dynamic movement that has been evolving over decades, if not centuries. Second, and perhaps more importantly, we must acknowledge that, despite this seemingly impressive steady march of progress, CSR has failed.

CSR has undoubtedly had many positive impacts, for communities and the environment. Yet, its success or failure should be judged in the context of the total impacts of business on society and the planet. Viewed this way, as the evidence already cited shows, on virtually every measure of social, ecological and ethical performance we have available, the negative impacts of business have been an unmitigated disaster, which CSR has completely failed to avert or even substantially moderate.

The Failure of CSR

Why has CSR failed so spectacularly to address the very issues it claims to be most concerned about? In my view, this comes down to three factors – call it the Triple Curse of Modern CSR, if you like:

Curse 1: Incremental CSR

One of the great revolutions of the 1970s was total quality management, conceived by American statistician W. Edwards Deming and perfected by the Japanese before being exported around the world as ISO 9001. At the very core of Deming's TQM model and the ISO standard is continual improvement, a principle that has now become ubiquitous in all management system approaches to performance. It is no surprise, therefore, that the most popular environmental management standard, ISO 14001, is built on the same principle.

There is nothing wrong with continuous improvement *per se*. On the contrary, it has brought safety and reliability to the very products and services that we associate with modern quality of life. But when we use it as the primary approach to tackling our social, environmental and ethical challenges, it fails on two critical counts: speed and scale. The incremental approach to CSR, while replete with evidence of micro-scale, gradual improvements, has completely and utterly failed to make any impact on the massive sustainability crises that we face, many of which are getting worse at a pace that far outstrips any futile CSR-led attempts at amelioration.

Curse 2: Peripheral CSR

Ask any CSR manager what their greatest frustration is and they will tell you: lack of top management commitment. This is 'code-speak' for saying that CSR is, at best, a peripheral function in most companies. There may be a CSR manager, a CSR department even, a CSR report and a public commitment to any number of CSR codes and standards. But these do little to mask the underlying truth that shareholder-driven capitalism is rampant and its obsession with short-term financial measures of progress is contradictory in almost every way to the long-term, stakeholder approach needed for high-impact CSR.

The reason Enron collapsed, and indeed why our current financial crisis was allowed to spiral out of control, was not because of a few rogue executives or creative accounting practices, it was because of a culture of greed embedded in the DNA of the company and the financial markets. Whether you agree or not (and despite the emerging research on 'responsible competitiveness'), it is hard to find any substantive examples in which the financial markets consistently reward responsible behaviour.

Curse 3: Uneconomic CSR

Which brings us to Curse 3. If there was ever a monotonously repetitive, stuck record in CSR debates, it is the one about the so-called 'business case' for CSR. That is because CSR managers and consultants, and even the occasional saintly CEO, are desperate to find compelling evidence that 'doing good is good for business', i.e. CSR pays. The lack of corroborative research seems to be no impediment for these desperados endlessly incanting the motto of the business case, as if it were an entirely self-evident fact.

The rather more 'inconvenient truth' is that CSR sometimes pays, in specific circumstances, but more often does *not*. Of course there are low-hanging fruit – like eco-efficiencies around waste and energy – but these only go so far. Most of the hard-core CSR changes that are needed to reverse the misery of poverty and the sixth mass extinction of species currently underway require strategic change and massive investment. They may very well be lucrative in the long term, economically rational over a generation or two, but we have already established that the financial markets do not work like that; at least, not yet.

CSR 1.0: Burying the Past

What would be far more productive than all this wishing and pretending that CSR is good for everyone and will help to solve the world's problems is to simply see it for what it is: an outdated, outmoded artefact that was once useful, but the time for which has past. We need to let the 'old CSR' die gracefully and give it a dignified burial. By all means, let us give it the respect it deserves – a fitting eulogy about brave new frontiers of responsibility that it conquered in its heyday. But then, let us look for the next generation of CSR – the newborn that will carry the torch forward.[2]

If we succeed in admitting the failure of CSR and burying the past, we may find ourselves on the cusp of a revolution, in much the same way as the internet transitioned from Web 1.0 to Web 2.0. The emergence of social media networks, user-generated content and open source approaches are a fitting metaphor for the changes CSR will have to undergo if it is to redefine its contribution and make a serious impact on the social, environmental and ethical challenges the world faces.

For example, in the same way that Web 1.0 moved from a one-way, advertising-push approach to a more collaborative Google-Facebook mode, CSR 1.0 is starting to move beyond the outmoded approach of CSR as philanthropy or public relations (which has been widely criticised as 'greenwash') to a more interactive, stakeholder-driven model. Similarly, while Web 1.0 was dominated by standardised hardware and software, but now encourages co-creation and diversity, so too in CSR, we are beginning to realise the limitations of the generic CSR codes and standards that have proliferated in the past 10 years.

CSR 2.0: Embracing the Future

If this is where we have come from, where do we need to go to? Let us explore in more detail this revolution that will, if successful, change the way we talk about and practice CSR and, ultimately, the way we do business. There are five principles that make up the DNA of CSR 2.0: Creativity (C), Scalability (S), Responsiveness (R), Glocality (2) and Circularity (0).

Principle 1: Creativity (C)

In order to succeed in the CSR revolution, we will need innovation and creativity. We know from Thomas Kuhn's work on *The Structure of Scientific Revolutions* that step-change only happens when we can re-perceive our world, when we can find a genuinely new paradigm, or pattern of thinking. This process of 'creative destruction' is today a well accepted theory of societal change, first introduced by German sociologist Werner Sombart and elaborated and popularised by Austrian economist Joseph Schumpeter. We cannot, to a paraphrase Einstein, solve today's problems with yesterday's thinking.

Business is naturally creative and innovative. What is different about the Age of Responsibility is that business creativity needs to be directed to solving the world's social and environmental problems. Apple, for example, is highly creative, but their iPhone does little to tackle our most pressing societal needs. By contrast, Vodafone's M-PESA innovation by Safaricom in Kenya, which allows money to be transferred by text, has empowered a nation in which 80% of the population have no bank account and where more money flows into the country through international remittances than foreign aid. Or consider Freeplay's innovation, using battery-free wind-up technology for torches, radios and laptops in Africa, thereby giving millions of people access to products and services in areas that are off the electricity grid.

All of these are part of the exciting trend towards social enterprise or social business that is sweeping the globe, supported by the likes of American Swiss entrepreneur Stephen Schmidheiny, Ashoka's Bill Drayton, e-Bay's Jeff Skoll, the World Economic Forum's Klaus Schwabb, Grameen Bank's Muhammad Yunus and Volans Ventures' John Elkington. It is not a panacea, but for some products and services, directing the creativity of business towards the most pressing needs of society is the most rapid, scalable way to usher in the Age of Responsibility.

Principle 2: Scalability (S)
The CSR literature is liberally sprinkled with charming case studies of truly responsible and sustainable projects and a few pioneering companies. The problem is that so few of them ever go to scale. It is almost as if, once the sound-bites and PR-plaudits have been achieved, no further action is required. They become shining pilot projects and best practice examples, tarnished only by the fact that they are endlessly repeated on the CSR conference circuits of the world, without any vision for how they might transform the core business of their progenitors.

The sustainability problems we face, be they climate change or poverty, are at such a massive scale, and are so urgent, that any CSR solutions that cannot match that scale and urgency are red herrings at best and malevolent diversions at worst. How long have we been tinkering away with ethical consumerism (organic, fairtrade and the like), with hardly any impact on the world's major corporations or supply chains? And yet, when Wal-Mart's former CEO, Lee Scott, had his post-Katrina Hurricane Damascus experience and decided that in future *all* Wal-Mart cotton products will be organic and *all* fish MSC-certified, then we started seeing CSR 2.0-type scalability.

Scalability is not limited to the retail sector. In financial services, there have always been charitable loans for the world's poor and destitute. But when Muhammad Yunus, in the aftermath of a devastating famine in Bangladesh, set up the Grameen Bank and it went from one $74 loan in 1974 to a $2.5 billion enterprise, spawning more than 3,000 similar microcredit institutions in 50 countries and reaching over 133 million clients, that is a lesson in scalability. Or contrast Toyota's laudable but premium-priced hybrid Prius for the rich and eco-conscious with Tata's $2,500 Nano, a cheap and eco-efficient car for the masses. The one is an incremental solution with long term potential; the other is scalable solution with immediate impact.

Principle 3: Responsiveness (R)
Business has a long track-record of responsiveness to community needs – witness generations of philanthropy and heart-warming generosity following disasters like 9/11 or the Sichuan Earthquake. But this is responsiveness on their own terms, responsiveness when giving is easy and cheque-writing does nothing to upset their commercial applecart. The severity of the global problems we face demands that companies go much further. CSR 2.0 requires uncomfortable, transformative responsiveness, which questions about whether particular industries or business models are part of the solution or part of the problem.

Instead, we frequently see the opposite, for example, when it became clear that climate change posed a serious challenge to the sustainability of the fossil fuel industry, all the major oil companies formed the Global Climate Coalition, a lobby group explicitly designed to discredit and deny the science of climate change and undermine the main international policy response, the Kyoto Protocol. In typical CSR 1.0 style, these same companies were simultaneously making hollow claims about their CSR credentials. By contrast, the Prince of Wales's Corporate Leaders Group on Climate Change has, since 2005, been lobbying for *bolder* UK, EU and international legislation on climate change, accepting that carbon emission reductions of between 50% and 85% will be needed by 2050.

CSR 2.0 responsiveness also means greater transparency, not only through reporting mechanisms like the Global Reporting Initiative and Carbon Disclosure Project, but also by sharing critical intellectual resources. The Eco-Patent Commons, set up by WBCSD to make technology patents available, without royalty, to help reduce waste, pollution, global warming and energy the donor exchange platforms that have begun to proliferate, allowing individual and corporate donors to connect directly with beneficiaries via the web, thereby tapping 'the long tail of CSR'.[3]

Principle 4: Glocality (2)
The term *glocalisation* comes from the Japanese word *dochakuka*, which simply means global localisation. Originally referring to a way of adapting farming techniques to local conditions, *dochakuka* evolved into a marketing strategy when Japanese businessmen adopted it in the 1980s. It was subsequently introduced and popularised in the West in the 1990s by Manfred Lange, Roland Robertson, Keith Hampton, Barry Wellman and Zygmunt Bauman. In a CSR context, the idea of 'think global, act local' recognises that most CSR issues manifest as dilemmas, rather than easy choices. In a complex, interconnected CSR 2.0 world, companies (and their

critics) will have to become far more sophisticated in understanding local contexts and finding the appropriate local solutions they demand, without forsaking universal principles.

For example, a few years ago, BHP Billiton was vexed by their relatively poor performance on the (then) Business in the Environment (BiE) Index, run by the UK charity Business in the Community. Further analysis showed that the company had been marked down for their high energy use and relative energy inefficiency. Fair enough. Or was it? Most of BHP Billiton's operations were, at that time, based in southern Africa, home to some of the world's cheapest electricity. No wonder this was not a high priority. What was a priority, however, was controlling malaria in the community, where they had made a huge positive impact. But the BiE Index did not have any rating questions on malaria, so this was ignored. Instead, it demonstrated a typical, Western-driven, one-size-fits-all CSR 1.0 approach.[4]

Carroll's CSR pyramid has already been mentioned. But in a sugar farming co-operative in Guatemala, they have their own CSR pyramid – economic responsibility is still the platform, but rather than legal, ethical and philanthropic dimensions, their pyramid includes responsibility to the family (of employees), the community and policy engagement. Clearly, both Carroll's pyramid and the Guatemala pyramid are helpful in their own appropriate context. Hence, CSR 2.0 replaces 'either/or' with 'both/and' thinking. *Both* SA 8000 *and* the Chinese national labour standard have their role to play. *Both* premiums branded *and* cheap generic drugs have a place in the solution to global health issues. CSR 2.0 is a search for the Chinese concept of a harmonious society, which implies a dynamic yet productive tension of opposites – a *Tai Chi* of CSR, balancing *yin* and *yang*.

Principle 5: Circularity (0)

The reason CSR 1.0 has failed is not through lack of good intent, nor even through lack of effort. The old CSR has failed because our global economic system is based on a fundamentally flawed design. For all the miraculous energy unleashed by Adam Smith's 'invisible hand' of the free market, our modern capitalist system is faulty at its very core. Simply put, it is conceived as an abstract system without limits. As far back as the 1960s, pioneering economist, Kenneth Boulding, called this a 'cowboy economy', where endless frontiers imply no limits on resource consumption or waste disposal. By contrast, he argued, we need to design a 'spaceship economy', where there is no 'away'; everything is engineered to constantly recycle.

In the 1990s, in *The Ecology of Commerce* (1994), Paul Hawken translated these ideas into three basic rules for sustainability: waste equals food; nature runs off current solar income; and nature depends on diversity. He also proposed replacing our product-sales economy with a service-lease model, famously using the example of Interface 'Evergreen' carpets that are leased and constantly replaced and recycled. William McDonough and Michael Braungart have extended this thinking in their *Cradle to Cradle* (2002) industrial model. Cradle-to-cradle is not only about closing the loop on production, but about designing for 'good', rather than the CSR 1.0 modus operandi of 'less bad'.

Hence, CSR 2.0 circularity would, according to cradle-to-cradle aspirations, create buildings that, like trees, produce more energy than they consume and purify their own waste water; or factories that produce drinking water as effluent; or products that decompose and become food and nutrients; or materials that can feed into industrial cycles as high quality raw materials for new products. Circularity need not only apply to the environment. Business should be constantly feeding and replenishing its social and human capital, not only through education and training, but also by nourishing community and employee wellbeing. CSR 2.0 raises the importance of meaning in work and life to equal status alongside ecological integrity and financial viability.

Shapeshifting: From CSR 1.0 to CSR 2.0

Even revolutions involve a transition, so what might we expect to see as markers along the road to transformation? Paternalistic relationships between companies and the community based on philanthropy will give way to more equal partnerships. Defensive, minimalist responses to social and environmental issues are replaced with proactive strategies and investment in growing responsibility markets, such as clean technology. Reputation-conscious public-relations approaches to CSR are no longer credible and so companies are judged on actual social, environmental and ethical performance (i.e. are things getting better on the ground in absolute, cumulative terms?).

Although CSR specialists still have a role to play, each dimension of CSR 2.0 performance is embedded and integrated into the core operations of companies. Standardised approaches remain useful as guides to consensus, but CSR finds diversified expression and implementation at very local levels. CSR solutions, including responsible products and services, go from niche 'nice-to-haves' to mass-market 'must-haves'. And the whole concept of CSR loses its Western conceptual and operational dominance, giving way to a more culturally diverse and internationally applied concept.

How might these shifting principles manifest as CSR practices? CSR will no longer manifest as luxury products and services (as with current green and fairtrade options), but as affordable solutions for those who most need quality of life improvements. Investment in self-sustaining social enterprises will be favoured over cheque-book charity. CSR indexes, which rank the same large companies over and over (often revealing contradictions between indexes) will make way for CSR rating systems, which turn social, environmental, ethical and economic performance into corporate scores (A +, B−, etc., not dissimilar to credit ratings), which analysts and others can usefully employ to compare and integrate into their decision-making.

Reliance on CSR departments will disappear or disperse, as performance across responsibility and sustainability dimensions are increasingly built into corporate performance appraisal and market incentive systems. Self-selecting ethical consumers will become irrelevant, as CSR 2.0 companies begin to choice-edit, i.e. cease offering implicitly 'less ethical' product ranges, thus allowing guilt-free shopping. Post-use liability for products will become obsolete, as the service-lease and take-back economy goes mainstream. Annual CSR reporting will be replaced by online, real-time CSR performance data flows. Feeding into these live communications will be Web 2.0 connected social networks, instead of periodic meetings of rather cumbersome stakeholder panels. And typical CSR 1.0 management systems standards like ISO 14001 will be less credible than new performance standards, such as those emerging in climate change that set absolute limits and thresholds.

CSR 2.0: The New DNA of Business

All of these visions of the future imply such a radical shift from the current model of CSR that they beg the question: do we need a new model of CSR? Certainly, Carroll's enduring CSR Pyramid, with its Western cultural assumptions, static design and wholesale omission of environmental issues, must be regarded as no longer fit for purpose. Even the emphasis on 'social' in corporate *social* responsibility implies a rather limited view of the agenda. So what might a new model look like?

The CSR 2.0 model proposes that we keep the acronym, but rebalance the scales, so to speak. Hence, CSR comes to stand for 'Corporate Sustainability and Responsibility'. This change acknowledges that 'sustainability' (with roots in the environmental movement) and 'responsibility' (with roots in the social activist movement) are really the two main games in town. A cursory look at companies' non-financial reports will rapidly confirm this – they are mostly either corporate sustainability or corporate responsibility reports.

However, CSR 2.0 also proposes a new interpretation on these terms. Like two intertwined strands of DNA, sustainability and responsibility can be thought of as different, yet complementary elements of CSR. Hence, sustainability can be conceived as the destination – the challenges, vision, strategy and goals, i.e. what we are aiming for – while responsibility is more about the journey – our solutions, responses, management and actions, i.e. how we get there.

The DNA of CSR 2.0 can be conceived as spiralling, interconnected, non-hierarchical levels, representing economic, human, social and environmental systems, each with a twinned sustainability/responsibility manifestation: economic sustainability and financial responsibility; human sustainability and labour responsibility; social sustainability and community responsibility; and environmental sustainability and moral responsibility.

CONCLUSION: THE PURPOSE OF BUSINESS

When all is said and done, CSR 2.0 comes down to one thing: clarification and reorientation of the purpose of business. It is a complete misnomer to believe that the purpose of business is to be profitable, or to serve shareholders. These are simply means to an end. Ultimately, the purpose of business is to serve society, through the provision of safe, high quality products and services that enhance our wellbeing, without eroding our ecological and community life-support systems. As David Packard, co-founder of Hewlett-Packard, wisely put it:

> Why are we here? Many people assume, wrongly, that a company exists solely to make money. People get together and exist as a company so that they are able to accomplish something collectively that they could not accomplish separately – they make a contribution to society.

Making a positive contribution to society is the essence of CSR 2.0 – not just as a marginal afterthought, but as a way of doing business. This is not about bailing out the Titanic with a teaspoon – which is the current effect of CSR 1.0 – but turning the whole ship around. CSR 2.0 is about designing and adopting an inherently sustainable and responsible business model, supported by a reformed financial and economic system that makes creating a better world the easiest, most natural and rewarding thing to do.

CSR is dead! Long live CSR!

NOTES

1. Earnings before Interest, Taxes, Depreciation and Amortisation.
2. At the launch of CSR International in March 2009, this is exactly what we did – we held a mock funeral with a coffin, out of which the new CSR baby was born. See http://www.csrinternational.org for a video of the ceremony.
3. This is a reference to *The Long Tail*, by Chris Anderson, as it might apply to CSR. I have written about this elsewhere.
4. The index has subsequently been reformed and now runs as a more integrated Corporate Responsibility Index. See http://www.bitc.org.uk

REFERENCES

Bowen, H. R. (1953). *Social responsibilities of the businessman*. New York: Harper & Row.

Carroll, A. B. (1979). A three-dimensional conceptual model of corporate social performance. *Academy of Management Review, 4*, 497–505.

Carroll, A. B. (1991). The pyramid of corporate social responsibility: Toward the moral management of organizational stakeholders. *Business Horizons*, July–August.

Carroll, A. B. (2008). A history of corporate social responsibility. In: A. Crane, A. McWilliams, D. Matten, J. Moon & D. S. Siegel (Eds), *The Oxford handbook of corporate social responsibility*. Oxford: Oxford University Press.

Carson, R. (1962). *Silent spring*. New York: Houghton Mifflin.

Hawken, P. (1994). *The ecology of commerce: A declaration of sustainability*. New York: Harper Business.

McDonald, L. (2009). *A colossal failure of common sense: The incredible inside story of the collapse of Lehman Brothers*. Ebury Press.

McDonough, W., & Braungart, M. (2002). *Cradle to Cradle: Remaking the Way We Make Things*. North Point Press.

Nader, R. (1965). *Unsafe at any speed: The designed – in dangers of the American automobile*. New York: Grossman Publishers.

Visser, W. (2011). *The age of responsibility: CSR 2.0 and the new DNA of business*. London: Wiley.

Visser, W., & McIntosh, A. (1998). A short review of the historical critique of usury. *Accounting, Business & Financial History, 8*(2), 175–189.

Visser, W., Matten, D., Pohl, M., & Tolhurst, N. (2010). *The A to Z of corporate social responsibility: The complete reference guide of concepts, codes and organisations* (2nd ed.). London: Wiley.

DYING OF CONSUMPTION? VOLUNTARY SIMPLICITY AS AN ANTIDOTE TO HYPERMATERIALISM

Hershey H. Friedman and Linda Weiser Friedman

The economic path we are currently on, which focuses on extreme materialism and overconsumption, is leading us to destruction. It is not sustainable and is destroying the true values that result in a healthy and happy society. After the financial turbulence of 2008, it is becoming very obvious that we need a new economics, one that is moral and considers more than profit and growth. This chapter examines the effects of hypermaterialism and overconsumption and proposes that one possible solution may be found in the movement toward voluntary simplicity. Voluntary simplicity can help lead us on a path toward sustainable development and away from the greed-is-good credo that nearly caused another Great Depression.

There are many indications that the drive to consume, which was considered an economic virtue 50 or 60 years ago, has led to an ingrained, extreme form of materialism. The consequences of this hypermaterialism on the financial industry, on the environment, on joblessness, and on our very happiness are myriad.

And now, our so-called affluent society has been shaken up by the current financial debacle. Millions of people have lost their jobs, many

Reframing Corporate Social Responsibility: Lessons from the Global Financial Crisis
Critical Studies on Corporate Responsibility, Governance and Sustainability,
Volume 1, 253–269
ISSN: 2043-9059/doi:10.1108/S2043-9059(2010)0000001017

are underemployed, and trillions of dollars in wealth have apparently disappeared. The U.S. unemployment rate in October 2009 was 10.2 percent, the highest it has been since the early 1980s. The broader measure of joblessness, which includes underemployment, is at a record 17.5 percent (Leonhardt, 2009a). Robert Reich, the former labor secretary, believes that most of the jobs that disappeared during this recession will not be returning. In July 2009, there were a record six job seekers for every position available – 2.4 million full-time jobs for 14.5 million unemployed laborers (Goodman, 2009a).

According to the U.S. Census Bureau (2009), the poverty rate in the United States was 13.2 percent in 2008, the highest it has been since 1997. The poverty rate will very likely continue to increase. On top of that, the gap between the wealthy and the poor is quite wide. Of course, this is not new. In fact, the phrase "affluent society" was coined by John Kenneth Galbraith in his 1958 book with that title. In his book, Galbraith noted the disparity between those in the wealthy and the poor strata. Over the past several years, low- and middle-income families made few gains in income. For those in the bottom quintile, average incomes fell by 2.5 percent. For those in the middle quintile, it only went up by a paltry 1.3 percent, and for those in the top quintile, income went up by a healthy 9 percent (Bernstein, McNichol, & Nicholas, 2008).

MATERIALISM

Materialism is a consumer value that stresses the importance of acquiring more and more material goods. Success is defined in terms of the type and quantity of goods one owns and happiness is expected to result from physical wealth (Beutler, Beutler, & McCoy, 2008). Materialism as defined thus is closely tied to the idea of the pursuit of rational self-interest that has been associated with Adam Smith (1776).

Is Self-Interest Really "Rational"?

The famous speech by Gordon Gekko in the movie *Wall Street* (Weiser & Stone, 1987) is based on the idea that the pursuit of self-interest is good for all of us:

> Greed, for lack of a better word, is good. Greed is right. Greed works. Greed clarifies, cuts through, and captures the essence of evolutionary spirit. Greed in all of its forms, greed for life, for money, for love, knowledge has marked the upward surge of mankind.

> And greed, you mark my words, will not only save Teldar Paper, but that other
> malfunctioning corporation called the USA.

Change the word "greed" to pursuit of self-interest and you have in effect what has been and continues to be taught to millions of business and economics students. Most of Wall Street still believes that the pursuit of self-interest (another way of saying materialism and greed) is good for society. However, many scholars and leaders warned of the dangers of raw greed. Interestingly, in 1937 – a year that feels awfully "familiar" to us today (see Krugman, 2010) – at his second inaugural address, President Franklin D. Roosevelt stated, "We have always known that heedless self-interest was bad morals; we know now that it is bad economics" (Roosevelt, 1937). Pitelis (2002) asserted that unrestrained capitalism that is obsessed with self-interest and unconcerned about the long run can lead to monopoly, inequitable distribution of income, unemployment, and environmental disaster.

Robinson (1978) made the point more than 30 years ago that the pursuit of self-interest has caused much harm to society and that Adam Smith does not deserve to be associated with this doctrine. In actuality, Smith believed that "society ... cannot subsist among those who are at all times ready to hurt and injure one another." Raw self-interest without a foundation of morality is not what Adam Smith is all about. Robinson (1978) ended a commencement address with the following warning: "I hope ... that you will find that the doctrines of Adam Smith are not to be taken in the form in which your professors are explaining them to you."

President Obama asserted the following about Adam Smith:

> Adam Smith, at the same time as he was writing about the invisible hand, he was also
> writing about the moral sense – that human ecology – that allows a market to work: the
> sense that if I bring my goods into the market, someone is not going to hit me over
> the head; the sense that because I am trading with this guy often enough that I know that
> the scales aren't tampered with. (Leonhardt, 2009b)

Smith was a believer in capitalism based on morality. Indeed, his second most famous work was *The Theory of Moral Sentiments*.

Lawrence H. Summers, currently serving in President Obama's administration as Director of the National Economic Council, remarked in a 2003 speech to the Chicago Economic Club:

> it is the irony of the market system that while its very success depends on harnessing the
> power of self-interest, its very sustainability depends upon people's willingness to engage
> in acts that are not self-interested.

The financial turbulence of 2008 brought home quite clearly what happens when self-interest and greed are allowed to go out of control. Of course, there were other factors as well, but there is no question that greed had a significant and material role. As one Indian banker explained, "It was perpetuated by greedy bankers, whether investment bankers or commercial bankers. The greed to make money ..." (Nocera, 2008). Vice President Biden had this to say about the Wall Street executives who were still trying to collect bonuses after nearly causing a depression: "I'd like to throw these guys in the brig. They're thinking the same old thing that got us here, greed. They're thinking, 'Take care of me'" (Stolberg & Labaton, 2009).

The root cause of the financial debacle that has nearly destroyed the world economy is gross materialism – in a word, greed. Materialism, greed, and self interest are all different ways of saying the same thing. There is no way in the world that Adam Smith would have condoned this kind of raw self-interest.

The Drive to Consume

After World War II, economists and business leaders believed that the only way to achieve growth was to do everything possible to encourage consumption. Earlier, John Maynard Keynes had advocated that the government should use its power (e.g., fiscal policy) to stimulate aggregate demand to ensure full employment. Consumption is a major component of aggregate demand. Keynes believed very much in government intervention as a means to bolster the economy when unemployment was unacceptably high (Davidson, 2007).

Victor Lebow encouraged making consumption a way of life: "We need things consumed, burned up, worn out, replaced, and discarded at an ever-increasing rate" (Barash, 2009). This is in fact what happened. Thus, for example, the average house today is more than twice as large as it was in 1949. Since 1940, the American people have consumed more mineral resources than all previous generations. Our country, in the last 200 years, has lost 99 percent of its tallgrass prairies and 95 percent of its old-growth forests (Barash, 2009). From 1950 to 1980, the personal consumption/gross domestic product (GDP) ratio was a stable 62 percent. Since 1980, it has surged to 70 percent. Personal debt also exploded from 55 percent of national income in 1960 to 133 percent in 2007 (Brooks, 2009). The national debt has mushroomed to a mind-boggling $12 trillion. As long as interest rates are extremely low, the cost of servicing this incredible amount of debt will be relatively low. However, the super-low interest rates will have to rise eventually, and the cost of servicing the debt will skyrocket.

The increasing budget deficit in the United States is not sustainable. China is holding approximately $1.5 trillion in dollar-based assets such as Treasury bills and is putting pressure on the United States to reduce its budget deficit. The United States has agreed to do this once the economy improves. Of course, reducing the deficit means less government spending and higher taxes (Landler & Sanger, 2009).

Ferguson and Schularick (2009) believe that China was able to quadruple its GDP between 2000 and 2008, create many millions of jobs, and quintuple its exports by purchasing dollars to keep the value of their currency low relative to the dollar. This allowed Americans to overconsume and undersave, and one-third of the overconsumption was on Chinese imports. Currently, the American trade deficit with China has been around $200 billion and China had to purchase 300 billion worth of dollars to keep its currency undervalued and exports inexpensive. Ferguson and Schularick refer to this as the 10:10 deal. America lives with 10 percent unemployment so that China can have a 10 percent growth rate. Of course, this arrangement cannot go on forever. The Chinese cannot continue to hold dollar-denominated reserve assets.

According to Tabuchi (2009), the Japanese used to be obsessed with luxury products and were buying vast quantities of items such as $1,000 handbags. Luxury boutiques were doing well. Then, economic stagnation hit during the 1990s, a period often referred to as the "lost decade." Today, the Japanese people are becoming thrifty, moving away from luxury products such as Louis Vuitton bags and Hermes scarves. They no longer care about ostentation and are focused rather on frugality. The global economic crisis together with the economic stagnation of the 1990s has changed the Japanese culture and many economists believe the change is permanent (Tabuchi, 2009). Similarly, it is quite possible that the U.S. consumer will also have to make adjustments and move away from luxury brands toward simpler and cheaper products.

In one episode of the television show *Sex & the City* (Harris & Taylor, 2002), the Carrie Bradshaw character discovers that, while she cannot afford an apartment in which to live, she nonetheless owns $40,000 worth of shoes. In her words, "I literally will be the old woman who lived in her shoes." She also remarks, "I'm homeless! I'll be a bag lady! A Fendi bag lady, but a bag lady!". This may be an exaggeration, but there is a great deal of truth here. Americans overspend on so many useless luxuries that they do not realize how empty and meaningless their lives have become.

Developed countries (United States, Canada, Western Europe, Japan, and Australia) with a total population of about 1 billion consume 32 times more resources such as oil and plastic than do those in developing countries with a population of 5.5 billion. According to Diamond (2008), population growth is not the real problem facing humankind, the big concern is overconsumption. If the entire world were to consume as much as the developed countries do, this would be the same as if the world population increased to 72 billion. No one believes that the world can support this many people. The solution is for everyone to reduce their consumption levels.

To make matters worse, the population of the world, currently at 6.8 billion, will probably increase to 9.3 billion people by the year 2050 (http://www.npg.org/facts/world_pop_year.htm), an increase of 2.5 billion people. Most of these people will desire the same middle class lifestyle that the typical American possesses. This is the conundrum of the "affluent society" on a global scale. Where will the resources come from to take care of so many people?

VOLUNTARY SIMPLICITY

One possible solution to the problems caused by overconsumption and hypermaterialism – that is, greed – is to promote the values of voluntary simplicity. There are many definitions of voluntary simplicity, but the basic idea is to become less materialistic and reduce consumption to lead a life that has more meaning and purpose (Johnston & Burton, 2003). It is, indeed, the antidote to greed and materialism. At this point, for the reasons noted earlier, living a life of purpose that is not focused on the acquisition of more and more material goods will be much better for the economy than predatory self-interest.

The 1980s and early 1990s saw the first wave of a movement toward voluntary simplicity, but it did not really take off at that time. Duane Elgin's book, *Voluntary Simplicity*, published in 1981 (later revised in 1993, and then again in 2010) became a sort of Bible for the movement. Shama and Wisenblit (1984) asserted that "The main goals of this lifestyle were rational moral behavior, spiritual growth and self-actualization, which together manifest the economic behaviors of low consumption, ecological responsibility, and self-sufficiency." Over the past few years, there seems to have been somewhat of a resurgence of this movement (see, e.g., Cherrier, 2009; Doherty & Etzioni, 2003; Etzioni, 2004; Huneke, 2005; Pellow, 2005; Salwen & Salwen, 2010; Shaw & Moraes, 2009; and, of course, Elgin, 2010).

With the havoc wreaked by the current global financial crisis and the ominous threat of global warming, we may have no choice but to encourage the philosophy of voluntary simplicity. A showy, overly ostentatious lifestyle does little to make people happy and is, indeed, no longer sustainable.

In the sections to follow, we attempt to explore the effects that a move toward voluntary simplicity and away from the hypermaterialism of the past several decades might have on our society.

Impact on the Environment

The phenomenon of global warming is making many of us aware that we may be heading for ecological disaster unless something is done – and soon. According to Gore and Blood (2008), "the challenges of the climate crisis, water scarcity, income disparity, extreme poverty and disease must command our urgent attention."

Similarly, the outdated view that the only way for us to prosper is through increased consumption of consumer goods is dangerous to our planet. Markham (2006) asked, How much longer can the United States with only 5 percent of the world's population continue to use 25 percent of many critical resources? Jencks (2008) also made a similar point:

> both the Democratic and Republican versions of the American dream will have to be rethought. They both focus heavily on income and material consumption. The idea that we can keep raising our material standard of living without making most of the planet too hot for human habitation is, I think, mistaken. Even the idea that we have 20 or 30 years to make the necessary adjustments appears wrongheaded.

Jencks concluded that we will have to redefine progress so that it does not focus on material goods but on things such as "physical health, material security, individual freedom, and time to play with our children and smell the roses." This sounds very much like the essential philosophy of the voluntary simplicity movement.

The cost of nonrenewable sources of energy has increased and will most likely continue to increase in the future. Contrary to what used to be considered common wisdom, many firms are discovering that they can actually increase profits by going green. A significant number of individuals are also trying to reduce energy usage. One study found that 75 percent of consumers claim that their purchasing decisions are affected by a firm's reputation with respect to taking care of the environment (Kotler & Lee, 2005, p. 12). Howard (1997) noted that "the lie that human nature demands that individuals maximize their self-interest, is particularly problematic for biological ecosystems." In fact, the "free market capitalist system, that encourages the current geometric rates of increase in population, production, consumption, and waste generation, represents a terrifying pyramid scheme. Eventually, we will overwhelm our ecosystems." Howard proposed that we reject this dangerous, consumption-oriented belief that is obsessed with maximization and materialism. According to Howard, people should believe in simplicity, moderation, and nonmaterialistic values and reject the idea of maximization.

A very simple way of helping the environment is to consume less meat. Meat is not only a relatively unhealthy and expensive way of consuming protein, it also has a serious negative impact on the environment. There are trillions of farm animals and they are responsible for more global warming than cars, buses, and planes; in fact, they generate 18 percent of the emissions that are implicated in global warming (Rosenthal, 2008). The flatus and manure produced by farm animals produce huge amounts of methane that trap far more heat than carbon dioxide. Methane is 25 times more efficient than carbon dioxide in trapping heat. Also, rain forests have to be cleared to have enough land to be able to grow feed for the cattle. According to one research group, "Producing a pound of beef creates 11 times as much greenhouse gas emission as a pound of chicken and 100 times more than a pound of carrots" (Rosenthal, 2008). Animal agriculture – thanks to factory farming – is now the number one contributor to global warming. It is also among the major causes of key environmental problems that include deforestation, air pollution, water pollution, and biodiversity decline (Foer, 2009).

Reducing meat consumption would not have a noticeable effect on one's lifestyle (except, possibly, for better health), but would have a greater impact on the environment than switching to a hybrid car (Rosenthal, 2008). There are towns in Europe whose populations refrain from meat one day a week to improve the environment (Kanter, 2009).

Consumers help the environment by leading a less materialistic life and consuming fewer and simpler goods. This means smaller and fewer cars, vacations closer to home, eating more fruits and vegetables, and so forth. True, the beaches of, say, Virginia Beach may not be as exotic as the French Riviera, but a Virginia Beach vacation is considerably less expensive and the people there are probably just as friendly as those on the Riviera.

Impact on Social Responsibility

Beyond taking seriously our roles as environmental stewards, the broader notion of social responsibility also encompasses ethical considerations as well as a profound respect for people, individually and in groups. Just as voluntary simplicity can help foster increased sustainability, it may also be an excellent way to frame and implement an organization's social responsibility program.

Corporate social responsibility (CSR) has become the latest mantra of the business world. Hundreds of papers have been written about it and many firms are trying to abide by it and even including it in their mission statements. Our definition of CSR will be the one cited in Hollender and Fenichell (2004, p. 29):

> an ongoing commitment by business to behave ethically and to contribute to economic development when demonstrating respect for people, communities, society at large, and the environment. In short, CSR marries the concepts of global citizenship with environmental stewardship and sustainable development.

Firms interested in CSR may have a variety of motives beyond, of course, the simple wish to do some good. Kotler and Lee (2005, pp. 10–11) reported that there are many benefits to being a socially responsible firm. These include, increased sales and market share; strengthened brand positioning; enhanced corporate image and clout; increased ability to attract, motivate, and retain employees; decreased operating costs; and increased appeal to investors and financial analysts. Regardless of motive, more and more firms have become interested in CSR. As important as CSR is to the business world, it is also important to consumers. Aburdene (2005) asserted that there are 70 million Americans – she refers to them as "values-driven consumers" – who prefer to buy from firms with values. These individuals are socially responsible and have concern for people and society at large. Socially responsible people and organizations care about the world. Voluntary simplicity is consistent with social responsibility. It is difficult to care for the world and society when one is obsessed solely with acquiring more and more material goods.

Patricia Aburdene, a renowned trend watcher and author of *Megatrends 2010*, asserted that spirituality in business is "converging with other socioeconomic trends to foster a moral transformation in capitalism" (Lampman, 2005). Aburdene (2005) claimed that we are moving toward "conscious capitalism," a new kind of capitalism that not only focuses on profits but also that considers factors such as social, environmental, and economic costs in business decision making (Lampman, 2005). Some of the major social trends identified by Aburdene (2005) include "the power of spirituality," "the dawn of conscious capitalism," "spirituality in business," "the values-driven consumer," and the "socially responsible investment boom."

Aburdene's findings are consistent with the theory of Fogel (2000), a 1993 Nobel laureate in economics, who stressed the importance of spirituality in the new economy. He identified 15 vital spiritual resources that include concepts such as "a sense of purpose, a sense of opportunity, a sense of community, a strong family ethic, a strong work ethic, and high self esteem." It may be obvious, but it is worth noting that it is hard to have a "sense of purpose" when one is obsessed with greed and materialism. The implication of his view is that capitalism should take spiritual values into account to survive in the new economy. It should also be noted that Fogel uses the term "spirituality" in a way that is not connected to any particular religion or group. Whereas spirituality may or may not be in decline in much of the Western world, other values such as environmentalism and CSR may be increasing in prominence.

According to Singer (2009), one of the great moral challenges of this generation is to do something about starvation in the world. Approximately 1.4 billion people live below the extreme poverty line of $1.25 per day. These people are hungry for much of the year and are also malnourished. The life expectancy of people living in the wealthier nations is 78 years; it is below 50 years in the poorer nations. Five percent of children living in these poor countries die before the age of 5; that is, 27,000 children dying every single day because of poverty. In India today, 43 percent of children younger than 5 years of age are malnourished and underweight (Rieff, 2009). The United States is among the developed countries that give the least foreign aid as a percentage of gross national income (0.16 per cent). As long as Americans define success by the number of possessions owned, it is difficult to be concerned with the poverty of others. In fact, traditional economists of the self-interest model are less likely to contribute to the needy (Lahart, 2010). On the contrary, "moral responsibility, spiritual growth, affiliation, and self-actualization" are characteristics of individuals who adopt a voluntary simplicity life style (Beutler et al., 2008).

Impact on Happiness

Is there a relationship between materialism and happiness? There is no question that people with enough money to take care of their basic needs are considerably happier than those who must struggle to survive. However, most scholars have found that increases in income do little to increase one's happiness once a person's basic needs are satisfied. What does seem to matter considerably more than absolute wealth is relative wealth. And expectations are also important in affecting happiness (Futrelle, 2006; Johnson & Krueger, 2006; Kahneman, Krueger, Schkade, Schwarz, & Stone, 2006; McConvill, 2005; McGowan, 2005; Myers & Diener, 1995; Myers, 2000; Wallis, 2005).

Those who study happiness know that individuals are very poor judges as to what will make them happy (Gilbert, 2006). They will, therefore, overestimate the joy that additional money will bring them and under-estimate the joy they will receive from having more time to spend with family and friends. For example, long commutes to work are rough on happiness; yet, people will change jobs to make more money – even if it means more time on the road – and end up with reduced happiness. In most cases, a person with an easy commute and a job that is not demanding in terms of time will be much happier than the person who has little or no time to spend with family and friends because of work. The same can probably be said of the joy from additional material goods. Does a person need four homes and six cars to be happy? One may safely assume that happiness will not be adversely affected by voluntary simplicity, especially if everyone is cutting back on the acquisition of material goods.

Layard (2005, pp. 48–49) described the "hedonic treadmill" that individuals and families often find themselves on. Their income increases, so they buy a bigger and better house, a nicer car, go out more. Within a few months, having adapted to the new lifestyle, they are no happier than before the raise in income. Firebaugh and Tach (2005) also concluded that Americans are on a hedonic treadmill: "working-age families must earn more and more over time to maintain a constant level of happiness." Myers (2000) observed that the inflation-adjusted income of Americans more than doubled from 1957 to 1998; yet, happiness did not increase: "We are twice as rich and no happier."

It is worth noting that the obsession with growth was partially responsible for the recent financial meltdown because it encouraged consumers to buy homes they could not afford and encouraged overbuilding (Goodman, 2009b). Barash (2009) noted that our relationship to the ecosystem is, in effect, a huge Ponzi scheme; we are all "Ponzis and Madoffs who profit from economic schemes that are fundamentally unsustainable and thus, in the deepest sense, frauds."

Materialism, while not conducive to happiness, is, in fact, correlated with several emotional problems such as lower self-esteem, a decrease in psychological well-being, and unstable self-esteem because it based on acquisition of material goods to achieve happiness. In addition, individuals who are materialistic are more likely than nonmaterialistic people to engage in behaviors that are risky and cultural fads (Beutler et al., 2008). Today, many adolescents see "happiness as the result of having the right image, the right things, or the right number of things." They often define their self-worth in terms of material goods (Beutler et al., 2008). Shifting over to a lifestyle that stresses true accomplishments rather than materialism can help adolescents as well as adults achieve a meaningful, fulfilling life.

A small number of economists believe that we should move away from models that focus on maximizing wealth (e.g., GDP) and instead use national indicators of happiness (Diener, 2000; Frey & Stutzer, 2005). One Buddhist country, Bhutan, plans on using "gross national happiness" (GNH) as a key economic indicator rather than the traditional GDP. Although there is no question that the overwhelming majority of economists do believe in growth, unfortunately, many of them have not considered that the resources of the world are limited and that the days in which we exploit the ecosystem will ultimately come to an abrupt and disastrous end.

Joseph Stiglitz and Amartya Sen, two Nobel Prize winning economists, in a recent study (Stiglitz, Sen, & Fitoussi, 2009; also, see Goodman, 2009b), have urged countries to move away from growth of GDP as an assessment tool with which to measure the health of an economy. They believe that focusing narrowly on the growth of GDP considers neither the incomes of average people nor the costs of environmental pollution. GDP is a poor measure of overall economic health, happiness, or social performance. An economy could be growing along with increasing pollution and a very high unemployment rate. If we keep stressing growth of GDP, we may find ourselves in a situation in which the economy is doing well but all our cities and rivers are polluted.

If happiness is ultimately our goal, running on the hedonic treadmill of materialism and consumption is not the way to achieve it. And if it is true that the more things change the more they remain the same, it makes sense then that thousands of years ago, Ecclesiastes (5:9) noted, "Whoever loves money will never have enough money; whoever loves wealth will not be satisfied with it. This too is futile."

CONCLUSIONS

If sustainability, organizational social responsibility, and happiness are critical goals of our modern world, then voluntary simplicity may be seen as one path to take toward the fulfillment of these goals. The other path, the one toward hypermaterialism and overconsumption, is not working out well. We have seen depletion of scarce resources, the buildup of toxins in the environment, acquisition of goods that borders on obsessiveness, and increasingly inequitable distribution of income. Clearly, these trends are not sustainable.

This global financial crisis was fueled by greed and a breakdown in ethics. It was not only the financial institutions that were behaving unethically. People were acting in a way that demonstrated no sense of personal responsibility. Individuals bought very expensive homes, with little or no money down, knowing very well that eventually there would be no way they could pay the mortgage. Greed is not good – and it nearly caused a world depression. Leading a simple life will help solve many of the world's problems. It will help reduce global warming and allow the rest of the world to catch up with the developed countries.

Perhaps, business schools and economics programs should rethink the self-interest paradigm. Recently, about 20 percent of the graduating class of Harvard Business School signed an M.B.A. oath that states that the goal of a manager is to "serve the greater good." The "greed is good" credo is being rejected by these students. They want to "act responsibly, ethically, and refrain from advancing their own 'personal ambitions' at the expense of others" (Wayne, 2009). Darlin (2009) observed that living a frugal life will be difficult not only because it asks consumers to forego many material goods but also because it asks people to abandon a "cherished belief about life." This is the belief that every person has to live better than his/her parents did. The authors feel that this belief is no longer sustainable and may not make much sense when a significant number of people have very extravagant lifestyles that include two homes, three cars, five television sets, and much more.

Back in 1997, it was becoming quite obvious that the global economy could not survive by following its current path, which focused on growth and profit, without considering other factors such as the environment and society. Robertson (1999) made the following observation:

> The growing sense in people around the world that modern society is not working now and is not sustainable in the long term, stems in large part from the tendencies of the global socio-economic system toward:
>
> – systematic destruction of the natural environment,
> – systematic destruction of community,
> – systematic transfer of wealth upward,
> – systematic marginalization of persons, communities and cultures,

 – systematic erosion and denial of the sense of the spiritual or sacred, and
 – systematic creation of learned incapacity and helplessness.

Voluntary simplicity is quite consistent with the M.B.A oath noted earlier and will help lead us on a path of sustainable development. Moreover, we may have no choice in redefining the American dream. It is quite likely that Americans will find that high levels of consumption will no longer be sustainable with the new postfinancial meltdown economy. Historians, in explaining the rise and fall of many great empires, have noted that "Wealth and power lead to affluence and luxury. Affluence and luxury lead to decadence, corruption and decline" (Brooks, 2009). The world needs a strong America to act as a stabilizing influence; the United States cannot be strong if it continues to take on more and more debt and wastes scarce resources. Voluntary simplicity may be the only antidote to materialism and greed.

Finally, voluntary simplicity is not an all-or-nothing movement of fanatical ascetics. Rather, it can be accomplished with a gradual shifting of priorities – less materialism, less consumption, more of a sense of responsibility toward the world we live in, and greater happiness.

REFERENCES

Aburdene, P. (2005). *Megatrends 2010: The rise of conscious capitalism*. Charlottesville, VA: Hampton Roads Publishing.

Barash, D. P. (2009). We are all Madoffs: Our relationship to the natural world is a Ponzi scheme. *Chronicle Review*, September 4, pp. B8–B9.

Bernstein, J., McNichol, E., & Nicholas, A. (2008). Pulling apart: A state-by-state analysis of income trends. Center on Budget and Policy Priorities and Economic Policy Institute. Available at http://www.epi.org/publications/entry/studies_pulling_apart_2008. Retrieved on 20 August 2009.

Beutler, I., Beutler, L., & McCoy, J. K. (2008). Money aspirations about living well: Middle school student perceptions. *Financial Counseling and Planning, 19*(1), 44–60.

Brooks, D. (2009). The next culture war. *New York Times*, OP-Ed, September 29, p. A39.

Cherrier, H. (2009). Disposal and simple living: Exploring the circulation of goods and the development of sacred consumption. *Journal of Consumer Behaviour, 8*(6), 327–339.

Darlin, D. (2009). A lesson in frugality, from the tenements. *New York Times*, Sunday Business, December 13, p. 10.

Davidson, P. (2007). *John Maynard Keynes*. New York: Palgrave Macmillan.

Diamond, J. (2008). What's your consumption factor? *New York Times*, OP-Ed, January 2, p. A17.

Diener, E. (2000). Subjective well being: The science of happiness and a proposal for a national index. *American Psychologist, 55*(1), 34–43.

Doherty, D., & Etzioni, A. (Eds). (2003). *Voluntary simplicity: Responding to consumer culture.* Lanham, MD: Raaaowman & Littlefield Publishers.

Elgin, D. (2010). *Voluntary simplicity: Toward a way of life that is outwardly simple, inwardly rich* (2nd ed.). New York: William Morrow.

Etzioni, A. (2004). The post affluent society. *Review of Social Economy, 62*(3), 407–412.

Ferguson, N., & Schularick, M. (2009). The great wallop. *New York Times,* November 16, p. A25.

Firebaugh, G., & Tach, L. (2005). *Relative income and happiness: Are Americans on a hedonic treadmill?* Working Paper. Penn State University, Pennsylvania.

Foer, J. S. (2009). Against meat: Or at least 99 percent of it. *New York Times Magazine,* October 11, pp. 68–75.

Fogel, R. W. (2000). *The fourth great awakening.* Chicago: University of Chicago Press.

Frey, B. S., & Stutzer, A. (2005). Happiness research: State and prospects. *Review of Social Economy, 62*(2), 207–228.

Futrelle, D. (2006). Can money buy happiness? *Money, 35*(8), 127.

Gilbert, D. (2006). *Stumbling on happiness.* New York: Alfred A. Knopf.

Goodman, P. S. (2009a). U.S. job seekers exceed openings by record ratio. *New York Times,* September 27, p. A1 +.

Goodman, P. S. (2009b). Emphasis on growth is called misguided. *New York Times,* September 23, p. B1 +.

Gore, A., & Blood, D. (2008). We need sustainable capitalism. *Wall Street Journal,* November 5, p. A23.

Harris, A. B., (Writer), & Taylor, A. (Director). (2002). Ring a Ding Ding. *Sex and the City,* Season 4, Episode 6, Perf: Sarah Jessica Parker, HBO.

Hollender, J., & Fenichell, S. (2004). *What matters most.* New York: Basic Books.

Howard, G. S. (1997). The tragedy of maximization. *Ecopsychology Online.* Available at http://www.ecopsychology.athabascau.ca/1097/index.htm. Retrieved on 6 October 2010.

Huneke, M. E. (2005). The face of the un-consumer: an empirical examination of the practice of voluntary simplicity in the United States. *Psychology & Marketing, 22*(7), 527–551.

Jencks, C. (2008). Reinventing the American dream. *Chronicle Review,* October 17, pp. B6–B9.

Johnson, W., & Krueger, R. F. (2006). How money buys happiness: Genetic and environmental processes linking finances and life satisfaction. *Journal of Personality and Social Psychology, 90*(4), 680–691.

Johnston, T. C., & Burton, J. (2003). Voluntary simplicity: Definitions and dimensions. *Academy of Marketing Studies, 7*(1), 19–36.

Kahneman, D., Krueger, A. B., Schkade, D., Schwarz, N., & Stone, A. (2006). Would you be happier if you were richer? A focusing illusion. *Science, 312*(5782), 1908–1910.

Kanter, J. (2009). Bottled water bans and meat-free days. *New York Times,* July 10. Available at http://www.greeninc.blogs.nytimes.com/2009/07/10/bottled-water-bans-and-meat-free-days/. Retrieved on 21 August 2009.

Kotler, P., & Lee, N. (2005). *Corporate social responsibility: Doing the most good for your company and cause.* New York: Wiley.

Krugman, P. (2010). That 1937 feeling. *The New York Times,* January 4, p. A21.

Lahart, J. (2010). Secrets of the economist's trade: First purchase a piggy bank. *The Wall Street Journal,* January 2, p. A1.

Lampman, J. (2005). Trend-watcher sees moral transformation of capitalism. *Christian Science Monitor,* October 3, p. 13.

Landler, M., & Sanger, D. E. (2009). China seeks assurances that U.S. will cut deficit. *New York Times*, July 29, p. A6.

Layard, R. (2005). *Happiness: Lessons from a new science*. New York: Penguin Press.

Leonhardt, D. (2009a). Jobless rate hits 10.2%, with more underemployed. *New York Times*, November 7, p. A1 +.

Leonhardt, D. (2009b). Theory and morality in the new economy. *New York Times Book Review*, August 23, p. 23.

Markham, V. (2006). America's supersized footprint. *Business Week*, October 30, p. 132.

McConvill, J. (2005). Positive corporate governance and its implications for executive compensation. *German Law Journal*, 6(12), 1777–1804. Available at http://www.german lawjournal.com/index.php?pageID = 11&artID = 677. Retrieved on 6 October 2010.

McGowan, K. (2005). The pleasure paradox: Money doesn't bring happiness. *Psychology Today*, 38(1), 52–54.

Myers, D. G. (2000). The funds, friends, and faith of happy people. *American Psychologist*, 55(1), 56–67.

Myers, D. G., & Diener, E. (1995). Who is happy? *Psychological Science*, 6(1), 10–19.

Nocera, J. (2008). How India avoided a crisis. *New York Times*, December 20, p. B1 +.

Pellow, D. N. (2005). Buying time and getting by: The voluntary simplicity movement. *The American Journal of Sociology*, 110(5), 1520–1523.

Pitelis, C. (2002). On economics and business ethics. *Business Ethics: A European Review*, 11(2), 111–118.

Rieff, D. (2009). India's malnutrition dilemma. *New York Times Magazine*, October 11, pp. 26–28.

Robertson, J. (1999). *The new economics of sustainable development: A briefing for policy makers* (Out of print. Available at http://www.jamesrobertson.com/book/neweconomicsofsus-tainabledevelopment.pdf. Retrieved on 16 August 2009). New York: St. Martin's Press.

Robinson, J. (1978). Morality and economics. *Challenge*, 21(1), 62–64. Available at http://www.economistsview.typepad.com/economistsview/2007/07/morality-and-ec.html, posted on 3 July 2007, accessed on 27 July 2007.

Roosevelt, F. D. (1937). Second inaugural address. Available at http://www.bartleby.com/124/pres50.html. Retrieved on 27 July 2009.

Rosenthal, E. (2008). As more eat meat, a bid to cut emissions. *New York Times*, December 3. Available at http://www.nytimes.com/2008/12/04/science/earth/04meat.html. Retrieved on 21 August 2009.

Salwen, K., & Salwen, H. (2010). *The power of half: One family's decision to stop taking and start giving back*. New York: Houghton Mifflin.

Shama, A., & Wisenblit, J. (1984). The values of voluntary simplicity: Lifestyle and motivation. *Psychological Reports*, 55, 231–240.

Shaw, D., & Moraes, C. (2009). Voluntary simplicity: An exploration of market interactions. *International Journal of Consumer Studies*, 33(2), 215–223.

Singer, P. (2009). America's shame: When are we going to do something about global poverty? *Chronicle Review*, March 13, pp. B6–B10.

Smith, A. (1776). *The wealth of nations: Inquiry into the nature and causes of the wealth of nations*. London: W. Strahan and T. Cadell.

Stiglitz, J., Sen, A., & Fitoussi, J. P. (2009). Report of the commission on the measurement of economics performance and social progress. Available at http://www.stiglitz-sen-fitoussi.fr/documents/rapport_anglais.pdf. Retrieved on 4 January 2010.

Stolberg, S. G., & Labaton, S. (2009). Banker bonuses are "shameful", Obama declares. *New York Times*, January 30, p. A1 + .

Tabuchi, H. (2009). Once a slave to luxury products, Japan catches the thrift bug. *New York Times*, September 21, p. A1 + .

U.S. Census Bureau. (2009). *Poverty: 2008 highlights*. U.S. Census Bureau, Housing and Household Economic Statistics Division. Available at http://www.census.gov/hhes/www/poverty/data/incpovhlth/2008/highlights.html. Retrieved on 6 October 2010.

Wallis, C. (2005). The new science of happiness. *Time, 165*(3), A2–A9.

Wayne, L. (2009). A promise to be ethical in an era of immorality. *New York Times*, May 30. Available at http://www.nytimes.com/2009/05/30/business/30oath.html. Retrieved on 26 July 2009.

Weiser, S. (Writer), & Stone, O. (Writer, Director). (1987). Wall Street, Perf. Michael Douglas, Twentieth Century-Fox Film Corporation, Gordon Gekko's speech. Available at http://www.americanrhetoric.com/MovieSpeeches/moviespeechwallstreet.html

CORPORATE SOCIAL RESPONSIBILITY IN DEVELOPING COUNTRIES: POLISH PERSPECTIVE

Justyna Berniak-Woźny

Since 2007, the world economy has been immersed in a financial crisis that has transformed into a deep recession. As with any complex economic phenomenon, this recession has not only economic perspective but also psychological, social, political, and ethical perspectives. One of the faces of the crisis is Corporate Social Responsibility and the impact it has on the future of the concept.

This chapter is aimed at presenting the specificity of CSR in developing countries in the financial crisis context. The choice to focus analysis only on the Polish context, even though the debate on CSR concepts' globalization is becoming more important for scholars and practitioners (McWilliams, Siegel, & Wright, 2006), is twofold: (a) research into CSR in developing countries is still relatively underdeveloped (Baskin, 2006) and it would be worthwhile to consider the opportunities and limitations of this concept in the post-communist country (b) CSR awareness in Poland is a relative new issue, compared to other nations.

The concept of Corporate Social Responsibility (CSR) is becoming increasingly popular in developing countries, both in academic circles through researching its theoretical foundations, and among managers and businessmen who want to put these theories into action in everyday business

Reframing Corporate Social Responsibility: Lessons from the Global Financial Crisis
Critical Studies on Corporate Responsibility, Governance and Sustainability,
Volume 1, 271–302
ISSN: 2043-9059/doi:10.1108/S2043-9059(2010)0000001018

practice. Nevertheless the global model of CSR cannot be replicated by developing countries without prior examination due to the macro-environmental conditions and country-specific contextual determinants. Simple transfer of CSR models from the developed countries may fail and slow down or even stop implementation of the concept in the rest of the world. The Polish case presented in the chapter demonstrates that successful adaptation and implementation of CSR concept requires continuous dialog and cooperation among all partners of the process. The number and type of partners are specific for every country or region.

The aim of this chapter is to analyze the level of CSR concept adaptation and implementation in Poland (as the example of a developing country). The analysis is the foundation for the recommendations of change (if necessary) and further actions to be taken in order to maximize the advantages of the concept.

The chapter covers relevant literature on Corporate Social Responsibility. It includes historical overview of the concept, the definition discussion, concept relation to stakeholder theory, and specificity of CSR in developing countries. The condition of CSR concept in Poland has been defined on the basis of previous cumulative knowledge, as well as the results of CSR research conducted on national and international level.

The discussion of the chapter is organized as follows: the first section contains literature review of CSR concept including specificity of the developing countries. The second section contains overview of CSR concept in the context of Poland and analysis of the engagement and activities of the most important partners in the process of CSR concept adaptation and implementation. The final section contains recommendations for further actions for all the partners whose activities were analyzed in section two.

CORPORATE SOCIAL RESPONSIBILITY

Corporate Social Responsibility (CSR), in the form of corporate philan-thropy or charity, has been practiced in the United States since the late 1800's (Sethi, 1977). Today's concept of CRS originated in 1953 with the publication of Bowen's book entitled "Social responsibilities of Business-men". In his book Bowen asked the question: "What responsibilities to society can business people be reasonably expected to assume?" At this time, the emphasis was placed on business people's social conscience, rather than on the company itself. Further on the academics became much more precise in defining the firms' responsibilities. Carroll (1999) divided companies' responsibilities into economic, legal, ethical, and philanthropic. Lantos (2002) narrowed down CSR to ethical, altruistic, and strategic responsibility. According to Davis (1973, p. 312) CSR refers to a company's concern for "issues beyond the narrow economic, technical and legal requirements of the firm."

Underlying the interest and concern for CSR is the fact that firms do not operate in a vacuum. Rather they can be viewed as "open systems" dependent on some actors and influential to others. Through exchanging output with the environment, for example the customers, companies impact, and transform society. In order to survive and prosper, sufficient resources must be retained to at least cover costs, and excess profit is considered advantageous (Vaaland, Heide, & Grønhaug, 2008).

Over the years, Corporate Social Responsibility (CSR) has risen as an important concept and research topic in the study of organizations (Moir, 2001; Lindkvist & Llewellyn, 2003; Margolis & Walsh, 2003; Valor, 2005). Since the 1990s, it has gained increased focus among practitioners on the political agenda and in daily press (Buhr & Grafström, 2004; Commission of the European Communities, 2001).

Although CSR is a well-established concept, there is no general consensus on the meaning of CSR in practice (Carroll & Buchholtz, 2000; Joyner & Payne, 2002; Roberts, 2003; Ougaard, 2004). From the 1950 onwards, business scholars and practitioners have provided various definitions of CSR.

One of the main factors contributing to the confusion about the nature of CSR is the large number of concepts used to describe largely the same phenomenon. The CSR concept relates closely to corporate citizenship (Bowen, 1953; Carroll, 1979; Mason, 1960), corporate social responsiveness (Ackerman & Bauer, 1976; Frederick, 1998; Strand, 1983), and corporate social performance (Stanwick & Stanwick, 1998; Swanson, 1999; Wood, 1991). Early on, authors referred to companies' public responsibility (Ackerman, 1975; Carroll, 1979; Davis, 1973; Preston & Post, 1975). These concepts interrelate and overlap, making it problematic to clearly distinguish between them (Waddock, 2004). Common to these concepts is the idea that organizations should not only be concerned about making profit but also engaged in "action scone that appear to further some social good, beyond the interests of the firm and that is required by law" (McWilliams et al., 2006, p. 1).

Most academics perceive CSR as an obligation of every present organization. According to Mosley, Pietri, and Megginson (1996) Corporate Social Responsibility refers to management's obligation to set policies, make decisions and follow courses of action beyond the requirements of the law, that are desirable in terms of the values and objectives of society. According to Robbins and Decenzo (2001), Corporate Social Responsibility refers to the obligation of a firm, beyond that required by law or economics, to pursue long-term goals that are good for society. Perrault and McCarthy (2002) also define CSR as a firm's obligation to improve its positive effects on society and reduce its negative effects.

There is a number of academics who are less radical in presenting the concept of Social Responsibility. Van Marrewijk (2003) defines CSR as company activities – voluntary by definition – demonstrating the inclusion of social and environmental concerns in business operations and interactions with stakeholders. Also for practitioners CSR is a voluntary action of every organization. The European Commission's Green Paper brings out in its definition of CSR the fact that these initiatives go beyond the legal requirements: CSR is a "concept whereby companies decide voluntarily to contribute to a better society and a cleaner environment" (Commission of the European Communities, 2001). World Business Council on Sustainable Development defines the concept as the commitment of business to contribute to sustainable economic development, working with employees, their families, the locals, and their quality of life.

Other definitions bring forward the importance of other stakeholders beside shareholders. Lom (2005) stated that "CSR is the acknowledgement by companies that they should be accountable not only for their financial performance." CSR and the concept of stakeholders complement and reinforce each other. Hopkins (2003, p. 10) is very specific about the relationship between CSR and stakeholder management and defines CSR as "treating the stakeholders of the firm ethically or in a responsible manner." Similarly, Smith (2003) stated that CSR is "obligation of the firm to society, or more specifically, the firm's stakeholders – those affected by corporate policies and practices." As it has already been mentioned, organizations exist within larger networks which consist of various stakeholder groups that exert pressure on them, such as employees, communities, customers. and suppliers, nongovernmental organization (NGO's). A good corporate citizen must address the concerns and satisfy (some of) the demands of stakeholders who, either directly or indirectly, can affect or be affected by the organization's activities (Donaldson & Preston, 1995; Waddock, 2001).

According to Hill, Stephens, and Smith (2003), an exact definition of CSR is elusive because beliefs and attitudes about the nature of the relationship between business and society fluctuate with the relevant issues of the day. Moreover, Carroll and Buchholtz (2000) argue that the difficulties with arriving at the definition of CSR partly have to do with the problem of determining operationally the managerial implications of such a definition. This is the major problem considering companies' differences in size, products, profitability, resources, societal impacts, etc. According to the research RESPONSE: Understanding and Responding to Social Demands on Corporate Responsibility, managers and stakeholders (including NGOs, shareholders, employees, customers, suppliers, and local government) were found to have divergent perceptions of what it means to be socially responsible, with an overwhelming majority of some 80% of managers viewing the issue from a passive "do no harm" perspective, as opposed to the proactive "do good" approach.

The success of the CSR concept implementation and development, both on the level of specific companies as well as the entire economy, depends on numerous situational factors – economic, social, cultural, and institutional. That is why promoting and implementing CSR should be adapted to particular conditions of a country (Lewicka-Strzalecka, 2006). The difference is reflected in CSR concept understanding and expectations. For example in Penn Schoen Berland 2010 research, the leading ways for firms to be perceived as socially responsible are: being environmentally responsible and creating energy-efficient products, treating employees well and giving back to the community. The similar research in Poland shows that being a socially responsible company means treating employees well, delivering good quality of products and services and obeying the law.

Over the past few years, Corporate Social Responsibility (CSR) has become one of the most popular strategies aiming at enhancing a company's image as a credible corporate citizen. This was relatively easy before the financial crisis when companies were making record profits, and needed to show a humane face. As the credit crunch started many academics and business representatives were convincing that this is the beginning of the end of Socially Responsible Business. The evidence of the past 3 years suggests that commitment to CSR is neither being reduced nor abandoned. According to KPMG (2008) the proportion of the world's 250 largest companies issuing annual reports on Corporate Social Responsibility increased from 50% in 2005 to 80% in 2008. The main drivers for implementing CSR strategies have been risk management on the one hand and ethical considerations on the other. But this is about the most economically advanced countries in the EU and attributes only to large companies. As the chapter focuses on CSR in Poland, review of factors characterizing this concept in developing countries is needed.

CSR IN DEVELOPING COUNTRIES

There are a number of reasons for considering CSR in developing countries as distinct from CSR in the developed economies. The most important of them are:

- Developing countries represent the most rapidly expanding economies, and hence the most lucrative growth markets for business (IMF, 2006).
- Developing countries are where the social and environmental crises are usually most acutely felt in the world (WRI, 2005; UNDP, 2006).
- Developing countries are where the globalization, economic growth, investment, and business activity are likely to have the most dramatic social and environmental impacts (both positive and negative) (World Bank, 2006).
- Developing countries present a distinctive set of CSR agenda challenges which are collectively quite different to those faced in the developed world. (Crane, McWilliams, & Matten, 2008, p.474).

According to Visser (Visser, Matten, Pohl, & Tolhurst, 2007) CSR in developing countries has the following distinctive characteristics:

- CSR tends to be less formalized or institutionalized in terms of the CSR benchmarks commonly used in developed countries, i.e. CSR codes, standards, management systems and reports.
- Where formal CSR is practiced, this is usually by large, high profile national and multinational companies, especially those with recognized international brands or those aspiring to global status.
- Formal CSR codes, standards, and guidelines that are most applicable to developing countries tend to be issue-specific (e.g., fair trade, supply chain, HIV/AIDS) or sector-led (e.g., agriculture, textiles, and mining).
- In developing countries CSR is most commonly associated with philanthropy or charity, i.e. through corporate social investment in education, health, sports development, environment, and other community services.
- Making an economic contribution is often seen as the most important and effective way for business to make a social impact, i.e. through investment, job creation, taxes, and technology transfer.
- Business often finds itself engaged in the provision of social services that would be seen as government's responsibility in developed countries, for example, investment in infrastructure, schools, hospitals, and housing.

- The issues being prioritized under the CSR banner are often different in developing countries, for example, tackling HIV/AIDS, improving work conditions, provision of basic services, supply chain integrity, and poverty alleviation.
- Many of the CSR issues in developing countries present themselves as dilemmas or trade-offs, for example, development versus environment, job creation versus higher labour standards, strategic philanthropy versus political governance.
- The spirit and practice of CSR is often strongly resonant with traditional communitarian values and religious concepts in developing countries, for example, African humanism (*ubuntu*) in South Africa and harmonious society (*xiaokang*) in China.

Research on CSR in developing countries is still relatively underdeveloped and tends to be ad hoc with a heavy reliance on convenience-based case studies or descriptive accounts. The focus is often on high-profile incidents or branded companies and a few selected countries (e.g., Brazil, China, India, and South Africa), with a general lack of comparable benchmarking data (Baskin, 2006). A relatively limited number of studies have emphasized comparative cross-country analysis, although these have largely been region specific or covered a relatively limited number of emerging market economies. The current state of CSR in a number of developing countries has been summarized by Baskin (2006). His generalizations are made with a strong caveat that each region is large and contains a wide variety of countries, histories, and experiences. This is the reason why this chapter employs national perspective and will be focused on Poland as the example of developing economy and example of post-communist country.

CSR IN POLAND

CSR is not a Polish concept and it came to Poland as the effect of the transformation. However, while the term CSR may not have existed in the respective vocabulary, social obligations of firms toward employees or wider society have long been recognized (Frynas, 2006). In Poland, like in most post-communist countries, the idea of company playing social role is not new. Under socialism state-owned companies built and maintained social, cultural, sporting, housing, and recreational facilities without any commercial cost–benefit analyses and goals. These activities were part of the communist ideology of guaranteed welfare and social protection; they were

---

Box 1. Polish Economy

Polish economy. Poland is at the moment of closing a transitional period from the centrally planned to the free market economy. Over the past two decades the country observed a stable economic growth. With the population of 38 million, Poland is the largest market in the Central Eastern Europe (CEE). Since 1997, Poland has been a member of OECD. In 2004 joined EU (presidency to be held in the 2nd half of 2011), which marks the turning point for the country. Services constitute per cent of GDP, industry per cent and agriculture per cent. GDP per capita is 14,000 EUR (17,816 $), per cent of EU average, which locates Poland among the poorest EU members (Eurostat). The date of joining Euro Zone has not been agreed yet; Polish Złoty (PLN) remains the currency.

---

not driven by factors of economic efficiency. When privatization began in the 1990s, most companies had to abandon these social obligations and focus on core business activities in order to survive in more and more competitive market (Box 1).

In contrast to the developed world (where civil society groups spurred companies to adopt CSR principles), in Poland (like in all post-socialist countries), the first big CSR wave came from foreign investors seeking to align their business practices in Eastern Europe with CSR principles at home. The CSR as such was brought to Poland as a part of PR and communications tools of large multinational corporations. Interestingly, an English abbreviation "CSR" is in use. As everywhere else, there is no common understanding of the term, no widely accepted definition (Piskalski, 2009). Specific circumstances of incomplete market reforms and opening to the global economy are the main reason why in Poland the process of developing and implementing strategies and standards of conduct toward all stakeholders (shareholders, employees, consumers, suppliers, local community representatives, and others) is at the initial stage. The social and political climate also does not facilitate the promotion and application of Corporate Social Responsibility in Poland (UNDP, 2007).

The concept of CSR originates from countries with stable market economy and still focuses on these countries. It requires appropriate implementation and adaptation to realities of a country with a different social system, religion, law, and politics. Consequently, if Corporate Social

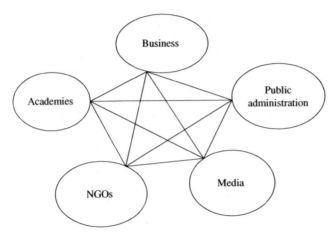

Fig. 1.   Partners Engaged in CSR Concept Adaptation and Implementation.

Responsibility is to take root in Polish society and business, Polish model taking greater account of the cultural background and historical identity of the country must be developed. The poor knowledge of global trends in social responsibility in Poland, as well as the necessity to seek new opportunities to gain strategic advantage opens up a new field to develop such model. A lot has been already achieved in this field, but it is necessary to remember that CSR is more than just a set of new obligations for companies. It is about a new role for the business in the society. In order to create the effective CSR model a continuous dialogue of all partners engaged in CSR concept promotion – not only enterprises and business organizations but also NGOs, educational institutions, media, and public administration (Fig. 1). The present engagement and activities of those CSR partners are to be presented.

Business

In Poland, like in any other country, systems of values are different for different people and different companies. The process of implementation of the CSR concept in Polish business practice continues to demonstrate that there is still a lot to be done (Gasparski, Lewicka-Strzalecka, Rok, & Szulczewski, 2004). According to TNS OBOP (2010) research, for over 60 per cent companies in Poland CSR concept is unknown. The application of tools and systems of social responsibility management is popular among

19 per cent of companies, out of which only one is Polish (UNDP, 2007). On the contrary, about 60 per cent of the researched companies are engaged in philanthropic activities (mostly donating money) (TNS OBOP, 2010). More than 50 per cent of Polish companies declare willingness to donate 1 per cent of CIT tax to NGOs.

Like in most developing countries, international corporations are leaders in CSR. However, small and medium enterprises are also beginning to participate, for example helping the poor, children, hospitals, etc. A large commercial certification campaign for SME's "Fair Play" is worth mentioning as it is one of the largest programs of this kind in Europe. It is also worth mentioning that it is more appropriate to use a term "responsible entrepreneurship" (which is also used by the EU Commission), as most CSR tools cannot be applied to SMEs.

It is possible to observe that the balance is slowly shifting from expressing mere interest and declarations of undertaking actions in the future to real implementation of ventures and programs tied in with responsible business (in the form of various social involvement programs, employees' voluntary work, codes of ethics, public reports, and the introduction of socially useful products to the market, as well as the implementation of best practice in corporate governance and investments for environmental protection). This trend is confirmed by the continuously increasing number of program descriptions submitted each year to the authors of Responsible Business in Poland (Koładkiewicz, 2009, pp. 98–99).

One of the weakest points of the CSR activity of Polish companies is promotion of such initiatives. Over 50 per cent of the Polish enterprises do not disclose information about their CSR activities, if there are any, on a regular and standardized basis. Only 30 per cent of them, including 7 of the 18 multinationals and 8 of the 21 large Polish companies, recognize the need not only to disclose information about CSR activities, but also to raise awareness and meet the needs as regards the transparency of communication on social responsibility activities (UNDP, 2007).

According to Edelman Trust Barometer 2007, the most important outlets people use to obtain information about companies' CSR activities are mainstream media (68.1 per cent), corporate web sites (57.3 per cent), NGOs (54.6 per cent), and CR reports (52.3 per cent). Two of the four mentioned sources of information may be controlled and shaped by the company (corporate web sites and CR reports). Surprisingly, according to BI-NGO (2008) research 41 per cent of the companies included on the list of 500 biggest enterprises in Poland has no information about social activity on their web sites. What is more, in 2009 only three companies (BRE Bank SA,

Grupa LOTOS, and PKN ORLEN S.A.) have presented social reports, prepared on the basis of GRI methodology (G3).

The latest crisis differs substantially from all the others as it is a consequence of a breach of trust. This situation was perceived as a great threat to CSR and there were predictions that companies will resign from social spending, especially in developing countries (including Poland) where CSR concept has not rooted yet. There is no doubt that corporations are engaging in less philanthropy, but that is not necessarily a bad sign. Although some cuts in CSR budgets are inevitable, companies can maintain their commitment by reviewing their approach in giving. As Mediplante research (2008, 2009) revealed (Kompendium, C.S.R., 2009), the Polish business engagement in CSR is not weaker, quite the opposite – per cent of entrepreneurs believe that business can be socially responsible despite the crisis. What is more, per cent of respondents declare building and implementing CSR strategy next year. There are four basic areas of business engagement in social responsibility: workplace, marketplace, environment, and community (Fig. 2).

Workplace

In the knowledge economy, which is based mainly on the people's intellectual potential, it is essential to treat employees as a priority, as a main asset. Formulation of the strategy of responsibility should not only consider investing in their development, stimulating them to pursue the company's goals, creating friendly relationships between employees and team-work spirit. It should also include the aspects of work-life balance, equal opportunities diversity and environment protection in order to build a respected employer's brand, recognized and preferred by potential employees.

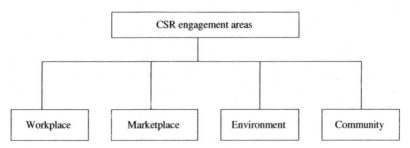

Fig. 2. Areas of Business Engagement in CSR.

Polish companies try to address those CSR goals and, for example:

- Protect needs of pregnant women and young parents – such programs have been introduced by Accenture (medical services, flexible work hours, working from home, etc.) or Bank Zachodni WBK (the bank guarantees young mothers work positions after maternity leave, possibility of part-time work, and no selling targets for certain time).
- Familiarize employees with a company's code of conduct and improving its functioning. Aviva Polska promotes an ethical code of conduct among employees, Danone engages its employees in working out partnership standards in the company, Provident Polska implemented *Employee's Forum* – project involving employees in decision processes, giving feedback and presenting one's comments (see the sidebar titled "Provident Polska – Employee's Forum") (Box 2).
- Promote equal opportunities and diversity – practices implemented by PricewaterhouseCoopers and Procter & Gamble which focus on age or nationality, gender equity, and cultural differences.
- Create or preserve job (especially important in the context of the high unemployment rate connected with the financial crisis). Autostrada Eksploatacja – trains and provides a number of nonfinancial benefits for its employees, reserves most jobs for the residents of local communities. LOTOS concentrated on creating favorable working conditions for highly qualified staff and on partnership with universities as a potential source of future employees.

Marketplace

The growing number of Polish managers understands that CSR is becoming one of the deciding factors of market differentiation. Consequently, the number of CSR programs addressed to consumers, suppliers, and other business partners has been systematically increasing. These programs are definitely pro-active within company's market or branch. However, they are still being implemented as a response to certain social or ecological incidents, law regulations, pressure, or consumers' needs and expectations.

The main CSR activities directed to marketplace are:

- Education of clients and consumers, for example: BRE Bank created a web platform Bizsupport, which aims at dissemination of business and

Box 2. Provident Polska – "Employee's Forum"

SITUATION/PROBLEM DESCRIPTION

In its business, Provident cooperates with approximately 2000 permanent employees and about 11,000 representatives in the field. Ensuring good communication and effectively functioning management system between the headquarters, employees, and co-operants presents a great challenge.

PROJECT DESCRIPTION/SOLUTION

The Project of the Employee's Forum enables involving employees in decision processes, giving feedback and presenting one's comments, offering streamlining proposals, integrating people, and promoting employees with the biggest potential.

The Forum is a series of recurring regional and corporate meetings coordinated by one specially designated person who daily stays in touch with a group of 70 field representatives who closely cooperate with the headquarters. Representatives collect ideas among the employees in their branch or subsidiary and then present them at the Regional Forum meetings. Then they take a joint decision which ideas should be shared on the Central Forum. The proposed solutions are discussed during the Corporate Meeting with the Board. The leader of the Forum is the vice president of the company. He participates in all the Corporate Meetings and in the majority of Regional Meetings.

Since the Forum was created (3 years ago) a number of improvements were introduced:

- The project was transferred from the HR to Communications Department, which generated greater interest and involvement of the part of employees. It also benefited from acquiring a complete communication strategy making the forum a main tool of internal communication in Provident Polska.
- The tenure of representatives was prolonged to 2 years, which creates opportunity for better emotional involvement in the proposed projects.
- New rules enable many terms in the office, which cut the rotation of representatives and contribute to higher quality of their work.

- Direct involvement of the board (vice president) brought higher involvement among employees and gave the sense of weight to the project.
- A new job (Forum Coordinator) was created for a person who exclusively deals with matters concerning the Forum.
- Giving feedback has been emphasized – there are clearly defined communication paths within the Forum and they take into consideration particular levels of analyzing ideas and informing the originator about the reasons for rejecting their ideas or about the effects of its implementation.
- Each edition starts with the meeting for all representatives and it is combined with the training which additionally motivates employees to take part in the Forum.

BENEFITS

- Employees feel they have impact on changes in the company as well as they have a chance to realize their ambitious projects, and by doing this they get new experience and prestige.
- It develops the company and initiates a better flow of information between employees and the board, also improvement in the operation has been observed.
- The project became the basis for twin projects realized in other worldwide divisions of the company and in the headquarters, from where the representatives contact coordinators of the project with request to share information and experience.

CHALLENGES

- Low innovative character of solutions proposed by employees.
- Decreasing interest among employees.
- Lack of support for the project from regional managers, who did not see benefits of sending a valuable employee to the Forum meetings.
- Insufficient communication about the Forum, especially of achieved successes.
- Ineffective territorial division made the representatives travel to remote places.

Source: Adapted form http://www.fob.org.pl

economy knowledge; Zakłady Mięsne PAMSO carried out an informative campaign on proper storage of meat products.

- Training business partners as a part of supply chain management – Coca-Cola trained its contractors on more efficient exploitation of sale areas, which has had a positive impact on the sales rate in stores. Schenker conducted trainings for drivers from collaborating carrier companies, which have improved their client relations abilities and had a positive effect on the mutual satisfaction from partnership, TP SA *Academy of Entrepreneurship* educates SME entrepreneurs within running and developing their businesses, transferring knowledge about telecommunication and tele-information products and their impact on the effectiveness of their businesses – (see the sidebar titled "Telekomunikacja Polska – Academy of Entrepreneurship") (Box 3).
- Support development of entrepreneurship – Michelin Development Foundation provides credit warranties for production plants that have innovative ideas, but do not qualify for credits in banks, as well as professional advice. Microsoft created a BizSpark program directed to companies that produce software, which gives them access to Microsoft tools and technologies, and gives the opportunity to establish contacts with partners throughout the world.

Community

Corporate Social Responsibility perceived as a strategy can become the source of social growth. When a company decides to invest some of its assets, like knowledge, abilities, means, etc. in its social partner it can be done in many ways. The typical activities directed to Polish society are:

- Activities related to health and safety, for example by creating programs and social campaigns on safety on roads (3M Poland, McDonald's Polska, Toyota Motor Manufacturing Poland, and Kredyt Bank/Grupa Warta), breast cancer prevention (Avon Cosmetics Polska), or heart-related diseases Polpharma – (see the sidebar titled 'Polpharma – Polscreen') (Box 4).
- Educational programs, for example – Bank Zachodni WBK and Eurobank carried out educational programs aimed at providing young people with knowledge and skills strengthening their entrepreneurship abilities. Citi Handlowy, GE Money Bank and Provident educated high school students, women, and families on finance management.

Box 3. Telekomunikacja Polska – "Academy of Entrepreneurship"

SITUATION/PROBLEM DESCRIPTION

Telekomunikacja Polska (TP) is a telecommunication company which attach significant value to the quality of communication and partnership relationships. Those in turn lead to rising effectiveness of services and hale impact on the image of the company and by that increase in revenue. This is why the company created a platform of direct communication between TP, sponsors (companies cooperating in this program) and Clients, both potential and current ones.

PROJECT DESCRIPTION/SOLUTION

Academy of Entrepreneurship aims at educating SME entrepreneurs within running and developing their businesses, transferring knowledge about telecommunication and tele-information products and their impact on the effectiveness of their businesses. The program includes the following activities:

- free educational and advisory program;
- meetings with consultants, advisors and experts in the tele-information field, examples of good practices and benefits which they provide to companies; and
- practical information on European subventions for e-business.

Academy is held in the form of workshops during which participants can exchange their opinions and views. Each workshop is run by an expert at European matters who moderates the whole meeting. Experts are chosen and invited to cooperation with the advisory company – Grupa BOSS on all matters concerning European endeavors. The Academy also hosts its mentors and during break there is time for individual consultations with a chosen expert. The choice of topics and companies invited is decided during the process of individual talks between the mentors' representatives and clients, questionnaires filled in by company's representatives at meetings and basing on the communication strategy of the mentors. The projects involves employees and managers of the Academy Mentors, i.e. TP S.A., Siemens, Intel, Microsoft, HP, Bank Millenium, and also local media and experts – representatives of government and local institutions.

BENEFITS

- Building responsible image among companies from the SME sector.
- Maintaining partners' relationships with companies – mentors – ask TP about it.
- Making direct contact and building relationships with companies – potential clients.
- Building market for modern tele-information solutions.

CHALLENGES

- Inviting companies and sponsors to the Project, which get involved and build a model solutions and offers for project participants.
- Obtaining financing for the projects.
- Transforming academy into a long-term project aiming at the on-going contact with the entrepreneurs.

Source: Adapted form http://www.fob.org.pl

- Creating equal opportunities for children and people marginalized on the job market – for example Cadbury Wedel, GlaxoSmith-Kline, Instytut Monitorowania Mediów, and Janssen-Cilag carried out programs for children, DGA-ran projects aimed at supporting people whose position on the labor market is uncertain and Grupa Pracuj conducted a series of trainings for young mothers in order to fight against discrimination of women on the labor market.
- Corporate volunteering – Aviva has increased the number of employees involved in voluntary work over 20 times in a 7-year period. PricewaterhouseCoopers offers pro bono services on tax, audit and business consulting for nongovernmental sector.

Environment

One of the most significant CSR fields is ecology. More and more Polish companies understand the need of activities connected with environment

Box 4. Polpharma – "Polscreen"

SITUATION/PROBLEM DESCRIPTION

An unblemished opinion and positive image are particularly important for companies such as Polpharma operating on the medication and pharmaceutical market. This is why the company's objective is to create and reinforce among its stakeholders the image of its involvement in social issues, activity, responsibility, and credibility. The Polscreen Program is a project serving this purpose.

PROJECT DESCRIPTION/SOLUTION

Polscreen is the largest in the world examination of a population aiming to evaluate the frequency of risk of heart-related diseases in the practice of doctors from basic health care. Thanks to this program, the doctors all over Poland have the opportunity to assess comprehensively the risk of a potential heart disease in their patients, implement modern treatment methods, and assess objectively effectiveness of this prevention program conducted in accordance with the recommendations of the Polish Cardiology Association.

Additionally, doctors can also participate in scientific seminars presenting the state-of-the-art achievements of cardiology. The program was prepared by the Prevention Commission of the Polish Cardiology Association and it is realised thanks to Polpharma's grant. Beside the financial commitment, Polscreen also involves the company's medical representatives who are in charge of providing leaflets and other materials for examinations.

Other medical personnel are also engaged in the project at the examination stage. The target number of examined patients is a million of Poles over 35 years old. Examinations will take place all over the country in the centres providing basic medical care and during special events and picnics and they are free of charge. So far, 825,000 of people have undergone the examination. The estimates indicate that the Polscreen Project helped to save the lives of several thousands of people.

BENEFITS

- Recognition from the medical profession – Polpharma has been awarded the title of Friend of Polish Cardiology by the Polish Cardiology Association twice, and also the Association's award Success of the Year 2003 in Health Promotion in the category The Achievement of the Year 2003 in Health Protection – Education and Training.
- The first place in the ranking conducted among pharmaceutical companies as a part of the GFK Polonia survey in the following categories: the most ethical and most patient-friendly pharmaceutical company and the second place in the category for the biggest involvement in health protection.
- Creating the image of an expert in cardiology, a credible partner, socially responsible company caring for patients' health.

CHALLENGES

High realization costs which were handled by encouraging medical personnel to participate and perform examinations in the Polscreen program free of charge.

Source: Adapted form http://www.fob.org.pl

protection. Most of initiatives concentrate on climate changes. Programs are usually aimed at reduction of water, energy, and paper use as well as waste management and renewable energy programs.

The range of such activities is very wide:

- Ecological education programs – Henkel Polska organized a "Green Grants" contest, IKEA Retail together with WWF built a "Green House." Employees ecological education was provided by Kompania Piwowarska, L'Oréal Polska, Pomorska Spółka Gazownictwa, and PricewaterhouseCoopers. RWE Polska runs social campaign "Conscious Energy," which promotes energy-saving behavior at home and in the workplace.

- Initiatives which focus on environmental protection by introducing integrated programs of energy saving, reduction of CO_2 emission, waste sorting, water, and paper saving. Such programmes were conducted by: Bank Ochrony Środowiska, Bielenda Kosmetyki Naturalne, PKN ORLEN, and TESCO Polska. Cartridges are collected and recycled by Hewlett-Packard (see the sidebar titled "Hewlett-Packard (HP)– Ecological Program" (Box 5)); Pryzmat and Eco Service.
- Taking care of national rivers, lakes, and forests – Barlinek protects environment by using raw materials for production with a forest management certificate and by planting a tree for each purchased pack of Barlinek floorboards. Alior Bank is planting trees for every customer choosing electronic instead of paper bank statement, PGNiG conducted a "Safe Mazuria" programme, which combined ecological education with promotion of water safety and taking care of Mazurian lakes' cleanliness.

Corruption

One of the crucial factors in Social Corporate Responsibility is corruption. The research results confirm that corruption is accompanied by economic stagnation and social decline. The high level of corruption discourages managers and businessmen from creating positive, long-standing relations with specific stakeholders, because the position of their companies is hardly dependant on their customers, employees, partners, and the local community. Instead, they are likely to get involved in corrupt deals with high-ranking state officials, in order to win tenders, ensure their access to the market or get various licenses, e.g., for exclusive supplies (Lewicka-Strzalecka, 2006, p. 443).

Corruption in Poland (beside universal causes) is driven by some factors specific for post-communist countries. In the 1970s and 1980s bribery was every day life reality. Such attitudes involved consent for "soft" corruption mainly (i.e. small bribe, protectionism and intermediary). The first years of political transformation after 1989 also created favorable conditions for growth of various forms of corruption. This complete reconstruction of the country's economic and legal systems was not accompanied by sufficient care for concurrent development of preventing anticorruption measures and control systems. Fast implementation of market economy rules, privatization, and transfers of enormous state property to the private sector at frequent government changes, periodic replacement of civil service

Box 5. Hewlett-Packard (HP) – Ecological Program

SITUATION/PROBLEM DESCRIPTION

Hewlett-Packard (HP) as the provider of technological solutions encompassing an extensive information infrastructure searches for solutions minimizing negative impact on the environment of its actions without compromising the high quality of provided services.

PROJECT DESCRIPTION/SOLUTION

In Poland HP runs Ecological Program, the purpose of which is to educate, support environment friendly attitudes, and promote the pro-ecological policy of the company. The program consists of several enterprises:

- A project of collecting and recycling cartridges for HP laser printers (for institutions and individual clients) and for ink printers (for institutions). Cartridges are then recycled in a process that is safe for the environment.
- HP initiated a countrywide ecological competition in Harmony with Nature which is addressed to nongovernmental organizations. The idea of the competition is to unearth the most interesting ecological initiatives and enable realizing them in forms of projects. The awards founded by HP are 30,000 zł (1st award), 15,000 zł (2nd award), 10,000 zł (3rd award).
- As part of promotion of pro-ecological attitudes among children and young people the company organized ecological competition for primary and junior-high and high schools. Schools are encouraged to propose practical projects concerning for instance waste collection and segregation, saving water and electrical energy, etc. The rewards in the competition are sets of HP computer equipment and printers.
- The topic of environmental protection and pro-ecological attitudes is promoted in media through another competition for journalists for the Reward of the Polish Journalists Association. The best publications relating to environment protection are awarded Ecos prize created by Professor Stefan Myczkowski from the Club of Environmental Journalists. The competition is organized under the auspices of HP.

BENEFITS

- Decreasing side effects of products and services.
- The company is more customer – and environment friendly.
- Finding new clients and building partner and transparent relationships with the interest holders.

CHALLENGES

- At the stage of creating the program, the biggest challenge was defining problems and target groups to whom address the campaign.
- At the roll out stage, the spreading information to program beneficiaries posed particular difficulties due to the limited promotional budget.

Source: Adapted form http://www.fob.org.pl

resources, administrative reforms, and unstable legal system were nurturing a corruption-friendly climate.

Consequently, in Transparency International 2005 and 2006 rankings Poland was recognized as the most corrupted EU Member State. However, in the past few years the index of Corruption Perception in Poland has not been deteriorating anymore. This means a breakthrough in a years-long trend of Poland's consistent decline in the ranking. This is the effect of both – *Corruption Control Programme – Anti-corruption Strategy* prepared and implemented by the Ministry of Interior and Administration and anticorruption strategies implemented by business.

Corruption is not a peripheral social concern that corporations can ignore or passively address – it is a bottom-line business issue that directly affects companies' ability to compete. Widespread in developing countries, corruption is becoming an increasingly important issue for business to address. According to Edelman Trust Barometer 2010 trust and transparency of the company is equally important for its reputation as the quality of products and services.

Business sectors are ready to embrace anticorruption as strategic Corporate Social Responsibility – moving beyond risk mitigation toward proactively solving social problems critical to the business. With a particular focus on the developing world, it suggests that corporations can build on existing models for compliance and collective action and take a greater leadership role in the broader anticorruption effort (Hills, Fiske, & Mahmud, 2009).

To reach that goal companies may implement four complementary approaches (see Fig. 1):

1. *Ensure compliance*. Corporations should continue to invest significantly in ethics and compliance programs to maintain or increase their level of integrity throughout all divisions and countries.
2. *Strengthen collective action*. Efforts need to shift from broad-based, diffuse declarations to more outcome-oriented pacts that can create effective incentives for members to change behavior.
3. *Engage demand-side forces*. Although the typical focus of corporate anticorruption work is on the "supply side" of corruption (the private sector), corporations should expand their efforts to influence the "demand side" (the public sector).
4. *Leverage corporate assets*. Corporations possess unique and powerful strengths in the fight against corruption, including communications power from the corporate brand, economic leverage, technical expertise, and cash resources for grant-making (Hills et al., 2009).

Corporations are not a panacea for all the problems the world faces from corruption. However, companies have a business imperative to reduce corruption in critical growth markets and can play an integral role in developing meaningful solutions to this challenge.

Public Administration

There are two basic reasons for public administration to engage in CSR: defensive and proactive.

The *defensive reasons* relate to minimizing the potential adverse effects of CSR on local communities, environments, and markets when it is imposed through international supply chains and investment. Governments may undertake a variety of initiatives to ensure that CSR practices with impact in their countries are tailored to national economic and social interests. This is particularly a concern when certification requirements, or the cost of meeting supply chain requirements, harm the local small or medium-size enterprises that represent the large majority of enterprises, and account for a significant part of employment in developing countries.

The *proactive reasons relates to* the opportunity to increase the domestic public benefits of CSR practices in economic, social, and environmental terms. Foreign investment offers potential to transfer technical expertise to local enterprises. Many large companies (encouraged by governments) are interested in exploring practical mechanisms for enhancing the input of local enterprises, and locally hired workers, into their projects. In some cases, this is encouraged through investment incentives or through the terms of foreign investment contracts.

In Poland, unfortunately, there is no official policy or document outlining the public policy toward CSR. The only action was undertaken in 2009 by Prime Minister who called an interministerial working group, led by Ministry of Economy, consisting of several ministries. This group has been in existence informally for some time, led by Ministry of Labor and Social Policy before. The goals and results of this body are unknown. Additionally, Ministry of Economy took some actions in order to promote sustainable development, i.e. commissioned a CSR management guide for SMEs. Consequently, the progress in that field depends on the measures which will be undertaken in the future by the European Union.

Nongovernmental Organizations (NGO)

One of the crucial background elements encouraging business to act for the public and environment is a strong civil society. Appropriate nongovernmental institutions can act as representatives of various groups of stakeholders, as partners in the dialogue with the business, as well as coordinators of company's cooperation with the local community. They can also initiate organized lobbying actions by citizens and consumers. However, the weakness of the nongovernmental sector and the civil society in Poland in general, makes them unable to fulfill these roles.

Polish civil society is still underdeveloped. Despite the success of the "Solidarity" trade union in the last years of communism, Polish society still believe that solving social problems is the duty of the Government and Church rather than business. Public opinion still has not implemented mechanisms enabling it to press business for responsible behavior. There is no tradition yet of watch-dog activities, fighting for human, and consumer rights. Developing Corporate Social Responsibility concept requires transfer of knowledge, not only to the managers, but also to the society which the company interacts with.

So far, there is a lack of "strategic philanthropy", business based foundations aiming at supporting specific cause are very rare and are usually connected with the biggest business organizations. It is worth to mention Akademia Rozwoju Filantropii for promoting philanthropy, Centrum Wolontariatu promoting corporate volunteerism, Responsible Business Forum promoting good practices (business NGO which is a part of CSR Europe network). Nevertheless the meaning of NGOs and business cooperation is growing, mostly because of the high society trust for this sector. According to Edelman Trust Barometer 2010, 61 per cent of Polish society finds NGOs trustworthy, compared to per cent in the EU and per cent worldwide.

The institutional and legal framework for NGO sector was initially set out in early 1990s and has developed since then. The latest law (the Act on public benefit organizations and volunteering) allows organizations – once they have passed a special registration procedure – to receive per cent of an individual's income tax, which can be declared to be granted to the chosen NGOs. Most of these resources are collected only by few biggest organizations and the companies' charities, which is a Polish phenomenon (Box 6).

Box 6. The Polish NGO Sector in Number

- consists of over 50,000 registered organizations;
- includes organizations of public benefit;
- most of active organizations operate in the fields of sport, social care, health protection, culture, education, and community development;
- a typical organization has an income up to 3,500 euro a year;
- 8 million Poles are members of organizations, 1/3 of the organizations employ staff; and
- 18 per cent of Poles are involved in voluntary activities.

Source: "NGOs in Poland– basic facts", Klon/Jawor Association (2004).

Academies

Academic research on CSR in Poland is still quite poor. It is most of all based on Anglo-Saxon approach to management, which do not necessarily fit well to the context of transition economy which Poland is. There is no scientific periodic on CSR, very few books have been published so far. CSR is rarely taught at higher schools, if so – as the business ethics. Recently, there have been attempts to launch postgraduate CSR programs, in which students are more and more interested. The number of students working on their thesis in different areas of CSR is still growing. Moreover, there are numerous conferences and seminars every year, organized by academic institutions together with business organizations, which is an optimistic perspective for the future of CSR concept in Poland.

Media

While examining the implementation of Corporate Social Responsibility, it emerges that there are not only structural but also communication barriers. That is why special attention needs to be given to the media.

Media in Poland have one of the highest social trust ratios. According to the Edelman Trust Barometer 2008, 45 per cent of the Polish society trusts the media, whereas in Great Britain it is only 19 per cent of the Britons. Such a high social trust ratio in Poland shows how significant is the role of media in raising social awareness.

The media are getting significantly engaged in CSR promotion. The number of articles on CSR-related issues keeps growing, and the discourse concerns various areas of Corporate Social Responsibility. As the FOB Report (2010) shows, the interest of media in Corporate Social Responsibility is rising. In 2009, 1,500 articles regarding corporate Social Responsibility and sustainable development were published, which is almost twice as many compared to last year. There is also a significant rise of articles on CSR in local and trade press. But this is sill insufficient. According to Iwona Kuraszko Research and Development Manager Responsible Business Forum, considering that Corporate Social Responsibility is gradually entering the public debate, media should not only observe and comment on the events, but also participate in the process of changing the role of business in civil society.

Currently, Polish media prefer to focus on negative aspects of business activity. This situation is probably caused by the low level of public trust toward business. According to Edelman's Trust Barometer (2010) results, the level of trust toward business declined by 5 per cent and accounts for 46 percent, whereas in the USA the rate increased by 18 per cent and accounts for 54 per cent. Situation is different in business press such as: Parkiet, Puls Biznesu, Gazeta Prawna, Rzeczpospolita, which publish numerous articles on CSR printed on "green pages" (dedicated to economic matters), and these are large texts and whole columns. Such tendency can be also observed in magazines like Forbes, CEO and Harvard Business Review Poland, Brief, Marketing w Praktyce. These titles occasionally contain information about important events: business conferences dedicated to CSR issues, public campaigns, etc.; supplementary inserts are sometimes added to the issues.

RECOMMENDATIONS

This section contains recommendations for further actions for all the partners whose activities were analyzed in the previous section.

Business

In order to implement CSR concept successfully Polish companies must reject corruption and unethical behaviors in business circles. Further on, Polish business organizations should increase their range of modern management methods by for instance introducing codes of conduct and implementing CSR strategies according to global CSR standards or applying the best standards of social involvement by partnerships with NGOs.

In such competitive and turbulent environment management sometimes must reconcile contrary needs as developing a socially responsible organization means creating the balance between profitability and other public goods. Carrying out CSR audits by independent organizations should be helpful in this process as they develop a general understanding of the social responsibility issues that affect their organization and industry.

Enterprises should also provide reliable and systematic information on social effects of business activities, mainly by developing CSR section on their web sites and presenting CSR reports based on international reporting standards.

Public Administration

The most important action that should be undertaken by public administration is acknowledging standards of responsible business as an important
component, together with economic effects, of business activity assessment,
e.g. as a part of managing the property of the Treasury, in the process of
privatization, in public procurement or in providing state aid. Moreover,
active participation in European discourse on CSR policy development is
needed.

Public administration should also promote and popularize CSR concept
by, for instance, rewarding best practices, supporting courses, and education
on ethics and Corporate Social Responsibility or promoting best practices
implemented by enterprises in Poland, with cooperation of NGOs,
employers' organizations, trade unions, academic institutions, and media.

Nongovernmental Organizations

NGOs in order to form a strong network supporting positive actions among
business organizations should engage more in CSR educational programs,
both formal and informal. Undertaking social initiatives encouraging
companies to act ethically and responsibly according to European standards
and promoting good CSR practices are also recommended.

As resources of Polish nonprofit organizations are limited and the
activities aforementioned are expensive it is suggested to carry out regular
research on business behavior and utilize the knowledge cumulated in
the organizations already engaged in CSR for example the UN Global
Compact, the Responsible Business Forum (in cooperation with CSR
Europe), the Business Ethics Centre CEBI (in cooperation with the
European Academy of Business in Society).

Academies

Universities in order to develop a Polish model of CSR and support
development of the concept among business should introduce obligatory
CSR workshops in business and business related faculties and support
research projects in the field of CSR.

It is also recommended to organize conferences and seminars in
cooperation with other CSR actors (business organizations, media, NGOs,

public administration, etc.) as universities should be a natural platform of the dialog between all the parties engaged in development and implementation of CSR concept in Poland.

Media

Polish media in order to promote socially responsible behavior among Polish business organizations should take part in motivating Poles to positive activities, cooperation, partnerships, and long-term development strategies. One way of reaching this goal is informing society about socially responsible activities implemented by business, especially about positive outcomes of CSR activities. Presenting good practices in media (especially mainstream media) should be an effective tool to encourage business to such activities.

CONCLUSIONS

CSR in developing countries must and will develop, as international business cooperation pays more and more attention to responsible business processes and awareness of international society continues to grow. But there is still the question about direction and pace.

Two things are very clear: CSR, as a strategic management tool, helps companies prepare for the future and equips them to deal with crisis situations. As a new mechanism for integrating companies more globally into society, CSR provides a way for business organizations to join the public administration and academies, media, and NGOs and work for the common good all over the world. Already, stirrings in developing countries have led to reduce corruption and to increase vigilance on human rights. Regions vary in this matter, however.

In the next few years Polish economy will have to face one of the most important challenges, which is social responsibility. In order to improve a companies' competitiveness and strengthen the brands, socially responsible operations will become indispensable. This requires change in quality of the CSR concept promotion (support from public administration, higher academic standards in CRS education, more attention from media, etc.). It may be very difficult, however, as CSR for the time being refers mostly to how a company's money is being spent (charity), instead of the way of achieving the gain, which is the essence of CSR. As CSR is a complex phenomenon it is very difficult to point on the leading organ responsible for the concept development. The analysis presented in the chapter demonstrates that the success of the CSR model depends on active participation and continuous dialog of key partners of the process.

REFERENCES

Ackerman, R. W. (1975). *The social challenge to business.* Cambridge, MA: Harvard University Press.

Ackerman, R. W., & Bauer, R. (Eds). (1976). *Corporate social responsiveness: The modern dilemma.* Reston, VA: Reston.

Baskin, J. (2006). Value, values and sustainability. Corporate responsibility in emerging market companies. Available at SSRN: http://ssrn.com/abstract = 1094573.

BI-NGO. (2008). Komunikacja społecznego zaangażowania firm poprzez Internet. Indeks Bi-NGO 2008. Accessed 15 February 2010.

Bowen, H. R. (1953). *Social responsibilities of the businessman.* USA: Harper & Brothers.

Buhr, H., & Grafström, M. (2004). *CSR edited in the business press – package solutions with problems included.* Paper Presented at the EGOS Colloquium, Ljubljana, 1–3 July.

Carroll, A. B. (1979). A three-dimensional conceptual model of corporate performance. *Academy of Management Review, 4*(4), 497–505.

Carroll, A. B. (1999). Corporate social responsibility. *Business and Society, 38*(3), 268–295.

Carroll, A. B., & Buchholtz, A. K. (2000). *Business & society, ethics and stakeholder management.* Cincinnati OH: South-Western Publishing.

Commission of the European Communities. (2001). *Green paper – promoting a European framework for corporate social responsibility.* Brussels: Commission of the European Communities.

Crane, A., McWilliams, A., & Matten, D. (2008). *The Oxford handbook of corporate social responsibility.* New York: Oxford University Press.

Davis, K. (1973). The case for and against business assumption of social responsibilities. *Academy of Management Journal, 16,* 312–322.

Donaldson, T., & Preston, L. E. (1995). The stakeholder theory of the corporation: Concepts, evidence and implications. *Academy of Management Review, 20*(1), 65–91. University of Toronto Press, Toronto.

Edelman Trust Report. (2010). *Corporate responsibility & sustainability communication.* Edelman. Available at http://www.edelman.co.uk

FOB. (2010). Responsible business in Poland. Good practices' Forum Odpowiedzialnego Biznesu, Warsaw.

Frederick, W. C. (1998). Business and society. In: G. L. Cooper & C. Argyris (Eds), *The concise Blackwell encyclopaedia of management* (pp. 54–56). Oxford, UK: Blackwell.

Frynas, J. G. (2006). Corporate social responsibility in emerging economies. *Journal of Corporate Citizenship, 24*(Winter), 16–19.

Gasparski, W., Lewicka-Strzalecka, A., Rok, B., & Szulczewski, G. (2004). Rules of ethics and social responsibility in practice of Polish firms ("Zasady etyki i spolecznej odpowiedzialnosci w praktyce firm w Polsce"). In: L. Kolarska-Bobińska (Ed.), *The economic awareness of society and the business image (Swiadomosc ekonomiczna spoleczenstwa i wizerunek biznesu)*. Warsaw (in Polish): Instytut Spraw Publicznych.

Hill, R. P., Stephens, D., & Smith, I. (2003). Corporate social responsibility: An examination of individual firm behaviour. *Business and Society Review, 108*(3), 339–364.

Hills, G., Fiske, L., & Mahmud, A. (2009). Anti-corruption as Strategic CSR: A call to action for corporations. Available at http://www.fsg-impact.org/ideas/item/Anti-Corruption_as_Strategic_CSR.html. Retrieved on 24 February 2010.

Hopkins, M. (2003). *The planetary bargain*. London: Earthscan.

Joyner, B. E., & Payne, D. (2002). Evolution and implementation: A study of values, business ethics and corporate social responsibility. *Journal of Business Ethics, 41*, 297–311.

Koładkiewicz, I. (2009). Responsible business in polish economic practice: The experiences of the camela s.a factory of clothing inserts. In: C. A. Mallin (Ed.), *Corporate social responsibility: A case study approach* (pp. 98–122). Cheltenham: Edward Elgar.

Kompendium, C.S.R. Mediaplanet. UNDP Poland, December 20 2009. Available at http://doc.mediaplanet.com/all_projects/4167.pdf

KPMG. (2008). *KPMG international survey of corporate responsibility reporting 2008* Available at https://www.kpmg.de/docs/Corp_responsibility_Survey_2008.pdf (last accessed on 15 February 2010). Geneva.

Lantos, G. P. (2002). The ethicality of altruistic corporate social responsibility. *Journal of Consumer Marketing, 19*(3), 205–230.

Lewicka-Strzalecka, A. (2006). Opportunities and limitations of CSR in the postcommunist countries: Polish case. *Corporate Governance, 6*(4), 440–448. Emerald Group Publishing Limited.

Lindkvist, L., & Llewellyn, S. (2003). Accountability, responsibility and organization. *Scandinavian Journal of Management, 19*(2), 251–273.

Lom, A. (2005). Balancing act. *The Daily Telegraph*, 8: December Issue.

Margolis, J. D., & Walsh, J. P. (2003). Misery loves companies: Rethinking social initiatives by business. *Administrative Science Quarterly, 48*, 268–305.

van Marrewijk, M. (2003). Concepts and definitions of CSR and corporate sustainability: Between agency and communion. *Journal of Business Ethics, 44*(2/3), 95–105.

Mason, E. S. (1960). *The corporation in Modern Society*. Cambridge, MA: Harvard University Press.

McWilliams, A., Siegel, D. S., & Wright, P. M. (2006). Corporate social responsibility: Strategic implications. *Journal of Management Studies, 43*(1), 1–18. Blackwell.

Moir, L. (2001). What do we mean by corporate social responsibility? *Corporate Governance, 1*(2), 16–22.

Mosley, D., Pietri, P. H., & Megginson, L. C. (1996). *Management: Leadership in action*. New York: Harper-Collins.

NGOs in Poland – basic facts, Klon/Jawor Association. (2004). Available at http://www.ngo.pl/files/01english.ngo.pl/public/Basic_facts_2004.pdf. Retrieved on 15 February 2010.

Ougaard, M. (2004). The CSR movement and global governance. In: S. Singh-Sengupta (Ed.), *Business-social partnership: An international perspective* (pp. 142–158). Jaipur, India: Aalekh Publishers.

Perrault, W. D., Jr., & McCarthy, E. J. (2002). *Basic marketing: A global-managerial approach*. Burr Ridge, IL: McGraw-Hill.

Piskalski, G. (2009). CSR in Poland. Briefing paper for the EU – LAC Forum, Buenos Aires, 27–28.10.2009. Retrieved on 15 February 2010.

Preston, L., & Post, J. (1975). *Private Management and Public Policy: The Principle of Public Responsibility*. Englewood Cliffs, NJ: Prentice Hall.

Robbins, S., & Decenzo, D. (2001). *Fundamentals of management* (3rd ed). Upper Saddle River, NJ: Prentice-Hall.

Roberts, S. (2003). Supply chain specific? Understanding the patchy success of ethical sourcing initiatives. *Journal of Business Ethics, 44*(2/3), 159–170.

Sethi, S. P. (1977). *Advocacy advertising and large corporations*. Lexington, MA: Lexington Books.

Smith, N. C. (2003). Corporate social responsibility: Whether or how? *Kalifornia Management Review, 45*(4), 52–76.

Stanwick, P. A., & Stanwick, S. D. (1998). The relationship between corporate social performance and organizational size, financial performance, and environmental performance: An empirical examination. *Journal of Business Ethics, 7*(2), 195–204.

Strand, R. (1983). A systems paradigm of organizational adaptations to the social environment. *Academy of Management Review, 8*, 90–96.

Swanson, D. L. (1999). Toward an integrative theory of business and society: A research strategy for corporate social performance. *Academy of Management Review, 24*(July), 506–521.

TNS OBOP (2010). TNS OBOP research for Bank Drugiej Ręki, Warszawa.

UNDP. (2006). *Human development report – beyond scarcity, power poverty and the Global Water Crisis*. UNDP.

UNDP. (2007). *Corporate social responsibility in Poland. Baseline study 2007*. Brussels: United Nations Development Program.

Vaaland, T. I., Heide, M., & Grønhaug, K. (2008). Corporate social responsibility: Investigating theory and research in marketing context. *European Journal of Marketing, 42*(9/10), 927–953.

Valor, C. (2005). Corporate social responsibility and corporate citizenship: Towards corporate accountability. *Business and Society Review, 110*(2), 191–212.

Visser, W., Matten, D., Pohl, M., & Tolhurst, N. (Eds). (2007). *The A to Z of corporate social responsibility: A complete reference guide to concepts, codes and organisations*. London: Wiley.

Waddock, S. (2001). Corporate citizenship enacted as operating practice. *International Journal of Value-Based Management, 14*, 237–246.

Waddock, S. (2004). Parallel universes: Companies, academics and the progress of corporate citizenship. *Business and Society Review, 109*(1), 5–42.

Wood, D. (1991). Corporate social performance revisited. *Academy of Management Review, 16*, 691–718.

World Bank. (2006). *World development report 2006: Equity and development*. New York: Oxford University Press.

World Resources. (2005). The Wealth of the Poor: Managing Ecosystems to Fight Poverty. United Nations Development Programme, United Nations Environment Programme, The World Bank, World Resources Institute, September, 2005.